BLOOD,
OIL
AND THE
AXIS

BLOOD, OIL
AND THE
AXIS

THE ALLIED RESISTANCE AGAINST A FASCIST STATE
IN IRAQ AND THE LEVANT, 1941

JOHN BROICH

Abrams Press, New York

Published in 2019 by Abrams Press, an imprint of ABRAMS. All Rights Reserved.
No part of this publication may be reproduced, stored in a retrieval system, or
transmitted in any form or by any means, mechanical, electronic, photocopy,
recording, or otherwise without permission in writing from the publisher.

Cataloging-in-Publication Data is available from the Library of Congress

On the cover: Arab Legion Chevys and machine gun crews pose for photographer
George Rodger and *Life* magazine in Amman, Transjordan, summer 1941. Chevys like
these had cut the rail line out of Baghdad and dueled the Luftwaffe. Absent is one destroyed by a Luftwaffe Messerschmitt Bf 110 in May.

Book design and typeformatting by Bernard Schleifer
Manufactured in the United States of America

ISBN 978-1-4683-1399-4

10 9 8 7 6 5 4 3 2 1

Abrams books are available at special discounts when purchased in quantity
for premiums and promotions as well as fundraising or educational use.

Special editions can also be created to specification. For details, contact
specialsales@abramsbooks.com or the address below.

Abrams Press® is a registered trademark of Harry N. Abrams, Inc.

ABRAMS The Art of Books
195 Broadway, New York, NY 10007
abramsbooks.com

This was not your land, or ours: but a village in the Midlands,
And one in the Five Rivers, may have the same graveyard.
Let those who go home tell the same story of you:
Of action with a common purpose . . .

—T. S. ELIOT, "To the Indians who Died in Africa"

Contents

Major and Minor Figures

Major Figures

Jack Bartlett. A twenty-one-year-old gardener and member of the Territorial Army artillery, or "Saturday soldiers," when World War II broke out, he fought in Belgium and northern France prior to escaping from Dunkirk. Recovered, he and his neighbors shipped out to the Suez Canal zone and on to Iraq, continuing into Syria. Two hundred thirty-seventh (Lincoln) Field Battery, 60th Field Regiment, Royal Artillery.

Harry Chalk. A seventeen-year-old tiler of very modest background from Southend-on-Sea. When World War II broke out he first shipped out to Egypt. After fighting on the Sudan frontier, he and his Southend friends were ordered to Palestine and later Iraq and Syria. First Battalion, First Essex Regiment.

Roald Dahl. Dahl was working for Shell Oil in Kenya and Tanganyika before volunteering for the Royal Air Force (RAF) in 1939 as a twenty-three-year-old. He trained at RAF Habbaniya in Iraq before being thrown into a desperate, losing campaign in Greece. His last combat missions were against the French and Germans over Syria-Lebanon in June–July 1941. Eightieth Squadron, RAF.

Jack Hasey. US citizen who made France his adopted home after failing at college; he yearned to fight the threatening Germans on the eve of war. Denied French citizenship, he campaigned in the United States for funds for volunteer ambulance crews and, informally, for America to prepare to fight fascist Germany. Returning to France during its fall, he fled to join Charles de Gaulle's Free French in Britain in 1940 before fighting in northeastern Africa and Syria. Thirteenth Demi-Brigade, Free French Foreign Legion.

John Masters. Born into a British family that had resided in India for many generations, Masters was an early career soldier in the Indian Army at the beginning of the war. While training Nepali recruits to the Gurkha Rifles and patrolling India's border with Afghanistan, he and his men and boys were sent to Basra, Iraq, early in the Golden Square Crisis. Second Battalion, Fourth Gurkha Rifles.

Reading. A young Palestinian from Haifa who worked as an interpreter for the British Army's Sixth Cavalry Brigade, headquartered near there. Suddenly pressed into field service during the improvised invasion of Iraq, Reading did some extraordinary improvisation of his own that seemed to contribute largely to the campaign's success. The name Reading was an alias he used for work; his real name is lost.

David Smiley. A wealthy, aristocratic member of the largely ornamental Royal Horse Guards at the outbreak of the war, Smiley volunteered as a commando operating on the Sudan frontier in 1940. He sought out similarly dangerous work in Iraq and Syria. Royal Horse Guards, First Household Cavalry Regiment.

Freya Stark. Having won renown as a traveler and writer in Arab and Persian lands in the mid-1930s, Stark volunteered with the British Ministry of Information at the outbreak of the war. She then traveled the Middle East, working formally and informally as an envoy, propagandist, organizer, and intelligence gatherer. Her goal was always to draw the British and Middle Eastern Arabs together in what she considered genuine friendship, while watching the forces of ignorance or imperiousness work against her.

Minor Figures

Moshe Dayan. A member of one of the semisecret Palmach strike teams of the Jewish Palestinian Haganah paramilitary who scouted the Syria-Lebanon frontier and accompanied an international team to disable a bridge wired with explosives on the eve of the Allied campaign there.

Henri Dentz. A general who had the misfortune of being tasked with offering the surrender of Paris to the Germans, Dentz was then sent by the Vichy regime to its colony of Syria-Lebanon as chief civil and military authority, only to be given the job of collaborating with Axis forces there.

Tony Dudgeon. Born in Cairo to a middle-class family, Dudgeon was a pilot placed in charge of a remote Blenheim bomber squadron fighting the Italians on the Egypt-Libya frontier as a mere twenty-four-year-old. Sent to quiet Habbaniya to recover from the constant stress and losses of pilots on the front lines, he found himself in the middle of a siege that wounded more than one psyche.

Santi Pada Dutt. A doctor's son himself, Dutt joined the Indian Army's Medical Service after getting his medical degree in Calcutta. He had sisters active in the anti-imperial Quit India Movement even as he served in a war many of his compatriots argued would only preserve the British Empire. He freely told British colleagues, meanwhile, that that was not his aim. He was steadfast in the face of grave peril to his Nepali Gurkha patients.

John Glubb. An army veteran of the Western Front in World War I, Glubb was then posted to Mesopotamia (later Iraq) for ten years before enlisting as an officer in the Arab Legion of Transjordan (later Jordan). His long-standing personal familiarity with the villages and Bedouin of the Iraq-Jordan-Syria frontier made him a valuable ally in the campaigns of spring 1941.

Fritz Grobba. Called not just an Arabophile but an Arabomaniac by one of his German Foreign Office superiors, Grobba had long dreamed of, and cultivated, an alliance between Germany and Iraq. When a cabal of army officers overthrew the Iraqi government, they immediately requested that Grobba hurry from Germany to act as liaison between the officers and their would-be Axis allies.

Rudolf Rahn. Envisioning himself as one who would nurture a new era of cooperation between France and Germany, the diplomat—and Nazi—

Rahn had the task of liaising with Henri Dentz in Beirut. His goal was to extract as much military cooperation from the Vichy French in Syria-Lebanon as possible, in the hope that this would strengthen ties and serve as a model collaboration for a new world order.

Abdallah Simon. A middle-class member of Baghdad's large Jewish population, Simon graduated from the American University of Beirut, only to find himself conscripted in the Iraqi Army as a second lieutenant in time for the Golden Square's military coup and war.

Bill Slim. An Indian Army officer wounded in northeastern Africa in early 1941, Slim was then tasked with leading Indian Army units north out of their base in Basra in May–June 1941. He'd fought in the plodding, bloody Allied advance up Iraq (then called Mesopotamia) in World War I, but in 1941 took bold measures to keep his mobilized advance progressing.

William Weallens. Having fought as a lieutenant with the Gurkhas in World War I, Weallens was languishing in the Indian Army Publications Department at the outbreak of World War II. The lieutenant colonel's adjutant, John Masters, came to admire how this somewhat old-fashioned, "brave and honest Edwardian gentleman" had some humanity to contribute to this dehumanizing war.

Note on Sources and Methods

THIS IS A WORK of professional history, and as such nothing is invented. If I write that George Orwell or Tony Dudgeon or an Assyrian Levy soldier *thought* something, it's because I have documentary evidence that they did so, whether in the form of a diary entry, a memoir, or an interview. Or, for example, if I write that a character *saw* something or *said* something, I draw from a unique archival document like a unit history, a letter, or some other source from an eyewitness. In the very rare instances in which I speculate about what someone or a group felt or believed, I make sure to signal this in my writing by stating something like, "they *must have been* afraid" or "*must have* imagined," or I might use the word "probably." I tend to avoid such instances, and indulge in them only when I'm not making a large leap of speculation, so that my reader knows he or she can trust that what I write is supported by quality evidence.

Such evidence comes from a wide range of archival and other sources, including a lot of communications between Cairo's intelligence center and London, Habbaniya, the Baghdad embassy, or elsewhere that are preserved in the National Archives in Richmond, England. The Special Operations Executive (SOE) files there were helpful and colorful, too. And, of course, the preserved Ultra intelligence relays (O.L. Files) were priceless. The National Army Museum in London held some personal papers that filled in details as well, including those of the campaigners in Syria. At the Imperial War Museum, the personal papers of a number of participants in the campaigns were invaluable, along with their recorded interviews. And some of the greatest treasures there were Harry Chalk's interview and his memoir, which his grandson helped him compile.

It was terrific to have such detail from a rank-and-file infantryman, all too rare in World War II histories, but alas the memories of Indian and Arab participants in these fights are chiefly lost to us. Thankfully, the officers of the Indian Army left writings, and I've certainly put those to use where possible. But the ordinary sepoy has left us little. You'll see in the endnotes where I've been able to draw on some interviews, but I had to rely on unit histories or, for example, the reports of people like doctor Sailendra Chaterjee who survived the Vichy siege on Mezze House and wrote vividly of it. Sadly, some of the unit diaries of those who participated in these campaigns are lost. And given the devastation of nearly entire companies of the Third Battalion, First Punjab Regiment and the Fourth Battalion, Sixth Regiment Rajputana, there were few individuals left to recall these scenes.

I've had to take great care in comparing and cross-referencing both primary and secondary sources per normal professional due diligence but also because official histories have their limitations and angles, as do memoirs, and because the first draft of World War II history— including those official histories—were all badly off base because the role of Ultra intelligence had yet to be revealed to the world. Further, the role of the Indian Army was badly underrepresented in World War II history until the past ten years or so—in ways that distorted the literature badly. The role of Arab cavalry in this campaign, both the Arab Legion and the Transjordan Frontier Force, was not only left out but sometimes erased.

If I hadn't read the memoirs from these campaigns with a critical historian's eye, I might not have realized the critical role of the interpreter Reading, who summoned a tank column out of thin air, a tank column that haunted the imaginations of the Golden Square or the officers defending Baghdad and, reports say, made Baghdad's defense appear untenable. Somerset de Chair, in his *Golden Carpet*, while often self-deprecating (he describes Brigadier Joe Kingstone's amusement with him pretty clearly), fails to state the obvious: that he could've accomplished nothing without Reading. This includes the evocation of the tanks that De Chair takes credit for in his memoir. Instead, De Chair frequently belittles Reading using Orientalist racial snubs. The story of Reading's background and eventual fate fascinate me, and I did my best to locate him, but to no avail. Instead of cutting him out of the story for a lack of data, though, I thought it most just to include him and work against the disparagement of De Chair and Reading's practical expungement from history.

Maps

Map 1
Circle of Fire

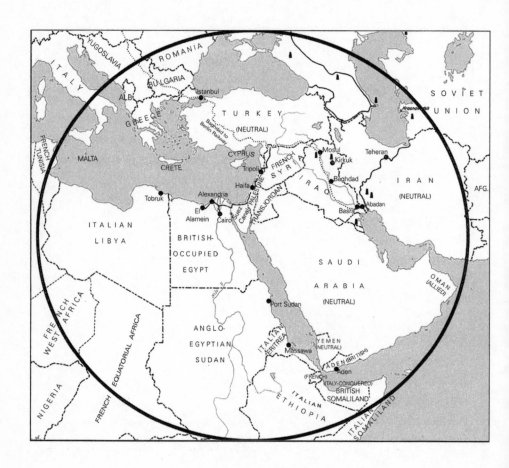

Map 2
Habbaniya Siege

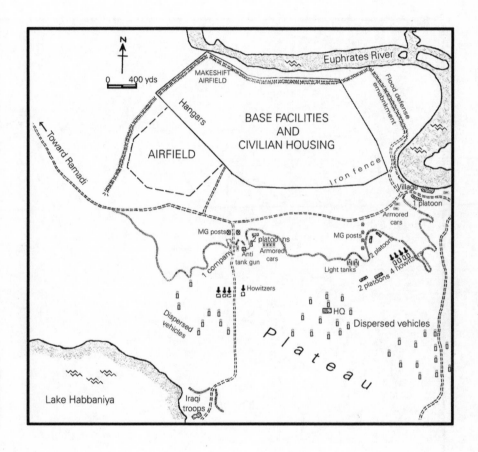

Map 3
Iraq and the Levant

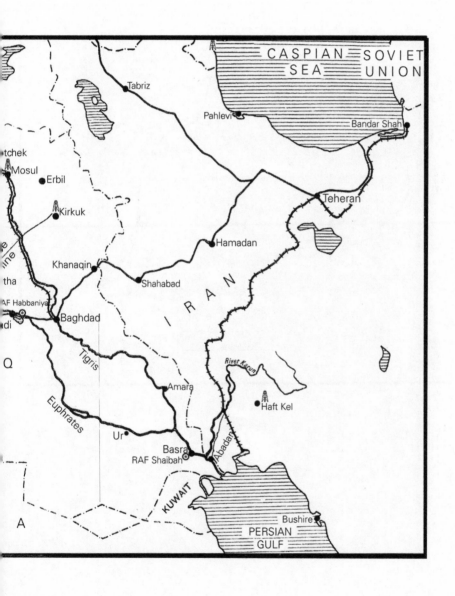

CASPIAN SEA

SOVIET UNION

Tabriz

Pahlevi

Bandar Shah

tchek

Mosul

Erbil

Kirkuk

Teheran

Hamadan

Khanaqin

Shahabad

I R A N

tha

AF Habbaniya

di

Baghdad

Q

Tigris

River Karun

Amara

Haft Kel

Euphrates

Ur

Abadan

Basra

RAF Shaibah

A

KUWAIT

Bushire

PERSIAN GULF

Map 4
Habbaniya to Baghdad

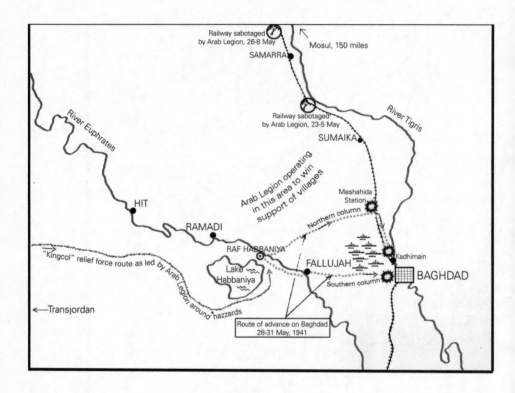

Railway sabotaged by Arab Legion, 26-8 May

Mosul, 150 miles

SAMARRA

River Euphrates

River Tigris

Railway sabotaged by Arab Legion, 23-5 May

SUMAIKA

Arab Legion operating in this area to win support of villages

Meshahida Station

HIT

Northern column

RAMADI

RAF HABBANIYA

"Kingcol" relief force route as led by Arab Legion around hazzards

Lake Habbaniya

FALLUJAH

Kadhimain

BAGHDAD

Southern column

←Transjordan

Route of advance on Baghdad
28-31 May, 1941

Map 5
Operations in Western Central Syria-Lebanon

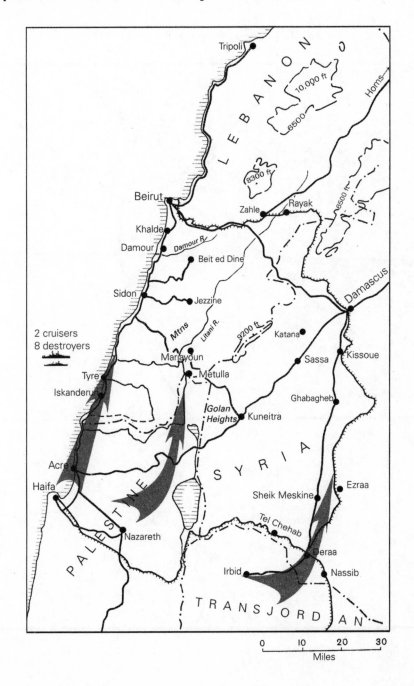

Tripoli

L E B A N O N

10,000 ft

6500

Homs

8300 ft

Beirut

Zahle · Rayak

6500 ft

Khalde

Damour · Damour R.

Beit ed Dine

Sidon

Jezzine

Damascus

Mtns

Litani R.

9200 ft

Katana

2 cruisers
8 destroyers

Marjayoun

Metulla

Sassa

Kissoue

Tyre

Iskanderun

Golan
Heights

Kuneitra

Ghabagheb

Acre

Haifa

P A L E S T I N E

S Y R I A

Sheik Meskine

Ezraa

Nazareth

Tel Chehab

Deraa

Irbid

Nassib

T R A N S J O R D A N

0   10   20   30
Miles

Map 6
Damascus Area

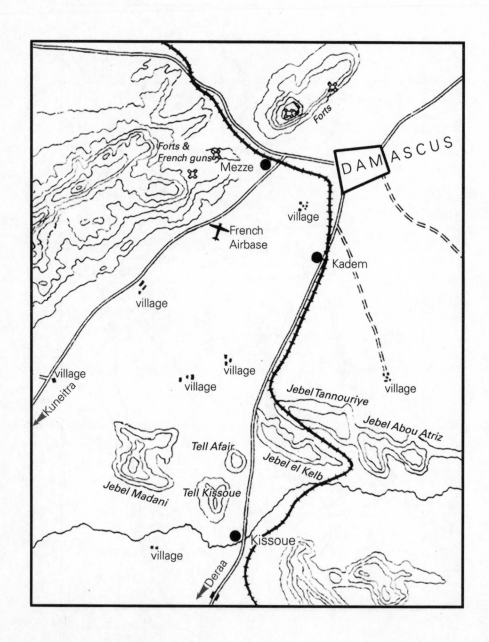

Forts

Forts & French guns

Mezze

D A M A S C U S

village

French Airbase

Kadem

village

village

village

village

Kuneitra

village

Jebel Tannouriye

village

Jebel Abou Atriz

Tell Afair

Jebel el Kelb

Jebel Madani

Tell Kissoue

village

Deraa

Kissoue

Map 7
Operations in Eastern Syria by Relief Force

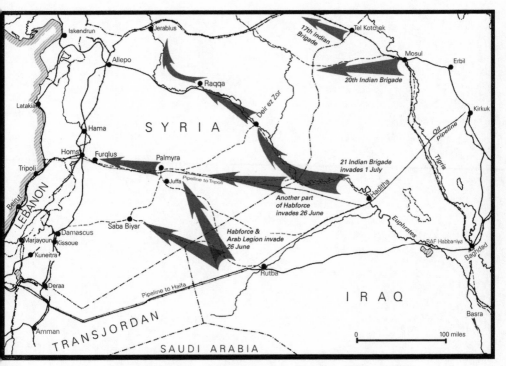

Routes of invasion of relief force from Iraq, from 26 June 1941.

1

"To Extinguish Peace from the Earth"

*Where the Middle East and the World Stood
in Spring 1941*

THIS IS THE story of how close the European Axis came to achieving a
massive triumph in Iraq and the Levant in spring 1941. Imagine Germany
and Italy acquiring an oil supply sufficient for all of their war needs along
with a pipeline that would deliver that oil to a convenient Mediterranean
port and to a rail network that could deliver the oil through Turkey to
the Axis-occupied Balkan States. Imagine in that moment the Axis gaining an ally with a modern, British-trained army of around thirty to fifty
thousand in the Middle East. Imagine that the Axis gained a port and air
base about thirty miles from the Allies' most important non-American
fuel supply and refinery in Iran. And imagine Germany suddenly commanding an army on the northern border of Palestine, with its population
of a half million Jews, and that army invading, perhaps holding the Jewish population hostage.*

This is not sensational conjecture; each of these things seemed on
course to happen in spring 1941. And they seemed bound to happen not
in the event of some grand or lucky stroke by the Axis but simply in the
absence of a quick reaction from the Allies. That is, all it would have
taken for this potential to become reality was the absence of a desperate

---

*Along these lines, the Germans practiced such hostage-taking techniques else-
where—for example, by inflicting collective punishment on civilian populations in
Axis-occupied territories like Yugoslavia, scenes from which will be described herein.
The Germans also exchanged their Jewish prisoners from neutral or Axis-allied countries for cash later in the war.

response by an extraordinary, makeshift alliance—the subject of this book.

The crisis in Iraq and Syria-Lebanon was a low point among a series of low points for Britain and its allies—allies that did not yet include the United States. It had been almost a year since the fall of France and the headlong flight of British forces from the beaches of Dunkirk before the German war machine. Prime Minister Winston Churchill had rallied Britain to keep up the fight—hardly a forgone conclusion—after the catastrophic loss of its chief ally, but since then had found no new ally to take France's place. Britain, therefore, could only toil at its own defense, not turn the tide back on occupied Europe, keeping its fighter planes close above its ports and cities, beating back German bombers as best they could.

The battle for western Europe was over, and the Axis had won. The battle for the world now pivoted on the Suez Canal and the sphere that orbited it, about two thousand miles in circumference. Where there weren't actual battles being fought, nearly every land within that circle struggled and strained in spring 1941—whether from propaganda wars or fierce internal debates about fascism versus antifascism (more on that below)—or was weighing its ability to maintain its neutrality in this viper pit. The circle included Greece, Turkey, and Mediterranean islands like Crete and Malta; Egypt, Italian Libya, and Sudan; the Red Sea and the lands adjoining it; and the Levantine lands of Lebanon, Palestine, and Syria, as well as Iraq and other lands.

The main prize in this fight was the Suez Canal itself, a choke point of world trade and Europe's gateway to India and points east. If the Axis could control the Canal and the Red Sea shipping lanes beyond, it would control a huge fraction of the world's shipping, police access to the Mediterranean, and halt its enemies' troop and logistical movements. The other main prize in this circle was neutral Turkey. If the Axis surrounded Turkey, it could force the nation into its fold and win its vital rail lines and Black Sea gateways.

In early spring 1941, therefore, the Axis and the Allies were battling all around this ring of fire. The Germans were blitzing and bombing their way across Greece and Yugoslavia despite the efforts of brave resisters. (The experiences of Royal Air Force pilot Roald Dahl will offer a glimpse of those desperate efforts in the pages to come.) The British and their allies, meanwhile, were fighting a seesaw desert war with the Italians and the newly arrived German Afrika Korps on the Egypt-Libya frontier. The Indian Army was fighting a brutal peak-to-peak battle against dug-in, veteran Italian forces on the fringe of the Red Sea. And Crete, an island of great tactical importance, was about to be overrun by German paratroopers.

But on the eve of the Iraq-Syria crisis there were other battles, less bloody but no less critical, between fascist and antifascist forces across the region. These were contests in the political or moral spheres between those who sided with the Allies, often called the Democracies, and those who sided with the fascist powers. These debates extended from the lands of northwestern Africa, the colonies of defeated France, now under the sway of the collaborationist Vichy regime, all the way across northern Africa through Italian Libya, British-occupied Egypt, through the Middle East to the neutral countries of Afghanistan and Iran, and into British-dominated India. The question of which side countries should support was mixed up with the question of how to free themselves from European domination or meddling. Nationalist leaders asked themselves whether their countries should adopt fascism, with all of its apparent vigor, or whether they should throw their lot in with the antifascists and strive for liberal democracy.

In retrospect it might seem that the choice should've been obvious: fight fascism and all of its evils. But that meant asking peoples who did not enjoy democracy—peoples whose freedom in any real sense had been denied by colonizers or meddlers—to fight for *other* people's democracies, and then hope that democracy was eventually extended to themselves. Besides, sources suggest that few people in those lands were well informed about the wider implications of fascist terrors like Kristallnacht or the early signs of the imminent Final Solution. It was far easier to see the Germans, who held no colonies in that broad region, as simply the enemies of their enemies—the British and French interlopers. The Germans, furthermore, were adding triumph to triumph by spring 1941, and had long courted public opinion across North Africa, the Middle East, and beyond through their propaganda channels and embassies, a fact exemplified in this book by the figure of German consular agent Fritz Grobba, envoy to Iraq. At the same time, Grobba's foil in this book, British Middle East emissary Freya Stark, lamented that British efforts at winning hearts and minds had been neglectful at best, and bullying at worst, in the region.

Debates about fascism versus antifascism extended well beyond this ring centered on Suez. Fascism was seductive, and before history revealed its genocidal nucleus to any with eyes to see, there were many—and many prominent—people taken by its simple, singular idea of power, the singular ruler, and the singular race. This went even for Britain, which was leading the fight against fascism in spring 1941, where there were infamous figures like the black-shirted Oswald Mosley, placed under house arrest during the fall of France, and press magnate Lord Rothermere, who peddled appeasement in the papers he owned and encouraged Adolf Hitler in his personal correspondence with the dictator before the war. These were notorious cases, but they represented a much broader, amorphous base of those attracted to fascism's antilabor and anti-Jewish currents.

George Orwell—a prescient observer if ever there was one—thought it possible, even after Churchill rallied the nation to keep up the fight, that the British public might still support a snap election to replace Churchill's coalition in spring 1940. As a journalist speaking with and observing his fellow Englishmen, Orwell sensed that working people who did not feel represented by the Westminster elite already felt subordinated, so why would it matter if a fascist new order swept away the plutocratic in Britain? Orwell asked an influential newspaper editor whether he thought the public would accept negotiations with the Axis. "Hells bells," the man replied, "I could dress it up so that they'd think it was the greatest victory in the history of the world." And amid an upper class whom he sensed already leaned toward authoritarianism, Orwell felt an unspoken, perhaps unconscious, hope that Britain would lose and so end the liberal democratic experiment with all of its noise, disorder, and labor sympathy.

In the United States, President Franklin Roosevelt was doing his best to outmaneuver isolationists in Congress and coax along a public that had no taste for what appeared to be a European matter and the concern of the unpopular British Empire. Two out of three American voters wanted no part in a war with Germany in the spring of 1940— even if Britain's life were at stake. So Roosevelt negotiated with Congress to win what concessions he could, to at least make the United States "the arsenal of democracy," by supplying some old warships to Britain in fall 1940, and winning the Lend-Lease Act, which started sending munitions across the Atlantic in 1941. In the United States there were many eager to fight the fascists, but there were also those who excused or even welcomed German warmaking. They said that Hitler was misunderstood, simply recovering Germany's World War I losses, or was a righteous champion against what they called Bolshevism or the "Asiatic" assault on "pure" Anglo-Saxon blood. The profascist radio giant Father Charles Coughlin, whose shows had audiences of many millions, praised fascist Germany and Italy and openly hoped for the defeat of Britain. Influential anti-Semites like Henry Ford and Anglo-Saxon racial supremacists in America First and the Silver Legion of America believed that Hitler was a much-needed corrective to an imagined global Jewish conspiracy and the expansion of the Bolshevik/Slavic horde. Jack Hasey, on the other hand, a young American who appears later in this book, was quite decidedly ready to fight the fascists. And while his compatriots stood by, he was battling for his life against fascist armies.

So the titanic brawl between fascism and antifascism wasn't just fought on the battlefield but was contested as a sort of spiritual civil war in most every nation. And this book tells part of that story while it tells about a particular high-stakes campaign in Iraq and the Levant. In those lands, too, there were those who embraced pluralism and democracy, and those who embraced authoritarianism. There were Palestinians who fought alongside the British; Iraqis who looked to Benito Mussolini's Blackshirts as models; Syrians who rallied to de Gaulle and the Free French; and Jews who offered to work for the Germans. And there were members of each of those groups who fought for the opposite side. In this story, the righteousness and choices of individuals get the spotlight, not the righteousness of nations.

Iraq, in particular, had its own struggle over which way to go in a world dividing between fascist and antifascist. And it was this cleavage that triggered the emergency portrayed in this book. In spring 1941, a group of four senior army and air force officers in Iraq, calling themselves the Golden Square, overthrew the government and decided to throw their lot in with the Axis. In part they were motivated by their personal authoritarian political leanings, essentially the idea that the whole country should be operated like an army with them at the top; and in part they were motivated by personal connections to Germans and Germany. They also believed that the Axis—which looked unstoppable—offered the best chance to bolster their position and snuff out long-standing British colonial meddling in the country.

Then, Vichy France agreed to allow Germany to use air bases in Syria and an obscure port in colonial Lebanon to allow the passage of arms to Iraq. Both the Iraqi revolutionaries and their new Axis partners envisioned Iraq being the heart of a new state or federation stretching from the Persian Gulf to the Mediterranean after the war. While those Iraqis believed the new kingdom would be allied with fascist Germany and Italy, the Axis was sure it would be a mere vassal state.

The Iraqi coup and French-Syrian complicity was a moment of grave danger to the Allied effort in North Africa, with the Iraqi oil supply—critical for the Royal Navy—closed off, the Suez Canal imperiled, staunch British ally Transjordan nearly surrounded, and the Jewish community of Palestine preparing for the worst—and in graver peril than nearly anyone could imagine since the Final Solution would be implemented in the lands that Germany conquered at the end of 1941.

Understanding this danger, and understanding how the Axis nearly established itself in Iraq and the Levant, requires a bit of understanding about North Africa and the Middle East on the eve of World War II. That great swath of the world, running from northwestern Africa to India and beyond, was mostly divided among European colonies; and where Europe did not preside over literal colonies, it oversaw spheres of influence. From the nineteenth to early twentieth centuries, the French took possession of vast areas of western and northwestern Africa, including Algeria, Morocco, and Tunisia, often replacing Ottoman influence there. Tunisia's neighbor Libya was attacked by Italy in 1911, and Mussolini finished its takeover by around 1934. Egypt, other than the Suez Canal Zone and a Royal Navy base at Alexandria, had won a large measure of independence from the British in 1922; but that came to an end with the coming of war, because a treaty with Egypt permitted Britain to reoccupy the country if another power threatened it—and the all-important canal that linked Britain to India. So Cairo became the British Empire's most important headquarters outside London. Northeastern Africa was divided between sparsely populated lands variously split between British and Italian over-lordship. The importance of these were that they harbored air and sea bases from which the rivals could compete for control of the Red Sea life-line to India and points east.

The Arabian heartland in the Levant had been divided among those who defeated the Ottomans there in World War I. To the British went Ottoman Mespotamia (later called Iraq) and Palestine, with little Trans-jordan given in turn to Britain's World War I ally, Sharif Hussein, and his son Abdullah, a key figure in this story. To the French went Lebanon, with its significant Christian Arab population, and Syria. These were theoretically granted to the British and French by the League of Nations as so-called mandates in return for those empires' "improving and up-lifting" them, a civilized fiction meant to put a modern, genteel burnish on the tarnished name of imperialism. In fact, Arab leaders throughout the region who'd long-resented Ottoman dominance dreamed of their own independent nations or a federation of states extending from the Mediter-ranean to the Persian Gulf now that the war was over. Meanwhile, British Mandate Palestine saw the growth of a sort of state within a state in the form of the new "Jewish national home" facilitated by British policy. This conflicted with Arab aspirations for their own independent national homes.

East of Iraq was Iran, which had fought ceaselessly to remain free of the Ottoman Empire and now, in the post-Ottoman world, carefully balanced its friendships with world powers to remain so. Iran enjoyed a large oil supply, with accompanying refineries right on the Persian Gulf, located very near Iraq's port of Basra. When World War II broke out, most British oil came from the United States, but the oil refined at Abadan, Iran, was another key source for the Allies. Iran also had a key rail corridor running north to south from the Persian Gulf to the Soviet Union, which later would become a key lifeline in the Soviets' resistance against Germany. The loss of Iranian neutrality to the Axis, perhaps because of an Axis victory in Iraq, would have been a terrible blow to the Allies.

East of Iran was neutral Afghanistan, and while it straddled no oil, it was long eyed with suspicion by the British as a potential staging ground for the invasion of neighboring India. At the beginning of World War II, before Stalin was betrayed by Hitler's Operation Barbarossa in summer 1941, the British feared Soviet meddling in Afghanistan. They would have done better to fear an invasion from an army led by Indian quasi-fascist Subhas Chandra Bose, who in spring 1941 was negotiating with the Germans for the financing and arming of just such a force. That story will resume in the pages to come.

India had a broad independence movement on the eve of World War II, which made a tremendous irony of the fact that the Indian Army played an irreplaceable role in the salvation of British democracy. There were many in Britain, let alone India, who argued that the British should exchange Indian independence for its help in defeating the Axis; but leaders from Churchill to the Raj's viceroy in New Delhi wouldn't hear of it, thus utterly alienating the majority of Indian leadership. It was a misstep that the British were lucky to survive. Its time-honored professionalism meant that the Indian Army nevertheless did its duty, while the attractions of pay, adventure, and glory attracted vast enlistment over the war years. (There was never conscription in India.) Still, centuries of coercion and the stubbornness of Churchill and others meant that pro-Axis figures like Bose made serious inroads among Indian listeners so that India, too, balanced on the edge of a choice between fascist and antifascist forces—external and internal—when the war began.

For the European Axis, this is how the war was supposed to go: Britain was supposed to realize that it was beaten, to fold on its responsibility to France as it had on Czechoslovakia, to turn its head once again as it had on Spain. The threat of a flotilla crossing the English Channel was supposed to cow the British people, and the Royal Air Force (RAF) was supposed to dwindle like the island's food and fuel supply. Then, after Churchill's coalition was voted out by a hungry and frightened populace and British resistance halted, the United States would see little point in joining the war in Europe. Hitler could turn his attention to stamping out the Soviets and the Marxism that the Nazi worldview cried out to eliminate as a violation of the "natural order" of social Darwinism.

Hitler and his inner circle of Nazi ideologues understood their war chiefly as the setting to rights of an imagined global racial order. That order was supposed to include high in its race hierarchy the English— presumably once their population had been purged of a list of racial "un- desirables." The purified English were not supposed to be eliminated, nor even removed from some parts of their empire; indeed, in 1940, Hitler still wanted the empire to persist as a stabilizing force. That is, the English or British, whom Hitler called a "Nordic" race, were to continue to police certain areas of Africa and Asia as they always had. Yes, the British would surrender areas of the former German Empire; and where the British had held informal ascendancy, Germany and to some extent Italy would replace them.

But it was central to Nazi theory that "low-ranking" races needed firm control, and in that the British, Hitler believed, had proven their ability in places like India. Hitler was supposed to love the film *Lives of a Bengal Lancer*, in which the British—embodied by American Gary Cooper—showed their worth as guardians of civilization against the "Asiatic horde." It depicted a unit of cavalry at a remote frontier station standing against an Indian frontier rebel. Though overmatched, the Lancers succeed against the rebellious forces fighting under an invented villain named Muhammad Khan. (In fact, there were probably hundreds of men with the commonplace name Muhammad Khan who fought against the Axis.)*

* One Muhammad Khan was in fact a Bengal Lancer, a risaldar, or cavalry cap- tain, in Skinner's Horse, a cavalry unit sometimes given that name. He served in Eritrea, North Africa, and Italy and was decorated for his leadership and pen- chant for tracking down hidden Italian soldiers and artillery.

It is nearly unimaginable, whatever promises Nazi propaganda made, that Hitler would have granted self-rule to India, or to British and French colonies or spheres in the Middle East. In the Nazi mind, that would have been like dismissing the guards and letting the inmates run the prison.

Britain and France had to lose some territory in the Axis's new world. In 1940, the plan was still for Italy to replace Britain in the lands surrounding the Mediterranean, which would become, as it had been in the classical era, a sort of "Roman lake." ("The world will once again hear the tramp of the dauntless Roman Legions. The flashing eagles have been raised aloft to restore to Italy her historic position in the world," said British Nazi William Lord Joyce, also known as Lord Haw-Haw, over the radio waves from Berlin.) That meant Italy would rule, directly or through its consuls, the countries and kingdoms encircling the Mediterranean in North Africa, the Balkans, and the Levant.[1]

So what would have happened if the Axis had created a vassal kingdom of Iraq and Syria? That will remain only a speculative game of "what if?" But what Allied and Axis leaders themselves envisioned, at least, is revealing. In early spring 1941, the British were watching developments in Yugoslavia with a chill, helplessly observing the fate of neutral countries surrounded by Axis, or Axis vassal, states. At the turn of 1941, Yugoslavia was bordered on the south by Italian-occupied Albania, on the north by Axis Hungary, and on the northeast by fascist Romania. Then on March 1, Bulgaria—Yugoslavia's directly eastern neighbor—joined the Axis. Judging itself surrounded, Yugoslavia surrendered itself to the Axis a few weeks later—"breaking all our hearts to see the gallant Serbian and Yugoslav people signing away their souls," Churchill wrote. Yugoslavia's fascist party declared triumph, but loyalist monarchists, socialists, and a group of Air Force officers took up arms against the new collaborationist government. Their revolt was brief, however. The Luftwaffe bombed Belgrade into submission and, Yugoslavia lacking the air force or army capable of withstanding them, the Germans overran the country in ten short days.

From April 1941 on, the experience of Yugoslavia offered another illustration of what might have been at stake in the fight for Iraq and the Levant in the same period. When Yugoslavian resistance fighters killed two Schutzstaffel (SS) officers in mid-April, the German Army rounded up thirty-six civilians who had nothing to do with the assassination and publicly executed them. Later that year, the German Army rounded up almost three thousand men and boys—including communists, Jews, Muslims, Romani, and others—to be shot after the Yugoslavian resistance killed ten German soldiers. Now it was as if all of Yugoslavia was held hostage. Had Axis vassal states surrounded Palestine, making the conquest of Palestine a relatively simple matter, would the Axis have held its hundreds of thousands of Jews hostage? That is a matter of speculation. Was the German military *willing* to do so? That is a matter of record.

The next worrisome spot on the map to British eyes was Turkey, and the Yugoslavian scenario is precisely what the British feared for that nearby country. Large, resource-rich Turkey was diligently preserving its neutrality in early 1941, having long-established trade relationships with World War I ally Germany, but jealous of its independence. Crisscrossing Anatolia was a well-developed rail network that reached to Soviet Armenia and Iran—a potential route for Caucasus oil to reach Axis Europe. With neighboring Bulgaria in the Axis, and Greece imperiled, Turkey's western border was deeply threatened. On its south side, Turkey bordered Vichy French Syria and Iraq. In the judgment of British observers, if Turkey were surrounded by German garrisons, as Yugoslavia was, it could only surrender to the Axis. It could not realistically resist, wrote a brigadier in the British diplomatic mission to Turkey; Istanbul would be overrun within "two hours against an assault by modern armour," he reported. So the British and even Roosevelt watched Turkey's tenuous position and would soon link Turkey's neutrality to the outcome of threats in Iraq and Syria.

Speaking of Roosevelt, in spring 1941 he and his top military brass watched developments across the globe, including those centered on the Suez Canal, very closely. While the President did not know for certain that the United States would join the fight against the fascists, he and his military were certainly preparing for it. He also maintained a constant correspondence with Churchill in which the two men exchanged thoughts on global strategy, including how and where American logistical material and troops would land in the Old World. The Suez, naturally, was key, but so was the critical Iraqi port of Basra at the end of the Persian Gulf, as well as the large British air base west of Baghdad, RAF Habbaniya. These were important enough for Roosevelt to send his son, a marine captain, to investigate them in secret. The story of Captain James Roosevelt being welcomed to Iraq by the fire of Luftwaffe Messerschmitts appears in the pages to come.

General Erwin Rommel, who had successfully cut a swath across France the previous spring at the head of a swarm of tanks, landed in Italian Libya in February 1941. Once the Tripoli cranes had lugged his heavy Panzers off their transports, Rommel eyed the map of Libya and British-occupied Egypt and saw opportunity. In France, the Low Countries, and Poland, Rommel had seen that success in tank warfare depended on surprise drives and audacious lunges. His Italian allies in Libya and his superiors at Army Forces Command in Berlin intended to wait until May before launching attacks to push the British out of their gains in Libya, but Rommel knew to lunge.

And so he did in late March 1941, catching the British off guard because the code decrypters at Bletchley Park had told the British command in Cairo that Rommel had instructions to stay put until May. The British believed that he would follow instructions, but he disregarded them. And the British were outmatched because the nucleus of their forces in North Africa had been rushed to Greece, thinking they had until May to return to defend against Italy and an expected German attack there. So Rommel pushed and pushed again, sending the British back toward their home ground of Egypt within a few weeks, and besieging Australian defenders in a key port in northeast Libya on which the Allies would have to depend to supply any eventual drive against the Germans and Italians westward across North Africa.

Rommel's object was to help the Italians make a "Roman Lake" of the Mediterranean, but it was also to seize the Suez Canal, eventually. Closing the Suez to Britain and its Allies would mean halting the flow of resources from the empire and commonwealth to the home islands, in turn halting the flow of weapons to India and elsewhere, and stifling the

Royal Navy. It would mean American and other neutral ships might be policed as well, denying more resources to the Allies. If the Suez were closed and the British could not reinforce the Royal Navy from the east, the German, Italian, and Vichy navies need only guard the Strait of Gibraltar in the west in order to control the Mediterranean, leaving the Axis able to move ships, men, and supplies at will. Meanwhile, with the Suez in German and Italian control, Berlin envisioned a contiguous naval network that would link the European Axis with the Japanese; it even recommended that the Japanese form a base on Madagascar from which it would dominate the Indian Ocean and guard against Allied shipping coming around South Africa. Then, with a secure Mediterranean at its back, the European Axis navies could focus their attention on the Atlantic sea lanes to strangle Britain. And, with the Suez Canal captured, the Germans and Italians might have rolled all the way to the oil fields of Iraq, to Turkey and beyond.[2]

Another potential consequence of the Suez being captured was the isolation of countries on the Red Sea, the Arabian Sea, and the Persian Gulf. Iran, Saudi Arabia, Yemen, and others were holding out, trying to navigate among the vast forces clashing around them, but they were in danger of finding themselves under pressure by the Axis with the Allies too distant, blocked from quickly coming to their aid. The same went for countries like Oman and Persian Gulf princedoms that sided with the British but had no realistic chance of holding out against Axis pressure without help. This is why Freya Stark, who worked with a fierce will but gentle touch to retain Arab friendship, will be so important to this story.

In April 1941 Mussolini and a German general sat down together in Rome to discuss the possibilities of capturing Iraq, which Mussolini called the linchpin—"the center," in his words—of the British Empire. In Italy's long-standing correspondence with its potential allies in the Iraqi government and military, it had always spoken vaguely about Iraqi and wider Arab independence in the postwar world. But out of earshot of the Iraqis, Mussolini could speak freely of "possessing" Iraq, and that is what he did that day in Rome. "Discussing the possibilities" does not capture it: he practically salivated at the thought of placing Iraq under the Axis. The Axis, naturally, would own the oil wells of northern Iraq, and the country would provide a staging ground for attacking the Suez from the east, Mussolini said; this would be mortal for the British Empire. Turkey, meanwhile, would be forced to capitulate to Axis demands. Success in Iraq, he summarized to the German general, "might have an even more profound effect upon the British world position than a landing in the British Isles themselves."

As ever, the outcome of the subsequent fight came down to the sum of individual choices, and this book in part examines why people made them. Had a few thousand—perhaps a few hundred—people chosen differently, the balance would have been tipped toward results that range from bad to horribly worse. Put another way, a few thousand choices, a few thousand lives, stood between a shocking Axis success and failure. The price of forestalling a Nazi-aligned federation in Iraq and the Levant was the blood sacrifice of several thousand fathers' sons: as any father knows, a price worse than his own death. It is fitting, then, that this harsh story revolves around the legendary birthplace of Abraham.[3]

2

"Snares around You. And Sudden Dread"

The Crisis Begins in Iraq: Linchpin

> Let me just deal with the oil thing . . . we may be right or we may be wrong. . . . But the oil conspiracy theory is honestly one of the most absurd when you analyse it. The fact is that, if the oil that Iraq has were our concern I mean we could probably cut a deal with Saddam tomorrow in relation to the oil. It's not the oil that is the issue, it is the weapons.
>
> —Prime Minister Tony Blair, in an interview on
> *BBC Newsnight*, February 6, 2003

IN FALL 1940, IN the thronged streets of Amman, a government car honked and coaxed its way through the crowds. Anthony Eden, secretary of state for war and Churchill's first lieutenant, was in Transjordan's isolated mountain capital. He had just come from Cairo, where he had seen tanks returned from patrols in deserts to the west, ground down by sand and battle. An officer pleaded with Eden for more, but Eden knew there were no more. It was an unsettled question as to whether there were enough at home to even mount a sufficient defense of England. And a tank sent around Africa and up the Suez Canal meant one less in Britain. Still, Eden was happy that the officer imagined there was a reserve, and he did not disabuse the man of the false impression. If this officer thought there were more tanks, then maybe Hitler thought so too.

The sergeant at the wheel pulled the car up to the emir's palace, and there at the door, surrounded by an honor guard of the Arab Legion, stood Abdullah I, a compact man with dark and thick eyebrows and goatee. Though a short man, and for many years now a sedentary politician, Abdullah had been an active revolutionary in World War I. With his father and brothers he had cooperated with Lawrence of Arabia,

T. E. Lawrence, in the Arab Revolt by attacking Turkish garrisons and blasting railways. Abdullah's little emirate of Transjordan, with a population of one million, was born of that successful alliance. It was effectively an independent state, but the British retained a set of foreign policy and trade prerogatives there. What they could certainly *not* do was order Abdullah to join their fight against the Axis powers. They could only ask, and that is why Eden was there.

Emir Abdullah I greeted Eden cordially, guided him into the palace, and over coffee and cigarettes the men spoke. Abdullah was neither a fool nor unaware of the dangers of throwing in his lot with the British. Western Europe had been swallowed by Germany, and the Germans and Soviets had apportioned eastern Europe. Hitler and Mussolini seemed poised to divvy southeastern Europe next. Turkey was neutral at the moment, but could very easily succumb to Axis pressure if backed into a corner. Collaborationist Vichy France had control of Syria-Lebanon, which bordered Transjordan directly to the north, and commanded at least thirty thousand troops, with rumors of more, while Italian delegations operated in Beirut and Damascus keeping an eye on things for the Axis. To Abdullah's east, straddling a great desert, were the Saudis, against whom he periodically skirmished and whose loyalties in the expanding world war were unclear. Iraq, on another of his borders, was quiet at the moment, but top politicians there made no secret of their opposition to Britain and had refused British requests to break off diplomatic relations with fascist Italy. A short distance from the Transjordanian port of Aqaba on the Red Sea was Egypt, which might very well succumb to Axis siege someday. Over the summer the Italians had pushed back the British in the Horn of Africa and threatened the security of the Red Sea shipping lanes, and from there might ultimately threaten to create a second front in the campaign against Egypt and the Suez Canal. At this date the British could not point to any significant victory in the war, and at best could claim to have held out against the new German air onslaught on London. Opinion on the streets of Amman, meanwhile, was that the Germans would occupy Syria in a matter of months. Churchill might have promised that Britain would ride out the storm alone, but Transjordan might very well find itself alone and surrounded before Britain.

With spreading clouds visible on every dry horizon, Abdullah, too, had to choose, and he did. He told Eden that he was more than ready to send Transjordan's soldiers to the Western Desert to take on the Italians. And even should their island fall as France had, the emir would fight on with the British. Abdullah was neither a stooge nor naive. And he had his differences with the British: he resented Britain's refusal to grant self-determination to the Arabs over the River Jordan in Palestine; and he hoped Palestine might then form a state in a new free Arab confederation. (Zionist-Jewish Palestinians might have their own province within it too; he had always demonstrated the acceptance of some sort of Jewish-Zionist home in Palestine.) But Abdullah was making a bet that the British, despite the seeming invincibility of the German tank corps, would ultimately win. Those who knew him thought he took pride in standing with an old, if difficult, ally when it had been knocked down and bloodied. And he was also making the sound bet that it was better to have British partners—even if they were often bumptious, sometimes meddling—than German or Italian bosses. The streets of Amman were rife with rumor and fear—speculation and hoarding made things hard on the soldiers whose wages were fixed—but Abdullah and his Arab Legion stood ready.

Before leaving Transjordan by air, Eden reviewed the Arab troops, and they raised his spirits in a time of retreat and uncertainty. "The toughest looking lot of Bedouin Arabs ever I saw," he recorded in his journal. All in good order, ready to fight, and backed by some armored cars. Eden planned to appeal to London for funds to give Abdullah to expand their ranks. After their plane lifted off, Eden and some officers skirted the frontier with Syria and discussed the military problem that the border represented. Abdullah had offered to send his fighters to defend Egypt. But Eden had told him to hold tight, and warned the Arab Legion's officers that, should the Axis appear on Transjordan's borders, they might have to stand alone against many tens of thousands of potential enemies on several borders.[1]

Around the same time, a conversation took place late in the day in a café in Palestine. The radio had just carried a broadcast from Radio Bari, the Italian propaganda station, offering the typical anti-British message it incessantly broadcast to the Middle East. German and Italian radio would periodically invent Muslim uprisings in India, relate tales of the British destroying mosques, and call Emir Abdullah I a Jewish puppet. This afternoon the Arabic speaker had declared that the Italian Navy reigned over the Mediterranean, that the British were afraid of the Italians, that Mussolini was the greatest friend of Islam, and the British government was made up of Jews.

An Arab youth applauded. An older man in a kaffiyeh spat with contempt. "They are oppressors, those Italians," he said, "slave people though they be. I have a cousin in Eritrea who in his letters tells me he has forever to be rising from his seat in front of his shop in order to salute Italian soldiers—the spawn of pigs!" He was a dignified man, a village elder, but at that moment he was indignant. "And our women—they violate our Muslim women. No woman is safe when Italian soldiers—or those who pretend to be soldiers—are near. They enter our mosques for no reason. They have no respect for our mosques." He spat again, and told how Mussolini had ordered a scimitar made for himself and declared it a gift from the Arabs that called him Protector of Islam. He told how Arab leaders who had refused to collaborate with the Italians in Libya had been thrown to their deaths out of airplanes over their hometowns. "That was in Libya, but so would they do in Palestine were they to rule here. . . . Ah, my brother, we Arabs have no love for the British. They are taking our country from us and giving it to the Jews. But better we have dealings with them than with the Italians."[2]

It's a dark irony that Axis radio propaganda sought to turn Arabs in the Middle East against the British at the same moment that Italian bombers were killing Arab children in Palestine and damaging mosques and cemeteries.

The Italians knew the vast importance of the oil refinery at the Port of Haifa in northern Palestine. It was this oil, pumped from nearby Kirkuk, Iraq, that fueled the Royal Navy fleet in the Mediterranean— and that fleet was the sole fact that stood in the way of Axis dominance of that sea. Haifa's naval base also facilitated the movement of arms and men that kept the war effort going. So when the Italians joined the Axis, they soon began launching bomber raids against Haifa. In July 1940, with the Italian Army massing on the frontier between Egypt and Libya, Supreme Command in Rome authorized the most deadly bombing run on Palestine yet. Around seven o'clock one morning, a flight of ten three-engine Savoia-Marchetti SM.79 medium bombers, planes that had already earned a reputation for speed and deadliness in France and elsewhere, lifted off from Italian-controlled Aegean islands for the two-hour journey. They approached above the clouds, and where sea met land they dropped around ninety bombs. Columns of water erupted in the Port of Haifa as a fishing boat was struck and two Arab fishermen were killed. Air wardens and police directed people as best as they could: a Jewish policewoman kept to her work as bomb shards flew around her, as did a Scottish police constable until he was knocked down. As anti-aircraft guns opened fire, stretcher bearers hurried some of the wounded to the hospital, while taxis carried others. The refinery was hit, and kerosene stores erupted into flame. Abdul Latif Abdullah, Ibrahim Bawakat, and Farid Khalil were killed, as was young Molly Kisch. Twenty-eight Arab men and woman, fifteen Jewish civilians, and Constable Peter Moran were dead.

In the weeks and months to come, the Italians and then the Germans returned, sometimes reigniting the refinery, often merely hitting residential areas, with eleven bombing runs in the year between July 1940 and June 1941. In one attack, bombs meant for warehouses and port facilities actually fell on houses and apartments in Jaffa and Tel Aviv, killing 125 men, women, and children in just three terrible minutes. The largest share of the dead were Jewish refugees, often crowded in flimsy tenements; but bombs also struck an Arab village, killing five children. Tel Aviv had no antiaircraft defenses, and the RAF presence in Palestine was nominal, since the thinly stretched force needed to protect the Mediterranean fleet. In the immediate aftermath of the bombing of Tel Aviv, Arab dignitaries attended Jewish funerals, Jewish dignitaries attended Arab funerals, and Arab and Jewish newspapers united in condemning the attack. People of all walks, meanwhile, seemed to take a measure of pride in ostentatiously carrying on with business as usual. The day after incendiary bombs ignited an Arab village's grain stores near Acre, a newspaper quoted a townsperson as saying, "we can take it. Our hearts go out to the people of England who are under constant attack." Children picked through the craters and rubble, collecting bomb fins and other fragments, perhaps at the same time as did children in London.

Despite the blitz spirit, the defiant display of normalcy, the danger to Palestine was real. In the same days that the Italians were bombing Palestine, the British were examining the potential of a new Middle Eastern front in the war. They knew it was a tempting prospect for both the Germans and the Italians: push through the Balkans; cross Turkey, with its acquiescence or not; or perhaps cross over the Greek islands, then push through Syria and Palestine to the Suez Canal. It would be a deadly right-hand pincer to meet the left-hand one closing in on Egypt from the west. In late 1940 military intelligence at the British War Office believed that the Axis was more than tempted; the office was convinced that Germany would drive on the Middle East to capture Iraq's oil. Italy's invasion of Greece in fall 1940 seemed to confirm this push, and the British looked nervously at Vichy Syria for signs that the Germans or Italians would use it as a foothold for invasion.

There was simply little the Allies could do in response to a larger attack on the Levant. They had few troops in Palestine: one infantry battalion of fewer than one thousand as 1941 arrived, and some inexperienced cavalry who would soon give up their horses and have to learn to drive trucks and fight as infantry. Emir Abdullah I could contribute less than one or two thousand war-ready soldiers from the Arab Legion. Meanwhile, in Syria-Lebanon there were at least thirty thousand Vichy troops—European troops, colonial troops, and an infamously hard core of the French Foreign Legion. There was also a modern air force of many scores of fighters and bombers. In Iraq there was a vast army—around thirty to fifty thousand, including some light tanks, armored cars, and fifty aircraft—and Iraq's attitude in the war was uncertain. Should an airborne assault occur, as the Germans were planning for elsewhere, or should Turkey turn or permit Axis passage across the Anatolian railway, Palestine could not offer much resistance. The British were making their stand far away in Egypt, where General Erwin Rommel arrived in February 1941, and in the Sudan-Eritrea borderlands. And as new crises were soon to appear in the Balkan States and Greece in these days, ships, planes, and men were siphoned off from these forces.

In early 1941 the British in London and Palestine gloomily sketched contingency plans in case Palestine was invaded—really, overrun, since there was little chance of a real contest for Palestine. The plan was to resist as long as possible with what few units were likely to be available, then scorch the earth. Then the nonmilitary administration and their families would most likely take to the lonely highway between Amman and Baghdad—assuming that remained open—and thence to Basra, near the Persian Gulf, and finally down the gulf to relative safety in India.

The British were well aware of the particular danger facing Palestine's Jewish settlers. While the unspeakable horror of the systematic destruction of Jewish Europeans—the Final Solution—had not yet commenced, the world nevertheless knew of Jewish repression, imprisonment, and executions in Europe. In Italian Libya, meanwhile, Jews had been maligned for years, but from 1941 on the Jewish community began to be deported, interned, and enslaved as laborers. The British in Palestine knew that the possible consequences of Axis invasion for Palestine's Jews only ran from bad to worse—even before the commencement of the full horror of the German extermination program in 1942.

But there were almost a half million Jews in Palestine, and no possibility of moving or feeding a half million refugees in the desert, nor putting them on ships, nor resettling them. Even the administrators of the Jewish community in Palestine admitted it, though they gave the British a list of several hundred Jews to be evacuated who they deemed would be particularly singled out by the Gestapo. Ultimately the British envisioned being able to move no more than a few thousand, the wives and children of Jewish members of the British colonial administration. The rest of Palestinian Jewry must be left to their fate.

As things grew darker in early 1941 the Jewish community prepared to fight an insurgency campaign of sabotage and guerilla warfare. With British consent and some training, the Palmach, a "strike company" drawn from the existing paramilitary, formed in secret. Its purpose was to work against the Axis where possible and prepare for rearguard attacks in case of invasion. As the seesaw struggle on the Egyptian frontier

continued and Rommel made headway, the British and Jewish administration in Palestine prepared a network of intelligence agents and radio
operators to work in occupied Palestine. The Jewish administration was
also able to pass to the British helpful intelligence on the military situation
in Vichy Syria-Lebanon from Jewish informants there. And leading Jewish intelligence figures and Arab leaders even met together in secret to
prepare to resist German occupation.

Another perverse irony is that even the Jewish Palestinian community contained those who sided with the Axis, judging the enemy of their
enemy to be their friend and sharing in their faith in fascism. The British
had governed Palestine after Allied and imperial troops pried it bloodily
from the Germans and Turks near the end of World War I. While many
in the Jewish community who chiefly arrived after World War I were dis-
pleased with the British colonial government for a variety of reasons, one
group was single-mindedly intent on seeing the British crushed. The fascist seduction had insinuated itself into Jewish parts of Palestine as it had
the world over, and a group of such fascists came together in 1940, calling themselves Lohamei Herut Israel (the Fighters for the Freedom of Israel), or Lehi. They admired the apparent unifying strength of European
fascism (some of them had studied in Mussolini's Italy in the 1930s), rejected democracy for authoritarianism, and scorned politics for brute
force. Their goal was to help the Germans or Italians drive the British
from Palestine and establish a fascist, yet purely Jewish, nation—an Axis
ally. The Axis countries would, in return, send the Jews of Europe to this
new state.

The successful Italian bombing raids seemed to signal the time was
ripe, and in late 1940 Lehi tried to form a pact with the Italians. British
intelligence and antifascist Jewish paramilitary intelligence worked together to intercept the first Lehi overture, however. Lehi instead sent representatives to Vichy Beirut, where they successfully met with a Reich
Foreign Office representative. The Lehi proposal was for the group to
undertake guerilla operations on the behalf of Germany in advance of
recruiting, they claimed, forty thousand men to help Germany drive
Britain from Palestine. (This army, they said, would only require Axis
training.) Again the plan was for the Germans to send Europe's Jews to

Palestine in exchange for their supporting a new fascist Jewish nation to be an ally, consolidating German strength in the postwar fascist-aligned Middle East. The Reich Foreign Office agent left Beirut with the proposal, but nothing is known about how it was received in Berlin. Though the story of Jews seeking to help the Axis reads like a perverse joke, there was little humorous about Lehi: while it numbered some hundreds, not thousands, there is no telling what effects it might have had in the event of an Axis invasion of Palestine. In any case, it undertook a deadly serious campaign of murder, bombings, and gun running throughout the war.[3]

Britain controlled Iraq from the end of World War I, having seized it—really a collection of provinces—from the Turks in a long, bloody struggle largely fought by the Indian Army. The British granted Iraq a large measure of independence in 1932, leaving it to the rule of Britain's old ally from the days of the Arab Revolt, Faisal I (brother to Transjordan's Abdullah I), along with a parliament. The British granted this semi-independence on many conditions: that Iraq remain its close military ally, that British political advisers serve in Baghdad, that two RAF air bases remain, that the British reserve rights of military transit across the country, and that British interests retain exclusive rights to oil extraction in the valuable north central oil fields. The British did not want to control Iraq directly, but wanted to maintain influence there as a regional linchpin, vital stopover en route to India, and source of oil. Naturally, this merely conditional independence was unsatisfactory to those Iraqis who wanted a truly free nation.

In the years between semi-independence in Iraq and World War II, one power block in particular rose: the military. Iraq was a peculiar, forced amalgam of sectarian and ethnic groups: Christians and Jews; Shiite and Sunni Muslims; Assyrians and Kurds, among many. Within its somewhat arbitrary borders were rival tribes and families, Bedouin and people of the mountains, and people of the wetlands. How to unite such a disparate country? The Royal Iraqi Army, created in 1921, had an answer: teach national unity through military service, a lesson its officers learned from Germany before World War I. Germany itself was a strange amalgam of Catholic and Protestant, mountain people and Baltic Sea people, bound together in a new nation in 1871. And part of the way Germany unified was by passing young men through its new army, formed around the ages-old powerful Prussian military. When Germany and the Ottoman Empire were close allies before World War I, young Arab men from what would become Iraq trained under these German officers in Istanbul.

This provided the seed of the idea of unifying the country through military service, and this crop of young officers eventually aged into the senior military officer corps. After 1921, when the British and Iraqis opened a military college in Baghdad, some of these men became instructors and began making direct comparisons between Germany and Iraq. Let the Iraqi Army, like the Prussian Army, lead the way in making one nation, they said; indeed, let them lead the way to a unified Arab Middle East. One of these former Ottoman officers trained under the Germans in Istanbul gave a speech in 1939, extolling how recent nationalist movements were only made possible through unified violence: Mussolini's Blackshirts in Italy were a prime example. He helped set a national policy that high school–age students of all ethnicities and religions across the country must dress in paramilitary uniform.

In the mid-1930s this movement to make the army the incubator of a unified nation achieved a major goal by securing national conscription. Iraq's many minority communities resisted, but the military violently put such resistance down. The Sunnis from cities like Baghdad and Mosul overwhelmingly dominated the officer corps, and did not hesitate to crush resistance from outlying Kurdish or Shiite areas. Soon the Iraqi military became more powerful and stable than its civilian government, and politicians had to court its senior officers to secure their influence.

At the turn of 1941 Iraq was officially at peace, neutral in the world conflict, but in fact it was the scene of straining forces pulling it in multiple directions. These tectonic stresses, accompanied by many violent shocks, had been building for over a decade and soon had to give. The death of King Faisal—Iraq's first king—in 1933 was the first blow to stability. And Faisal's son did not have the personal force of his father nor his father's political acumen; a series of coups—army interference in politics, assassinations, and constant intrigue—followed. When this next king crashed one of his Italian sports cars into a lamppost in 1939, the crown prince was just three years old, so a regency followed. Another blow.

Under all this political instability lay in Iraq, as throughout the world, two main currents that were pushing against one another: there was the movement toward liberalism, pluralism, and democracy, and there was the movement toward authoritarianism as symbolized by many at the top of the Iraqi officer corps. There was a debate that coursed through newspapers and schools and politics: Were "real" Iraqis just Arabs? Just Sunni Muslims? Or could a real Iraqi patriot be Christian, Jewish, or Shiite? There were young Jewish teachers who promoted Arab nationalism to their students; there were Shiite teachers who publicly rejected the anti-Semitism and anti-Kurdism of some fellow teachers. And just as there were militarist and fascist Iraqis, there were Iraqis on the far left who argued that race did not define a nation and were instead united in a common struggle against imperialism and capitalist economic exploitation. Such groups, like the Committee for Combating Colonialism, clear in its opposition to anti-Semitism, were made illegal in the years before the Golden Square coup, thus helping rid the field of its opposition.

Left or right, political groups of nearly all stripes desired greater freedom from British intervention in Iraqi affairs. There were no fewer than eighteen permanent British secretaries across Iraq's government ministries, and British spying in the country—especially via RAF intelligence—was an open secret among Iraqi officials. Among Iraqi politicians and power brokers, reactions ranged from the slow and tactful politics of Faisal's family to revolutionary militancy lodged in the army. There were those who saw some kind of relationship with Britain as a boon to the country, and there were those who believed that the day of the British Empire was over and the day of fascist Germany and Italy had dawned.

Enter Fritz Grobba—a small man, prim, proper, and pleasant-looking— whose role it was to convince the Iraqis that the day of Germany and its friends had dawned. Grobba was a World War I veteran of the Western Front and Syria, possessed a doctorate in law, and was a longtime diplomat working on Middle Eastern affairs. He spoke Arabic and Turkish, and was a veteran of postings in Afghanistan and Ottoman Palestine.

A genuine Arabophile, Grobba truly believed that the Arabs of the Middle East and the new Germany should be staunch allies. Upon Iraq's nominal independence in the early 1930s, the Reich Foreign Office sent Grobba as head of its legation in Baghdad.

If wooden and formal in appearance, Grobba acted with great energy, cultivating friendships with teachers, students, lawyers, and civil servants and hosting them in the legation's Baghdad house for champagne and elbow rubbing. Grobba bought space in Iraqi newspapers to spread the gospel of the fascist renaissance and the anointed Hitler. He arranged for scholarships for Iraqi students to study in Germany, as well as other cultural exchanges. He met with Amin al-Husseini, the Arab revolutionary who sought German assistance in his fight against the British and the Jews (more on him later). And he was particularly successful at increasing commercial links between Germany and Iraq, screening industrial propaganda films and discretely delivering bribes. On the other hand, Grobba had to placate Arab nationalists who feared that Germany's own prewar policy of repatriating its Jewish citizens to Palestine stood in the way of creating an independent Palestinian Arab state there. At the same time, Grobba also met with leaders of Iraq's large Jewish community to convince them that reports of atrocities afflicting German Jewry were overblown.

Grobba's bureaucratic mandate and his personal inclination was to strengthen the bonds between Germany and Iraq. But his orders forbade him to directly attack the British, even in the later 1930s. As late as 1940, Hitler's vision of the new world order had the British Empire, once cowed, serving the Reich as imperial caretakers in India, the Middle East, and elsewhere. It would not do to utterly undermine them. But convince the Iraqis that they had a true friend in Germany? By all means.

The "German option" appeared increasingly viable as the 1930s progressed. It was hardly the case that Grobba waved a wand and hypnotized Iraq with Aryan race nationalism. Indeed, Grobba grew more and more frustrated that his führer's anti-Semitic statements included Arabs, hampering his ability to unite Arabs and Germans. For years he worked to overcome the Nazis' infamous race ordering while trying to ally with Iraqi Arabs—not to mention that *Mein Kampf* had clearly denigrated Arabs. (Hitler later permitted an Arabic translation to cut such passages, but behind closed doors Hitler called the Arabs "half-apes.") Given the Nazis' well-documented racism—which Arab anti-Nazis highlighted—the pro-German party in Iraq was more misguided than Lehi only in degree.

Competing liberal Iraqi activists wrote that, whatever the shortcomings of imperial Britain, it could not be compared with Nazi Germany's animal aggression. And should Britain fall as France did, there would be nothing to stop fascist colonialism over the globe. This opposition extended to other Arab lands too. In Egypt there was a broad current of anti-Nazism in these crucial days, with a number of newspapers railing against the inhumanity fundamental to the Nazi worldview and the brutality of Mussolini's Italy. Muslim leaders in Britain, meanwhile, leant their voices to the argument that Islam was the natural ally of democracy.

When Britain declared war on Germany in late 1939, Grobba's work of ingratiating the Arabs came to a halt. The Iraqi government politely invited Grobba and the German legation to go home. So he continued his work from Berlin, no less passionately, with some of his Foreign Office superiors finding his enthusiasm for the Arabs unhealthy, even calling him an "Arabomaniac."

On the other hand, it was a good sign for the Germans that, when Italy joined the war, the Iraqi prime minister did not invite the Italian legation to go home. This was a bold move meant to make a show of independence to Iraqi nationalists of the authoritarian bent. While on the surface it was a bad sign for the Allies, it turned out that it was to the advantage of the British that the Italians stayed in Iraq, because before long British cryptologists were reading radio transmissions sent from the Italian consulate in Baghdad to Rome.[4]

These decrypted messages of March and April 1941 described how a group of senior Iraqi officers known as the Golden Square—Colonel Salah ed-Din es-Sabbagh, Colonel Fahmi Said, Colonel Kamal Shahib, and Royal Iraqi Air Force colonel Mahmud Salman—wanted to join the fight against the British in exchange for Arab independence in Iraq and the Levant in the new world order. The colonels, Ottoman veterans trained under the Germans decades earlier, wanted German weapons, ammunition, and perhaps officers in advisory roles. Meanwhile, Allied intelligence agents placed in Iraq reported that, as Europe fell to the Germans and the British grew increasingly isolated, there was a feeling on the streets of Baghdad, Basra, and Mosul that the Germans were the inheritors of the earth. Iraqi representatives met with Germany in neutral Turkey, meanwhile, to win support for independence. Intelligence analysts in Cairo and Whitehall took this very seriously, assessing the ways in which the Germans might reinforce Iraq, eying Vichy Syria as the best way in. The only problem was that British leadership could do very little about it.

Then, on March 31, 1941, the Golden Square made its move, the army officers' men trying to seize the four-year-old king and his uncle, the regent. The two stayed a step ahead of their pursuers, however, first sheltering in the American consulate, then speeding—smuggled—in a car to the RAF base west of Baghdad, then flew to Basra, and eventually on to a British warship. But though they escaped, the coup proceeded. The Golden Square dismissed the country's prime minister and installed its own choice, a former prime minister who would happily work with Germany if it meant personal power, independence from Britain, and ultimate independence for Arabs in the Middle East.

Though they failed to actually seize the child king or disappear the regent, the pro-German military leaders were as confident as the British were unprepared. With the British falling back from Italian Libya and the Germans rolling through Greece, they had launched their revolt at the perfect moment. (The Italian ambassador heard their apparently freely offered expressions of self-assurance and passed them on to Rome.) Their Axis partners, the Iraqi officers said, would soon appear in Iraq to help drive the weakened British from the Middle East.

The new prime minister, the officers' man, was Rashid Ali al-Gailani. Fifty years old, bespectacled with a trim mustache, al-Gailani was a capable politician, a lawyer and former prime minister. He had been a member of the proindependence movement since entering politics as a younger man, and for over a year he had been communicating with the Germans through intermediaries seeking their support for a break from British interference.

Now, in early April 1941, he was shrewd enough to know that he could not consolidate power on the basis of his colonels' confidence alone. In Berlin, Joachim von Ribbentrop's Foreign Office began to organize the arming and funding of the new Iraqi allies. Meanwhile, al-Gailani was taking steps to buy the time he needed for that German aid to arrive. The ousted pro-British prime minister, the child prince, and the pro-British regent had all eluded capture and apparently escaped the country. Al-Gailani could not know how the British would react to the loss of these friendly figures, but it wouldn't be well received. The most powerful leaders in the Iraqi Army and Air Force—all pro-German— were with him. But other influential figures and politicians in Iraq ran the gamut from profascists to prodemocracy liberals.

And Iraq was a deeply divided country of forcibly combined communities. Outlying populations and the religious leadership of the Shiite majority had not declared loyalty to the new regime. Could al-Gailani shore up his legitimacy in the eyes of the Iraqi people and stave off a British counterstroke until his appeals to the Germans and Italians bore fruit in the form of arms, planes, and men?

It was this question that motivated al-Gailani to summon the Iraqi Parliament one day in early April. And by the end of that day of speeches and negotiations, he had succeeded: he convinced the parliament to name a new regent for the boy prince (never mind that the prince was in hiding outside the country), a man who was both a distant relative of Emir Abdullah I in Transjordan and amenable to cooperating with the new regime. Al-Gailani thus succeeded in undermining arguments that he had dishonorably disowned the Hashemites of their dynastic rights in Iraq.

Second, al-Gailani shrewdly announced that the new government would indeed continue to honor British treaty rights in Iraq. These included the right to keep an RAF air base and flight terminus at Habbaniya, west of Baghdad, and another near Basra. They were not major bases of war operations; they were mainly used for training and refueling (and, as forthcoming pages will show, as spy centers). The more important right was to pump oil from Kirkuk to a refinery in Haifa, Palestine, where the Royal Navy refueled. (Another pipeline ran from there to Vichy Lebanon, though that pipeline had been shut down after the fall of France.)

Britain's prerogatives included the right of the British to move troops across Iraq, a provision meant to address the potential of the Suez Canal being seized. Nor, for now, did the new prime minister call for the return of the German embassy delegation—though, in fact, Iraqi representatives were in frequent contact with Rome and Berlin, and "Herr Gehrcke" (that is, Grobba) was soon on his way.

"This national movement is entirely an internal movement having no connection whatever with any foreign state," said al-Gailani before the Iraqi Parliament. With all this, the new prime minister hoped that he had neutered the threat of any immediate intervention on the part of the British.[5]

March 1941 was a low point for Britain and its allies. The Germans rained more bombs—including incendiary bombs—on London than ever before, with the ports of Bristol, Glasgow, and Portsmouth also hit. Britain's war effort was sustained by a lifeline of convoys that crossed the North Atlantic from American, Canadian, and Caribbean ports, carrying industrial resources, invaluable oil, even Spam. In March 1941 the German *Kriegsmarine* sent more convoy ships to the bottom of the Atlantic or back to port than ever before, just edging out its previous record of February as measured by volume.

By April 1941 it had been almost a year since the British and their imperial and commonwealth allies had made the fateful choice to fight on without France—one year, and still little good news. Erwin Rommel, who had a year earlier blitzed across France, now blitzed across Libya, sending the British scurrying. Then Germany bombed and invaded Yugoslavia, overrunning it in less than two weeks with over eight hundred tanks. Next came Greece. Churchill had envisioned making a stand in Greece and opening a southern front to threaten occupied Europe's "soft underbelly." A force of almost fifty thousand Australian, British, and New Zealand troops were there. But in about three weeks in April the Germans had chased them all—save the seven thousand they took prisoner—to the sea and into all shape of boats and ships in a desperate scene reminiscent of Dunkirk.

On an early April late afternoon, the War Cabinet gathered at 10

Downing Street to learn of the new threat of an Axis-allied Iraq flanking Egypt, Suez, and Palestine. Churchill, Clement Atlee, Ernest Bevin, and the Chiefs of Staff—all the top hats and brass—heard reports of the German bombing of Belgrade, the alarming rate at which ships were being sent to the bottom of the Atlantic; and now this news of Iraq. It was not that the threat to Iraq was entirely a surprise; the men on the ground in Cairo and New Delhi had already envisioned the danger of the scenario— the port at Basra key for disembarking troops, the Iraq oil field and the nearby Persian oil fields, the air entrepôt at Habbaniya. But even to many who watched developments in Iraq closely, the actual coup was a surprise and so a reaction had to be improvised. After learning of the success of the Golden Square, London wired Cairo to see what kind of military intervention might be sent to Iraq.

And now the War Cabinet heard Cairo's response. Battered by Rommel, stretched thin by responsibilities in Greece, and fighting the Italians in northeastern Africa, the Middle East Command had almost nothing to devote to Iraq. Even in the worst-case scenario all it could do was send a single battalion garrisoning Palestine across the desert road to Iraq—aided, perhaps, by the very few modern warplanes stationed at the RAF base west of Baghdad. "Any other action," the reply stated, "is impossible with existing resources." Churchill was unhappy, and ordered an appeal to India to see what kind of response it could offer. With the question of what to do about Iraq unanswered, the meeting dispersed under the light of the lengthening spring day. But once darkness fell that night, the German bombers came, passing over England, passing over neutral Ireland, to bomb Belfast and its dockyard.[6]

Al-Gailani hoped that his political maneuvers had neutralized the threat of any immediate intervention by the British before Axis support arrived, but intervene was exactly what General Claude Auchinleck wanted to do. Auchinleck was one of those bygone figures who, if certainly not truly Indian, was not entirely British either. His father was a lifelong artillery officer in India and, except for some school and the Royal Military College in England, Claude Auchinleck lived nearly his whole life in India as well. Beginning his army career in 1903, he spent the bulk of it in the

Punjab. Among other languages, he learned a number of dialects of Punjabi from his comrades. Out on the frontier between Afghanistan and India where he spent many years he was known for striking up conversations with gray Indian veterans. His fluency helped lower barriers to understanding and, more important than his tendency to participate in village gossip, he learned far more than most officers of Hinduism, Islam, and Sikhism as practiced by ordinary people. This learning and understanding helped make Auchinleck an outspoken opponent of race prejudice in the Indian Army and a proponent of greater numbers of Indian-born officers. Now he was commander in chief in India.

It seemed he learned a cagey wariness in his years of policing and fighting in volatile places like Mohmand, too; perhaps that is why he was raising the alert today. He was worried about signs that London intended to take a wait-and-see attitude toward Iraq. Immediately after the coup, he had convinced his political superiors to redirect two troopships that were preparing to leave for Singapore to the main Iraqi port of Basra at the end of the Persian Gulf instead. He had succeeded.

But then the British ambassador in Iraq sent a coded message to Whitehall declaring that the British had been outmaneuvered by Rashid Ali al-Gailani's moves to consolidate power and buy time. If, argued the ambassador, the Iraqis made clear their intention to honor Britain's treaty rights, Britain could not very well land troops in the country. The new Iraqi regime should be somehow tested, and if it proved intransigent, only then might the matter be pressed militarily.

The military Chiefs of Staff in London agreed and, though the troopships *Varella* and *El Madina* had already set sail for Basra from Karachi, with the *Devonshire* and *Lancashire* about to follow, they judged the ships should be halted at allied Bahrain to see how things played out.

When General Auchinleck learned of these developments the next day, he leaped to object. He immediately wrote to the viceroy's office in New Delhi, "Acceptance of the ambassador's advice to defer action for the securing of Basra may very well result in our never getting Basra at all." He argued that securing a base in Basra might determine Allied success or failure in the entire Middle East. If they stopped to parley, there was a deadly risk "that Rashid [Ali al-Gailani] will use the breathing space [British ambassador Kinahan] Cornwallis proposes to consolidate his position and, probably, to invoke German aid, which might even take the form of airborne troops and aircraft." Auchinleck had no idea at the time how prescient he was; the German Foreign Office was at the same moment beginning to organize Luftwaffe support for the Iraqis.

Auchinleck was pressing for risky action, but he did so knowing what he was asking of the boys and men he wanted to hurry to Basra. In 1914 he and his Punjabi battalion were on a transport bound for Europe when it was hurriedly diverted to the Suez Canal. The Turks were making a thrust for the canal, and young Captain Auchinleck and his riflemen fended off the attack. They then reversed the attack, crossed the canal, and stormed the Turkish trenches. Not long after, the unit was sent to Basra. In the campaign to drive the Turks from Baghdad, his battalion slogged through sodden mud in flooded countryside, was beset by lice and flees, and was hurled against dug-in machine gun posts by superiors in scenes reminiscent of the Western Front. Auchinleck's press for a rush to Basra in 1941 was not an uninformed act of swagger and bluff but based, sadly, on experience.

The viceroy agreed with Auchinleck and sent his recommendation on to London. There the War Cabinet was won over, and the transports were ordered once again to proceed directly for Basra.[7]

Soon representatives from the military, their chosen prime minister Rashid Ali al-Gailani, and the Grand Mufti, Amin al-Husseini, met with the Italians at their consulate. The Italians, in turn, would act as a go-between with the Germans. It was time to work out a concrete deal by which the Axis would help the Iraqis throw out the British in return for concessions.

Of course, what the Iraqis had to offer the Germans and Italians was their oil. They offered to cancel British oil rights and create a national oil board on which German and Italian representatives would be in the majority. Oil would immediately recommence flowing through Syria-Lebanon for Axis use, and the new oil board could build more pipelines from Iraq's northern oil fields to the Mediterranean. They also offered the Axis options to lease land, sea, and air bases in Iraq.

In return the Germans and Italians offered to support a single state encompassing Iraq and the Levant—what the treaty called the United Kingdom of Iraq and Syria. It is unclear whether the terms of the alliance included Lebanon, with its significant Christian Arab population, under the category of Syria. It could be that the Axis intended to leave it to the Vichy French as a vestige of their colonial presence in the region; more likely it was to be subsumed again under Syria. The Axis would also have lease rights to navy bases on the Mediterranean.

To realize this, the Axis powers would fight beside their new allies, sell them heavy weapons and planes, give the Iraqis credits toward more purchases, and provide one million Italian lire in cash immediately. Besides oil, the Germans promised to import commodities like Iraqi cotton, wool, and millet to make up for the loss of British purchases shortly after the war began in 1939.

Shortly after this, the German and Italian Foreign Offices signed an agreement to split their new Iraqi oil windfall fifty-fifty. This was in keeping with their shared understanding, worked out since allying, that in the new world order they would share in exploiting the oil, economic benefits, and transportation opportunities of the Arab Middle East. And while they would emphasize the Axis's shared interest with certain Arab nationalists in throwing out the British, they would decidedly *not* promise independence. In fact, an internal memo circulated in the Italian Foreign Ministry in late 1940 made its plans for Iraq clear: "our policies . . . after England is displaced from its positions . . . will not be much different from those already existing between Great Britain and Iraq." In other words, Italy would simply replace Britain as informal colonial interloper. Naturally, they didn't tell the Iraqis this.

The Golden Square immediately sent troops to the oil fields of Kirkuk, ordering the pipeline sending oil to British Palestine shut down and the pipeline to Vichy Tripoli, Lebanon—shut since the fall of France—reopened. The army was placed on standby and reinforcements started arriving in Baghdad. So the die was cast. For the colonels of the Golden Square, the pressing question was whether Axis aid would arrive in Iraq before Allied troops could easily stop them.[8]

3

"When They Ride in the Ships, They Call Upon God"

The Indian Army Comes to Iraq

> When we landed in Basra it was like a meat wagon of hairy infantrymen wearing body armour and helmets spilling onto the tarmac. The intense heat hit me like a sledgehammer . . . something that we all had to look forward to for the next six months. . . . We gathered together and listened to an RAF full screw waffle on about keeping safe, adhering to procedures, then we piled into a bus and headed for our new base at Shiba [Shaibah].
> —Dean Bailey, British Army sniper based in southern Iraq, 2007, in *Crawling Out of Hell: The True Story of a British Sniper's Greatest Battle*

TURNING THE CALENDAR back to 1938 reveals John Masters, not yet a captain, trying to outrun a war by train. Twenty-four years old, he had a dark mustache under his Roman nose, a tall forehead above that. He was a lieutenant in the Indian Army's Fourth Gurkha Rifle Battalion. Masters was descending from the highlands on the Afghan border, riding the *Frontier Mail* over the rails toward Bombay, where a liner awaited. It was September, and in the foregoing months the battalion mess radio had piped the voice of the German führer in a shrill crescendo. Adolf Hitler had made increasing demands to add German-speaking parts of Europe to his Reich. Now, even as John Masters rattled south, it appeared Hitler would get his war over Czechoslovakia. The armies of France and Germany, meanwhile, faced each other over the Rhine. And British prime minister Neville Chamberlain strove to keep Europe from falling, again, into depravity. At train stations along the southern route, Masters scanned newspaper headlines and eavesdropped on radios for news. He willed the war to hold off; he needed to get on his ship and away from India before an irruption and the Indian Army stopped all leave.

Masters was no coward. Far from it; he had already fought the legendary Pashtun fighters of the frontier tribal areas on their own ground. As a professional soldier he welcomed the chance to do his job and lead his men, and to humble the hectoring boss of Berlin. But it just so happened that Masters was due for his career's first furlough at precisely this moment when hell threatened to break loose in Europe. He was sure that there would be plenty of war left for him to fight once he got back from his nine-month leave.

He had a plan for seeing America. His army travel allowance provided enough for a first-class return trip to England, and for a fraction more, he calculated, he could travel east instead of west, crossing the United States overland. He had dreamed of it for years, nurturing visions of the Great Plains, Rocky Mountains, cowboys, New York City. At his battalion's alpine station he spent many a night reading about the American Civil War by the light of a smoky hurricane lamp to the music of the wailing wind pouring through the mountain passes in search of the plains below the headquarters of Bakloh.

Finally Masters arrived in Bombay and hurried from the train depot to the pier where his ship awaited. Then he was at the gangplank. He made it; he would escape.

"Lieutenant Masters, Fourth Gurkhas," came a hail over a loudspeaker, "to the stationmaster's office!"

Masters knew what that hail meant, and he turned to go receive word that all leave had been canceled and collect his ticket for the return to his post. As he did, he wondered all the while when he would get another chance at his American adventure in a world about to be plunged into war.

Some days later, back at the frontier, John Masters nursed the sting of surrender to Germany over Czechoslovakia and trained his Gurkha riflemen in case Hitler's signature did not, in fact, promise "peace in our time." Masters's riflemen were called Gurkhas for the Gurkhali language they spoke. They were Nepalis, boys and men from that mountain-bound kingdom above India. When the East India Company quarreled with the

Hindu kingdom in 1814 it learned to its cost how tenacious were the Nepalese fighters. The "Honourable Company" was lucky to fight the King of Nepal to a draw; it was luckier still that he later agreed to allow his subjects to enlist in the company's army. Since that day, Gurkha battalions had fought beside British from France to India and points in between.

And John Masters deeply admired them. On the whole, he found the Gurkhas relished life, greeting it with a warm sense of humor. They tended to be proud, and especially proud of their fearlessness. Whatever life or duty dictated to the Gurkhas, they nodded acceptance—but not, it seemed to Masters, because they were servile or browbeaten. Still, Masters was smart enough to avoid painting the Gurkhas with the broad strokes with which white sahibs in India tended to paint the various "races" of the Indian Subcontinent: this one dimwitted and martial, that one lacking manly strength, and another inclined to rebellious cunning. No, Masters had observed that the *lance naik* (lance corporal) with the most sinister set of eyes south of Kashmir could be angelically honest, and the most begrimed peasant *jawan* (private) a genius at electronics. And he observed that the usually dutiful and proud men could become slaves to their love of rum, gambling, or women. Masters, in fact, understood India to comprise saints and sinners, ugliness and beauty, in various degrees. It was not inscrutable and picturesque, as writers and tour companies portrayed, nor as simple as MGM projected on the silver screen.

Before long, the army reinstated leave and Masters rode the rails again down to Bombay. There, as he awaited the sailing of the liner *Canton* for points east, he was entertained by his Indian friend Reggie Sawhny. Reggie had sold him a car not long before, and the two had hit it off. Masters tended to be open to new friendships and, besides, Reggie was witty and loquacious. The car had kept running, so the friendship had too. Reggie sped John Masters around Bombay in his new car, a long red Bugatti with sweeping fenders, and they met up with Reggie's friends for drinks. The group included those who identified as Indian and as mixed Anglo-Indian. Introduced, one of them told John Masters that he had just been, in his words, "home" to England for a visit. Reggie inquired politely, "What happened to your face, old boy? Fall into the

Black Sea on your way out?" Amid laughter, friends old and new began to talk about how an Indian—even one who considered himself an avowed nationalist—could call England home. And these friends were all nationalists. They acknowledged the joined pasts and destinies of India and "home," but they wanted to see India independent. When one of them said he wanted the British to leave at the earliest possible moment, he noticed the flash of hurt on Masters's face; he hurried to assure Masters that he did not mean *him*—*he* was welcome to stay as long as he liked.

As they spoke, Masters came to realize that he was deeply sympathetic to their arguments. Before then he had not stopped to consider his individual position in British domination of India. He had been born in Calcutta into a family that had been in India for many generations. And, while he had done his upper schooling in England, India felt like home. Besides, by a soldier's inclination and Indian Army protocol, he brushed off politics. Now, in the mouths of Reggie and his friends, the arguments for letting Indians chart their own path were convincingly thoughtful and undeniably just.

Before long it was time for the *Canton* to sail, and after one last drink with Reggie on its deck looking at the lights of Bombay, Masters was off. Through warm seas past Singapore, the Gibraltar of the East, and up to Hong Kong the *Canton* steamed. Then a crossing to Japan and onto a train for a quick tour of Tokyo before heading across the Pacific. Two inquisitive men who entered Masters's compartment between Osaka and Tokyo were obviously not-so-secret-police interested in the travels of an Indian Army officer. In this, in displays of authoritarian efficiency, in instances in which Western tourists were conspicuously demeaned, Masters thought he divined something about the "harmonious new order" that Japan promised East Asia.

Next stop: Honolulu. Steaming eastward across the Pacific on the *Empress of Japan*, Masters befriended Herman Geschwind, a young Jewish man from New York. In Hawaii they spent a week together, by day sprawled on the beach, trying their hands at surfing, and by night rushing around Oahu with two young American women from the ship. Masters was struck by what he observed in American girls: the diametric opposition between their raucous behavior and their stalwart virginity. Related to this phenomenon, one night Masters and Geschwind went out without their friends to find a den of iniquity. They succeeded, only to depart immediately, pursued by police whistles as the place was raided.

Then on to Los Angeles. Masters and his friends toured the same MGM studios that produced fantastical "Indias" for the silver screen. He saw in person the Queen of the Movies, Joan Crawford; he listened to jazz bands led by Gene Krupa and Louis Prima. After a December week under the palms, Masters went to the railway ticket office; he had a ticket for crossing the United States to New York, but he got it refunded. Then he bought a 1932 Dodge that he named Ol' Man Mose after a popular jazz tune. Telling Herman he would meet him in New York, he pointed the Dodge toward the dawn and up into the mountains. *How like the continent-spanning trunk roads of India*, he thought. Except that, were this India, most of the people on the road would be walking; here everyone drove.

Up and down the mountains he forced the fast-aging Dodge, collecting snow in the heights and dust in the lowlands. Depending on altitude, he lugged on and off his poshteen—a knee-length coat lined with tanned goatskin from the Afghan frontier. Much of the landscape of the Southwest made him feel like he had never left Afghanistan.

Past desert and sagebrush he rolled into Texas, where he befriended some US cavalrymen. He took to them as he took to nearly everyone he met on his American odyssey, but he was struck by the differences between American and Indian soldiers. The Americans seemed fit men, but hardly ready to fight the looming war. In India, the turban-wearing lancers earned their spurs, meanwhile, patrolling frontier stretches of infamous danger or fighting little wars. The cavalrymen took him out to a bar where two lean gray-whiskered men drank at the rail. After a while, one of them leaped up in a flash, planted his boots, and threw his stool through the window. Thus did John Masters realize his lifelong dream of seeing real cowboys have a bar fight.

Outside New Orleans, Ol' Man Mose broke down along the highway. Used to long marches, Masters set out unperturbed in search of a mechanic. It was the night of a big prizefight and, with almost no interruption, Masters was able to listen to the match on the radios of cars speeding past in both directions.

In New Orleans he saw out 1938, a year that he could only rate a disaster. But, for now, there was sailing on Lake Pontchartrain, an American football game curiously called the Sugar Bowl, and as much jazz as he could care to listen to. Some Americans he met asked him about Britain's abandonment of Czechoslovakia, parts of which Germany had absorbed, going so far as to ask why the British had "crawled" before that monster, Hitler. By now Masters had decided that what would appear rudeness among the British was an invitation to a teasing game of give-and-take among Americans. So he countered that the League of Nations had not acted like a hero either. But the fact was that he truly did not understand the apparent capitulation. He did, however, believe that the world was rushing toward war despite the complacency he saw around him in the United States. He therefore drank and danced like one going to meet fate. At New Orleans' Hotel Charles the band played "That's a Plenty" as many times as Masters requested, the melody spinning manically like the world.

Then, into the South. At a gas station, while attendants swarmed over his Dodge, the man behind the counter took one look at Masters's poshteen coat and politely asked exactly what part of California he was from. When Masters reached the East Coast and turned the car north, he wondered at the small distances between the sites of Civil War battles he had read about in huts on the other side of the world. In North Carolina he recoiled at the widespread evidence of Jim Crow. Some nights he would pull into an auto camp where he would wind up the gramophone that had traveled from England to India and all the way to exotic America. From the case came the grave tone of Paul Robeson, singing as Joe, a laborer on the Mississippi River. "What does he care if the world's got troubles?" he asked of Old Man River. "What does he care if the land ain't free?"

In New York Masters reunited with Herman amid "glittering crowds in canyons of steel," and sold the Dodge for what he could get so the two young men could live the nightlife at the Belmont Plaza, the Onyx Club on Fifty-Second Street, and Radio City. The money went fast, and as Masters waited for the day of departure for England he made the dollars stretch on coffee and hamburgers (which he found colossal). His favorite—and most affordable—pastime was sitting on a bench in Central Park watching the city, his poshteen shielding him from January.

Then the night came for the good ship *Manhattan* to steam under Manhattan's lit towers and turn toward England, though the ship's last port of call was Hamburg. As always, Masters sought to befriend the Americans around him. Though he tried and tried again, he failed to connect with the bearded Bohemian college students on board; meanwhile, the professors on the ship were too professorial, the table of rabbis too prophetic. The ship's crew were largely German and with one, a Hitler supporter, Masters argued loudly. Embarrassed, the stewards were especially deferential toward Masters thereafter. And so, a ship carrying American freethinkers and German Hitler backers, rabbis and an Indian Army officer, crossed what would soon become the battlefield of the Atlantic.[1]

Back in India, with his escape to America well behind him and the war fully underway, Masters was appointed adjutant, a kind of chief of staff to the man leading his battalion, a lieutenant colonel. It was a harried job of doing all the record keeping and management necessary to keep his unit fed, clothed, armed, and transported while also playing the role of severe, eagle-eyed presence that allowed the lieutenant colonel to be more aloof.

So in early spring 1941, there was John Masters at his desk outside his lieutenant colonel's office, being harried and acting severe, when a young, lanky Indian man approached him, smiling in his overlarge uniform of the Indian Medical Service (IMS)—daring to smile, that is, in the presence of the apparently hard-hearted adjutant. His uniform showing him to be a lieutenant, the young man said his name was Dutt and that he'd been sent as the battalion's medical officer.

"Name?" asked Masters, frowning as he pulled out a clean officer's record sheet.

"Dutt. I just told you."

"Christian names?"

"None."

Masters set the pen down. "I am very busy, and . . ."

"I am not a Christian," Dutt said, smiling again, "so how can I have Christian names? I am Hindu, and my full name is Santi Pada Dutt."

Doctor Santi Dutt was a twenty-six-year-old man of Calcutta, one of a large, middle-class family, well educated and prosperous. His father, too, had been in the IMS during the Great War; he'd served in the searing quagmire of Mesopotamia, now called Iraq. The senior Dr. Dutt had not wanted his son to enlist; but travel and adventure lured his son, even though he and his six siblings hoped for Indian independence. A pair of sisters even marched in triumph when news spread in Bengal of the escape of Subhas Chandra Bose from British house arrest.

As a professional, as very comfortably middle class, and as supremely educated, Dutt was not one to kowtow before a British man, even one doing his best to appear impatient and fierce. Dutt dared to smile. He was the first non-British medical officer to serve in the battalion; in the coming months and years, Indians like him would quickly swell the ranks of the Indian Army, given the massive needs of wartime. And the significance for the imminent freedom of India was also massive.

"Have you seen the colonel yet?" asked Masters.

"No, I am looking forward to that pleasure."

"Wait here." Masters went into Colonel William Weallens's office. "Our medical officer's arrived. . . . I think he's going to be a good egg." Masters showed Dutt in, and as he closed the door a smiling Weallens was striding over to shake the young doctor's hand and inquire whether he knew Doctor So-and-So of the IMS.

Not long after this, word came from Indian Army headquarters that the battalion and others in its division should prepare to dispatch to Malaya and Singapore. Had Dutt and Masters gone there, their fates and those of their riflemen would have been only death, utmost misery, or service in the army of Bose, a Japanese ally.[2]

Wartime casts light on the hidden doings of the fates, with their spinning, weaving, and cutting of threads. One life is spared, while another life is cut short. One unit spends the war close to home; another is decimated

at the front line; another is made prisoners of war. And often the difference between these destinies seems due to nothing but the fates' whims.
So it seemed that they had taken notice of John Masters, Santi Dutt, and
other soldiers in April 1941.

From Bombay and Karachi Harbors, the fates sent some men west
and some east: some to a bitter fight in Iraq and Syria-Lebanon, and some
into the hands of the Japanese in Malaya and Singapore. But their destinies were almost very different. One group that was about to be sent to
the desert had been training in preparation to go to the jungles of Southeast Asia. Those who went east in their place were later captured by the
Japanese. One battalion that sailed to Malaya in April 1941 instead of
being diverted to Basra was captured, then joined Bose in fighting alongside the Japanese in what was called the Indian National Army. On one
of the transports a young man from southern India was overjoyed when
he learned his ship was turning toward Singapore because it was considered the unassailable Gibraltar of the East. A year later he became a prisoner of the Japanese, in whose hands he suffered horribly. Such were the
whims of the fates.

In April 1941, large troopships lay at anchor in Bombay and
Karachi Harbors, and while only the seniormost officers on board knew
it, they were headed west instead of east. On the long *Devonshire* was a
battalion of the Thirteenth Frontier Force Rifles, trying to get used to an
alien element. This unit of riflemen, who specialized in ranging over hills,
traced their history through Afghan campaigns, brutal fighting in France
in World War I, and beyond to the so-called Indian Mutiny of 1857. It
comprised four companies, each of a different ethnic or religious background. There were around one hundred riflemen each of Dogras (mainly
Hindus of Kashmir and the far north), Pashtun Muslims (from Afghanistan
or of Afghan descent), Punjabi Muslims, and Sikhs. Like most battalions
in the Indian Army, the seniormost officers were British. But some company commanders were Indians, including Punjabi Muslims. Only a few
days before, they had received an abrupt order to cut short a training exercise and to hurry to Bombay for embarkation.

The Frontier Force Rifles had only just given up their horses and
mules for trucks; they still did not have steel helmets. Literally days be-

fore they came down from Poona to Bombay Harbor they had been hurrying to learn how to effectively load their new trucks with all the gear they would need for the desert. Among them were teenagers from the mountains bordering Afghanistan who had never seen a highway, let alone traveled in a motorized vehicle. But before being thrown into a global war they had to be trained to drive and service internal combustion engines.

Their rushed transformation was typical. In these months, things were changing rapidly in the Indian Army. Its most experienced units were already in northern and northeastern Africa, fast becoming the some of the world's most battle-tested at places like Eritrea. Often remaining veterans in India were moved about the subcontinent to form the nuclei of new units. Meanwhile, enlistment efforts were feverish. Tea planters' sons joined up, as did coffee planters' sons. And in the coming year or two, more and more Indians ascended to high leadership positions. Within the year Punjabi captains commanded British officers in a Frontier Force battalion and a Baluchi battalion. Old ways and old weapons were being swapped out, but at a painfully slow pace; modern weapons like antiaircraft guns, antitank guns, and mortars were rare.

Down from Risalpur had hurried the Thirteenth Lancers. They, too, had only recently surrendered their horses for armored cars built on Rolls Royce chassis. In fact, the troopers, or *sowars*, as they were known, had only surrendered their lances themselves less than a decade before and the officers their sabers. Theirs was a 140-year history, and its foregoing generation had been among the first troops to enter Baghdad—on horseback—in the Great War. (There were plenty of World War I veterans among the men on these transports.) The Thirteenth Lancers comprised turbaned Pashtun, Muslim Rajput, and Sikh drivers, gunners, and mechanics. While their noncommissioned officers were Indian, the seniormost officers were British—though that would change very quickly with the demands of world war. Over the past year, the men had trained with armored cars and trucks on the Northwest Frontier just south of the Khyber Pass. But that was cut short by a call to hurry south.

Aboard the *Devonshire* was John Masters, Santi Dutt, and their Gurkhas, who had also hurried from their station on India's Northwest

Frontier. There they fought "savage wars of peace" on the restless border and stood ready for any fickleness on the part of the inscrutable Soviets. While the battalion mustered and marched in the alpine snow, they read with nagging envy of the exploits of other units in their division in the deserts of northern and northeastern Africa like the First Punjab Regiment and the Sixth Rajputana Rifles. They did, though, take some comfort that no Gurkha battalions had beaten them into the war. They maneuvered, trained under live machine gun fire, preparing to fight a jungle war. Only very recently had they been reissued desert khaki and desert-fighting manuals. A cousin battalion of Gurkhas had also received a telegram to rush from Quetta to Karachi and the transports.

A group of gunners, of artillerymen, also left Quetta for the SS *Varella* in Karachi. They were all British men, the Third Field Regiment, attached to the Indian Army. And in the rush, they left both their guns and their signalmen. They couldn't fire, and had they fired, they couldn't communicate with their spotters, so they would not have known where their shots had fallen; for the moment they were quite theoretical gunners only. (The very transport that bore them west to Basra, the *Varella*, turned around immediately and picked up Sikh units bound for Malaya and their fate at the hands of the Japanese.)

In Bombay and Karachi Harbors there was hurry and waiting; finding berths, stowing, and cleaning; drilling at submarine defense, drilling at air defense. For most of these several thousand, the vast majority of whom were sons of the northern hills and mountains, it was their first time at sea. They pointed at the porpoises, excited, and watched the flying fish in Bombay Harbor. The quartermasters of the various units worked to provision their men with food suitable for each of their respective castes and creeds—Christians, Nepali Hindus, and Sikhs—and jury-rigged galleys multiplied. Someone procured mangoes. Meanwhile, news of nightly bombings of London came over the radio. A soldier learned that his young cousin had died under the collapsing roof of the Café de Paris where she was dancing with her husband, an RAF pilot.

In moments of relative quiet after the *Devonshire* weighed anchor, some of the British and Indian officers discussed India's and Indians' place in the war. Mostly professional soldiers who tended to do the job they were ordered to do, the British officers admitted that they did not think much about the issue. Sure, the time for leaving India might come soon, and they would obey the order to pack up, like any other order.

Meanwhile, some of the Indian officers on those transports made clear that they were hardly fighting to preserve the British Empire, but only to make sure that it was not replaced by German power over India. So said Santi Dutt one day on board, matter-of-factly. Satyen Basu, another officer of the IMS, then steaming west on another transport, had thought at the beginning of the war, "I'm not going to be party to an imperialist war." Let the European empires fight it out; what's the distinction between one and the other, anyway? Yet the young man was too tempted by the possibilities of travel and adventure and good pay, while frustrated at his low income as a beginning doctor in Calcutta. But the opinions of those Indian officers who sailed for the Middle East varied widely. One who had gone to northeastern Africa to treat the wounded of the Battle of Keren identified more so with the British: their war was his war. Statements like Dutt's could rankle some of the British officers, others not at all; and in any case, such talk did not seem to lessen the popularity of those Indians who said it.

Finally, after the ships pointed west, the men on board learned where they were heading: there was trouble in Iraq.[3]

Things settled into a routine on the troopships *Lancashire* and the *Devonshire*, the latter following some days behind. When they boarded, some of the Gurkhas' officers overheard the *Lancashire*'s captain make racist predictions about the cleanliness of his ship now that it carried Indians. But on the first morning of the voyage the captain made his usual inspection of the ship; when he arrived on the troop decks he found the companies seated in ranks in their respective places. When the captain approached, company commanders gave a shout, and the companies shot bolt upright. All was spotless, everything stowed tidily, and the captain at least had the honesty to admit to the Gurkhas' commanding officer that he had never seen such smartness in all his years of trooping.

Things were routine—that is, until word came that the ships were headed for Basra and to a potentially deadly welcome from the Iraqis.

The ships had been hurried to sea equipped for a peaceful landing in Singapore, not an opposed landing in Iraq. There were no marines, and the *sepoys* and *sowars* were not trained at this sort of operation; they had no assault landing craft, and almost no ability to cover the landing with significant guns. The brigade staff sent company commanders plans for an assault landing, and the various companies drilled—as best they could on the deck of their troopships—at making the landing under fire. The landing craft were to be lifeboats, with the men boarding them on deck and then lowered over the sides. The lifeboats had levers that controlled hand-powered propellers at their sterns. The rehearsing riflemen were cheerful, some laughing, at the ridiculousness of the situation. Captain Masters of the Second Battalion, Fourth Gurkhas dearly loved the cheerfulness of his men and boys but feared the joke would be on them. Some of them would die needlessly, he feared, because of some brass fool's overoptimism about their ability to force their way into Basra in lifeboats.[4]

In April 1941 the men of the Indian Army descended the gangplanks hung on the Basra quay at 10:15 a.m. They carried their rifles, watching the roofs and alleys of the city, but no shots came—for now. The Basra police watched, while the famously strong Basra porters went home; let the British and Indians unload their own ships.

It was hot and humid as the first brigade of the Indian Army unpacked itself in Iraq. The ship provided the only shade, and then only when the sun descended to a certain point. A turbaned Sikh regiment filed down the gangplanks, a Gurkha regiment. The Third Field Regiment came down the gangplanks but had no field guns to unload; they were either still in India or bound for Singapore. A member of the IMS rejoiced when, unloading, he found that charpoys—beds made of wood frames stretched with nets that kept the sleeper off the ground and cool—designated for Singapore arrived instead with them in Basra. There was no green except some distant date palms, and flies commanded the day while mosquitoes ruled the night.

In these days, at the small RAF airstrip on the edge of Basra, there was a series of unusual arrivals. There were several US planes, and a few aged, high-winged airliners from Imperial Airways. They were shuttling in infantrymen, a battalion of the King's Own Royal Regiment, British men and boys attached to the Indian Army. They had started in Karachi, paused at Bahrain while the politicians debated their landing in Basra, then continued on. Four hundred of them crammed into the small planes, representing what was probably the first significant British military airlift. Some of their Indian civilian staff came too; for the one-eyed steward, Dunga, his first time overseas combined with his first time in the air. After they landed, the men and boys of the King's Own heard over Axis radio that they'd been shot down.

Some American airplane mechanics in Basra who'd been employed by the Royal Iraqi Air Force took the arrival of the Indian Army as a sign to get out of Iraq. By way of encouragement, they told some of the King's Own that the Iraqi Air Force planes were notorious for getting sand through their air filters. And with that, the Yanks hopped a lift back to Karachi on one of the American airliners.

From Baghdad, Rashid Ali al-Gailani watched the arrivals in Basra. His army partners could have stopped the landings with ease; their British-provided, British-trained artillery would have ravaged the thin-skinned civilian transports. But that would have forced a war before Axis support could arrive, so al-Gailani and the Golden Square waited to hear whether the Indian troops disembarking in Basra were heading toward the Baghdad–Haifa Highway and thus on to Palestine and Egypt. If they were passing through, the Iraqi forces had time; if not, they might be forced to act.

Al-Gailani also kept in close contact with the Italian embassy, through whom he communicated with Rome and Berlin.[5]

As April proceeded and al-Gailani and the Golden Square colonels saw no signs that the Indian Army that had landed at Basra was proceeding north out of the country, they felt increasingly like they had been tricked by the British. Prime Minister al-Gailani sent a list of demands to the British embassy, calling for the troops in Basra to proceed to Palestine, and that no more should land until those had departed, and that in the future the government should be given early notice of such landings. The demands were passed up to Westminster, and British prime minister Winston Churchill replied to the Foreign Office that he hardly cared what a group of usurpers demanded, that the Allies would not promise anything about the troops moving to Palestine, and that the ambassador in Baghdad should not trouble himself giving explanations. The Foreign Office smoothed the sharp edges of this Churchillian response, telling the ambassador to "express the hope that further cooperation by the Iraq authorities may provide evidence of their desire to fulfill the alliance and thereby allow the establishment of formal relations."

That dodge seemed to chill the new Iraqi regime. The timeline on the hard break with Britain and full cooperation with the Axis had to be pushed up.

A few days later, the British ambassador to Iraq sent al-Gailani a formal note indicating that another set of troops would land at Basra the next day as permitted under the terms of the Anglo-Iraqi Treaty. But the first set of troops had not proceeded out of the country, as al-Gailani had insisted. The Iraqi prime minister now knew that the British were there to throw him and the Golden Square out. Al-Gailani sent his complaints to the British ambassador, telling him that the landing was a violation of the treaty terms; but the time for diplomatic objections, in truth, was over. Al-Gailani and his army allies prepared for imminent war.

His own army, at least throughout the country, outnumbered the British force in Basra many, many times over—as many as fifty thousand Iraqis to about thirty-five hundred British and Indians—but they were not in position. Plus, sparking the war now would mean that Axis support could not arrive in time to make the difference. So in late April's 110-degree heat the second set of Allied troop transports landed and came down the gangplanks carrying the white flag since, for now, they were not a hostile invasion force. Around three thousand men—rifle battalions, some cavalry with armored cars—joined the roughly three thousand who in the previous days had occupied the dock area, sorting and guarding supplies, setting up a hospital, suffering the flies.

When al-Gailani summarily rejected the second round of troop landings at Basra, the British embassy figured the game was up. It sent messages to all British families in Baghdad stating that women and children would be flown out of the country. British men and civilians from Allied countries were to report to the gated embassy with one suitcase and all the food they could carry. It was soon hosting 350 men, women, and children in every nook and cranny. The American ambassador, meanwhile, opened the doors of the US embassy to 150; 250 drove off for the RAF base at Habbaniya, fifty miles west of Baghdad, in buses or their own cars. From there the plan was to fly them to Basra and then India beyond.

It was too late for the Golden Square to fight off the second troop landing, but what it could do was try to bottle up British forces and prepare the way for the aid they were most eager to see: the Luftwaffe.

So it was that at 2:00 a.m. on April 30, the morning after the second Indian troop landing in Basra, the British embassy in Baghdad sent an urgent coded radio message to the Habbaniya RAF base: soldiers were pouring out of Baghdad's barracks and into trucks heading in Habbaniya's direction.[6]

4

"Hemmed In by the Desert"

The Siege of Habbaniya

> I was based . . . just south of Habbaniyah, in between Ramadi and Fallujah. A suicide truck-bomber had exploded in a crowd of families going to mosque and Marines brought the wounded onto base. . . . It was the first time I'd ever seen anybody . . . who had those kind of injuries. Bombs do very, very bad things to human bodies; it's incredibly shocking to see.
>
> —Marine public affairs veteran Phil Klay, deployed in Iraq, 2007–8, on National Public Radio's *Fresh Air*, March 20, 2015

IN LATE 1940, twenty-four-year-old Antony "Tony" Dudgeon found himself commanding a small RAF squadron based in the desert west of Alexandria. Its job was to raid Italian convoys in the Mediterranean and battle their defenders in the air. Week in and week out, Dudgeon took to the air or sent his pilots up to try their luck against other young men determined to kill them. It was an isolated squadron, operating from tents, alone in the desert hinterland. And that isolation gave Dudgeon the feeling of sole responsibility for what happened to his pilots. Each condolence letter that he sent back to England was agony, while the strain of maintaining an airman's cockiness pressed and pressed on him. The memory of outfoxing an equally young opponent in the sky, resulting in the Italian's crash in the sea and drowning, weighed Dudgeon down with guilt. Finally he lost the ability to sleep, for which a doctor sent him— and his Dachshund Frankie, who flew with him—packing for some quiet little corner of the British Empire, a flight school where he could settle his nerves while he taught the next generation of pilots. The place was both a school and an air base: RAF Habbaniya.

Habbaniya was a strange place. It sprawled between the Euphrates River and a wide glinting lake, with the appearance of a postwar Arizona suburb of about ten thousand. Yet its roads had conspicuously English names like Cranwell, Grantham, and Uxbridge. There were stables, a polo field, a chapel, and a small golf course; it had its own a power station, school, and hospital. But this was the desert, the temperature was in the nineties in late April, and coaxing green things to grow in its many vegetable plots took intense care.

This curious pseudosuburb was multicultural, in a way. The majority of residents were British—civilians far outnumbering RAF personnel, while security for the base was provided by around twelve hundred Iraqis. Called the Levies, there were two companies each of Christian Iraqi Assyrians, Iraqi Arabs (drawn from the River Tigris lowlands of southeastern Iraq, particularly), and non-Arab Iraqi Kurds. The Levies' married men brought their families as well. There was also a signal company that mixed communities. There were Goanese cooks and Persian horse grooms; Indian tailors and clerks. There was plenty of segregation; each community had its own barracks or bungalows, prayer rooms, and mess hall. And, as always, officers further separated themselves. But all reports suggest these widely diverse communities lived and worked well together.

This isolated RAF base was in profound contrast to RAF bases in southern and eastern England that at that moment were the front line of Britain's defense. There pilots perpetually scrambled to airstrips to mount their Spitfires or Hurricanes to meet the next Luftwaffe incursion: at RAF Tangmere they struggled to defend Portsmouth that spring; at RAF Biggin Hill they tried to fend off London's attackers—and tried to fend off attackers of their own air base.

RAF Habbaniya had no flashy Spitfires or tight-turning Hurricanes. Most of its warplanes were biplane Audaxes, with a top speed of 170 miles per hour, that would soon officially be declared obsolete; its most "advanced" aircraft was the biplane Gladiator, outdated by German advancements and retired from frontline use back in Britain. The bulk of its craft were twin-seated trainers.

RAF Habbaniya was considered "nonoperational"—that is, war operations were not usually flown from there. Before the war, it was a stopover for commercial flights that landed in the great lake beside it, as well as planes on RAF business. And it was a communications—and intelligence—relay. But its main role was as a training school. Its slow biplanes were forgiving of flight students from Britain, Poland, and other Allied countries. The base would have to become a key lifeline if the Germans and Italians shut the Suez Canal; but few foresaw the base playing an important wartime role in spring 1941.

It was built during peacetime, after Iraq received its semi-independence, around 1930, and that seemed to contribute to a layout and placement that made it nearly indefensible. When the British war secretary wrote the air secretary with such concerns on the eve of construction, the Air Ministry responded, "no hostile act by the Iraqi Government against our forces could reasonably be contemplated, [and] they were pledged by Treaty to come to our aid if needs be." The base had a seven-mile perimeter to guard and only an iron fence as a barrier. There were some brick blockhouses at some corners, but they were meant to deter bandits, not withstand artillery.

On the evening of April 29, people on the ground in Habbaniya were not particularly anxious. They thought the rumblings in Baghdad echoed a minor power struggle in the Iraqi Army. A week earlier, Habbaniya's twelve hundred Iraqi RAF Levies were reinforced by about four hundred men of the King's Own Royal Regiment who flew up from RAF Shaibah, outside Basra, to bolster Habbaniya's defense, just in case. But their arrival by air meant they did not have any heavy weapons. The base's strongest ground weapons were six armored cars dating from 1915 at the latest; they were strong enough against rifle fire, but no match for anything more powerful than that.

When the British embassy in Baghdad radioed its message warning of the approaching Iraqi Army to Habbaniya, the base duly sounded its alarms. But there was little it could do beyond that. The base commander ordered all of his pilots and ground crews out of bed to grab every pick and shovel on base. For the next four hours they dug trenches at what they hoped were defensible points, built machine gun nests spread around the wide perimeter. In that predawn dark Tony Dudgeon shook his head at the hopelessness of such measures against a modern army.

As the sky lightened in the east on April 30, Dudgeon saw that the Iraqi Army had arrived. To the south, about six or seven hundred yards outside the base's iron fence, there was a long plateau rising two hundred feet above the floodplain. On top, there was movement; with binoculars, Dudgeon could see guns and vehicles; and there were more coming up the road from Baghdad. As it lightened further, the base commander sent up an Audax to have a better look, and the pilot reported that there were about one thousand men on the plateau already, with many more constantly arriving and digging in. They had an antiaircraft gun, field guns, and howitzers. Armored cars were approaching, and some light tanks were taking position near the base of the plateau.

At about six o'clock that morning, an Iraqi officer approached the base's main gate under a white flag, was led to the base commander's office, and left a short time later. Dudgeon learned soon after that the officer brought a warning: the Iraqi Army was occupying the plateau "for the purpose of training," and while the exercise was underway no one was to leave or enter the air base, including by air. Now the Iraqis at Habbaniya had answered British lies at Basra with their own. And, again, there was little danger of either side being deceived.

The RAF commander sent back a message stating that the occupation of the plateau put the base completely at the Iraqis' mercy and could not be tolerated. He then radioed the embassy in Baghdad asking for political directions to be relayed from Whitehall. Should he hold tight, preemptively attack the plateau, or threaten to bomb the government office in Baghdad?

As the base commander waited for a response from Britain, a rush of orders went out to all corners of the besieged base. Men jury-rigged an operations room in a small office in one of the hangars farthest away from the plateau and its Iraqi guns. Others jury-rigged bomb racks onto the trainer planes suitable for carrying real bombs. Men distributed ammunition and bombs to different dumps around the base. Someone drew up a list of pilots who could conceivably fight, and the number came to just thirty-nine. Of course, most of the pilots were instructors, many of whom who had never dropped a bomb in anger. A few were Greek flight students who spoke no English. (They were now without a country, since

Greece was being overrun by the Axis at that very moment.) A couple others were pilots sent to Habbaniya to rest, like Tony Dudgeon.

Civilian volunteers joined ground crews. Planes were pushed to positions slightly better obscured from the plateau. Someone pointed out that the pair of World War I–era field guns, now serving as decorations in front of the officers' mess, might be made to work if some historic ammunition could be found.

Dudgeon was placed in charge of twenty-seven aircraft, trainers, and aging fighters; a friend was put in charge of twenty-one old biplane bombers. But the haste of improvising flight and ground crews and modifying planes could not keep Dudgeon's mind from their open vulnerability. A single Iraqi light tank could at any moment simply drive up to the base commander's quarters and poke its gun through his office window, he thought, and there was little anyone could do to oppose it. As the day wore on without definite instructions from RAF brass and London except to reply to fire with fire, the young man worried that a night attack by the Iraqis would also be unanswerable and brief. While no one seriously doubted their loyalty, the RAF's Iraqi Levies had no means for assaulting the kind of force besieging the base. The King's Own Royal Regiment numbered only four hundred and had no answer for an Iraqi tank. The only answer could come from bombing runs, and they could not target their bombs in blackness.

Signals between Habbaniya, the Baghdad Embassy, Cairo, India, and London flashed inconclusively all day on April 30. The Iraqis sent another messenger to Habbaniya's gate now saying its instructions were to enforce a no-fly policy until the Indian Army at Basra had respected the treaty requiring it to pass through the country. To everyone's relief, no attack came in the dark of night. And no attack came on May 1, while men with shovels leveled the small golf course to act as a backup landing strip in 110-degree heat and civilian volunteers were instructed in their duties and shown their positions. Middle East Command was being pressed hard in Libya, Greece was falling, and those men retreating needed cover from the RAF. But Cairo promised some modern bomber reinforcements if the siege turned into active war. Meanwhile, the number of Iraqi troops surrounding the base climbed to around seven thousand with around twenty-eight guns now dug in and more armored cars and light tanks materializing.

On May 2 Whitehall agreed that Habbaniya could not possibly fend off a ground attack. In that case, the entire base population might be ransomed for British withdrawal from Iraq—which would practically mean that Iraq would become an partner and oil supplier to Axis. The base's only mode of defense was offense. Now the government and top brass gave Habbaniya's leaders free rein; but, stated a wireless telegram sent by Winston Churchill, "If you have to strike, strike hard."

And so they did, striking first as soon as there was light to take off that morning, thus starting a fight that would span two and a half months throughout the region.* In the minutes before the surprise attack, in the dark, flight instructors climbed into their cockpits guided by hooded flashlights, with students acting as rear gunners in the open cockpits of the Audax biplanes. Some planes took off from the main runway outside the base's gates, practically under the muzzles of the Iraqi guns; others took off from the polo field, which had been transformed into a second runway. They sped through the dark, unguided by lights (which would have alerted the Iraqi artillery), and they throttled up fast and pulled back hard, trying to get away from the earth that the pilots knew would soon be riddled with shells.

Soon, dozens of planes were above the occupied plateau, shoulder to shoulder, until—with the 5:00 a.m. light just enough to make out the guns and machine gun nests below—they dropped their bombs and started a war.

Iraqi antiaircraft fire opened up from below immediately, and holes began appearing in wings and cockpits, though at least the tracers showed the makeshift bombers where to target. Artillery and machine gun fire started falling among the base's buildings. An Assyrian soldier of the RAF Levies watching from one the brick blockhouses at Habbaniya's perimeter saw the entire plateau above the base light up with a shimmering that he thought looked like a sky of flashing stars.

* The BBC told listeners in Britain that the Iraqis had struck first and that the Indian Army had indeed landed in Basra with the intention of passing through the country or "opening a line of communication" to Palestine.

Habbaniya had sixty-four planes, most of which were trainers that could not carry much bomb weight. But at least Middle East Command in Cairo came through with its promise of modern twin-engine bombers, ten Wellingtons, which would meet Habbaniya's improvised air force over the plateau as soon as it was light enough to see that morning. Except for these ten modern bombers, Habbaniya's sorties were very short, with their bomb loads so limited, lasting only a matter of minutes. Then it was the awkward matter of landing a plane while being shot at. The teacher-pilots found creative ways of approaching the runway and polo field landing strip from paths that limited their exposure to Iraqi guns until the last minute, and hurried their planes behind hangars or screens of trees as soon as possible when on the ground. When the Iraqi Army saw the approach that the RAF was adopting, they sent out riflemen and a few machine guns under the path, right on the bank of the Euphrates. So the Levies—Iraqis themselves—scrambled to the opposite bank of the Euphrates and, after a fierce exchange, flushed the Iraqi Army out and back up the plateau.

Still, RAF planes were being constantly pocked by fire. At a steady rate, planes and the pilots themselves were being hit from below. Jimmy Broughton was shot in the jaw; "Wad" Taylor was grazed in his cheek and eyebrow by a bullet screaming up from the plateau; Dan Cremin landed his open-cockpit Audax with fifty-two bullet holes in it, but none in him. One pilot, hit three times from below, lost consciousness and collapsed on the flight stick. With the plane nose-diving, the student gunner behind him pulled him off the stick and held him up. The pilot came around in time to pull the plane out of a dive and even land it on the polo field before losing consciousness again. An Oxford trainer was shot down, killing its crew of a teacher and his two pupils. One pilot was shot down twice that day, the second time crash-landing on the base's golf course, flipping his plane in a sand trap and burying his head therein until his gunner dug him out.

One of the precious Wellington bombers experienced mechanical trouble on the runway and was ripped apart and set on fire by the Iraqi guns just after a few of the base's armored cars escorted its crew to safety. Then the modern Iraqi Air Force soon appeared on the scene, dive-bombing and burning two of Habbaniya's irreplaceable planes on the ground before throttling away. Unlike most of Habbaniya's planes, the Iraqis' planes were more modern and far faster.

The Iraqi artillery up on the plateau mainly targeted the base's planes, runways, and hangars—apparently avoiding obviously civilian areas—but shells inevitably fell all around. When one of the mess halls came under fire, an Iraqi cook rushed to find something solid to get behind. The corrugated roofs of the buildings offered no protection, though, and shrapnel struck him. The Iraqis avoided the hospital, with its broad red cross on its roof, and an ambulance soon appeared to stretcher away the bleeding cook. Indeed, that ambulance spent the day rushing to all corners of the base, bringing in the bleeding. In the hospital, the wives of the pilots and wives of embassy staff from Baghdad who refused to be airlifted away to safety worked amid the blood, heat, and hurry.

The base commander had told his officers that he expected the Iraqis would break and run after three hours of constant bombing. It was a statement of classic colonial arrogance along the lines of, "These primitive natives will run for cover in the face of our modern weapons." After three hours of bombing, the Iraqi Army showed no signs of moving from the plateau, and by the end of daylight, it still showed no signs of retreating. Meanwhile, there were thirteen RAF dead and twenty-nine wounded, and the base commander was on his way to a nervous breakdown under the incessant Iraqi shelling.[1]

MOST URGENT
ANKARA
MAY 2, 1941
10:10 pm

The Iraq Minister read me the telegram from his Government which had just arrived. According to this, fighting began today between English and Iraq troops at the Habbaniya airfield, and consequently war is in progress. Relations with England have been broken off. The Iraq Government requests that Minister Grobba be sent to Baghdad at once so that diplomatic relations may be resumed. It also requests immediate military aid. In particular a considerable number of airplanes in order to prevent further English landings and to drive the English from the airfields. The English have a total of 8,500 troops on Iraq territory, including the recently landed forces, and the Iraqi have 50,000 men under arms. They want to raise another 50,000 and weapons for them are urgently needed. The Iraq Minister asked for an answer by tomorrow if in any way possible. I should be grateful for immediate radio instructions.

Hans Kroll, German Embassy, Turkey[2]

As war began in Iraq, the head of Middle East Command, General Archibald Wavell, fought a hydra. In the past few weeks, his forces had been driven almost completely out of Libya by German general Erwin Rommel, Yugoslavia had been lost, and then—just in the last few days—Greece had collapsed. Malta, a key air and sea base for stalking Axis shipping to North Africa, was being pummeled. Now Wavell was trying to come up with a way to hold on to the key island of Crete, which commanded the Aegean Sea. The Fifth Indian Division, meanwhile, was at any hour about to start yet another battle against professional Italian units defending a fortress literally carved into an Ethiopian peak.

When, a few weeks earlier, coded messages had arrived from London asking what strength Wavell could lend to Iraq in case of trouble, he responded that he had nothing to give. Send a roaring squadron of bombers over Baghdad to rattle the windows, he suggested; have the ambassador mediate some acceptable outcome.

The moment the shooting began at Habbaniya, the Chiefs of Staff in Whitehall appealed once again to Wavell in Cairo to send some strength in that direction. Could he secure a path from the Indian Army in Basra to Habbaniya, about 375 miles to the north? Could he send a battalion in Palestine to Habbaniya? "I have consistently warned you that no assistance could be given to Iraq from Palestine in present circumstances," he signaled back, having just returned from the Western Desert and a review of efforts against Rommel. "My forces are stretched to limit everywhere and I simply cannot afford to risk part of forces on what cannot produce any effect." The only option was to threaten war and back up threats with a naval blockade and bombing, if pushed.

London wrote back that "positive action as soon as forces can be made available will be necessary" if there was to be any hope of restoring the Kirkuk–Haifa pipeline. Churchill, Wavell, and the Chiefs of Staff in Whitehall went back and forth over the next hours and days. Things grew heated. Handed another in a series of proddings from Churchill, Wavell shouted, "he must face facts!" For his part, Churchill mumbled to those around him that Wavell "gives me the impression of being tired out." The War Office signaled that the Golden Square's success depended on German weapon supplies and air support, but that "our arrival in Basra forced [al-Gaylani] to go off at half-cock before the Axis was ready." Finally, Churchill and the War Office stated that they would take personal responsibility for the outcome if Wavell would organize a relief column for Habbaniya and, after that, a push to Baghdad (though it was far from certain the Allies had sufficient force to go all that way).

And, though Wavell thought the kind of troops he could scrounge out of those lightly garrisoning Palestine would be too little, too late, he read it as an order. So he radioed the major general in charge of Palestine and told him to start scraping men together. Shortly after that, as the next chapter will show, Jack Bartlett, Harry Chalk, David Smiley, and the Arab Legion were in motion.[3]

In the moments leading up to the siege of Habbaniya, British spies in Iraq were struggling to learn how much support al-Gailani and the Golden Square had in the military and general population. Things were murky. Down in Basra, where the Indian Army was digging in and waiting for action, the chief British spy gathered that there was some turmoil among Iraqi Army leadership. The local Iraqi commander at Basra was frustrated that he was in the dark about moves in Baghdad. And the British agent was dubious about the devotion to the revolutionary cause among some sections of the military in the area. Still, he had an informant from a unit of Iraqi Euphrates gunboats who identified some senior officers in the area siding with Germany. On the other hand, he learned that Nasiriyah and Suq-ash-Shaykh, two towns up the Euphrates toward

Baghdad, appeared unwilling to cooperate with al-Gailani's regime. In the days before fighting began at Habbaniya, British intelligence at Basra struggled to pin down concrete information about the likelihood and timing of an Iraqi first strike. Sources suggested that the Iraqis were unlikely to attack first at Basra, but that rioting seemed to have been arranged, probably to slow an Indian Army advance on Baghdad.

The matter of British spying in Iraq, the RAF base at Habbaniya, and the Golden Square coup itself were all tied closely together. That's because those British spies in Basra were reporting their findings to Habbaniya, which was not just an air stopover en route to India and a training center; it was an intelligence center and, after Cairo and Jerusalem, the most important intelligence center in the Middle East. It was where the British tried to influence the scrum of Baghdad politics, watched for meddling from Iraq's neighbors and Britain's rivals, tried to protect the flow of oil, and kept tabs on Iraq's sheiks and power players in outlying areas. Or, put in the ages-old colonial lingo, from here the British could watch for "tribal unrest." And it was natural that the place from which planes could keep an eye on things, where the RAF conducted "air policing," would become the place where the intelligence officers worked.

An important RAF intelligence agent, called an air attaché, worked from the British embassy in Baghdad, whose ambassador was an intelligence linchpin himself. And besides Basra, there were other intelligence officers stationed in important provincial cities like Mosul, and some British advisers to Iraqi ministries played a double role as intelligence observers.

A group of RAF intelligence agents in the guise of ordinary RAF personnel euphemistically called air liaison officers traveled the country visiting airfields and befriending Royal Iraqi Air Force officers. In 1938, with war approaching, they tried to step up their efforts to find out where sympathies lay in the Iraqi military. They bought their information and friendship with gifts: this official might get hunting gear, that official might receive medicine. All of this was illegal; the treaty between Great Britain and Iraq gave the British no rights to spying. The Iraqi government, well before the Golden Square coup, did its best to keep its eyes on such RAF figures, fully aware they were meddling and documenting their comings and goings in various regions, as well as the sorts of gifts they bestowed. And, of course, it spurred broad and deep resentment. It was this resentment that helped breed support for a break from the British and a closer relationship with Germany.[4]

On the first day of the RAF Habbaniya countersiege Tony Dudgeon's little air force of trainers and legacy bombers—along with the precious few modern Wellingtons helping out from Cairo—had flown 193 frenzied sorties. When darkness fell, they had to stop flying since they dared not illuminate a taxiing path nor the runways. In the hangars, or in sheltered spots they hoped were out of view of the Iraqi gunners, mechanics rushed to patch and repair the punctured planes all that day. They had lost a third of them—crashed, burned, or punctured beyond return to the air. At some point the question of courage would be overridden by attrition.

After nightfall, Tony Dudgeon and his superiors reorganized their remaining planes into two patched-up units and planned the next day's effort. Curiously, the base's chief officer was nowhere to be seen, and hadn't been seen by any of those officers that day. And when Dudgeon and his unit's leader went around in the dark just before midnight to visit and encourage the mechanics, there was no sign of the commanding officer then, either.

The morning briefing was at 4:00 a.m., so Dudgeon went to his hut to let Frankie the Dachshund out briefly and get at least a few hours' sleep. But the Iraqis up on the plateau thought otherwise, and between midnight and 3:00 a.m. fired at the base at a rate of about one shot per minute. Dudgeon could hear the arc and spin of the shells as they soared toward him and, midway through this sleepless three-hour vigil, the shells started landing nearer and nearer: first, two hundred yards away, and then close enough to blow in a window on one side of his hut. Before the next one arrived, he was under his bed, where he met Frankie, whom he promptly accused of cowardice, not long before a shell blew in a window on the other side of the hut.

The RAF armored cars, World War I–era Rolls Royces that were older than most of their crews, were constantly at work. They sped to signs of trouble along the perimeter, raced alongside departing craft to kick up dust, led sorties of the King's Own Royal Regiment and Assyrian Levies against Iraqi defenses. But they were outmatched against modern machine guns, mortars, and artillery. It was too much for one of the armored car officers: he shot himself in the toe in order to be spared the constant hellish exposure.

Before dawn Tony Dudgeon was at the daily briefing when, with just the barest light, the battle began again. The first task of the day would be to get up in the air and escort in a DC-3 from RAF Shaibah, the small airstrip outside Basra, coming to airlift women and children evacuees and some badly wounded back to Basra and then to Karachi. (The women had been practically racing to contribute what they could on the base—laboring hard, nursing under bloody conditions—before they were forced to fly off.) The plane was too large and unwieldy to do any sly maneuvers to approach the Habbaniya runway safely; it would have to come in right over the heads of the Iraqis on the plateau. The plan was for a group of dive-bombers to strike at the besiegers at the right moment to keep them covering their heads while the DC-3 sailed over.

Up in the air, Dudgeon and the others saw the transport approach from the southeast, snub-nosed, with seven windows to a side. He was not alone in his Oxford; after Frankie's agony over the shells the previous night, Dudgeon didn't have the heart to leave him on the ground to suffer throughout the day. From then on the Dachshund went up in the air on most sorties, appearing perfectly content, apparently enjoying watching the ground rush by on takeoff and landing, and snoozing while up in the air.

The Habbaniya planes bombed away as the DC-3 landed, and the plan worked. Now on the ground, the transport took on its refugees; eventually 250 women and children were airlifted from Habbaniya. Among them, accompanied by a doctor, was an air vice marshal: the base commander whom neither Dudgeon nor, it seemed, anyone else had seen since shortly after the battle began. The World War I veteran had broken down under the shellfire; now sedated, he was gently guided onto the plane and away from his nightmare.

That day the mission of keeping the Iraqis pinned down and exacting a price for approaching the base continued. When the Iraqis pulled a two-pounder antiaircraft gun behind a brick outbuilding it was in position to easily shred a landing DC-3 at point-blank range or even open up one of the thin-skinned RAF armored cars. One of Habbaniya's most skilled bombers, "Horse" Evans, promptly asked for a 250-pound bomb under his yellow Gordon biplane and took off. To be safe from the pompom gun he shielded himself with the same brick building that it hid behind. That meant he charged the position at such a flat angle that he barely skimmed the packed Euphrates silt. He dropped the bomb, almost sliding it at the gun, and had to pull back hard on the stick to clear even the one-story building. The bomb's fuse delayed the blast seven seconds while Evans throttled away and, after the explosion, the position was silenced.

That day another plane was struck at takeoff, another pilot survived three bullets, and ground crews did their indispensable work under wailing shells. Tony Dudgeon was utterly weary, yet the constant work of his curious air force appeared to make the Iraqis more cautious. After hours of deadly visitations from the air, the Iraqis were less willing to expose themselves and their big guns. But Dudgeon also knew that the gunners could do their work at night at less risk, with the RAF planes grounded by darkness. The base could not light its hangars or the runway safely. So that day he and the other officers leading the countersiege decided that they must try to take off and land after dark. There were three pilots, Tony included, with experience in pitch-black operations with no runway lights, and the plan was for a single RAF plane to stay aloft at all times between moonset and dawn. It might not amount to much offensive power, but with each plane armed with eight bombs they could avenge any muzzle flashes or at least drop them intermittently, keeping the Iraqis on the plateau as sleepless as Dudgeon and Frankie had been the night before.

Ten minutes after the moon descended, Tony Dudgeon and a bomber climbed aboard their Oxford, engine running, all lights switched off. A couple of hooded lanterns dimly marked the exit through the iron gate and, passing through, they were now in complete darkness. Tony could make out nothing except a few stars above. He had to avoid colliding with a burned-out plane wreck and a burned-out tractor, relying on memory and luck. He rolled to what he hoped was the right starting point for takeoff, based on timing, then turned and throttled. He felt the packed sand rumbling underneath him, but could see no movement out of the canopy. It was disturbing to see no motion, though the phosphorescent instruments showed him gaining pace. When they indicated the right speed, Dudgeon pulled back, bracing himself for impact with the raised Euphrates embankment somewhere ahead of him in the blackness

The impact never came, and he began to discern more stars above and barely make out the Euphrates' shade of black from the desert's. This let him reckon the position of the plateau beneath him, and he began two hours' patient harassment. He saw very few gun flashes.

Then came time to try to get back on the ground. There was even less of a margin of error than when he had taken off, the earth having no give. He circled around, trying to orient himself via the faint impression of the river and his phosphorescent compass dial. Dudgeon called to his bomber to start his stopwatch, and then he began his descent. The first task was to clear the plateau, yet drop quickly after passing over it, since he would be exposed to rifle fire during his descent. The bomber called ten seconds, and Dudgeon dropped to one hundred feet, again bracing for disaster in the blind darkness. Thankful to have cleared the ridge, he then dropped to fifty feet. If he sought out the ground too quickly, he might catch the lip of the ditch surrounding the airfield. When instinct and instruments told him that he was about to touch down, he dared to flip on his landing lights, hoping one of the burned ruins on the runway didn't lurch out of the night. Then his wheels found earth; he switched the lights off and throttled back.

Then came a voice. "Are you okay?"

It was the voice of Dudgeon's bomber. Dudgeon snapped out of the spell of some strange animal terror; he was panting, shaking, sweating as if he had run a long distance. He had been calm in the air, under control during the landing, but a sort of insensate panic struck him after the plane rolled to a stop.

The pilot and his bombing partner who took that night's third patrol were dead before they got in the air, but mercifully never knew it. When they taxied out of the iron gate, turned, and headed for the end of the runway, they did not taxi far enough. So, though he couldn't see to know it, when the pilot throttled down the runway in the opposite direction he didn't have enough distance to get up in the air and over the ten-foot levee that protected the base from the Euphrates. His wheels caught it, the Oxford flipped end over end, pounded into the marshy bank, and instantly burst into flames.

The next day, after a very short sleep and the morning briefing in the dark, Tony Dudgeon and several others were up in the air pointed toward Baghdad. There they would rendezvous with some modern Wellingtons flying up from Basra's Shaibah airstrip at dawn. They wanted to let the Golden Square know that the siege of Habbaniya would have consequences for Baghdad. On the ground in Baghdad—actually, on a balcony overhanging the River Tigris, Freya Stark—British explorer, sometime spy, sometime propagandist—would see him and his squadmates make their bombing run and her heart would lift. She was in a sort of prison there, as chapter 6 will tell.[5]

5

"Summon the People from All Over Israel"

*Where They Were When They Were Called to Iraq:
Jack Bartlett, David Smiley, Harry Chalk, and the
Arab Legion*

THIS IS WHERE Jack Bartlett, David Smiley, Harry Chalk, and the Arab Legion enter the story. In the first days of the siege of Habbaniya, General Archibald Wavell ordered his general in command of Palestine to cast about for the odds and ends that would have to form a relief column for the RAF base. These young men of vastly different stations and origins were the "odds and ends" on which the outcome of this crisis turned.

Twenty-one-year-old gardener Jack Bartlett was in Belgium a year before this, in May 1940, desperately trying to hold back the German blitzkrieg with his neighbors from Lincolnshire amid scenes of desperation and chaos.

Theirs was a group of Territorial Army artillery; Saturday soldiers, they were called, because they trained on Saturday evenings when they didn't have to work. Bartlett had an open, boyish face—truly a gardener's face, not a gunner's. A coworker from the estate he worked and lived on joined Bartlett after the lord of the manor came to them in the darkening days of 1938, saying, "I'd like you lads to think about volunteering to serve your country in some way." They weren't sure whether this was a suggestion or an employer's demand. The other Lincolnshire gunners were butchers, dairymen, mechanics, and grocers. The second lieutenant worked for an insurance agency. They called each other, even the officers, by their first names; it would have felt presumptuous to call familiar townsmen Sir, or Bombardier, or Gunner.

In spring 1940 Jack Bartlett was situated by a narrow river and several hundred yards from a bridge linking Belgium and France. The Lincolnshire neighbors were isolated and outmatched, their four old field guns lacking armor-piercing shells for the antitank role they were supposed to play. The retreat of British and French infantry was underway, and the young men marched past Bartlett's position looking hungry and dead on their feet, while the gunners stayed put to buy them time.

Bartlett and his friends had orders to destroy any tank trying to cross the bridge below them—the hope was that the tank's wreck would make the bridge impassable for those coming up behind it. What, Bartlett, wondered, was to become of the Belgian refugees currently clogging the bridge? They crossed in a constant stream, hungry, and Bartlett and his battery—who themselves were short on food—could not resist giving the hungry children what they could.

Soon the Luftwaffe arrived and began bombing the Belgian town and their battery's position. One bomb struck the town asylum and its patients, dressed in hospital robes, emerged from the bricks and began wandering the war zone. Another bomb blew the front off of a grocery store, temporarily solving the problem of the battery's slim rations. At one point the gunners' sentries focused on a car hovering nearby and driving around with no apparent destination. Suspecting the passengers of being German artillery spotters or other scouts, the sentries fired warning shots in the air and confronted them. When the car still didn't stop, the men opened fire on the car, only to discover that those inside were civilians. They were lost, couldn't distinguish the warning shots from the sounds of war; a young woman inside was dead, and another was wounded.

In the coming days Bartlett and his friends withstood more bombing, sniping, and artillery as they covered the constantly retreating Allies until they, too, were ordered to retreat, first spiking their guns and burning their trucks. After that it was a bleak odyssey westward to share the miserable fate of several hundred thousands of others, waiting on the crowded beaches of Dunkirk for rescue.

Nine months later, Jack Bartlett left the cold River Clyde on a commandeered Cunard liner in a blizzard. Ten weeks after that, he and the Lincolnshire gunners landed in Alexandria, having gone the long way around Africa and up the Red Sea. They then moved to a huge camp called El Tahag spread across the desert west of the Suez Canal. A few weeks after settling into the great canvas city, Bartlett's new artillery arrived with some large trucks—called quads—to pull them. There were four new field guns that lobbed twenty-five-pound shells from snouts that thrust out from big steel plates that would protect the crew from rifle fire, though not the fire of tanks that dueled these guns. The quads and guns had been a little battered in their long trip around Africa, unloaded and reloaded in a number of ports. Still, they finally had modern weapons.

Talk in the camp was about Rommel's tanks and the Egyptian frontier, but the Lincolnshire men had just sent off two of their guns and crews in the other direction, across the Mediterranean to Crete. Then, in the first week of May, word reached Bartlett that they were needed immediately in Palestine, where they would join a force headed into the desert for Iraq.[1]

In February 1940, while Jack Bartlett and his neighbors were freezing cold on the Belgian border, awaiting the German invasion, a young man who would fight beside him in the desert was en route to Palestine. David Smiley came from circumstances that were dramatically different from those of the working-class gardener; descended from baronets on both parents' sides, his life was about horse riding, hunting, piloting his personal plane, and motoring in his Bentley. His father had been a cavalryman, so military college at Sandhurst seemed the thing to do. Then Smiley enlisted in the most elegant unit possible, the Royal Horse Guards, or "Blues," in 1936, where among his fellow troopers in his squadron were "Lords," Honourables," and "Dukes." Between horse parades at Knightsbridge or Windsor, he had plenty of time for racing his own horses and seeking dalliances. David Smiley was in little danger of doing anything useful in the world.

Occasionally other soldiers directed wry observations at these posh Blues who traditionally performed ceremonial duties outside Buckingham Palace. The various companies of Horse Guards would swap barracks— Knightsbridge for Windsor, Windsor for Knightsbridge—every six months, and Smiley heard jokes that, for the Horse Guards, moving between barracks—crossing Hyde Park and its lake, the Serpentine—constituted "overseas" service. But when war came in 1939, his life of ease and luxury was over. And he chose to end it: Smiley was one of those who used his privilege to place himself in harm's way in war to do something useful.

Spring 1940 found twenty-four-year-old David Smiley patrolling British Palestine on the back of his Cavalry Black. Cavalry horses were well suited to hilly Palestine, where Smiley would occasionally talk horses with a village mukhtar between policing bandits, or gun runners, or hashish smugglers. But in fact, Smiley agonized over being away from the fighting in northern and northeastern Africa, a feeling only strengthened by seeing Italian bombers set the Haifa oil refinery ablaze. He pled with his superiors for a fighting assignment and—thanks to the fact that his aristocratic family was friends with General Wavell's—got himself and some fellow Blues posted to the Abyssinia-Sudan border. There he harassed the Italians throughout the winter of 1940–41 as a commando, doing hard and dangerous work while dodging the malaria endemic to the region during the rainy season. He operated behind Italian lines, attacked supply trucks, ambushed enemy posts before slipping away. He was no longer a mere parade trooper.

With the assignment over in early spring 1941, Smiley found himself back north in the port of Alexandria doing a job he found far less pleasant than stalking the eastern Sudan steppe for Italians: wrangling Australians. The Allied retreat from Greece was underway, and day after day all manner of ship deposited evacuated soldiers on the Alexandria docks between Axis air raids. Some units marched down companionways in good order, looking largely unscathed; others were in disarray, their weapons and equipment gone—and sometimes their morale and discipline.

The soldiers were supposed to shuffle onto trucks bound for desert camps like Jack Bartlett's to be braced up and refitted. But many of the Australian young men had ideas more along the lines of wine, women, and song. So David Smiley and his friends from the Blues had to track them down in Alexandria's shadowy places and bars. Cornered, the strays would often put up a terrific fight.

It was in one of those Alexandrian dives that Smiley heard a pair of rumors. First there was a horrible rumor about the Royal Horse Guard back up in Palestine: their faithful black geldings had all either been given away or put down. Trucks had arrived to replace them. The modern battlefield was no place for a horse, according to someone in Whitehall; and the price of feeding and caring for the horses could not be borne.

The other rumor was that the Blues had been put on notice of an imminent move: they were bound for a fight in Iraq. David Smiley and the other Horse Guards on loan to Egypt begged to be retransferred, and they were soon speeding back to Palestine before they missed the action.[2]

Harry Chalk, from Southend, Essex, was even farther removed from David Smiley's world of plumed helmets and polished riding boots. Chalk grew up hungry, his father a bookie and black marketeer, his mother taking in lodgers. He left school at age thirteen so he could work as a tiler to help support his family. In 1937, at age fourteen (and giving a false birth year), he enlisted in the Territorials, the Saturday Soldiers, for extra money, and because his employer implicitly threatened to not give work to those who didn't enlist. Though the money was indeed helpful during the Depression, Harry Chalk wasn't happy to enlist, because his father had lost a leg in the last war, and an uncle had died three days before the Great War's Armistice. Still, the new uniform deeply impressed his friends who were still in school, even though Chalk was tremendously slight and boyish even in the smart costume.

During the Munich Crisis, when it seemed Britain might go to war over the German annexation of Czechoslovakia, Chalk switched from the Territorials to the regular army. He had just turned sixteen and was now an infantryman of the First Essex Regiment, the recruiter immediately sending him to a barracks. His mother now had one fewer mouth to feed, and he was happy to be out of reach of her beatings. His soldier's pay was unlike any he'd ever seen and, when he was shipped out to Egypt and got an even higher wage, he couldn't believe his luck.

Though Chalk's upbringing was a far cry Smiley's, Chalk and the First Essex Regiment, like Smiley, fought across the borders of Sudan,

Ethiopia, and Eritrea in late 1940. There Chalk saw his friends Sammy Jay, "Baldy" Warner, and "Toughie" Clark shot and killed in August 1940 when the Essex was ordered to charge across four hundred yards of open desert toward Italian positions one morning. The Italians (Chalk and his friends called them "Eye-ties") opened up with machine guns, bullets humming like bees around Chalk's ears, as his captain and his friends were killed, the rest pinned down with no cover. Eventually a British truck appeared from somewhere behind them, rushing in reverse with two men working a machine gun mounted on the back. Their fire gave Chalk and his remaining friends a moment to scramble back and out of the sun-blasted shooting gallery, though so many never left that place. Until then, Chalk thought of shooting, and being shot, in terms of the cowboy films on which he'd grown up—a cowboy would get shot, but he'd keep riding. But he had a new understanding now.

Near the end of 1940, Harry's First Essex staged for a big combined assault on an Italian fort. Gallabat, perched on a high rock commanding the Ethiopia-Sudan border, would be a very tough target. With the Essex was a Baluchi and a Garhwali battalion, some artillery, and even about a dozen light tanks. Six small bombers—out of date and retired from every other theater—and six Gladiator biplanes would provide air support.

Before the attack the always polished Anthony Eden appeared in the desert, his plane having descended under the escort of a wing of fighters. Here was the secretary of war himself, on tour of North Africa and the Middle East just then. He gave a speech to the assembled soldiers, and Harry Chalk caught some words about how "England had its back to the wall," and though the men were underequipped and undersupported, "they must do their best with what they had." Harry Chalk was never one to be impressed by the upper crust.

Then, watching Eden "bugger off," in Harry's words, taking his "lovely warplanes" with him, Harry felt deserted by the "top wig."

Nevertheless, after a night of rain, at zero hour, 5:10 a.m., the Essex stormed the rock of Gallabat under Italian artillery and mortar fire from above. Most of the British light tanks accompanying the Allied assault were removed quickly, hitting mines or breaking tread pins among the boulders and ridges, while the truck carrying the tools and spare parts was destroyed, its three mechanics badly hurt. The six RAF biplanes providing cover were all destroyed or forced down quickly. And yet the Essex worked its way upward and took the fort after several hours of hard fighting. The Italians withdrew to a rearward hill to keep raining artillery on the fort, while Allied and Italian bodies, along with those of many mules, quickly attracted legions of flies.

Without the six fighters to harass Italian bombers, Chalk and his friends occupying the newly captured fort were badly exposed. Bombers started arriving from all corners of Italian East Africa, wave after wave.

The Essex boys and men tried to find cover, but while the fort dominated the passes and valleys around it, it had no protection from the air. The Italian artillery contributed air-bursting shells to the bombers' onslaught. For many hours the ground shook under Chalk; shrapnel whizzed around him; a friend had his leg destroyed; "Tug" Wilson, smaller and even younger than Chalk, was killed.

The Essex was cornered—from above—and it seemed to inspire the frenzied fear of a wild animal cornered, until, from Harry Chalk's point of view, "the Essex had enough." In the middle of the afternoon, they broke and scrambled back down the hill they had won at such a high cost to them and their Indian partners of dozens of lives and over a hundred injured.

Still streaming down and away on the road below, they encountered an Indian captain and some soldiers at a crossroads who ordered them back to the fight. They, in turn, let this Captain Chaudhuri know that they would shoot him if he tried to stop them. By rights, he could have shot those men with impunity for desertion, but instead he never reported the incident.

After this, the First Essex was withdrawn to the rear in Sudan and then moved up to Palestine to recover and regroup. Their barracks were at a point just south of Haifa Bay, and from the barracks it was only steps to the shimmering Mediterranean. Some days Harry Chalk would walk out in the waters there, the hills rising up at his back, and a quiet Carmelite monastery watching over it all.

The quiet came to an end in the first days of May, when orders to move east into Iraq found Chalk and his remaining friends.[3]

• • •

When the commanders of Chalk's, Bartlett's and Smiley's units were summoned to Jerusalem for a briefing on the impromptu mission to Iraq, so was John Glubb of the Arab Legion. John Bagot Glubb, nicknamed Abu Hanik, or Father of the Little Jaw due to the wrecked jaw he had received in World War I, was one of those figures, like Gertrude Bell, T. E. Lawrence, and others, who identified with the Arabs of the Middle East, loved them, was sure in his heart that he was their ally. Yet he loved them on British terms, on terms that could not easily be reconciled with regional aspirations for independence. Glubb had patiently learned an encyclopedia's worth of geography, dialects, history, and memories in the region; yet before he became Transjordan's Emir Abdullah I's servant as head of the Arab Legion, one of his roles had been to visit and threaten "recalcitrant" Iraqi sheiks with the destruction of their villages by the RAF.

Now Glubb—also called Glubb Pasha by many—was summoned from Amman to Jerusalem and he made the quick crossing of the River Jordan valley from Amman. The new general in command of Palestine was Henry Wilson, called Jumbo for reasons obvious to anyone who saw his huge frame. General Wilson had just overseen the evacuation of British troops from Greece ahead of a German onslaught, but he was smiling when Glubb and other officers were ushered into his office in the King David Hotel in Jerusalem.

"More trouble, gentlemen, I'm afraid!" The general laid out his plans for the march on Iraq by forces from Palestine, already barely defended. Jumbo Wilson enumerated the hodgepodge of units available, including Glubb Pasha and the armored cars and trucks of the Arab Legion.

"Will the Arab Legion fight?" the general asked Glubb.

"The Arab Legion," he said, "will fight anybody."

The legion was loyal to Emir Abdullah I of Transjordan, who was one of Britain's first and fiercest allies against the Germans and Italians. And the Golden Square coup in Iraq had been a personal outrage to him. The coup plotters had chased the emir's nephew, the ruling regent Abdul Ilah, out of the country as their first act; Britain had installed his branch of the Hashemite family in Iraq after World War I. Now the emir's nephew and the six-year-old king of Iraq, Faisal II, were sheltered in one of Abdullah's homes in Transjordan.

Abdullah and his court watched developments in Iraq closely in the first days of May 1941. There was little chance that the Arab Legion and the Transjordanian Frontier Force—lightly armed and mainly an antibanditry police force—could resist a division of an Axis-allied Iraqi Army descending on Amman. Nor could they put up much of a defense against bombing. The more nervous among Transjordanian officials watched the British in the capital closely to see whether they would evacuate. The incensed Abdullah, meanwhile, had to be talked out of personally leading the Arab Legion across the desert to Baghdad to knock some heads and reinstall his nephew. As a British ally, Abdullah had done hard desert campaigning against the Ottomans in World War I as a thirty-four-year-old; but he was almost sixty now.

Meanwhile, legionnaires recruited from Iraq and all the region's countries, like Daud Hassan, trained at motorized combat. Hassan drove with a zeal that suggested he thought his fate was already written in heaven's Book of Time, regardless of the care he took. And Mutr Fuqaan and Mubrad Sulaiman trained at loading and firing the Lewis gun they mounted on a tripod in a Chevy truck's bed. Those trucks and the armored cars that patrolled the deserts with them were an American presence in this war. Having watched the terrifying efficiency of German mobile warfare in 1939 and spring 1940, John Glubb had sent a telegram to Dearborn, Michigan, ordering over one hundred trucks. In those Depression days, the Michiganders happily built them and sent them over the Atlantic to the port of Haifa. (The Arab Legion, though, never quite received them all; a good many ended up on the bottom of the Atlantic courtesy of the German Kriegsmarine.) A small number of the trucks received armor plating from a Wagner's Engineering and Metallurgy in Jaffa, which bolted armor onto them in the form of two sheets of steel sandwiching plywood. Then they crossed the deep Jordan valley to Amman. Indeed, those trucks and armored cars embodied a uniquely combined American, British, Jewish-Palestinian, Transjordanian force in the war, and would play an indispensable role in the fights to come.[4]

6

"He Guides Whom He Pleases"

How Freya Stark Came to Iraq

> We didn't understand the culture, we didn't understand the language, we didn't have a corps of people we could rush there. . . . We had bad intelligence.
> —Frank Miller, head of the US National Security Council's Iraq Group in 2003, quoted in Special Inspector General for Iraq Reconstruction, *Hard Lessons: The Iraq Reconstruction Experience*

THIS BRINGS US to the story of Freya Stark, whose destiny would eventually lead her to a balcony in Baghdad from which she watched Tony Dudgeon on a bombing run, but who found herself in the crosshairs of an Italian bomber in late 1940 while passing up the Red Sea. There, with Italian-held Eritrean and Somalian coasts to port, Stark sailed amid a vast convoy moving under broadening morning. There were cruisers and destroyers, giant troopships, little merchantmen; a vast conglomeration carrying trade, resources, supplies, and the Fifth Indian Infantry Division. The Fifth comprised men of mixed experience—some Great War veterans who had sailed this way to France in their youth, others who had fought in periodic bloody campaigns against Pashtun tribesmen on India's Northwest Frontier, and some green recruits. There were mule drivers, signalmen, and too few artillerymen, but most were riflemen, coming from all corners of the Indian Subcontinent; roughly one in four came from the Punjab, and at dawn prayed toward Mecca, not so far away up the Red Sea.

Among all these men, a woman: Freya Stark. Dark-eyed, dark-curled, small of figure, and forty-seven years old. She might have been somewhat out of place in this flotilla bringing war to Africa, but she had never given a whit about being out of place. At age thirty-four she had decided to escape a blind alley of a life and a domineering mother; she sailed to the Levant, learned Arabic, and began a life of very successful exploration and writing.

Indeed, it was Stark's not caring a whit, her polite failure to conform, that allowed her eventually to succeed at both. She appeared a typical middle-class English tourist, if unusually colorful, and a "mere woman," after all. This had led to her first of many successful explorations, and her first book had been about the unique Druze peoples in what was then the south of French colonial Syria. Having fought against colonial occupation for years, the Druze were blockaded by the French in their mountain homeland. When Stark took it upon herself to pierce the French blockade to learn about the little-known Abrahamic sect, she simply set out with a friend and a muleteer from Damascus. With affected credulousness she passed through a region under martial law in the guise of a tourist who had innocently wandered off the beaten path. And where a military-age male would have been detained by French authorities, police simply directed the young woman out of the war zone and carried on, taking little notice. She succeeded at reaching the Druze, who noted with approval that she'd been stopped by the French and thus were willing to speak with her, and from that Stark wrote her first success. Next she did the same in Iran, where she successfully sought out a long-forgotten stronghold of the Assassin sect. And later she identified ancient incense trade routes in Yemen at the base of the Arabian Peninsula. In a fifteen-year career that only began in her midthirties, she had become a bestseller as well as a sought-after and celebrated personality in London.

It was off Yemen where Freya Stark had joined this convoy en route from India to Sudan. It was not safe for Allied ships to move through the Red Sea unescorted because of the threat of Italian dive-bombers and submarines based in Italy's colonies there. And this is why the Indian Army's Fifth Division was coming: Britain's holding the Suez Canal was only so important if the Italians could threaten India's lifeline and half the world's trade from its Red Sea bases. Some of the best Italian troops garrisoned these places in seemingly unassailable mountain headquarters, places from which they could attack British Sudan or Egypt. There these Italian forces might meet up with the German and Italian tanks that were encroaching on Egypt from the west. The Indian soldiers were to place themselves between the Italians and Egypt at Port Sudan.

On the little ship *Amin*, leant by a powerful friend in Aden, and sailing under the heels of the cruiser *Leander*, Freya Stark thought of London, laying at the mercy of German bombs. She worried for friends, even those whose homes were out in the green suburbs, where sometimes bombs fell shrieking too.

On this morning an Italian reconnaissance plane emerged from the sun on the horizon, swept over the flotilla, and turned back into it. At their breakfast, the *Amin*'s captain predicted that the bombers would appear in about three hours. Afterward, Freya saw that two Sikh signal officers, who before that morning had been dour, now combed out each other's hair, smiling. Finally, a fight.

Rattling and popping announced the arrival of the bombers midmorning, and Stark politely declined the captain's advice to go below as she watched great plumes of water erupting amid the convoy surrounding the *Amin*. She counted four bombers above, flying high. And she watched with a kind of elation as the cruisers and destroyers opened up with everything that could be pointed skyward, which made the ships appear to be draped in sparkling gold like heroic things. Even little *Amin* joined in: a World War I–era machine gun had been set up above the bridge among a nest of sandbags and was adding its own little bit of defiance. Up there, too, were the Sikh officers firing away with their rifles. There was something about being in harm's way, like people were in London, that assuaged some unhappy feeling in Stark.

Though the bombs fell close amid the convoy, the glittering defensive cloak forced the bombers high, and none of the boats were hit. The *Amin* remained unhit when the bombers returned as the convoy docked in Port Sudan—a village, really, with no real antiaircraft defenses, only relying on blackouts at night—but the port suffered.

After that, Stark was soon steaming up the Nile River toward Cairo, the pivot of the war in that half of the world. The city housed Britain's Middle East headquarters, and the citadel defending the Suez and its vital land bridge between Africa and the Levant. And Cairo was a city on edge; the Egyptians had won a measure of national independence in 1922, but Britain had maintained troops in the Canal Zone, as well as the right to involve itself in Egypt's foreign affairs. With war, the British had come pouring back in, to the resentment of a country that had only recently seen them leave. The kingdom hardly welcomed German or Italian domination over British domination, but neither did it make sense for it to cast its lot with an old foe that hardly seemed incapable of standing against the Axis war machine that was chalking up victory after victory. Besides, Axis radio promised that it would respect Egyptian sovereignty in the new world order. Meanwhile, there were some tens of thousands of Italians still living in the country, some of them serving in the king's court. On the other hand, the British had a paltry propaganda campaign of their own at this time.

That's why Freya Stark had come. The beginning of the war had found her in London, being fêted for her writing and exploration, jealously sought after as a guest whose RSVP could guarantee an evening's success. Some of those with whom she dined and danced were intelligence officers, and before long the question among intelligence and consular agents was not *whether* Miss Stark would be employed in Arab lands, but *where*, exactly. First Stark went to Yemen at the base of the Arabian Peninsula. The Germans and Italians were hard at work there trying to convince the Yemenis that Axis victory was assured and the British should be scorned. The British, whose base at Aden was an utterly vital naval bastion, had little to offer in terms of proof that they could defeat the Axis. So when Freya Stark arrived in Yemen all she could do was talk to people. She thought of her role as providing a sensible, humble counterpoint. While the Germans and Italians used bombastic accounts of military victories over the radio to puff themselves up and belittle the British, Stark started with chats over tea. Soon after she had arrived in Yemen, a cook explained to her that "all things in Arabia are done by the harem; get them to wish what you wish, and you will get it." Stark, therefore, started by speaking with the wives of influential members of Yemeni society.

Whether via an introduction from a sympathizer or due to curiosity about the colorful Englishwoman, Freya would receive an invitation from a household. On arriving, she would be ushered into the wives' quarters among cushions and rugs. Her favorites were the older ladies who were beyond the usual years of childbearing and threw off their care for prettifying and dainty behavior. Cheerfully, one asked Stark to guess her age, and when she underestimated forty-five in perfect honesty, the woman revealed her breasts to show they were "as firm as a girl's!" Stark found it all pleasant and it made her think of the various forms that freedom could take. The wives were supposed to be isolated here in their chambers, but every delivery of tea brought intelligence from the town, while windows were for spying from the shadows.

Between cups of tea or having her fortune read, Stark simply chatted and gossiped with the women. Unobtrusively she might remind them of something good the British had done in the country, or she might gently turn the conversation to Italian outrages in Abyssinia or Libya. She might describe a talk that she had had with an imam who believed in the basic democracy of Islam—a religion of many nations with no priestly hierarchy. Yet she was not above mentioning that Hitler had been a wallpaper hanger or that Mussolini's father had been a blacksmith. She sought to be liked and to remind those with whom she spoke of what she usually found to be true: that they themselves simply liked the British more. By the time the wives' husband entered the harem rooms, the women's chatter silencing, Freya Stark often felt that her work was already done.[1]

She had come to Cairo to continue her work of cultivating friends of Britain and the democracies. It was a cosmopolitan city, and she did not have to influence powerful men from a distance through their wives in Cairo as she had in Yemen. Sometimes it was champagne cocktails sipped around fountains in a shaded courtyard. But tea remained her weapon of choice, and she still liked to make her first inroads among the women. It was not always easy since, in those days, with eastern Europe joining the Axis and German bombs falling on British cities, the odds seemed to be with Germany.

Stark recruited Egyptian university students, longtime British residents of Alexandria or Cairo, and others to host their own talking circles. She would appear at these, but as they proliferated she would also write and distribute talking points and responses to Berlin radio propaganda for use at such gatherings. The collection of circles she called the Brotherhood of Freedom as a conscious verbal foil to the anti-British Muslim Brotherhood.

In Cairo her chiefs at the embassy gave Stark a partner in Lulie Abul-Huda, a highborn young woman of Egyptian-Jordanian-Syrian-Turkish Arab background who was already on her way to becoming a formidable activist for Arab feminism and independence. Her father served Emir Abdullah I, and she had grown up in Amman, where she stood out for her liberal spirit, refusing to cover herself—to her parents' chagrin. As a mere high schooler in Jerusalem she helped start a club for young women advocating for Arab Palestinian rights. As a student at Oxford University, probably the first Muslim female to attend, Abul-Huda moved in liberal anticolonial intellectual circles. After graduation, she was recruited by one of the government propaganda branches and posted to Egypt.

The twenty-one-year-old was a vivacious and intense foil to Stark's unassuming and relaxed ways. In Cairo, Stark's approach was to assume that everyone with whom she spoke was naturally inclined toward democracy and the Allies yet might need to be reminded of why they liked them and should distrust the Axis. Young Lulie spoke with more passion. When she spoke of what the Allies idealized, her words streamed; when a young man was dismayed at German and Italian advances, Lulie chastened him. Freya was charming, but Lulie turned heads. Freya was extraordinarily independent, but never considered herself the feminist she thought Lulie was. Freya loved her, and saw in her the future of Arab lands. In sum, she wanted an Arab Middle East fit for Lulie, and one that would be friends with Britain.

The pair visited girls' schools, went to the hinterlands and ate roast lamb with villages of horse traders, had tea with Emir Abdullah I when he visited Egypt, and dined with princesses. General Archibald Wavell, who was responsible for defending the Suez as head of Middle East Command, found Freya good company, in part because she had the good grace not to talk to him about the war. One evening when the two hosted the Wavells for dinner, the general quoted Oscar Wilde:

The almond-groves of Samarcand,
Bukhara, where red lilies blow,
And Oxus, by whose yellow sand
The grave white-turbaned merchants go:
And on from thence to Ispahan . . .

Stark had visited Isfahan years earlier en route to searching for the lost valley of the Assassins, a success for which she had been given an award by the Royal Geographical Society. She would try to return to Isfahan very soon, before disaster intervened.

She started down that fated path in early March 1941 when her chiefs decided to try to expand her Brotherhood of Freedom circles in Iraq to counter German influence. Freya and Lulie's other helpers could take over the program in Cairo, their fellowship having now over five hundred registered members, as well as informal participants. Stark left Egypt just as General Erwin Rommel renewed the Axis threat in the Western Desert and General Wavell was forced to send thousands of troops from the Libyan front to eventual disaster in Greece. She flew to Jerusalem, relieved by the sight of spring greenery on the hills. Then she made the brief crossing through the Jordan valley rift and back up to Amman, where she stopped for tea with Emir Abdullah I.

As a traditionalist, the emir seemed to want to put on a brave face for the lady, saying that he was unconcerned that the French in Syria-Lebanon—right on his border—had sided with collaborationist Vichy France.

"Let them go," he told her. "It will mean a year or eighteen months more. But England will be alone at the peace." (Yet when he was not putting on a chivalric face for Stark, Abdullah was realistic about the fate of his country in the event of a Vichy incursion. He and the country's tribal leaders did not waver, but knew there could be only one outcome if that large army invaded.)

Stark then made the long crossing through the Iraqi west, her car driven by a RAF captain who was young for his rank. The new highway made with Iraqi tar smoothed out the miles—except, that is for those incomplete segments in the middle. She was not used to long passages so easily crossed by highway and feared it gave one a false sense of mastery over the landscape. Emerging from the desert at Ramadi and crossing the Euphrates on a modern bridge at Fallujah, Stark arrived at Baghdad in the evening, following a string of lights on the Tigris.

Only a few days later, the Golden Square and Rashid Ali al-Gailani launched their coup. Even afterward, Stark continued to make her social rounds and to visit the bazaar as she always had; she was a compulsive treasure hunter. Her sense on these outings was that ordinary Baghdadis did not pay the coup much notice. Yet she was very disappointed to hear so many anti-British—and, she thought, German-inflected—rumors spinning about. And the newspapers she found to be supremely pessimistic about Allied chances. When she asked them whether they knew about the recent Allied success in Eritrea, people in the bazaar had no idea what she was talking about. It did not help that, soon after, news of Rommel's capture of the strategic port of Benghazi, Libya, came over the radio. She held little hope of creating Brotherhood of Freedom cells in the short term, she conceded, yet they were badly needed there.

One early April day Stark went to the riverfront Hotel Zia to meet her friend George Antonius, a liberal pan-Arab nationalist. Born in Lebanon, but having adopted Palestine as his home, Antonius had been a civil servant in the government of British Mandate Palestine before becoming a proindependence envoy to the world. Antonius believed that the British had stood in the way of an independent Arab confederation in the Middle East despite what he and many others viewed as Britain's World War I–era promise. Still, he did not consider himself anti-British and certainly did not support Germany in the war.

To her surprise, Stark found Antonius conversing with Amin al-Husseini, a Jerusalem-born pan-Arab nationalist who, unlike Antonius, had long ago abandoned diplomacy for blood. He had helped lead an armed rebellion against the British in the Palestinian hinterlands for years in the mid-1930s before it failed and he fled the country. And where George Antonius easily imagined a Jewish national home embedded in a welcoming, even protecting Arabian federation, Amin al-Husseini had devolved into a bitter Jew hater. At the sight of Stark's approach, a few bearded men in the party looked at her with undisguised disgust. But al-Husseini, in a spotless white robe, greeted her with excited interest, his blue eyes twinkling.

"I am delighted to meet you," said Freya Stark, pleasant. She was well aware that he had been financially supported by the Germans through Fritz Grobba, that he was an old friend of one of the Iraqi coup plotters, and was a pro-German player in Iraqi politics. "So few of us British have a chance to do so now." While his entourage glared, al-Husseini himself smiled at the joke. Soon the two were speaking of Arab literature.[2]

In mid-April 1941, before the fighting erupted at RAF Habbaniya, Freya Stark slipped away from the Golden Square's Baghdad for Persia, passing through fiercely sublime alpine landscapes. Black hills contrasted with white snow, all interspersed with wet red and green, like the heather and ferns of Scotland in fall. The rain exposed the poverty of the people that she encountered in the countryside, those with little to protect themselves against the elements. She almost looked on this poverty among the wild places as picturesque, but caught herself: poverty wasn't quaint, it was hunger.

She arrived in Tehran and consulted with the consulate's intelligence circle about her efforts. She stayed at the British ambassador's home in Tehran, over which the gloom of the Allied retreat from Greece hung. But soon she was ready to depart Tehran for several days' happy exploration of Isfahan, eulogized by Oscar Wilde and General Wavell, the supremely ancient city thronged with synagogues, Zoroastrian temples, minarets, palaces, and bazaars. Then, still on the eve of leaving Tehran for Isfahan, Stark awoke somehow certain that if she did not return to Baghdad immediately, she might never again enter it, or at least not enter it before the war was decided one way or another.

So Stark hired a car and practically ran for the border with Iraq, sure that it would close soon. When she reached it, two young Iraqi soldiers checked her papers, saying, "Every night we pray to God for a victory for you." They sent her on her way into Iraq.

At the first real town over the border, though, she was stopped by police officers who couldn't help but notice a lone Englishwoman. One of them hopped on the taxi's running board and directed it to a police post. Inside, a middle-aged lieutenant politely but firmly told Stark that she could not continue toward Baghdad. The post had just received a telegram that ordered travelers to be stopped.

Stark immediately responded with her usual opening gambit: "Did your telegram say that women as well as men were to be prevented from going to Baghdad?" Surely there was a distinction; a mere English-woman, after all, could be no threat.

"No. It said travelers. It said nothing about women at all."

Stark was far from winning the argument, but she believed that she had planted a seed of uncertainty.

So began hours of chatting—over tea, naturally. From the officer she drew out that he had been trained as a cadet by an English colonel, and she helped the police lieutenant remember him as a good man and teacher.

"All of this is a pity," he soon said. More progress.

Some more tea and then sandwiches followed as Stark learned that there was some kind of trouble at the RAF air base west of Baghdad. (It was the first of May, and the real battle would begin the next morning.) And Stark learned that the oil wells of the Iraq Oil Company near the town had been seized by the Iraqi Army, the British employees of the largely American company arrested.

At some point in their conversation Stark shook her head at the misfortune of all of this for her new protector. "Of course, you would have to find me a maid," she said. "You would wish to do it all in a civilized way—you are not Germans, after all."

The thought of all that must be involved in arresting an English-woman in a civilized manner finally proved too much for the lieutenant. And a few hours later, chivalrous, he escorted her to her sleeping carriage on the train to Baghdad, shaking her hand before it steamed westward in the evening.

Stark didn't know it, but just as the sky was lightening and the minarets of Baghdad came into view, the battle at Habbaniya began; the war was west of the city, and she entered from the east. Stepping onto the platform, several Baghdadi police met her, but not to arrest the harmless woman. They assumed she was a guest of Harry Chapman Sinderson, head of the Baghdad Medical School, and placing her baggage aboard a horse-drawn cab, pointed the driver in the direction of the house.

"No. I am going to the embassy," she explained.

"Don't go to the embassy," one said with an ominous tone.

But Stark insisted, and the nervous driver eventually pointed his horse that way, down empty streets where even the shrewd cats knew that now was a time to lie low. At some point along the way, they came upon leaflets flickering in the breeze as if, it seemed to her, animated. The driver grabbed one, but he couldn't read it because someone, probably a British intelligence officer, had composed it in his very finest Oxford-learned Arabic—an Arabic the common man couldn't read. Freya perused it; the pamphlet was full of threats. Stupid, she thought; and just the opposite of her approach. If the British really were fighting this war for liberalism and democracy, they should have faith in the Arabs and appeal to those values in them. It was yet another sign that intelligence and persuasion in Iraq had been badly mismanaged by the British.

The horse cab arrived at a sealed-up embassy in the early morning, went past a group of Iraqi police in front of its gate, and pulled up to a side entrance. Stark paid the driver extra given the uneasy circumstances, and she knocked at a small postern in a wall. Eventually a guard opened the door and, seeing this small woman standing outside, seemed barely capable of mentally processing what was happening. A consul who knew her by sight was summoned, and they let the surprise guest enter.

The stir of Stark's arrival spread, and the young Iraqi embassy attendants soon crowded around to greet her. The few British inhabitants who were awake asked her how she managed to reach the embassy.

"In a cab," she said, striking them dumb or indignant.

Over three hundred extra residents were there, people of Allied and overrun countries whose peculiar fates had dropped them in Baghdad in spring 1941. There was the Hindu priest, a widow from Warsaw with her nine-year-old son, a Yugoslavian prima donna. All the Iraqi embassy staff was there; their unprotected houses were no longer safe. Persian gardeners, Kurdish and Arab Iraqi attendants, and Kurdish grooms for the stable of six horses were all there.

The embassy spread over about two acres of manicured grounds of palms, cypresses, and flowering vines, with a low, white-walled house and outbuildings. A gravel drive stretched from the main gate, now flanked by barbed wire, to the house steps, and some of the refugees' cars were parked along this. Freya thought they looked like barricades.

At this early hour many were still sleeping in odd corners and beside a fountain. In one courtyard a great pile of papers was burning, a young man prodding it and sending cinders floating to keep the papers' contents from Iraqi hands if the embassy was overrun. Among them, for example, was a file containing details of Britain's Iraqi oil extraction that would be "inopportune" to have public. Secrets turned black, curled on themselves, and fell apart in the flames.

The embassy was also a clearinghouse of secrets and intelligence assessments, and a host to several RAF intelligence and Special Operations Executive (SOE) officers. The night before Freya arrived at the embassy, the chief RAF intelligence officer was seen dumping small bundles down an old well on the grounds, vital components from some Royal Iraqi Air Force planes that some agent had provided.

The embassy was also the headquarters of a military mission comprising servicemembers who worked with the Iraq military to encourage cooperation. Their work was not secret, but the line between interacting with Iraqi officers and snooping on them was a fine one. The fact that members of the military mission were currently under house arrest and at the mercy of the Iraqis spoke ill of their success at making inroads. (The embassy would later learn that many of the "air liaison officers" around the country were the first arrested by the new regime in April, and treated about as roughly as might be expected of spies. Many Iraqis were arrested, too: those who served the air liaison officers as staff, drivers, and the like. They were also usually robbed by the police. This thievery foreboded some horrible events to come weeks later.)

The rooms of the ambassador's compound were subdivided into cramped dormitories, though many residents sought out stray breezes on the lawn or roof. The Muslims had their own mess area, the Hindus theirs, and they soon spread breakfast on a Ping-Pong table. Sandbags multiplied in spots that a gray major general imagined were defensible, and tin cans filled with sand had been distributed to be used in case of fire. The electricity had been cut, as had the phones. The police had confiscated the two-way radio and peoples' personal radios. One of the cars on the lawn had a radio, though, and there was another hidden in the house. Efforts to jury-rig a transmitter for a two-way radio resulted in loud popping sounds and had to be abandoned.

There were a good number of Stark's old friends from Cairo and intelligence circles, and they filled her in as best they could. Rumors of trouble at Habbaniya slowly became details. The fighting had started, but the last word was that the woman and children evacuated from Baghdad a few days before had still not been flown from the base. British staff who had not reached the embassy in time were arrested as enemy aliens. The American embassy, meanwhile, was sheltering around 150 British and Allied family members.

At some point during the day, the British ambassador to Baghdad, Kinahan Cornwallis, opened a grand piano and lifted out a large number of rifles, which were then distributed. Cocktail hour—rationed at one cocktail per day—took place at six o'clock for the officers.

That night Stark was shown her sleeping place, a spot on one of the compound's balconies over the Tigris, which moved swiftly with the snowmelt from the mountains of Armenian Turkey. She spread a rug there and was far more comfortable than she'd been on many of her travels.

An Iraqi police boat was stationed below, and as was her way, Stark worked to befriend the police guards the next day. Food was being brought into the embassy only with difficulty—the shopkeepers were afraid, too—and she arranged to buy fish from these policemen, who had brought their fishing poles.

Stark was there to do a job as a translator and a sort of diplomatic relations agent, to strengthen British-Arab friendship; but in the present debacle her main goal was to save RAF and other intelligence offices from making more mistakes like their rain of bombastic, threatening leaflets. There were like-minded people locked in with Stark, like her old friend Seton Lloyd, forty years old, a successful archaeologist and adviser to

Iraq's Ministry of Antiquities. Before being trapped in Baghdad, he had written Arab-language public relations material for broadcasting from Jerusalem and hosted salons for liberal-minded Iraqis in a similar vein as Stark's Brotherhood, though informally. Another friend was the tall, charming Irishman Adrian Bishop. He was in fact a monk, Brother Thomas, but his experience as a linguistics genius and longtime oil company employee in Persia in earlier days meant that at middle age he had been recalled to the army, then sent to the SOE. In the coming days, Stark and Bishop took long walks together around the grounds, discussing how things in Iraq got into this state and how to cultivate good feeling between Britain and Iraq in the future while respecting Iraqis' feelings of nationalism, which they both deemed perfectly natural.

Others trapped in the embassy embodied the darker side of British colonialism in the Middle East: men who had ordered or even participated in bombings of Arab villages as "communal punishment" for rebellion in their area. Still others in the embassy blurred the lines between wanting, for Iraqis' sake, to help the new, widely multicultural nation realize peace and prosperity on the one hand and seeking to maintain British power and oil interests there at whatever cost.

Freya was no bomber, but she was no pacifist, either, and she had some rather uncordial thoughts for Amin al-Husseini. The bloody revolutionary, the so-called Grand Mufti with whom Stark had spoken with unflappability weeks before at the Hotel Zia, tried to commandeer the battle against the British and to make it a holy war. He harangued and rhapsodized over the radio in in the public square. Once he managed to send a mob bearing banners and beating drums to the gate of the embassy, but that's as far as it went. Freya Stark was happy to see that he could not make the Golden Square's fight the people's fight. But she wrote to her chief at the Ministry of Information that al-Husseini should be "removed."[3]

As Tony Dudgeon and his fellow airmen tried to keep the Iraqis on the plateau sleepless, Freya Stark lay on a rug draped on a balcony over the Tigris. At one point in the night the arms of the Polish widow appeared above her, leaning on a railing the floor above. They gestured as the woman spoke about her layered miseries.

Just before dawn the eastern horizon lit faintly green behind the riverside villas of some wealthy Jewish merchants on the other side of the river. (These were shut up tight against the uncertainty of the city, Jewish history offering a long list of horrors that might descend on a Jewish home in a time of war, crusade, or upheaval.) Stark heard engines and, looking right down the river she made out bombers approaching through the dimness. Soon they passed up and over her at about a thousand feet. Then she heard the low echoes of bombs, followed by the higher pitch of antiaircraft fire. She didn't know it, but Tony Dudgeon and his RAF colleagues had just wrecked many Royal Iraqi Air Force planes at its air base near the city.

The attack continued as the RAF planes passed over the airfield and passed again. When they wheeled near the Tigris, some among the police patrolling the river shouldered their rifles, the shots briefly silencing the birds. Freya would have her usual tea with the same police later that day.[4]

7

"Lift Up a Banner against the Walls of Babylon!"

Cleveland Buses and the Luftwaffe Invade Iraq

> Everyone was assigned a brand-new Mercedes truck and fully loaded
> trailer. I think there were seven or eight of us who were going to form
> our convoy. . . . The convoy commander discussed hazard identification
> and talked about dangers we might encounter. We ran final checks on
> our trucks and made sure all of the drivers were prepared. We were told
> that we would follow another convoy into Iraq. . . . On the same day,
> another convoy that was coming down from the north of Baghdad
> along our route was attacked.
>
> —US civilian contractor Thomas Hamill, whose convoy was attacked
> in Iraq in April 2004, in *Escape in Iraq: The Thomas Hamill Story*

IT WASN'T EASY getting all the sprinkled-about and disparate components
of the Allied Forces for Iraq started on their way in the first week of May
1941. Some were in Haifa, some at Lydda, in Palestine; some in northern
Transjordan. And some RAF armored cars for the force were still in
North Africa. Orders flew fast, were rescinded, reissued: this unit would
fly to western Iraq; now it would go by train to the end of the line; now
it would go by truck. Transport was insufficient, and sometimes improvised. It was such a hard task to contrive an invasion with sufficient
water, fuel, and other logistics that the generals ordered a flying column
to rush ahead of the main body of the force in the hope of getting to RAF
Habbaniya before it was too late.

Finally, the lead column set off from Palestine, descending deep into
the green, sultry Jordan valley rift, and back way, way up. The Arab

Legion met it on the Iraq-Transjordan frontier, going first in their open Chevys and some of their homemade armored cars. Gunner Jack Bartlett and his Lincolnshire neighbors rolled along in their new, modern hump-backed quads, trailing their guns. The Fourth Cavalry Brigade, including David Smiley's friends, still wearing their high cavalry boots, pointed east toward Baghdad and Habbaniya in their trucks. (As cavalrymen, they were unrivaled, but only about 5 percent were experienced drivers; hardly more than half had spent more than a couple dozen hours behind the wheel of their trucks on training or exercises.) Harry Chalk and the First Essex Regiment followed in their trucks, along with some three-tonners of the Royal Army Service Corps with water, supplies for the invaders, and supplies for the besieged at Habbaniya. There were some ambulances and a field hospital truck, and there were also some trucks manned by members of the Second and Third Field Squadrons of the Royal Engineers and filled with TNT earmarked for the oil wells of Kirkuk, if things came to that. Eight RAF armored cars that had rushed from Egypt played a critical role in guarding the flanks of this spearhead group.

Also on that desert track leading out of Transjordan was a caravan of buses wrangled off the streets of Haifa, their drivers with them. These were sad, threadbare, secondhand things, with painted names like "Cleveland" and "Philadelphia" still visible in spots. Many of their tires were bald, and various parts were held on with wire. They carried water and other supplies as part of a column sometimes stretching seven miles along a desolate road that, one of the men of the First Essex said, looked like a "piece of black ribbon pinned on a sandtable." Even a taxi from Haifa was "requisitioned" to serve as the staff car of the leader of the Household Cavalry.

At this hour came another moment of division, another choice— one of the countless choices that, all tallied, would determine the outcome of this battle for Iraq and the Levant. One more unit was supposed to join in the ragtag phalanx but was absent: a truck-borne squadron of the Transjordan Frontier Force. The TJFF was a force of mounted constabulary, really; a British unit based in Transjordan, made up of Iraqi, Jordanian, and Palestinian Arabs. Jews had once been enlisted, but relations between the Jewish and Arab Palestinians broke down badly in the mid-

1930s. At the upper levels, the force was officered by British men, though a significant share were Arabs. The TJFF's main role was to police crime, including gun running and other kinds of smuggling, to watch for revolt, and to keep an eye on the three frontiers of Iraq, Palestine, and Syria.

When orders came to the force posted at the oil pipeline pumping station not far from the Iraq border to join the campaign in Iraq, one unit began murmuring. The murmurs built until, confronted by their British officers, the men complained that it was not their job to march on other countries to make war. Pressed, they admitted that they had heard voices on Axis radio exhorting Arab soldiers to refuse to make war on one another. The British were concerned, actually almost panicked about this. Was this a mutiny? How far did it spread? What should they do with the ringleaders? For the moment, this particular squadron of the TJFF was stood down and, rather than making martyrs of them, the ringleaders were quietly given their retirement. Unaffected units of the TJFF will reappear later in this story.

Also notably absent in the Iraq spearhead was air cover—the RAF was trying to cover the Royal Navy and the ongoing retreat from Greece. The column rolling east would have only some limited bombing support from Gladiator biplanes until it reached the Iraqi frontier. Also missing was armor—nearly every tank outside Britain was in Egypt and Libya stalking and sparring with Rommel.

In total, the force departing Palestine and Transjordan at the end of the first week of May was six thousand men, with the name Habforce, the force for the relief of Habbaniya. But the flying column ahead of the sluggish body numbered not quite two thousand.

The first Iraqi target of the advance group was a village and fort just over the border along the pipeline that ran from the oil fields around Kirkuk to the refinery at Haifa on the coast. The lonely desert station called Rutbah Wells, now occupied by a small number of Iraqi troops, had a water supply, some lodging and offices for Iraq Petroleum Company workers, and a high-walled stone fort. Located on a dusty flatland, it was formerly an Imperial Airways stopover, and it could double as an air base. Leaving it in their flanks in the hands of the Iraqis was not a good option.

Three hundred fifty of the speedy Arab Legion reached it first; this was their backyard, really, and some of them were born in the Western Desert of Iraq. They found the fort occupied and barred against them. Their World War I–era machine guns were no answer. The Iraqi soldiers within began firing from behind medieval-style loopholes, wounding a legionnaire. And John Glubb and his men had to retreat to some dunes bordering the village, surround the fort, and watch. They radioed Transjordan to ask for bomber support and waited.

When a couple of bombers arrived, they failed to hit the fort. One, though, was hit by a lucky rifle shot and it turned toward home; but it didn't make it, sputtering to death over the desert and burying itself in the sand. When news of this was radioed back to Baghdad by the Iraqis, word was repeated jubilantly over the airwaves, though the report stated that John Glubb was among the dead. This was repeated in Berlin, and was subsequently picked up by the BBC. Monitoring the BBC over the radio secreted on the embassy grounds in Baghdad, Freya Stark and her friends winced at the news.

As it happened, the RAF armored cars caught up to the Arab Legion at Rutbah a couple of days later. Afraid of being trapped in a siege, the Iraqi occupiers of the fort slipped off, driving eastward toward Baghdad in the dark of night. Glubb later learned that one of his men had a brother among the Iraqis who'd shot at them from the fort. This fight, at the local and global scale, turned brothers against each other many times over.

Behind the Arab Legion trucks and RAF armored cars, the relief column made its slower trip east into the desert down the black ribbon. Engines seized and radiators burned, trucks stopped, and men tried to slake their thirst. Some of the buses, which had served dauntless in snowy American cities, laid down at last and died beside that road. The long train reached Rutbah, where the Household Cavalry, the Essex, and others camped and resupplied. The well there was most welcome, since water discipline had been strict: one gallon a day per man and per vehicle in heat that reached 120 degrees. Some of the units had carried their water all the way from Egypt, water which now looked like someone had spilled ink into it.[1]

• • •

At Rutbah, on May 14, an inconspicuous figure entered the story. He was little noticed, and little respected, then, but during this campaign, at a key moment, he would summon as if by magic a force that would strike fear into enemy colonels, even German agents. He was an Arab Palestinian with the incongruous name of Reading. It was an alias, a name he used for work, because he was a British Army interpreter. To some of his compatriots he would look like a collaborator with the colonial rulers; and about five years before these events, those rulers had put down an Arab revolt in Palestine with often indiscriminate brutality. Hence the alias, which was probably borrowed from the Reading Power Station in Haifa.

Reading was shanghaied, or practically so. One day he was in Haifa, probably at the cavalry headquarters just outside the town, at Hadera; the next he was hurried in the back of a staff car and driven up into the hills, down into the green Jordan valley, back up and into the dry uplands of Transjordan, and plunged into the Iraqi desert plain. The force rolling toward Habbaniya needed interpreters. It seemed it hadn't occurred to them before leaving Palestine that it might be a good idea to have some people along who spoke Arabic. Even the Household Cavalry's intelligence officer didn't speak Arabic; he was a good fit for the Life Guards and Household Cavalry—wealthy, a fine pedigree, a Tory Member of Parliament, an enthusiastic but terrible hand at poetry—but he was far from a good fit for performing intelligence in Iraq; he knew not a whit about the Arab Middle East, let alone Arabic.

Reading was summarily dumped at this man's feet outside the oil company fort at Rutbah. Reading's personal bag, his shaving kit, everything was lost en route, except for the clothes on his back: his topee hat, shorts, shirt, and high socks. It was an inauspicious start to two months of heat and hardship, joyous exploits, almost dying more than once, and overwhelming fear.[2]

The new Iraqi government requested the return of Fritz Grobba, and he was soon informed of his triumphant return to his beloved Iraq, operating under the alias Herr Gehrcke. The Luftwaffe put thirteen transports at his disposal, even though they were needed for the approaching invasion of Crete. Grobba called together a large support staff, files, officer equipment, cameras, and cash. Other transports carried Luftwaffe mechanics, radio transmitters, and a chemical laboratory for testing and refining aviation fuel. Five bombers and three fighters would closely follow this initial mission. In an impressive feat of logistics, everything was assembled from different bases in Germany, and the planes were shepherded to occupied Athens; then, thirty-six hours later, flying in the dark and under radio silence, they landed outside Damascus en route to Baghdad. There they were met coolly by French officers: men of conquered France, men who had been ordered to accept the German landing, but they didn't have to like it. (More on that story to come.) The next stage took the German mission to Mosul, Iraq.

Soon afterward, in the second week of May, a Habbaniya pilot returned to base to tell an outrageous story: north of Baghdad he had seen a Messerschmitt 110. At first few believed him. It couldn't have been; it didn't have the range; from where was it supposed to be operating? The pilot responded that cannon and machine gun fire that he took from it were rather convincing. Nothing in the Royal Iraqi Air Force had the 110's distinctive and mighty firepower. Fear replaced disbelief among the Habbaniya pilots.

Tony Dudgeon took off, pointed west, and located the relief column—Reading, and Jack Bartlett, and Harry Chalk among them—still far from Habbaniya at Rutbah. Landing, he shared with them the news that the Luftwaffe was in Iraq.[3]

But a British aircraft was the first to strike the Allies: a British plane flown by an Iraqi pilot, that is. A day out from Rutbah, now staying off the incomplete Baghdad–Haifa Highway and feeling their way across the desert, the Royal Iraqi Air Force spotted them. A twin-engine British-made bomber opened with its cannon and bombed the trucks moving the First Essex. One truck was hit, and three men badly hurt. The bomber wheeled, unopposed, and returned home. It was just a small, bitter taste of things to come.

On a break along the route, Jack Bartlett and his friends were

brewing tea in the shade when one of them decided on some target practice. The man hung some jars on a telegraph pole around seventy-five
yards distant and banged away, inflicting no damage on the jars. Soon an
Arab Legion half-ton Ford came tearing up, responding to the gunfire. A
legionnaire stepped out in his buff robe and red sash, dagger at his belt,
and covered by a red-and-white-checkered kaffiyeh. He took in the scene,
saw that there was no fight to be had here, and without a word unslung
his rifle and, shooting from the hip, shattered the distant jars in succession.
He smiled broadly and wordlessly sped away as quickly as he had come.

Soon after this the column ran into a region of soft sand. Many of
the big, fifteen-ton supply trucks burrowed their wheels into the dust.
Since the Iraqis now knew where they were, the British were sitting ducks
from the air. The water was on those trucks, ammunition and food; all
of their supplies were in peril. And not only from the air: Ramadi, reportedly held by a strong contingent of the Iraqi Army, was only about
fifteen miles east of this point.

The men struggled all day to move the big vehicles and heavy guns,
even while the heat was so intense that the metal of the hulks they wres-
tled couldn't be touched with bare hands. By nightfall, they had all but
two of the big vehicles out of the sand trap, but a maze of dust still stood
between them and Ramadi, with Habbaniya not far beyond it. Water was
low, too, because some of the water tanks in the trucks had to be dumped
to lighten the vehicles and free them from the sand.

"We have enough supplies of water to stay here one more day. After
that, we go on or go back," the no-nonsense brigadier told his captains.
In other words, after one day, either they needed to find their way
through the sand and reach Habbaniya or turn around.

While the vast collection of big trucks were extracted from a sea of dust,
Reading had his first experience as a sort of provisional intelligence officer. The Arab Legion were out scouting for safe paths around the dust
trap, paths that did not pass near the Iraqi garrison close by in Ramadi,
and Reading's boss got orders to search for a new water supply, so desperately needed. Reading, his British officer, and the officer's driver-
servant set out into the desert by car, looking for an abandoned village

that John Glubb of the Arab Legion said should be nearby. It was Reading's first experience in the US-built yellow car that would become his home for the next two months. Before long, the three found the so-called village, little more than a single stone house, that stood among a vast field of natural tar. Amid that tar was a pool of water.

Reading knew of such places in Iraq. "It is no use for drinking. It is Sulphur water," he said. "People come for many miles to bathe in such water."

Reading, his officer, and the driver searched out the source of the water, a spring that welled up cool in the otherwise tepid pond. This was the first time, too, that Reading experienced his boss's near fixation on bathing. It was as if the man wanted to maintain here, in this world of dust, the squeaky bodily cleanliness he kept in the House of Commons. For within minutes of finding the spring, the officer had stripped off his clothes—save his pith helmet—and stepped through the oozing tar to have a bath. Reading laughed.

As the officer and driver were getting dried off (they had to use gasoline to clean the drying tar off their feet), Reading sighted some movement on the horizon: two figures watching them. The three jumped into the yellow car and sped toward the two men, who were not happy to be pursued.

"We would be safer to pretend that we are Iraqi soldiers trying to get back to Ramadi, for they would not speak to us if they thought we were British," said Reading before they reached the strangers.

His boss was dubious. "Do you think you can get away with it?"

"Of course." Reading told him that an Iraqi officer might very well be as fair as him and that he might very well drive an American-made staff car. All the officer and the driver had to do was remain in the car as Reading approached the men. Besides, Reading had family in Baghdad and could imitate an Iraqi Arab accent.

When Reading interviewed them they told him they knew nothing of any war. And after searching this countryside further, Reading found more Iraqis to interview, assuming a haughty, official manner, summoning villagers or Bedouin to come to him rather than approaching them. He was hosted to tea in one tent encampment, where someone told him there were fifty thousand Englishmen in the country; another said the Iraqi Army had passed through a week earlier, pressing all the men of fighting age into service; a fiery woman showed Reading her large knife, with which, she said, she would greet any British soldier who came near.

Reading and the others made another discovery about a factor that would shape the whole Iraqi campaign from this point on: the Iraqis had cut sluices through the embankments that held the Euphrates River in place, resulting in widespread floods that covered the road into Habbaniya. The floodwaters made the approach to Ramadi difficult, and at certain points cut off Fallujah, east of Habbaniya. In other words, the main routes into and out of the base were underwater. To those they interviewed, Reading sometimes played the role of an Iraqi officer trying to get back into Ramadi by way of discovering routes that were still open.

After hours of Reading playing the spy, the three were just about ready to return to the Allied column with the news of a water source for the vehicles, as well as news of the flooding. But first the British intelligence officer insisted on his second bath of the morning, this time in the Euphrates.

When Reading and the others eventually got back to the sprawling camp of dusty vehicles, they were met there by a dark Luftwaffe Heinkel bomber circling above. The spray of rifle and machine gun fire seemed to keep it at a high altitude, and its bombs rattled the stone and erupted the dust of the desert floor, but the vehicles escaped impact.

Then the Arab Legion came into camp, reporting that it had found a path to Habbaniya that avoided the soft sand and sidestepped the Iraqi force at Ramadi and the flooded spots. The next morning, woken before dawn by the mournful cries of desert birds at the edge of their vast encampment, the caravan began moving again. They either had to reach Habbaniya that day or their vehicles would die of thirst.

Watching from among the rank and file of the First Essex Regiment, Harry Chalk was not impressed with the commanding officer of the Arab Legion, Glubb Pasha, whom Chalk thought was a fat little man. But the Arab Legion? He thought they were "tip top" for finding them a way out of the morass of sand.[4]

•   •   •

Fritz Grobba and his staff were delayed en route to Baghdad by the prowling of RAF planes around Mosul. But by the morning of May 11 they were housed on the grounds of the presidential palace in Baghdad, where they almost immediately met with Iraqi chiefs of staff to review the military situation. Then Grobba presented Rashid Ali al-Gailani with ten thousand silver dollars (the prime minister, in turn, reminded him that the Italians had promised him one million). And Grobba presented Amin al-Husseini twenty-five thousand Reichsmarks. Al-Husseini accepted, but politely asked that future payments be made in silver—"more usable." He assured Grobba that the money would go toward fomenting a major rebellion in Palestine.

Grobba surveyed what he had to work with. He had few German soldiers, just the Luftwaffe technicians and pilots. He did have a network of Germans in the capital and other Iraqi cities; they were civilians, and really only useful in providing observations and relaying propaganda. And Grobba had some agents and saboteurs from the Sicherheitsdienst (the Nazi party's intelligence agency) based in Tehran who would be tasked with attracting some hinterland Iraqi tribes to their side and would prepare to sabotage Iraq's oil fields, if necessary, to deny them to the British if they could not be secured.

Grobba knew that if he could only maintain Berlin's focus on Iraq, if he could get even minimal investment from armed forces high command, he could tip the balance in favor of the Golden Square and an Axis-aligned Iraq. It would be the culmination of his professional life's work and make him, he hoped, a kind of German Lawrence of Arabia.

So the main allies he needed were Foreign Minister Joachim von Ribbentrop, and, through him, the führer himself. Grobba radioed back to Berlin that Rashid Ali al-Gailani enjoyed the wide support of Arabs and Iraqis everywhere; he reported that Arabs from Palestine and Syria were pouring into the country to aid the patriotic cause, and that Saudi Arabs were soon to pour into British ally Transjordan and cause chaos. None of this was true.

What Grobba really needed, he wired Berlin, were planes: "Imme-

Arab Legionnaires pose at a makeshift airstrip near a Kirkuk-Haifa oil pipeline pumping station in Transjordan.

(*Credit: © H. Hensser, courtesy of Imperial War Museum Collections*)

Jack Hasey speaking in Boston about his experiences in Finland and making the case for coming to the defense of France. (*Credit: © Jack Hasey*)

Members of Jack Hasey's Free French Foreign Legion platoon. Many having fought against Franco's Nationalists in Spain, it had a particularly anti-fascist bent. (*Credit: © Jack Hasey*)

Freya Stark, 1938.
(*Credit: © Royal Geographical Society*)

Harry Chalk (bottom left)
and friends, 1939.
(*Credit: Courtesy of James Hills*)

Dr. Santi Pada Dutt, 1941.   (*Credit: Courtesy of Leila Sen*)

John Masters, 1942. (*Credit: © John Masters*)

A "hijacked" Palestinian bus, broken down on the road to Baghdad.

(Credit: © Dr. Eviatar Reiter)

Buses shanghaied off the streets of Palestine en route to Iraq.
(*Credit: © Humphrey Wyndham*)

Reading,
Fourth Cavalry interpreter.
(*Credit: © Somerset de Chair*)

diate appearance of German planes, if only for purposes of a demonstration, is essential for military and political reasons."[5]

West of Ramadi, four planes sped toward their targets, a column of soldiers encamped on the undulating dust and gravel of central Iraq. They
were staging to drive eastward in the direction of their ultimate target,
Baghdad. The rear of this column was poorly protected, with no air cover,
no real surface-to-air weapons, its main defense a single American-made
truck retrofitted by the Arabs with some steel plating, a machine gun
mounted on its back. By any standard, this was a pathetic defense against
the four modern warplanes sweeping low over the desert, four state-
of-the-art craft from the mightiest air force the world had ever known.

When the dusty men on the ground heard the sudden onrush of
the planes coming over the horizon, most scattered and jumped for
cover. But not the Arabs in the converted Chevy, Mutr Fuqaan and
Mubrad Sulaiman, who leaped to the rear of the truck and swung
around their machine gun; far from afraid, they were eager for a
chance strike at these invaders. The two had been training as a team
with this gun for many months, and this was their first chance to put
it to action. Those who saw them then later told of how fervor blazed
in their eyes.

Quickly the planes reached their target and opened up with their
cannon, tearing the surface of the desert and generating great clouds of
dust. Fuqaan and Sulaiman answered with their machine gun, which rattled and spit its shells. But as it consumed its magazine, its noise was lost
in the far greater roar of the planes as they rushed over. The planes were
untouched, not leaving. But though they knew them, the two Arab men
did not shrink from the odds; they seemed to relish having the duel all to
themselves.

"New magazine!" shouted Fuqaan to Sulaiman in Arabic. "Here
they come again!" The planes wheeled, straightened, dipped, and started
their second attack. Mutr Fuqaan's kaffiyeh blew off and his long black
hair flew as he shouted a challenge and racked the slide. Again the desert
erupted in dust and sand and those men on the ground were deafened.
And again the men at the machine gun watched the planes for any sign

that they had been hit, but no flames appeared, no smoke. Mutr Fuqaan called for another magazine and prepared for another face-off.

On this last pass it seemed one of the planes had zeroed in on the truck and targeted it. The cannon shells tore into sheet metal, splintering the body, shredding the radiator, even piercing the heavy engine block. When the dust cleared, Mutr Fuqaan's body lay facedown under the twisted remains of his machine gun, and Sulaiman crouched nearby, his face torn by flying metal, streaming blood. The planes, never hit, had expended their ammunition and so sped away. The Luftwaffe's Messerschmitt Bf 110s had drawn first blood from the Arab Legion.

The legionnaires flagged down the yellow staff car in which Reading and his boss rode. Reading heard and translated the story of the duel while the others summoned the ambulance truck. The doctor arrived, and while he was tending Suleiman's wrecked face, a truck brought up three wounded troopers of David Smiley's Household Cavalry. One of the young men, Smiley's assistant, or "batman," soon died. And so the blood of cavalrymen from worlds apart mixed on the doctor's hands.

The Luftwaffe had begun making its mark in this battle, but it would have been a disaster if German planes had found this column clumped with its wheels buried in the sand a little more than a day earlier.[6]

The fifth day of the Iraqi siege on Habbaniya was the turning point: one side or the other was going to win the day. It ended up being decided by bad luck, misunderstanding, divided loyalties, and harried effort. It ended in ruin and a horrible, fiery death for many hundreds.

For Tony Dudgeon the day started before dawn yet again as he made a shocking tally of his squad: of around two dozen twin-engine Oxfords that had started the battle, he now had nine—most riddled, one with seventy fabric patches. He was down many killed and injured pilots, including four whose nerves had finally broken under the constant gauntlet of fire they ran upon taking off and landing. But for Dudgeon there was nothing for it but to keep going until help arrived from Basra or Transjordan, and once again his friend Arthur loaded his Oxford with that morning's ration of bombs—they had to make them last.

There was some good news: those decorative World War I–era field guns from the front of the officers' mess hall had been stripped of many layers of paint, a number of spokes replaced, and some cases of appropriate ammunition found in Basra and flown in along with some Royal Artillery men familiar with the museum pieces. When the old guns were first tried, an observer from the King's Own Royal Regiment couldn't guess who was more surprised that they fired—the Allies or the Iraqis. The two guns now went in to action, and though they weren't heavy artillery, the Allied men on the ground took a special satisfaction in being be able to answer the incoming fire from the plateau.

Then came very bad news. The morning reconnaissance flight returned from the east, its pilot leaping out in a hurry and rushing to report that a column of reinforcements was approaching from Fallujah, not twenty miles distant: armored cars, several batteries of heavy guns, many cars and trucks. The long-feared ground invasion had arrived. This changed things, and Tony and the others rushed out new plans for a counterattack.

When the Royal Iraqi Air Force appeared soon thereafter that morning, making its heaviest bombing run of the siege, it seemed confirmed: the moment had come for the Iraqis to make their final assault on the base. As long as Tony and his friends could keep the besieging men pinned down on the plateau, they had a chance; but if the Iraqis rushed the base, with only its iron fence guarding it, there was no way for the British and the Iraqi Levies to hold them off. It would be a street-by-street fight with no certain outcome. All thought of rationing bombs and bullets evaporated, and the pilots and students of Habbaniya took off in a constant stream, landing only to reload, never turning off their engines.[7]

At the same moment, Abdallah Simon watched from up on the plateau. Simon was the middle son in a middle-class Jewish family; they were Baghdadi, but like Reading's family, Simon's was really dotted all over the region, from Baghdad to Cairo to Beirut. In many ways, he was typical of Iraq's Jewish urban middle class of over 150,000, who were civil servants, merchants, railroad managers, and sometimes even government ministers. Young Abdallah had gone to college at the American University of Beirut, and then it was his time to serve in the military, as required of all other Iraqi young men. As an educated, cosmopolitan citizen, he was selected as officer material and was enrolled in the Royal Iraq Military College in 1940, that supposed incubator of a coherent, patriotic nation. That's where he was, five months into his studies when he was peremptorily given a commission as a second lieutenant. With his Sam Browne belt and khaki shorts, the urbane young man cut quite the figure, looking like nothing more than a young British officer; indeed, by the terms of its treaty with Britain, Iraq had to buy the majority of its military gear from the United Kingdom.

Before dawn one late April morning, Simon and his infantry company had been ordered onto trucks for the drive west out of Baghdad, over the Euphrates at Fallujah, and up onto the heights above the British air base at Lake Habbaniya. There he was surrounded by thousands and a war began. The British bombed them first, then the Iraqi gunners bombarded the base below, day after day. Meanwhile, Simon sensed that the senior leadership lacked the courage to order the ground assault.

So the exchange dragged on until, after several days, a rumor made its way all the way down to the green second lieutenant: the British had sent a vast relief force from Transjordan, and it would arrive the next day. (It was not, in fact, vast, and it was many days away.) In the dark before dawn, the Iraqi force on the plateau around Abdallah Simon began to disintegrate. Not to be left behind, he managed to throw himself in the back of a pickup and it raced, with a broken cavalcade of the entire force, down the Fallujah road in the direction of Baghdad and home.[8]

At some point in the early morning, as Tony Dudgeon and his colleagues kept up their constant attack on the forces driving westward from Fallujah, someone noticed the plateau overlooking the base had grown quiet. They then spotted the besieging force on the plateau evaporating eastward in every possible vehicle, as if they were routing. Gear was abandoned, even many artillery pieces. Dudgeon had no idea why it was happening.

Coordination among the Iraqis seemed to collapse, or perhaps the seniormost officers in the west-driving force had very different ideas from those in the east-driving, for in the middle of the stretch between

Fallujah and Habbaniya these two columns collided. It was a traffic jam, with vehicles bumper to bumper, those at its center unable to warn those at its ends.

Now the airmen who had thought that morning that they were on the edge of disaster saw where the disaster truly lay: they had a packed, miles-long, single-file target beneath them, unable to resist. The patched planes took off for Fallujah, found the columns, and lay their bombs down the row in a straight line. Vehicles exploded and burned, ammunition stores popped, men burned. Some of the caravan from Fallujah were able to turn around and escape back to the large garrison dug in there to protect the Euphrates crossing, but most of the vehicles retreating from the plateau were destroyed, while around a thousand men died in a matter of hours. A pilot reported to the operations room at Habbaniya that a 250-yard-long stretch of the highway was a solid sheet of flame. Meanwhile, several hundred Assyrian infantrymen of Habbaniya's Levies and the King's Own Royal Regiment rushed to the scene to collect prisoners, including many officers, amid the charred metal husks and horse corpses.

Somehow Abdallah Simon's pickup dodged the fire and shattering steel, and the sallying infantry, and he made it home to his brother and father in Baghdad.

Had the Royal Iraqi Air Force or Luftwaffe appeared at the right time, they might have turned the fight back onto the British air and ground forces; but there coordination had broken down, too. The Iraqi bombers did reappear in the sky above Habbaniya at the end of the afternoon, however, with a particularly heavy attack. Tony Dudgeon happened to be preparing for his next sortie to hunt down scattered vehicles still continuing east, the engines of his Gladiator still running as his friend Arthur was making his last check of the bombs under the fuselage, as he had done countless times. Dudgeon was on his way into his squadron's operations room for his last check-in with his senior officer when a particularly loud hammer blow landed outside. After days of such blasts, Tony didn't take particular note. But when he returned outside to his Gladiator, its engines still running, he saw a sight that never left him. He remembered in detail his friend's position on the ground: on his side, with his knees drawn up to his chest like a sleeping child. He never forgot the particular color of his skin, the yellow and faintly blue shadows that showed that his heart no longer beat. There was just a small hole in the young man's chest above his heart.[9]

Why had the forces besieging Habbaniya retreated so precipitously, leading to disaster on the highway to Fallujah? Abdallah Simon remembered a rumor of an approaching British force of thousands, and there is no reason to doubt that the rumor spread through Iraqi forces. And if the Iraqis on the plateau imagined tanks among this approaching two thousand, that would have been reason for concern. Still, artillery at a height above the approaching tanks, which could be seen a long way off, should've felt relatively confident. And, in fact, at this moment the leading vehicles of Habforce were still a week from arriving at Habbaniya.

There is no definitive answer for why they retreated, but there are clues. One was that a colonel of the Golden Square itself had a mental breakdown under the falling bombs, like so many did during that war, on the plateau overlooking Habbaniya. Colonel Fahmi Said was in charge of mechanized forces and was there observing the siege when he collapsed and had to be evacuated to a Baghdad hospital. Reportedly, there were eventual desertions from the Habbaniya siege as the RAF bombs continued to rain. And the makeshift Habbaniya air force had succeeded in penalizing approaching Iraqi supply trucks so harshly that they only dared move at night, throttling the flow of food, water, and other supplies to the plateau, which delivered a further blow to morale and readiness. And captured Iraqi officers later suggested that when the two refurbished World War I–era guns started firing on the heights some believed the British had managed to fly in artillery.

There appeared to be divisions, too, within the armed forces themselves about whether the proauthoritarian, pro-Arab, pro-Sunni coup leaders should be followed. Their narrow ethnic nationalism left out the Kurds, for example, and the Shiite Arabs of the Euphrates hinterlands. The army rank and file were far from all Sunni.[10]

The battle for Iraq was still just beginning, though. The siege of Habbaniya was lifted, but Habbaniya's base security forces and the King's Own couldn't possibly remove the Golden Square from power. The Luftwaffe was about to arrive, claiming Mutr Fuqaan's life, and its aircraft were superior to the vast majority of Habbaniya's planes. Meanwhile, the Germans were hurriedly arranging for the delivery of weapons and ammunition to Baghdad and Mosul. In these hours and days, back in London, Prime Minister Winston Churchill worried about airborne troops landing at Baghdad—as they had in Norway and during the blitz across northern Europe the previous year—and helping the Iraqis dig in. His Middle East forces had little strength to throw in the direction of Baghdad if the fight there was drawn out. Fallujah, where at least a thousand soldiers of the Royal Iraqi Army were dug in along with guns and armored cars, was the next obstacle between the Allies and Baghdad and the ouster of the pro-Axis government. Iraqi tanks were somewhere in the country as well. It was still not clear to General Archibald Wavell, commander in chief of Middle East forces, that he could drive on Baghdad with enough force to compel the Iraqi colonels to do anything.[11]

At the British embassy in Baghdad, Freya Stark was at work in the office she shared with other propagandists and translators when a great roar shook the place and sent a colleague diving under his desk. Stark discovered that a Gladiator biplane had skimmed the palms of the embassy grounds to drop a letter from Habbaniya. It reported that the air base was safe, the Iraqis having retreated to Fallujah with heavy losses that day. And it stated that the vast majority of the embassy staff's family members had been safely airlifted out.

Stark spoke with the ambassador, Kinahan Cornwallis, a man with decades of experience in Cairo and Iraq as an intelligence officer and adviser to Iraqi royalty. How had they so lost touch with the feeling of the Iraqi on the street? How, wondered Cornwallis, had Fritz Grobba outplayed them in recent years? Part of the answer for Stark was that the British seemed to encourage the aspirations of those who wanted a Jewish nation in Palestine while discouraging those who wanted a Palestinian nation or pan-Arab federation in the region. Meanwhile, she found a number of the diplomatic staff boorish and imperious—just the opposite of what was needed, and the opposite of her own approach. And now

what? Could they play up the fact that German aid hadn't been sufficient
to prevent the Iraqi setback at Habbaniya? Whatever the move, thought
Stark, now was neither the time to threaten supporters of the Golden
Square nor crow. She was more right than she knew, since Allied forces
were far from threatening Baghdad and the Iraqi military that vastly outnumbered them, more German planes were arriving, and the Vichy
French in neighboring Syria were about to make terms with the Germans
that would promise more military equipment to the Iraqis.[12]

For John Masters, the Gurkhas, and the other Indian Army forces camped
at the Port of Basra, the morning after the siege of Habbaniya broke was
the moment to break out of their bridgeheads and secure wider Basra.
They had already secured the docks on the wide Shatt al-Arab estuary
that flowed down to the Persian Gulf. And they had secured the tiny RAF
landing ground inland, past the outskirts of town, where the airlifted
families of Habbaniya and Baghdad embassy personnel had stopped en
route to Karachi. But those were just small footholds; it was now time to
try, at least, to push inland into the city and upcountry, time to plunge
into the narrow streets of Basra and a neighboring town to the north,
Ashar. That northern suburb was occupied by Iraqi soldiers and police,
their machine gun nest visible from the wide estuary and canals around
it. If those forces were loyal to the Golden Square, they could not be left
in the rear of any Allied force that hoped to march north on Baghdad.
Plus, these Iraqi units could reclaim the Shatt al-Arab docks, attack the
nearby RAF base, or even provide a base of operations for attacking the
all-important Abadan oil refineries only thirty miles downriver in Iran.
Furthermore, the Indian Army needed wheels: Masters and his senior officers hoped to find transport at Ashar for their drive north, either by rail
or truck. Many of the trucks that were supposed to land with the force
were on their way to Singapore—and eventually destruction or capture
by the Japanese.

First, hundreds of the turbaned men of the Eleventh Sikh Regiment
moved out of occupied Iraqi barracks into Ashar well before dawn. They
took strategic bridges and searched for Iraqi police or soldiers who might
oppose their expansion in the Basra suburbs. Meanwhile, the Frontier

Force Rifles, with Hindu, Muslim, and Sikh companies totaling about 750, occupied a hospital and other positions, though things got a little tense when a Frontier Force company surprised a Gurkha company; they couldn't warn them of their approach because Iraqi defenders had cut the telephone lines. The mosquitoes, for their part, propagated by the flooding Tigris, gorged themselves on the young Nepali Gurkhas guarding the banks of the estuary, planting malaria among them as they did, which would soon occupy Dr. Santi Pada Dutt.

Then Masters's and Dutt's Gurkha Rifles battled some dug-in Iraqi soldiers in the clogged heart of Basra until the Iraqis retreated in the face of superior numbers. When they inspected the abandoned Iraqi position, everyone was happy to find the British-issued mortars that the Iraqis left behind. Masters had been pleading with his superiors for mortars for a long time, but in early 1941 most modern weapons were still directed toward rebuilding the British Army at home. John Masters then oversaw the placement of machine gun nests to defend their expanding zone of control, one on the roof of a dismal brothel. (When Colonel William Weallens learned of this particular placement, he asked Masters whether it was really proper that the impressionable young men should have to scale the brothel stairs to reach their post.) They set up another machine gun near a date mill; rations were slim, and the riflemen were happy now to have some dates to eat. When Masters saw that they were pitted by no machinery but the front teeth of women who sat in long rows within the building, he asked the doctor whether they were in danger of contracting something. Dutt told him to relax.

Over the coming week, the Gurkhas and the rest of the Indian Army expanded and expanded their control through Ashar and Basra. Doctor Dutt negotiated with an Armenian teacher who allowed him to use her school as a hospital for the injured and those falling victim to malaria. Meanwhile, Masters and his Nepalis patrolled in the tropical heat under the palms and among jungle thickets and by boat in the flooding creeks. A few riflemen collapsed from the jungle heat. The overgrown twists and turns meant that sometimes they startled upon the Iraqis, and one day they walked straight into machine gun fire, with three Gurkhas falling. Yet a main objective—transport—was not to be found; the trucks and trains they hoped to find in Ashar for their drive north on Baghdad had been pulled out ahead of them.

Eventually the Gurkhas and others found the hard center of Iraqi resistance at a stone house, a makeshift fort, that overlooked the Shatt al-Arab and the main road running north toward Baghdad. So one early morning the Gurkhas and Madras Sappers made their attack on the place they dubbed the Big House. Artillery firing from the RAF airstrip joined in, while an Australian sloop in the mist down the Shatt al-Arab contributed its four-inch shells. The young men of Madras and Nepal had to win a bridge that allowed access to the Big House, but it meant advancing into the teeth of Iraqi machine gun fire, and some were thrown back, dying, into the swollen river. Meanwhile, more Gurkhas steamed up the Shatt al-Arab in Australian launches, thudded on the beach, and attacked the Big House from its other side. The fire from the sloop ricocheted strangely against thick stands of palms around the Big House, and it was barely touched by the shells. Still, the Iraqis were forced to flee under the lobbed grenades and Bren machine gun fire. The Indians seized the headquarters.

When John Masters, his colonel, and some artillery officers hurried up to the roof of the Big House, they could see through their binoculars a flotilla of small boats retreating northward across a vast flooded area. John Masters told the artillery officer to fire on them, and the man got on his radio, set to call in the coordinates to the guns at the distant RAF base. But then Colonel Weallens told him to stop. It seemed to him that there was a village obscured somewhere to the north and that some of the boats, at least, originated there. "There may be women and children in those boats, too." Almost as he spoke, women and children were being ferried out of Basra to Karachi by air. Masters replied that if there were women and children in the boats, there were certainly Iraqi soldiers in them. The artillery officer shared Masters's opinion. They strained to fire.

Colonel Weallens was born in 1896, and had been a captain with the Gurkhas in the Great War. He had been brought out of semi-retirement at Delhi headquarters for this second global war, which was in the most basic ways the same, but in horrible details different, from that first one.

"Don't fire on those boats," he said, and turned away.

At the moment, John Masters was disgusted that his colonel would be so precious in his morals, and imagined those same men getting away in the boats would kill even more of his Gurkhas in the weeks to come. But soon, after he had cooled off, Masters thought Weallens was right and loved him for what he considered his old-fashioned honor, so out of place in this depraved war.

John Masters then went with Doctor Dutt to see those they'd lost that morning in the rush on the Big House. Six men of Bangalore, Madras Sappers, and six Gurkhas were dead. Masters's old friend Jemadar (warrant officer) Sakas was among them, wet from having fallen in death into the river, his face now graying.

After this, Masters and his Gurkhas were summoned north to the RAF base at Habbaniya. There was still no secure route, nor sufficient transport for getting there. Besides, the flooded Euphrates added to the difficulty of moving upcountry. So for the first time the Gurkhas were going to be airlifted. Masters had only ever flown once, and had not appreciated the experience at all, but he had to act like flying was perfectly natural for humankind. His young Nepalis, he thought, who had been unfamiliar with motor transport until only a few years earlier, must know for certain that man was not meant to fly. So Masters sat them down and explained how an airplane worked, told them that they might vomit and that they were to use paper bags for this, told them that they must stay seated calmly, no matter what came over them. A picture of Gurkhas running around the plane's hold, hysterical, troubled him.

Then the moment came for the Gurkhas to board the roaring plane at the Shaibah airstrip, weighed down with new gear, until it sped and lifted just above the date palms. Masters soon saw the Big House, which had claimed the lives of six Gurkhas, and the vast flooded plain beyond, across which the small boats had escaped. The plane soon banked to take a westerly course to Habbaniya away from where German Messerschmitts were likely to prowl, and Masters turned to his Gurkhas, putting a practiced, unperturbed mask on his face. But they didn't see it; they were all asleep.[13]

8

"Set Thy Face against It, and Besiege It"

The Battle of Fallujah

> How can I begrudge the resistance in Fallujah for killing my friends, when I know that I would have done the same thing if I were in their place? How can I blame them when we were the aggressors?
> —Ross Caputi, US Marine veteran of the Second Siege of Fallujah, 2007, in "I Am Sorry for the Role I Played in Fallujah," *Guardian*, December 22, 2011

THEY ROLLED IN, dusty, through the iron gates of Habbaniya: scores of heavy trucks bringing welcome supplies; the humpbacked quads of the 237th Field Battery, pulling their modern, snub-nosed guns on limbers and carrying gardener Jack Bartlett and the grocers and dairymen of Lincolnshire; the Arab Legion guides in their Chevys; Harry Chalk and around two hundred other young men of the Essex Regiment in their quaking American buses. (Harry Chalk mistakenly thought the so-called Brylcreem Boys—the posh and soft-handed RAF pilots—must have been pretty grateful at their deliverance. Tony Dudgeon and his friends, meanwhile, had taken to calling them the Phantom Column, since they were said to be approaching for so long, yet no one could see them.)

Most of the guns and armored cars that had besieged the base now lay in crumpled ruins and burned-out husks on the plateau above the base and on the hellish road to Fallujah. But the war for Iraq was far from over, and Habbaniya was not yet out of danger, as John Masters and his friends were about to find out.

Through the window of the transport Masters had watched the desert pass beneath him, captivated at the dim signs of ancient civilizations: walls and reservoirs, highways and city grids. After darkness fell, the plane approached a blacked-out Habbaniya, which turned on its runway lights only just before the plane completed its descent. With most of the Gurkhas not bothering to wake even for the landing, the plane taxied toward its appointed hangar, and Masters prepared to rouse the men and boys to gather their things. Then the door flew open, desert heat rushing in, and a voice shouted, "Out, quick!" Twin-engine Heinkel medium bombers had appeared over Habbaniya about the same time as had the Gurkhas. The bombs began to drop, and Masters shook his men awake and out the door to nearby shallow trenches. Welcome to Habbaniya.

The days after "relief" arrived in Habbaniya were a strange time. There was no immediate threat of the base being overrun, but it was still subject to periodic bomber attacks and strafing runs of German fighters that streaked across the desert sky with startling speed. Some twin-engine Blenheim fighter-bombers did their best to chase them away, a pair of modern Hurricanes had even arrived, but they were insufficient to win mastery over the sky above. Desperately needed supplies had arrived with Habforce, but food still had to be strictly rationed. Alcohol was actually more forthcoming than fresh food, so that John Masters and his men still relied on dates, but happily washed them down with whiskey and tepid water.

Yet whiskey contributed to a tense situation that almost started a second battle of Habbaniya. After the barricades were lowered at the base officers' club, and blackout rules eased, the spot became a gathering point for middling officers of a range of services and regiments. One night in the club's bar, an Indian Army officer on his third drink broke into song, apparently to see what would happen: "Deutschland, Deutschland über alles / Über alles in der Welt!"

Habbaniya's RAF officers in the room had seen a drunk clown letting off steam before and, though they gave him some looks, they let it go. Then, some of the singers' friends joined in. They didn't deserve to win the war, the officers said loudly; they were decadent and effete. They didn't want to fight their German friends; in fact, they didn't want to fight *anyone*. Unknown to the boozy men, there were officers from the First Essex Regiment in the bar; men who, like Harry Chalk, had fled down a barren slope on the Sudan border from the Italian fort they had captured at bloody cost. They had been pounded by exploding shells and unopposed Italian bombers for hours until they couldn't take it anymore. Their faces reddened with anger, and they loosened their uniform buttons in preparation to fight.

But instead they laughed. The Indian Army lieutenants had started a new tune, just in time:

> Ours is not a happy household, no one laughs or ever smiles
> Mine's a dismal occupation, crushing ice for father's piles
> Jane the underhousemaid vomits every morning just at eight,
> To the horror of the butler, who's the author of her fate.
> Sister Sue has just aborted for the forty-second time.
> Uncle James has been deported for the most unusual crime.

Instead of pounding them, the Essex and RAF officers demanded to know the words of the vulgar verse and were soon encouraging the Indian Army men with even more drinks.

Such boorishness was beneath Reading's superior, the member of Parliament turned intelligence officer, who in these days continued his obsessive bathing, now in the wide Lake Habbaniya. He and other cavalry officers formed a permanent fixture there like malformed and sunburned fountain nymphs. One day, the officer stood, mouth open, up to his waist in water, transfixed by the display of speed from Messerschmitt 110s streaking over Lake Habbaniya on a strafing run. The same Messerschmitts that cometed over the Household Cavalry bathing in the lake sped under the feet of the Lincolnshire gunners, who were up on the plateau watching the strafing run of the low-flying Luftwaffe.

Adding to the strangeness of these days, the United States arrived on the scene in the person of a tall, thin young man in a marine's tropical uniform: Captain James Roosevelt. The president's son arrived from Cairo, only the latest stop on his tour of British and Allied bases. His role was to encourage those fighting the Axis that President Roosevelt hadn't forgotten them and was doing his best to aid the effort. Jimmy Roosevelt, traveling with a veteran marine major, was also there to make serious observations of the logistical and offensive situation throughout the region in the hope that Americans would soon join the war and bor-row British and Indian facilities. He stopped in Crete, Karachi, and even Basra, where his meetings were interrupted by casualties arriving from a firefight with the Iraqis like the one Masters's Gurkhas and the Madras Sappers had fought. Around this time in mid-May 1941, Winston Churchill wrote a letter to Jimmy's father explaining that part of the stakes in winning Basra back from the Iraqis was using it as a port that would be critical if Roosevelt could bring the United States into the war. In Habbaniya, on one of its strafing runs, the Luftwaffe shot up the house in which Roosevelt was staying on the base. The attack was said to have interrupted, but not entirely ruined, cocktails and supper.[1]

More strange story lines crossed at Habbaniya when Jimmy Roosevelt was involved in another German attack. One day, as he was crossing the base in a staff car, Roosevelt and his driver saw another car bombed by a German raider as it drove toward the base. They rushed to the scene of smoking ruin. Inside an Indian Army officer was obliterated, and another had lost his legs; an army officer was fast dying of his wounds, and an-other young soldier was shaken but all right. The dying man's ID card showed him to be one Captain Ben-Moshe, apparently a Jewish Pales-tinian member of the British Army.

Only his name wasn't Ben-Moshe, nor was he—nor the other young man apparently of the British Army—in the British Army. They were spies and saboteurs. They were also terrorists, by most definitions, sworn enemies of the British, and members of the Irgun, an underground organization that had bombed cafés and marketplaces, striking at British police and Arab civilians, killing over one hundred people in the previous decade in Palestine. The Irgun had declared a truce with the British when the war began, unlike the more right-wing Lohamei Herut Israel (Lehi), which had tried to make common cause with the European fascists against the British.

Captain Ben-Moshe was really David Raziel, one of the Irgun's founders. In spring 1941 he was in a British prison in Palestine when, to his surprise, he was let out on the condition that he undertake a mission for the British. The target was the oil refinery in Baghdad, a refinery that might distill the special aviation fuel required by the Luftwaffe; the British feared that bombing it from the air—bombing the city of Baghdad—might lead to Iraqi retaliation against those besieged in the British embassy like Freya Stark. And because Britain's Iraq spymasters were locked up in the embassy with no way to contact their operatives and informers outside its gates, the Secret Intelligence Service headquartered in Cairo had to improvise. They needed operatives with experience in explosives who could pass as Iraqis.

The operatives requested, and were given a free hand, to eliminate Amin al-Husseini, the bloody Palestinian revolutionary who had long been a thorn in the side of the British. The desire for murder was mutual. It was al-Husseini with whom Freya Stark suddenly found herself chatting about Arabic literature with such sangfroid one day in Baghdad's Hotel Zia; he, who she recommended to her handlers be assassinated. Al-Husseini successfully acted as a go-between for the Golden Square and Axis capitals, and the British knew he was in their pay. There was a debate about this in Westminster, the people with Middle East experience warning against making a martyr of al-Husseini, while the military brass pushed for assassination, arguing that it would be a show of strength at little cost. When Churchill signed the authorization, he used ambivalent language that gave him plausible deniability of sanctioning murder; when the reluctant Foreign Office passed it on to Cairo, it warned that British personnel should not be used.

As it happened, the four Irgun operatives could not kill al-Husseini, could not even advance much beyond Habbaniya because of the Iraqi garrison dug in at Fallujah and because the flooded Euphrates made other routes very difficult. The agents were able to do some scouting in the guise of Arabs—and were briefly held as spies, though they talked their way out of it. So the British did in fact have to rely on the RAF for bombing the Iraq Petroleum Company refinery, with Freya Stark watching the refinery's flames brighten the sky above Baghdad from the embassy.

It was only bad luck for David Raziel and his British handlers that the Luftwaffe came upon his car outside the base, ending his life and ending a potentially incendiary subplot to this war.[2]

The Arab Legion stayed in Habbaniya a few days before pushing east-northeast. Their target was the Baghdad–Mosul railway. The Luftwaffe was known to be flying from Mosul, far to the north, and the Morse code secrets bouncing around the stratosphere whispered to the young ladies and men of Bletchley Park that weapons were arriving there too. Plus, the thinking in Habbaniya and Cairo was that the Golden Square, if it felt threatened in Baghdad, might move to Mosul, in proximity to Vichy Syria, protected by German air staff and an Iraqi Army brigade. For the Allies, that would require another epic advance of 260 miles north across Iraq.

John Glubb and eighty of the legionnaires set out in their pickups, a couple of their homemade armored cars, and a pair of RAF armored cars. They brought along a member of the Royal Engineers, one of those experts at wrecking or building as needed. First they had to be ferried over the Euphrates, since the nearest crossing, the iron bridge over the river at Fallujah, was being guarded by the Iraqi Army. Then the cluster of twelve vehicles set out into a burning hot desert. As they got farther from Habbaniya, they got farther from any support if they should come upon Iraqi tanks or German planes. At one point they huddled amid some dry bushes as the Luftwaffe passed overhead before continuing, going up and over the remains of ancient earthworks, now dry, that once dominated the Euphrates in the name of some king of kings.

In the dark that night, Glubb and his men reached the Baghdad–Mosul highway that ran roughly parallel to the railway. It was busy with headlights. Some legionnaires crept forward to look at the traffic and reported back that it was civilian. There was a discussion during which they considered halting and burning some of the trucks in order to stir alarm that the British had arrived and the route north was unsafe. But Glubb and the others feared that this might drive ordinary Iraqis, fearful, to the side of the Golden Square. So instead they pushed past the highway toward the railway. In the small hours of the morning the Royal Engineers dismantled a stretch of rails before the force faded back into the desert in the dark with no headlights. (They didn't know it, but they were being watched at their work by Iraqi eyes.)

In the morning they crossed the tracks of a pair of trucks that had headed toward Ramadi. Glubb rushed the strike force to a position where they expected to cut them off and, sure enough, the two trucks soon appeared where they were expected. The legionnaires shouted a war cry and descended on the trucks, which sped off but were overtaken in a few minutes. The prisoners, an Iraqi captain and some junior officers, were soon being served tea by the Arab Legion as a courtesy before they were driven to Habbaniya. Back at the base, these and some other prisoners reported that the situation in the Iraqi military was very confused, with loyalties uncertain and information scarce. Some units that went to Habbaniya had been told they were going on an exercise—the Golden Square apparently didn't think they had to convince them to start a war with the British since they hadn't believed they would need to fire on the base to get the British to come to terms.[3]

After about two weeks of regrouping and resupplying at Habbaniya, it was time for the Allies to push eastward in the direction of Baghdad. Cairo and London hadn't given the go-ahead to besiege the capital itself—there might simply be too few men to threaten the vastly larger Iraqi Army; but the force commander at Habbaniya wanted to seize the most important Euphrates crossing in the region and eliminate Fallujah as a prime operating base for the Iraqis. With not even two thousand men to put toward the effort, compared to several tens of thousands, at least, in the Iraqi Army, they were still badly outmatched. And the Iraqis still had armored cars and at least six tanks in the area of Baghdad, probably more. Meanwhile, there was still a significant Iraqi force at Ramadi, west of Habbaniya, that Habforce had sidestepped. The air situation was uncertain, but at least the RAF—treasuring its sole surviving Hurricane and four modern Blenheim fighter-bombers—was now able to carry out operations around the country from Habbaniya, since the Iraqi Air Force had been both sabotaged and defeated. But the small but modern Luftwaffe force on the scene was still making bloodily successful strikes on the RAF base while ground forces operating away from Habbaniya were in danger of being discovered by the four Heinkel bombers still operating and eight Messerschmitt fighter-bombers stalking them in mid-May. In the face of flooding, and lacking sufficient transport, the Indian Army units down in Basra still could not join forces with the those in Habbaniya except through piecemeal air transport, as the King's Own Royal

Regiment had very early in the war, and as had John Masters's and Santi Pada Dutt's Gurkha companies.

In the dark of night on May 18, it was time to break out of Habbaniya and push on Fallujah. Five teams of infantry, totaling around a bit under fifteen hundred, made up of the King's Own, Assyrian companies of the RAF Levies, and a company of Gurkhas, crept from the iron gates of Habbaniya. A few armored cars and artillery pieces followed. Their destination was Fallujah's iron bridge, guarded by at least one thousand Iraqi Army soldiers well dug in there. These, too, enjoyed a direct line of supply and reinforcement to Baghdad.

For the roughly fifteen hundred boys and men slogging to Fallujah in the dark, there was no such direct line. Weeks before, in an effort to buy time for more Axis help to arrive, the Golden Square had ordered some Euphrates embankments breached in order to keep the Allies from Fallujah. Now, at key points, sheets of water stood between the RAF base and the town twenty miles to its east, with its all-important Euphrates bridge. This was the first obstacle that the men in the dark had to overcome. They could move through the flood waters for much of the distance along an embankment that remained uncovered. But the troops would have to wade several hundred yards through waist- and even neck-deep water. A leading group of the King's Own and Assyrians crossed the gap in small pleasure boats borrowed from the Habbaniya's "yacht club." (The Assyrians had practiced amphibious landings for the first time in the base's large swimming pool only days before.) The armored cars and artillery—lightweight guns only, captured Iraqi pieces—would have to ford a gap in the embankment over a ferry. Jack Bartlett's modern twenty-five-pound gun could not cross.

The Allied force had no bridge layers or amphibious vehicles so, in classic style, some Madras Sappers and Miners improvised, jury-rigging a pontoon out of oil barrels from Habbaniya. Then they floated a coil of wire cable across the Euphrates at a place they hoped the Germans and Iraqis would not discover and strafe them, secured the looped wire to both banks, hooked the pontoon onto the cable, and pulled it, hand over fist, across the flood waters. It took hours for the force of over a thousand to cross the floodwaters in the darkness.

While they did, Tony Dudgeon and the other pilots of RAF Habbaniya did their part, cutting the phone lines to Baghdad to keep the Iraqis in
Fallujah from raising the alarm. Where there was a single wire, they simply flew an old Audax biplane through it; where they feared the plane
would give before multiple wires would, the pilot landed, engine left running, scrambled out on his upper wing and cut the wires with a pair of
shears while the rear gunner kept watch.

After the Assyrians, some of the King's Own men, and Gurkhas
were in place, the last piece of the siege was airlifted into place when a
pair of old biplane transports landed on the packed desert floor east of
Fallujah. Out of these came rushing a small company of now very battle-
tested King's Own Royal Riflemen who would do their best to prevent
reinforcements arriving from Baghdad if word reached there of the Allies'
surprise attack. If word had gotten out, the German fighters and bombers
would be along soon to terrorize them too. There was little a few dozen
men could possibly do to withstand a German-Iraqi counterattack.

The battle began when an Audax dive-bombed Fallujah's radio
station mast to keep the garrison from warning Baghdad. Now the
Assyrian-Iraqi men of the RAF Levies, along with the Gurkhas, besieged
the town but dared not try the bridge, where they knew they would be
funneled into a hopeless shooting gallery. From another direction, one
company of Assyrians was particularly glad to rush the town, emerging
from a date palm grove where they'd suffered the horrible smell of the
corpses of Iraqi Army horses killed on the Fallujah road many days
earlier.

Then the Habbaniya planes began their blitz on Fallujah too. The
goal was to avoid at all cost a protracted siege, a deadly charge on the
narrow iron brigade over the Euphrates, and a house-to-house battle for
the town. Some of the RAF bombs were retrofitted with fins that would
create the whistling sound that so rattled many Londoners in those same
days. The RAF targeted Fallujah's Iraqi defenders, it didn't carpet-bomb
the town in the style of total war, but inevitably the bombs fell far and
wide in the small, dense riverside town. And inspiring terror was most
certainly part of the plan.

Meanwhile, the ground forces at the perimeter of Fallujah probed the Iraqi defenses and found them standing firm. After a first demonstration of bombing by Tony Dudgeon and his colleagues, the RAF dropped leaflets demanding surrender within a half hour. When none came, the Allied fighters and bombers continued the attack.

Coordination between ground and air was poor, but eventually word got around to the headquarters at Habbaniya that the Iraqi defenders could not be seen. One of the pilots risked his neck by flying low and slow over the town to see if he drew fire. The arrival of a coordinated attack by a wing of Messerschmitts at this moment would have been devastating; but no attack came from air or ground. So in the early afternoon the Levies rushed across the bridge, hurrying in case the Iraqis blew it up underneath them, but again nothing happened. Some Iraqi defenders surrendered at the Fallujah hospital, others discarded their uniforms and went home, and still others snuck through Allied lines and dispersed to countryside villages.

Afterward, Fallujah was a scene of blasted mortar and smoke, its townspeople having been at the mercy of terror and death from above for hours, just like Londoners on the other side of the world. An observer compared it to the ruined towns of Flanders in World War I. The RAF flew 134 sorties from Habbaniya, dropping over nine tons of bombs in a day. But despite the ruin, it was considered a victory, as none of the Allied troops had been killed and the Euphrates bridge was seized intact.

A strong company of the RAF Levies from Habbaniya took up defensive positions around the town, along with two companies of the King's Own Royal Regiment. And now that the river crossing was secure, it was a matter of consolidating and getting prepared for the possibility of a push eastward to Baghdad if the brass in Cairo chose such action. It would be slow going in any case because, while the Euphrates bridge was in Allied hands, the approach to Fallujah was still flooded, meaning muddy slogs and piecemeal crossings by reinforcements from Habbaniya on the Madras Sappers' pontoon.

The Iraqi desert usually cooled dramatically after sundown, but on this night, the third after Fallujah was taken, it was particularly warm, which added to the smell of death still hanging in some quarters. There was no moon, and the whole battered town was without electric light. So it was easy to see the strange lights coming over the horizon to the northeast well before dawn: the headlights of Iraqi trucks and armored cars. Before them came a pair of tanks.

Assyrian-Iraqi and British soldiers rushed for cover in stone houses, while a surprised headquarters in Fallujah radioed back to Habbaniya on its sole wireless set at 4:00 a.m., asking for help. The brigadier in charge of Habforce, in turn, woke Harry Chalk and the First Essex in their borrowed barracks. Another frantic message woke the Household Cavalry, sleeping under canvas by the shore of Lake Habbaniya.

The Iraqi tanks were soon at Fallujah's makeshift outer defenses, and they easily shoved aside the King's Own and Assyrian sentries and shouldered their way into the cramped town. Behind the tanks an Iraqi infantry brigade group charged Fallujah in trucks. The Allies immediately suffered badly from the attack, men falling fast to the tanks, to mortars, and to infantry whose advance was sharp and successful. Some of the Iraqi troops set up their own rifle nests that commanded broad reaches of the town and made some streets certain death. Despite all this, observers recalled the Assyrians throwing themselves at the Iraqi tanks with a fervor, as if they wanted to peel them open like cans.[4]

This was a rage nurtured by history. In 1932, when Iraq received a measure of independence from Britain, Iraq's Assyrian minority approached the League of Nations with aspirations and fears. They aspired to their own country in their homeland north of Mosul; they feared that if Baghdad were given free rein, the Nestorian Christians would be disenfranchised at best, attacked at worst. That's because they had called for independence for a long time: their ancient homeland had been divided between several countries by the redrawing of borders after the Ottoman defeat in World War I, like the Armenians, who found themselves in postwar Turkey and subsequently suffered at Turkish hands. Iraqi Assyrians' calls for sovereignty antagonized those Iraqi nationalists who called for unity over all, and enraged those antipluralist fascist-leaning nationalists coming on the scene in the early 1930s. Who would try to break away next, they asked, the Kurds or Shiites?

In the eyes of certain nationalists, too, the Assyrians were associated with the resented British because they had served as RAF soldiers, the Levies, since the 1920s.

After the Assyrians' appeal to the League of Nations failed, they felt so split from their Iraqi compatriots, and so reviled, that their leadership called on all Assyrians around the country—including the armed RAF Levies—to come back to the small Assyrian homeland in the north to defend themselves. To the heads of the new semi-independent country of Iraq, and to the heads of the Iraqi military whose ethos was unity through the military, this situation offered an opportunity. To them the Assyrians were rebels, and crushing them was patriotic, unifying, a warning to other minorities, and an opportunity to flex their muscle for the first time independent of British oversight. It wasn't quite as simple as a Muslim majority taking pleasure in the crushing of a Nestorian Christian minority, because the capital, the heart of nationalism, had many thousands of Arab Christians who did not suffer at the time. This was in large part about the integrity of "the nation."

In 1933 the Iraqi Army had headed north and confronted the Assyrians. Eyewitnesses disagree about who fired the first shot, but the question pales compared to what followed: systematic murder, rape, looting, and terror throughout many villages of the Assyrian heartland, a litany of monstrous acts against humanity. At minimum, three thousand civilians were massacred.

But back in Baghdad it was reported in newspapers as simply the defeat of a breakaway rebellion, the first major campaign of the independent army, a kind of victory over Britain itself since many considered the Assyrian Levies British toadies. On the victors' return, there was a parade through the streets of Baghdad, and the brigadier general who led the slaughter was hailed as a hero.*

---

*The brigadier general, Bakr Sidqi, was a main mover behind the mission of unifying the nation through the army, and he became the most powerful man in the country in 1936. Sidqi was assassinated the next year for a number of reasons, including the fact that he was half Kurdish and appeared to favor Kurdish officers in the army. Nationalism, it seemed, was a treacherous tool that could cut its wielder.

The Iraqi Army's terrors extended over many villages, but one suffered particularly, with as many as a few thousand slaughtered: Simele.* An Assyrian veteran of the battles for Fallujah in May 1941 described the ferocity of the Assyrian Levies this way: "Our boys wanted revenge for Simele; the enemy had two choices, stay and die or run."[5]

Help for the Assyrians and the King's Own, who were falling to tanks in Fallujah, was slogging toward them. Harry Chalk and his friends sloshed, waded, and swam the six-hundred-yard-wide floodwaters standing in the middle of the road between Fallujah and Habbaniya; so did the Household Cavalry, tugging antitank rifles and an antique three-pounder gun in the pleasure boats from Lake Habbaniya and on the Madras Sappers' oil drum pontoon. It took over two hours for the British troops to cross; even the pontoon could only carry about a dozen at a time. Meanwhile, the Iraqis had advanced through Fallujah to within sight of its Euphrates bridge.

Finally, Jack Bartlett and his friends drove their twenty-five-pounders into position to help in the counterattack. With their tremendous range, the Lincolnshire gunners didn't have to get close; they dragged their guns to within five miles of Fallujah, fully a mile closer than their maximum practical range, then they pounded away, guided by spotters overlooking the battle, hurling 250 rounds to keep any Iraqi reinforcements at bay and away from the bridge. It was exactly a year since they had been covering bridges in Belgium and France for the retreating British Expeditionary Force.

Arriving after a seven-mile walk dragging their equipment from the floodwater ford, the Essex and Household Cavalry were divided into platoons and were immediately thrown into the bloody effort of house-to-

---

*When the Iraqi troops left the plateau above Habbaniya and retreated to Fallujah, the Assyrian Levies sallied forth from the RAF base to attack along with the strafing and bombing planes. The Levies were rounding up straggling prisoners when they heard a wounded artillery officer speaking their language: he was an Assyrian. For a few tense moments it seemed the Levies would execute him on the spot as a turncoat, until a young man among the Levies, who said the officer was from his village, intervened.

house fighting to help the Assyrian Levies and the King's Own: precisely the sort of fighting the Allies wanted to avoid in their initial attack on Fallujah. It meant turning blind corners into machine gun nests, or stumbling upon entrenched Iraqi infantry. The Essex hunted down snipers and assaulted barricaded houses. Harry Chalk and a platoon were given their target, and they battled through a cemetery, the bullets whirring by him. "Pretty decent fighters," Harry thought. The gravestones provided good cover, though, and the Essex pressed on. They had run from Gallabat when there was no cover from the Italian exploding artillery and bombs— run when subjected to an unanswerable torment that few human psyches could bear for long; but now, even though the enemy fire was accurate and unyielding, they advanced and advanced. They were not cornered; they had a chance. And while they must have been afraid, it wasn't a broken animal dread.

In another corner of the town, three young men of the Assyrian Levies found themselves confronted by an Iraqi tank and dropped to the ground. They racked the bolt on their long Boys antitank rifle, a massive thing like an elephant gun, roughly the same length as the men themselves. They sent round after round at the tank, the recoil of the gun nearly crushing the shoulder of the shooter, but without much hope that their bullets would penetrate. To their shock, the tank heeled suddenly rightward and into a ditch and to a stop. Some lucky shot had landed.

Machine gun sections of Assyrians did their best to slow the Iraqi advance through the town and toward the bridge. They hustled their heavy Lewis guns of World War I provenance up the narrow roads of the town, sometimes coming under fire from rooftops, once turning a corner and running into Iraqi Army soldiers unloading gear from trucks who turned around and gunned down the shocked Assyrians. Sometimes the Levies were pinned by fire coming seemingly from all sides, and steeling their courage for a spring from their trap, were shot upon rising to run. Sometimes they emptied their Lewis guns and fought on with pistols; other times, they picked up the Iraqis' dropped Bren machine guns, superior modern guns that had been sold to them by Great Britain in the run-up to the war.

While it tried, the RAF could be of little help in such close-quarter fighting, but the German Messerschmitts didn't appear either. And Iraqi artillery firing from the east did not do much other than terrorize the sheltering townspeople.

Brigadier Joe Kingstone, who arrived from Habbaniya via a boat coming down the Euphrates, saw the brutality of the house-to-house fighting and arrived at a conclusion. He gathered the chief men of the town and gave them an ultimatum: at a certain hour, every noncombatant in the town must be in its mosque. After that, anyone on the streets would be fired upon. (Later this ultimatum transformed into a rumor that the British had actually blown up the main mosque in Fallujah.)

The fighting wore on throughout the long day of driving heat and swarms of mosquitos. More and more bleeding young men—Assyrian, British, and Iraqi—were dragged out of the alleys of Fallujah. A King's Own private had his legs shattered; the commanding officer of the King's Own in Fallujah, observing from a rooftop, fell to an Iraqi Army sniper. But with Allied reinforcements, now more Iraqis fell, while others barricaded in stone strongholds and hung out the white flag.

The next morning an Iraqi counterattack resumed, this time with Luftwaffe support; but it was too little, too late. That day, too, Iraqi artillery at some distance in the east tried to hit the Euphrates bridge, but missed, killing instead three Assyrian soldiers and eight of their Iraqi Army prisoners. But the British had reinforced the town successfully, the RAF could successfully harass the Iraqi artillery, and the counterattack was not strong enough. This battle of Fallujah was over.

When the Iraqi commander of the attack was interrogated, he revealed that their nearly successful assault on Fallujah had followed plans, the "solution," drafted by General G. G. Waterhouse of the British military mission to Iraq. The Iraqis had practiced the attack in a military exercise not two years earlier.

Among the ruins the young men of Essex were delighted to come upon an abandoned Bren carrier, a car-size tracked vehicle that could carry about six men and mount one of the modern Bren machine guns. It was another instance of the Iraq Army being better equipped—with British-issue weapons—than the Allies fighting them. Bren carriers could not stand up to tanks or artillery, but they shrugged off rifle fire and were particularly useful for rushing to the rescue of a fallen man in a firefight to carry him back to safety. The Essex painted their prize desert khaki and named it after home, "Southend" now stenciled on its side.

They carried their friends—seventeen of them—back to Habbaniya to be buried in the cemetery there, one of those green places nurtured from the desert with Euphrates water. The King's Own carried back Ernest Classon, age twenty-two, from Moreton, near Liverpool, Charles and Ellen's son; they carried John and Annie Wilson's son, Cliff, age twenty-five. There they joined John Rooney, age twenty-six, son of Beth, originally from Dublin, who had been killed earlier at Habbaniya, along with John Adshead, during the siege. Carried back to Habbaniya with them were the young Assyrians who shared with them their last living day, May 22, 1941: Khaskiel Enwia, Pithyou Eshu, Binyamin Tooma, and several others.[6]

Meanwhile, in Baghdad, Fritz Grobba was desperately trying to keep the Golden Square on the offensive until he could get more planes, weapons, and Wehrmacht boots on the ground in Iraq. He had about two dozen Luftwaffe craft, but needed more—and fast. The Royal Iraqi Air Force should have had a greater number of modern planes, but its sixteen American-made 8A-4 ground attack planes, which could have devastated both Habbaniya and the Allies operating around Fallujah, had vital components go mysteriously missing. The planes would have outpaced, out-climbed, and had a far greater range than the vast majority of Habbaniya's planes. Still, Grobba cajoled the Iraqis and his Luftwaffe counterparts to keep the pressure on, at the same time radioing Berlin with rosy approximations of success if only it would hurry more aid.[7]

The day after the Allies fought off the Iraqi counterattack on Fallujah, a remarkable meeting took place to the south, in Basra, between two men who were carrying the weight of the world on their shoulders—Generals Claude Auchinleck and Archibald Wavell. Auchinleck had responsibility for the defense of India and for the Indian Army, which he knew would be essential to any Allied victory; Wavell had responsibility for defending the Suez Canal and the Allies' most important bases in the world war in Egypt. Over several hours, the two debated which course the war for Iraq would take. While they frankly disagreed about what to do, they showed each other the patience that was decidedly lacking in General Wavell's reception from Churchill around that period.

Wavell's eyes were on the Egyptian-Libyan frontier, where a misstep in his contest with Rommel could mean disaster. He worried about the defense of the key Libyan port of Tobruk; and he worried about the constant effort to block German supplies crossing the Mediterranean. In those exact hours, the Allies were being driven from Crete—centered in the eastern Mediterranean—whose capture was about to imperil the Royal Navy and make it harder to deny supplies and reinforcements to the Afrika Korps.

Auchinleck, on the other hand, viewed Iraq as just outside the gates of India. The Axis powers, in moving planes to Mosul—even from a great distance, even while they were busy with Crete—had proven they could do it again. And perhaps next time there would be airborne crack troops with them. If they landed in Baghdad, the Germans could lead the Iraqis on Basra and hit the utterly vital Allied oil supplies at Abadan, Iran.

Wavell countered that the Axis must be far more interested in Syria than Iraq, at least for the moment. The invasion of Crete certainly suggested it. From bases in Crete and Syria, the Axis could command the Aegean, cow Turkey, and loom over the Kirkuk oil fields in northern Iraq. Yes, the defense of Egypt and Palestine would be badly hampered by an unfriendly Iraq, and the Abadan oil badly threatened; but Vichy Syria becoming a base of operations for the Axis was an even worse scenario.

Auchinleck argued that the forces sallying out of Habbaniya and coming up from Basra could manage to seize Baghdad, capture the Golden Square, install a friendly government, and dig in for the duration of the war. Wavell put the odds of two or even three thousand Allied troops defeating perhaps several tens of thousands of Iraqis at fifty-fifty. Better to hunker down at Habbaniya and Basra, consider Baghdad and the oil fields lost to the enemy for now, and focus on denying them Syria, which the Axis would need in order to consolidate power in Iraq and ship the captured oil, in any case.

But soon Auchinleck won Wavell to his view. And command of the Iraq campaign, which Wavell never wanted in the first place, officially passed to Auchinleck, who bet his career and so much more that Habforce and the Indian Army could capture Baghdad. Wavell flew back to Cairo and a world of other worries, and Auchinleck began to set in motion the final attack on the Golden Square.[8]

9

"That My Wonders May Be Multiplied"

The Battle for Baghdad

> In the afternoon, we had news that the Americans crossed the bridge with about 150 tanks and armored vehicles. . . . Our forces were shaken. . . . It was a terrible night, because the crossing of the Americans on the Euphrates were speeding up the advancement of the enemy to its strategic goal, which is Baghdad.
> —Lieutenant General Raad al-Hamdani, Iraqi Republican Guard, 2003, in an interview on PBS *Frontline*

AFTER THE SECOND battle of Fallujah, John Glubb and several trucks of the Arab Legion patrolled the desert north of Habbaniya. There was still an Iraqi Army brigade fortified in Ramadi, and it was not a comfortable thing for the Allies to leave it to their rear. So, leaving the green, palm banks of the Euphrates, they rolled north across pebble-strewn desert. They watched for movement coming from Ramadi, eyed any advance by rail from the north, where many thousands of Iraqi troops were, and kept a lookout for the Luftwaffe.

One fiercely bright morning, the legionnaires came upon a couple dozen tents pitched between the edges of the desert and a green stretch. Sheep meandered around them, and hobbled horses kicked at the arrival of the legion's loud pickups. A young Arab on a chestnut mare rode past, singing through his black kaffiyeh as if to calm the horses. By the time the legionnaires had dispersed their trucks widely in case a German plane appeared, the men of the camp had already gathered in the largest tent, its four sides flung open to admit the visitors, whom they hosted cordially. These were seminomadic Sunni, shepherds and farmers, a tribe of the Dulaim people.

Over tea they talked. It was "unlucky," said one the hosts, that two governments had chosen to fight their battles on Dulaim land. They cared nothing about a revolution or the matter of Germany; that was for the political types in Baghdad, Basra, or Mosul. What mattered was that the Iraqi Army, in cutting the Euphrates embankment between Fallujah and Habbaniya, had flooded many Dulaim crop fields. And it mattered that the British, for their part, had hurt many civilians in their bombing of nearby Fallujah, warning leaflets or no. One man said that even the Turks, renowned for their brutality, had never shelled "a town full of women" as the British had done in Fallujah. Among the gathered men was one who'd been working in a Fallujah shop when the RAF blitz took place; he, like many other people of the town, now homeless, had taken refuge with a hinterland tribe. Some in the tent also placed outsize blame on the ruin of Fallujah on the Assyrian companies of the RAF Levies.

But amid this talk of "politics" jeopardizing their hospitality, someone veered the conversation toward shared reminiscences among themselves and the guests. For John Glubb, the Arab Legion's commander, this was a better course for a conversation. But he would have to gently wend the drift of conversation toward a fighting alliance between the Dulaimi and the British if the upstarts in Baghdad could not be finished quickly. And if old friendships and memories didn't suffice, Glubb had a purse of silver to help things along.[1]

In the early darkness of May 28, 1941, Jack Bartlett, David Smiley, Harry Chalk, the Arab Palestinian known simply as Reading, and Glubb and the Arab Legion began their approach on Baghdad. After garrisoning Fallujah and Habbaniya, the Allies had just under fifteen hundred men—Arab, British, and Nepali—to send toward Baghdad. The Iraqi Army in the region had, spread between Ramadi and Baghdad alone, about twenty thousand; thousands more could arrive by train from Mosul, two hundred miles to the north, also the main regional base of operations of the Luftwaffe.

The Assyrians, some of the British and Gurkha troops, and a handful of armored cars had the hard task of occupying the Iraqi troops still hovering in the Habbaniya hinterlands, numbering probably in the low thousands as compared to the Allies' low hundreds. There was every chance, meanwhile, that the Allied force set toward Baghdad would be exposed as far too small for the job. The thirty miles between Fallujah and Baghdad were a gulf of risk.

The force leaving Fallujah and Habbaniya was split into northern and southern columns. The southern group, made up of 750 men of the Household Cavalry, including Reading, two companies of the Essex Regiment, a few armored cars, and two guns of Jack Bartlett's 237th Field Battery, drove due east down the Fallujah–Baghdad road. The second group of seven hundred veered north before heading east, so they could approach Baghdad from above and block the escape route to Mosul and also, they hoped, block reinforcements from Mosul (of course, it was almost as likely that the Allies would be caught in a vice from these two directions). This northern group consisted of Glubb and the Arab Legion in addition to more Household Cavalry, two more twenty-five-pound guns, two more companies of the Essex, and three armored cars. Some Royal Engineers rode along to try to sabotage railways and highways.

The Indian Army force would eventually advance on Baghdad from Basra in the south, but in the interest of maintaining momentum, the Allied attack from Fallujah and Habbaniya would precede them. In the meantime, some of the Indian Army rolled out of the Basra area westward. This group was slowed by the flooded Euphrates and lack of transport, with just a handful of trucks and armored cars lifted out of ships' holds on the Shatt al-Arab docks. Earlier the Iraqis had forced civilian trucks and the trains out of the Basra suburbs to slow the Indian Army.

Directing things in Basra was Major General Bill Slim. He had just recovered from being shot in the buttocks by a strafing Italian fighter in the brutal Eritrea campaign in which he helped lead the Indian Army—part of the campaign in which the Essex Regiment suffered so terrifyingly. Slim was a veteran of World War I, and he had passed through Basra then as a twenty-seven-year-old. Having spent most of his career as an officer of Gurkhas and a teacher at staff college in India, he was a son of a Birmingham family of little means, had started his adult life as a school teacher, and wrote magazine stories under a pen name to supplement his Indian Army pay; he wouldn't have known how to act the haughty general if he wanted to. Out of a sense of pride and confidence, Slim wanted to get his Indian Army men into the thick of the action, but the problems of transportation meant that, for now, their way north was badly hindered.

Still, Bill Slim sent what force he could into the heart of the country about the same time those heading toward Baghdad left Fallujah, aiming them overland toward the town of Ur—the site of the ancient kingdom and legendary birthplace of Abraham. The ancient kingdom turned to ruins, the sort of ruins John Masters wondered at from the air on his flight to Habbaniya, Ur was now a humble village set beside the old stones, about eighty miles north and west of Basra. Yet, though the village itself was small, it stood at an important crossroads about one-third of the way toward Habbaniya.

Slim's Thirteenth Lancers, at least, had transportation; they were an old cavalry regiment from Bombay, and like so many Indian units, this was a return to a country in which their fathers had fought the Turks in World War I. Back then, they still had their horses. Now, as had happened to the Household Cavalry, their horses were gone, having parted in 1938. The lanceless Lancers now drove armored cars built on Chevy chassis, though they retained their traditional turbans.

Laden with water and rations, they left Basra first, followed by a column including Madras Sappers and Miners, a field ambulance, a handful of modest guns, and as many Gurkhas as the limited trucks allowed. A group of Sikh signalers crammed in Fords too small for their long legs followed in a cable truck unspooling a new phone line to keep in touch with the headquarters outside Basra.

The column left the sultry, green Basra area and ranged over a rough track, fording soft sand, until they neared the crossroads village in the midafternoon and three machine guns opened up on them from ahead, with about a hundred riflemen of the Iraqi Army joining in. The Lancers pulled back to a point a mile outside Ur and waited for the small artillery battery to catch up with their Gurkha escort. A few hours later, the Indian guns started firing on the Iraqi machine gun defenses. The spiritual grandchildren of Abraham were trying to defeat each other, Christian, Muslim, and—if there were some among these units of the Iraqi Army—Jews alike. With the light artillery at work, the Iraqi Army was retreating north in the direction of Baghdad before long, and the Indians drove in to occupy the town without losses. In the next hours and days they set out to make sure there were no dangers lurking in the neighborhood and to probe the route toward Habbaniya, eventually linking the two Allied bases.[2]

Meanwhile, in the area west of Baghdad, the two small assault forces were making their approach on the capital. David Smiley was with the Household Cavalry in the northern group, whose goal it was to cut off any retreat of the Golden Square and their supporting units toward Mosul, where the Iraqis might carry on the fight. But ahead went Glubb and the Arab Legion in their trucks and armored cars, watching for unpleasant surprises from the Iraqi Army. After them was the Household Cavalry in a long line of one-ton trucks spaced out in case the Luftwaffe discovered them, led by a World War I–vintage RAF armored car. Two quads, with Jack Bartlett in one, pulled their sole pair of modern twenty-five-pound guns. (It had taken enormous manpower and time to ferry the heavy guns and quads over the ferry east of Habbaniya; only later would more guns follow).

The Arab Legion came upon the Baghdad–Mosul railway and were greeted by Iraqi machine gun fire from a nearby train station, a squat, dense structure built in the 1910s as part of the cooperative venture between the Germans and the Ottomans, the Berlin–Baghdad railway. Such stations were meant to serve the double purpose of a defensive outpost and a small fort, and from behind dark slits came the Iraqi shots, now.

The Arab Legion remained to deal with this machine gun fire while Smiley, some more cavalry, Jack Bartlett and a pair of guns, and an RAF armored car turned south on the track running parallel with the rails in the direction of the next station down the line toward Baghdad. The River Tigris, lined with date palms, was now visible about a mile on their left. After a while, Smiley and his group came to the next train stop, as puffs of dust and ricochets near the wheels of the trucks alerted Lieutenant Smiley to another brusque greeting, and he ordered his men into the ditch, the trucks out of range. After he and some other troopers crawled behind a dusty embankment, approached the fort, and split into groups, he ordered the charge, accompanied by an armored car. But by the time the cavalry got near, the Iraqis had driven off down the line toward Baghdad, to a spot where they'd eventually put up their determined defense. Still, Smiley's men happily took the Iraqi flag that had been flapping above the station as a trophy.

Back to the north along the rail line, as the Arab Legion were preparing to deal with the Iraqi defenders of another station-fort, a strange car rushed upon them from the direction of Mosul. Challenged by the Arab legion's armored car guard, the civilian vehicle spun around to flee. The armored car gunner fired a few controlled rounds, and the car suddenly swerved and stopped. The legionnaires hurried to it. Inside the Iraqi Army driver was bleeding out his last, while a well-dressed civilian was shot through his hand; the civilian turned out to be the mayor of Baghdad.

The Arab Legion medic treated the hand as the mayor volunteered that the Golden Square was watching the Baghdad–Mosul railway very closely. The Iraqis had heard of the handiwork of the Royal Engineers, whom the Arab Legion had escorted and guarded as they disassembled a length of track some nights before. And the Golden Square had sent the mayor and an Iraqi colonel—the now dead driver—to investigate these enemy attacks on the rail line and plan its protection. Without the railway, reinforcements could not easily arrive for the defense of Baghdad, nor could the Golden Square and its supporters retreat to Mosul if necessary. The mayor and the colonel were on their way back to Baghdad when they stumbled upon the Arab Legion, he said. Then the exhausted man was given his rest and tea while John Glubb thought about what to do with him.

Shortly after this, a shallow gash opened on the face of one of the Royal Engineers in the company. It took some moments to dawn on him that he had been grazed on the cheek by a bullet. He and the legionnaires leaped for cover and scanned for the source of the fire: a copse of willows up the line. While the bleeding engineer hunkered down in an irrigation ditch, an Arab machine gun team readied their Vickers gun. An Arab Legion armored car went to work with its gun, too, and Corporal Ferhan led a crouching team down another irrigation ditch, heading to a position flanking the Iraqis in the willows. Once all were in position they attacked, and a brief exchange of well-organized fire forced the Iraqis' surrender, but at the price of two legionnaires' lives.

Led slowly through the heat back to the rest of the legionnaires, the prisoners revealed that they had been sent in two trucks from their unit several train stops to the north to scout. But this conversation was quickly interrupted by a sight that made John Glubb's heart sink: a train arriving from the north, from the direction of Mosul, where there were known to be thousands of Iraqi troops. At the moment, the Arab Legion, the Household Cavalry, and two batteries of Lincolnshire gunners were operating in a narrow corridor between the Tigris and the Euphrates floodwaters. They were, in short, penned in and could not flee a force arriving from the north except to go due south and into the awaiting Iraqi Army in Baghdad. Glubb ordered one of his two armored cars to race to the south and warn the others: they might very well be trapped.

The train approached, puffing steam, pushing before it an open flatbed car crammed with soldiers, while an unknown number of soldiers rode within. The Arab legionnaires swung their Vickers gun and armored car turret to a new position, targeting a stretch of track a few hundred yards away. When the train was almost at its nearest point, the legionnaires preparing to pull their triggers, the train braked to a stop. Soon it was reversing to the north toward the stone station-fort. For some unknown reason, some Iraqi officer had thought better of pushing forward—warned of trouble, perhaps; or wondering at the absence of the forward scouts whom the Arab Legion had just captured; or unsure of the size of the Allied force down the line.

The legionnaires, outnumbered (and quite possible vastly so), crept unseen to the north to keep an eye on the station up the line, as the train soon rolled to a stop next to it. There was no possibility Glubb could take this large an Iraqi force. Dusk was coming on, and all the legion could do was watch the enemy.

Desert night came on, and both Glubb's men and David Smiley's group south of them set guards and dug in to sleep. At 2:00 a.m., some Iraqi raiders shot up the Household Cavalry camp with machine gun fire.

But a carefully placed Hotchkiss machine gun post viciously answered the Iraqi attack with no one hurt. These Iraqi raiders, however, left behind several Ford V-8s and a modern Bren machine gun. These were far better than a flag trophy, and one of the Fords was sent back to the unit's commanding officer to replace his staff car, which had been a taxi hijacked from the streets of Haifa.

In the next morning's darkness, Glubb and the legionnaires in the north prepared to move on the stone train station and the menacing troop train. They wouldn't have dared had Jack Bartlett not arrived with one of the twenty-five-pound guns of the 237th Field Battery. With that, they hoped to put some holes through the threatening train. But when the group got close enough to see, they discovered that the Iraqi train was gone, reversed to the north, along with the fort's defenders. Jack Bartlett at least got to put some holes through the stone station, just to be sure, before the legionnaires carefully approached, searched the place, and prepared to defend it. When a rumbling later came from outside, it turned out to be a large farm truck, loaded with crates of eggs. These were commandeered for critical war service, to everyone's delight, and breakfast was served, with a bill for the eggs arriving in Amman not long after, addressed to Glubb Pasha.

For the Household Cavalry, RAF armored cars, and gunners down the rail line it proved a bitter day. After a short advance down the line toward Baghdad, not far from the shadows of the Kadhimiya mosque's minarets, David Smiley and his men got badly bogged down. The Iraqis had chosen the place of their defensive stand well, and rained mortar and artillery fire and sprayed machine gun fire on the approaching British from a dug-out brickworks. An RAF armored car had its turret destroyed by a shell. The trucks had to reverse out of range, and the British men had to dig in among some dunes that flanked the road, one man savaged by a shell in the process.

The 237th went to work, with Jack Bartlett and his gun that had joined the Arab Legion eventually returning south to throw its weight too. But a heat haze in the direction of Baghdad made targeting very difficult, along with no good spotting, and they were under strict orders to avoid Kadhimiya's Shiite shrine at all costs. The Iraqi artillery, which rained all day, seemed to have a far greater range than the British had expected, a mystery solved later when the men heard that the Germans had somehow supplied the Iraqis with better, modern guns—indeed, they would prove to be French guns. The Allied advance from the north was over.[3]

When Bartlett's gunners, Smiley's troopers, and Glubb's legionnaires left Fallujah to approach Baghdad from the north, Reading and another company of Household Cavalry troopers, along with Harry Chalk and two companies of the Essex, headed due east, straight toward Baghdad. They had four more guns of the 237th Field Battery with them, a handful of Royal Engineers, and three RAF armored cars. They were only about 750 men in total.

They left Fallujah before 5:00 a.m., following a map that pilot Tony Dudgeon had made for them by photographing the route the entire way to Baghdad. An early landmark just east of the town was the burned husk of an RAF bomber haunting the dawn. As the morning wore on, the column made only slow progress toward the rising sun. It took a half day to cross the twenty-five miles from Fallujah to the place they expected their first trouble spot: a stone police outpost along the road, surrounded by a green, irrigated stretch that contrasted sharply with the pale yellow dust lands they'd crossed all morning.

The boys and men of the Household Cavalry fixed their bayonets and charged the police outpost, passing up and down irrigation ditches for cover as they ran. Most of the place's Iraqi defenders melted away, back in the direction of Baghdad, but some, apparently less enthusiastic about the Golden Square, gladly surrendered. Either in their own English or to Reading in Arabic, they offered a warning: just to the east, where a mile-wide sheet of shallow floodwater had been spread by the Iraqis, there were deep ditches hidden beneath the shimmering surface—tank traps.

Near the police fort was an irrigation station with a set of well-kept white bungalows, among flowering oleanders, perhaps for the long-departed irrigation staff. Reading followed some officers into one of these houses, including his chief, who had split his shorts in the course of the morning not having really done anything strenuous. They picked through the rooms and came upon a telephone switchboard. Reading looked at the member of Parliament, who suggested they give it a try, and the young Palestinian took up the receiver.

Reading was startled when a voice came over the line in Arabic, frantic: "I've been trying to raise you for two hours. What's the matter?" Reading translated for his intelligence officer, who had him respond that the area was surrounded by the British and that British tanks had gone around the floods in the direction of Baghdad. Reading conjured his best Iraqi accent and panicked timbre and told the Baghdad headquarters of an Iraqi Army division that British tanks would soon roll on the city.

But his work had only begun, because more voices began to stream across the switchboard circuits. For the next several hours, Reading translated at a dash, a one-man Enigma machine betraying the secrets of the enemy. His officer, in turn, passed these secrets on to his superiors and then onward via wireless back to the regional general at Habbaniya. Reading relayed information on troop locations, on the mood of officers, and on where Iraqi units were digging in. At one point he overheard Baghdad issue an order to reconnoiter these approaching British tanks and, to the surprise of everyone listening in the little white house, those Iraqi observers confirmed the presence of fifty tanks. (Of course, there were none.) Later an Iraqi artillery officer actually reported he was engaging five tanks. The officers around Reading thought the Iraqi commander was most likely trading fire with a pair of RAF armored cars (with their conical towers), or some of the Lincolnshire gunners with their humpbacked quads.

Reading worked for hours at his great subterfuge until for some reason all the lines went dead. Then, with the cavalry having been warned about the hidden traps under the smooth floodwaters, the trucks advanced slowly eastward toward Baghdad. They went single file, spotters with long poles out front feeling for the pits. Where they came upon them, they laid the steel ramps under the water and proceeded with supreme care. At one point an impatient one-ton truck tried to pass the one in front and, of course, ran into a trap, being instantly partially submerged and muddily squelching. Its occupants learned a lesson in patience as they crawled up the back of the truck with their gear and had to wait all day to be rescued by an armored car that eventually, laughingly, came back for them.

By the end of the day the southern column had cleared the flooded area toward Baghdad and dug in amid some low ridges for the night, while the shells of the 237th howled overhead toward the Iraqis, also well dug in, to the east. The next morning they would continue the advance, but would have to jury-rig a bridge over a canal twelve miles outside Baghdad, since the Iraqis had blown up the main bridge, at a place called Abu Ghraib.[4]

In the British embassy in Baghdad, Freya Stark heard the thudding guns from dawn on May 29. By 8:00 a.m. they were shaking the window-panes, and sharper. In her diary she struggled to find words for the mo-ment. To her, the sound of approaching guns promised change, the arrival of fate, even if that fate was uncertain and possibly bloody.

She and hundreds of others had been trapped within one square acre between the Tigris and a stone and iron fence for a month, languish-ing, uncertain whether they would be hauled away to a darker prison, perhaps even attacked in retribution for the next RAF bombing run; a weird mix of torpor and dread and a feeling they'd been forgotten. Mean-while, over the secret car radio came recent reports of the final Allied de-feat at Crete.

Now the wind carried the sound of small-arms fire from the direc-tion of the main bridge out of Baghdad.[5]

Fritz Grobba was losing control of the situation. Iraqi government min-isters were contriving reasons to leave the country. The minister of de-fense, whose job it was to defend the country, after all, left it for Constantinople claiming he needed to speak with important contacts. The foreign minister and two other officials made their excuses, too, and left for Tehran. The officer in command of the Luftwaffe squadron was en route to Athens to get sand filters for the engines of the remaining German planes.

There was very little air power left to throw at the approaching British (Grobba never considered them part Transjordanian, nor part Iraqi—just British). There were two Luftwaffe bombers remaining, the few remaining Messerschmitts were ailing, and aviation fuel was low and could only slowly be distilled by the lab they'd airlifted all the way from

Germany. At least the Italians had just arrived with some fighter planes that outmatched most of the Habbaniya aircraft.

In these final hours of Iraqi resistance, Grobba sent off a string of fictional messages to Berlin casting about for some reaction. Glubb of the Arab Legion was dead, he reported; the valiant Royal Iraqi Air Force had downed close to one hundred RAF planes; the Iraqis had overrun RAF Shaibah, near Basra, killing 150. The Iraqis could win this, he insisted, if only a little more help was sent by Berlin.

Then a report arrived at the presidential palace that a British armor column was approaching down the Baghdad–Mosul road. "Perfectly unbelievable . . . utterly false," he assured those around him.*

But while Grobba could encourage and reassure, what he mainly did was fume, suspecting that the Reich's armed forces high command was holding up his requests to the führer for help in Iraq in favor of their preferred focus on Crete, suspecting that the Luftwaffe was trying to thwart him out of some kind of personal animosity, and suspecting also that his remaining hours in Baghdad were few.[6]

Meanwhile, the diehards in the Golden Square, their chosen prime minister, and other loyal officials planned for how they could continue the fight. On May 28, the first day of the two columns' drive on Baghdad, the inner circle met and agreed that they should move the government and their loyal army units 170 miles due north to Kirkuk. The treasury was duly emptied and sent under heavy guard northward. But by the next day, before Rashid Ali al-Gailani and the Golden Square could retreat north, word came that the officers in the field leading the defense of Baghdad were beginning to disappear. There were rumors, too, that some of them had taken their private cars down the highway toward Iran. Soon myriad government and military officials were fleeing eastward, the only direction available, blaming everyone else for having been the first to run. Thus the prime minister and several of the Golden Square boarded a train eastward along the same route that Freya Stark had taken one month earlier when she hurried toward Baghdad.[7]

*While Fritz Grobba reassured his Iraqi colleagues that it was impossible that a column of tanks was approaching from the north, he did believe that the Allies had tanks among their columns to the west.

MOST URGENT
May 29, 1941
Special Security Handling

The English attack on Baghdad continued last night and today with an increased number of armored cars and tanks.

On the advice of the Minister President I left Baghdad at 6:00 a.m. with escort and arrived at Kirkuk at 3:00 p.m.

All local Germans left here this morning via Mosul; as I have heard from Mosul, all German military persons there left the city today by plane. The reason for their sudden departure is not known to me.

When the sudden departure of the German air force personnel becomes known it will mean a tremendous disappointment for the Minister President and the people of Iraq, unless there are compelling reasons for it, and German prestige will suffer for a long time. This outcome can be prevented only if the Luftwaffe is committed again quickly. Of the Italian fighters three were committed today, and one of them was shot down.

. . . The defense of the Mosul area is urgently in the German interest and should therefore be attempted by the necessary German commitment.

I intend to proceed to Mosul tomorrow morning, and hope to find there a promise of a renewed commitment of German planes.

Gehrcke [Grobba][8]

The Iraqis had a strong system of defense on the east bank of the Abu Ghraib canal, with trenches and air-raid shelters, and they'd dynamited the bridge over the canal itself. So there was little for Reading to do the morning of May 29, though machine gun fire sounded in the direction of the Iraqi line.

Things got a bit too interesting all of a sudden when a fast-moving biplane fighter shot low toward him and his party, which had stopped near a mud-brick coffee house. The Italian streaked past, aiming at another target, but not long after, the sky seemed full of dogfighting planes and RAF bombers pointed toward the dug-in Iraqis. Amid all this an enemy biplane coughed out a trail of black smoke and cast itself toward the ground close by, a parachute appearing that seemed to drift toward Reading. He took off running in the direction it seemed bound, along with his intelligence officer and several others. The parachute's landing spot, though, seemed to move farther and farther away, so that what looked like a short run turned into a run of two miles—in the direction of the Abu Ghraib bridge and the fighting. But Reading kept going.

Both the parachute and the plane came down on the opposite side of the canal, and Reading and his officer swam it in their clothes, on the other side finding the pilot tiredly dragging his parachute away from the smoking wreck. It was a type of plane that Reading had not seen before in this fight, bearing the markings of the Royal Iraqi Air Force. But when he and his boss caught up to the stumbling pilot and challenged him, they received in return a weary Italian fascist salute. The plane was in fact Italian.

The men led the pilot back to the wreckage, which they searched for any useful maps or other intelligence, though none turned up. They took the parachute, with its valuable silk, and Reading kept for himself the plane's beautiful gray Italian leather seat cushion (which for the next month would serve as an elegant chair when he placed it on any crate or gasoline can at hand). Then ammunition started popping amid the wreck's slowly spreading flames and, on the edge of hostile territory and miles from help, Reading and the others led the pilot back to camp. Later, somewhat revived by tea, the Italian explained that he had been in Rhodes not twenty-four hours earlier; had refueled in Vichy French Syria and again in Mosul; and had flown straight into an air battle on arriving at Baghdad.

After that Reading and two officers went in search of an alternative to the blown-up Abu Ghraib bridge, since the day was wearing on and repairs to the bridge were slow. First, their open car came upon a Bedouin who told Reading that there was another bridge to the south, though it was hard for the interpreter to understand the man's explanation of the distance. So the three drove along the canal until a modest concrete bridge did indeed come into sight, not too many miles to the south. There was a village on the other side of the bridge and a road that stretched from there eastward to the horizon in the direction of Baghdad. Reading saw, though, that many men were gathered conspicuously on the opposite bank as if guarding this road. He and an officer, both armed with pistols, approached these dozens of armed men with as much swagger as they could muster. Reading was not warmly welcomed, but not threatened either, and he asked whether the road that passed through the village was flooded farther on, and whether it connected to the main road leading into Baghdad. After the strangers reluctantly confirmed this, Reading once again conjured his British legions and tank corps, warning them of the vast British forces in the area and of their crushing of the Iraqi Army at the main Abu Ghraib bridge. Only then did he turn to leave.

Hours later, when Reading returned with an armored car and two trucks of troopers to further inspect the bridge, the guard melted away as if Reading's promise of an overwhelming British force had materialized out of the Iraqi dust.[9]

The next day, May 30, was the last day of the battle for Iraq. Back toward Fallujah, some of the First Essex was working with the RAF to hold down Iraq units in the rear of Habbaniya and faced determined resistance. In fact, Habbaniya was never really out of danger from the Iraqi Army at Ramadi if those units had made a serious, coordinated ground assault. The southern column of Harry Chalk's First Essex, Lincolnshire gunners, and truck-born cavalry meanwhile crossed the repaired Abu Ghraib bridge (not the one discovered by Reading, probably to his disappointment) at midday and fought a series of hard battles against the well-entrenched Iraqis. At one point the men of the Household Cavalry scrambled out of their trucks as Iraqi machine gun fire evenly sprayed the flat terrain over which they advanced, which meant hours of creeping in irrigation ditches to try to flank Baghdad's defenders. A company of Essex was also strafed by an Iraqi Gladiator biplane, which expended its ammunition and flew off under a hail of Essex rifle fire.

In this fight the twenty-five-pounders of Jack Bartlett's neighbors were horribly effective, and on top of that the RAF flying out of Habbaniya dropped more of its modified screaming bombs. Yet the Iraqis answered with their own effective artillery, at one point missing the column's leader, Brigadier Joe Kingstone, by a matter of yards. That day Reading was in the staff car waiting for his officers when there was suddenly an approaching whine, then a metallic *wonk*. An enameled tea mug on the car's hood flew in the air. An eighteen-pound Iraqi shell had hit its target—the front quarter of Reading's staff car—perfectly, but had not exploded, instead ricocheting over Reading's head and into the desert behind him. The passenger side front mudguard was no longer round, and the car had a bright, metallic divot in the middle shorn of buff paint. "What are we staying here for?" asked Reading, when the others came to see what had made the colossal noise.

Reading's close shave was not unique, and the Iraqi artillery there, just west of the city, and where David Smiley was fighting just to the north was pinning down the Allied advance. In truth, had the Golden Square committed a mass effort at this point, perhaps making a wide flank of Allied positions, the secret of the tiny size of the attack force might have been revealed.[10]

Midmorning on May 30, Freya Stark noticed the Iraqi police erecting sandbag defenses at their guard posts outside the embassy gates, apparently for the protection of the embassy inmates, but from what threat Freya did not know. Then, in the middle of the afternoon, word came from a delegation of Iraqi politicians that they would like to come to the embassy and discuss terms of an armistice with the British ambassador.

They duly arrived at 6:00 p.m.: anti–Golden Square politicians, police, and army officials. There was an Iraqi official in a stylish gray suit, a Mosul army commander who was less inclined to smile, and a very happy Baghdad officer who had trained at the eminent Indian Army staff college at Quetta, Baluchistan, where Generals Auchinleck and Wavell, as well as many others on the "other side," had trained. The American ambassador also arrived from his embassy where he, too, sheltered hundreds of refugees from Allied countries, though America itself was still neutral in the world conflict. Freya Stark wondered at his cool appearance, as if he'd just stepped off his yacht.

To the Iraqi delegation and all the embassy inmates the British ambassador gave a speech in Arabic from the steps in the spirit of friendship and letting bygones be bygones, the exact spirit Stark herself would've adopted. The embassy could now remount its radio mast, and the ambassador radioed Habbaniya for permission to negotiate the armistice. And after sunset, he worked out the terms with Iraqi Army representatives: hostilities were to cease the next day at dawn.[11]

And so the fighting did end the next morning, with most of the Allied force never entering Baghdad but stopping three miles west and five miles north. The terms of the cease-fire embodied the idea—to some degree fictional, to some degree real—that the entire episode had been a case of a small coup of several officers, not a general revolt. For this reason the Iraqi military was allowed to keep its weapons, though the armistice required that they disperse from Baghdad to peacetime garrisons. And Emir Abdullah I's nephew, regent for the Hashemite child king, drove in from Amman, Transjordan, and entered the city under an honor guard of loyal Iraqi soldiers. Yet the Foreign Office and the ambassador very consciously withheld British troops from the city in order to maintain the fiction that the regent's restoration was by Iraqi choice. (Freya Stark thought maintaining this pretense was nonsense; no one was fooled.)

From the point of view of the Allied commanders on the ground, staying away from Baghdad had the critical advantage of hiding the tiny size of the Allied striking column; if its size were revealed, Iraqi officers still inclined to fight might take advantage of it. (In the coming days, the striking force's commander went so far as to buy his supplies from different Baghdadi merchants in order to disguise the force's small needs.)

Later, the British held a ceremonial flag raising at their embassy. The Iraqis had required them to lower it during the war, and rehoisting it doubled as a thank-you celebration for the troops who lifted the siege. The embassy hosted a few representatives from the various units that had driven on Baghdad, including representatives of Jack Bartlett's Lincoln gunners. Harry Chalk himself formed part of the honor guard, though he thought to himself that he would gladly trade all the solemnity and ceremony for just a cool beer. For his part, he was just glad that he and his friends from the Essex, including several Jewish pals, came through Iraq largely intact.

Amid all this, Freya Stark watched Arab Legion troopers poke about the grounds. They seemed cheerful, somewhat amused by the colorless inmates, and amused by the big house and its elaborate trappings, as if what was considered luxurious to the denizens of the embassy was simply eccentric in their eyes.

Meanwhile, rumors, incorrect, swirled around the lawns and halls of the embassy that the Golden Square, the prime minister, and Amin al-Husseini were all imprisoned and Fritz Grobba was in Mosul. And a newspaper reporter took the opportunity to ask a representative from the new Iraqi government what had led the Iraqis to surrender. How, answered the man, could Baghdad stand against fifty tanks?[12]

It was not true that the Golden Square and its allies were captured; some had successfully fled in a number of directions, but it was true that Fritz Grobba was exiting the country through the north. So it was once again time for John Masters and his Gurkha friends and soldiers to duck into a transport plane and hurl themselves into the air northward to Mosul. The Gurkhas—some of the mountain men suffering heatstroke in consistent 120-degree weather—had spent the past few days in the hinterland north of Habbaniya to dissuade any possible rear action by the Iraqi Army, a rear action that might have discovered the weakness of the Allied advance. Now the Gurkhas were in the more familiar light air of the clouds. But John Masters was worried about what they might be getting into in Mosul, since no one had tested whether the Iraqi Army commanders there were as content with armistice as those in Baghdad; after all, there was no ghost column of British tanks approaching them.

As the transports packed with sleepy Gurkhas approached their landing, Masters looked down and counted about twenty antiaircraft guns defending the Mosul air base, all the while imagining that those men manning the guns were no more certain about whether they'd fire than Masters was. A pair of modern Hurricanes, at least, escorted the transports this time; but what the Hurricanes were supposed to do in response to twenty antiaircraft guns was anybody's guess. Eventually the transports touched ground without a shot fired, and Masters hurried down the aisle, shaking his riflemen awake so they could rush off the plane as quickly as possible. "Prepare for action!"

They rolled out of the plane and dispersed, and the clinch in Master's gut eventually released. His friend, Subedar Major (Warrant Officer) Sahabir, scanned the place as if hoping they'd left Iraq's blazing heat behind but, disappointed, murmured, "bad climate."[13]

John Masters and the Gurkhas did not know it, but David Smiley and a company, or troop, of Household Cavalry had arrived in Mosul already. They had found the local Iraqi commander very angry and had indeed feared that things would get out of control quickly. So the landing of the Gurkhas meant a sigh of relief for Smiley, too.

But Smiley found no sign of Grobba, and the only signs of the Luftwaffe were some burned shells of German planes on the tarmac and a Heinkel bomber in one hangar, its swastika painted over and Royal Iraqi Air Force symbols added. A few questions to the locals returned rumors that Grobba had already left overland for Turkey.

Grobba had in fact raced to Kirkuk first, south and east of Mosul, where he found a cold reception by the Iraqis who now knew the outcome of this war. (The many native Jews of Kirkuk had been distressed at the German pilots and staff walking freely through their town over the previous few weeks, as if Adolf Hitler's Germany had come to Iraq.) Grobba then proceeded by car to Mosul and tried to rally the Iraqi officers there to fight on. But former allies now refused to speak with him, and a disappointed Grobba flew north to Aleppo, Syria, with the last of the Luftwaffe ground crew, just ahead of their Allied pursuers.

Smiley got orders to head Grobba off at the pass. First his trucks pointed east to Erbil, the many-times ancient town on a hill, an important center to a half dozen former empires, and now the Kurdish provincial capital. Erbil was welcoming; the hill even offered some relief from the flatland's heat, and over a cup of coffee the chief of police explained that the Golden Square's war was never with the Kurds. They frankly hated their Iraqi overlords as much as they had hated Ottoman overlordship and as much as their Kurdish cousins in eastern parts hated Iranian domination. They wanted an independent Kurdistan.

Smiley and his troopers searched the area in the vain hope of bagging the most wanted man in the region, rolling through deep gorges under red cliffs and passing clear rivers churned by trout. They were welcomed in a vine-covered coffee shop on the Iraq-Syria frontier where they conversed with the locals through their interpreter. Everything about Kurdistan pleased Smiley, and he was sorry that he could not imagine how it could easily become free, divided as it was among three countries.[14]

West of Baghdad, the day after the cease-fire, Reading was back at the white bungalow where, days before, he'd summoned the ghost tanks that helped conquer the capital. He had a horrible feeling. Why was it that the Household Cavalry was sitting here west of Abu Ghraib while there was no Allied force keeping the peace in the city? The regent was returned with a modest honor guard of loyal Iraqi soldiers, but there was little sense of who was in control of the civilian government, the police, and the elements of the army that followed the Golden Square. Reading had relatives in Baghdad, which gave him some sense of the pulse there and a great sense of ill ease about the threat of anarchy.

He approached one of his officers. "Why do our troops not go into Baghdad? Already there might be looting, I know. There will be people killed if our troops do not enter."

"Are there not Iraqi troops enough in the city, now loyal of course to the new Government, to keep order?" Reading's intelligence officer replied. That man routinely talked down to Reading, not merely as his inferior, but as a mere "Oriental," and thus not sharing his British rationality. But in this instance even he was concerned at Reading's warning.[15]

Reading's fear was warranted, and what proceeded was a horror. Looters attacked shops and houses, targeting the minority Jews in particular. British-looking people who had gone to banks or shops to get money or supplies after the month-long siege instead had to hide or run for their lives, sometimes under gunfire. Freya Stark listened to reports that filtered through to the embassy switchboard. A British intelligence officer observed police and soldiers smashing and grabbing. Others told of people streaming in over the Tigris bridges, coming in from the countryside to take part in the pillaging, then streaming back laden with spoils.

Some Jews were murdered in the streets. Some mainly Jewish alleys and courts were set upon by large mobs. There were muggings, stabbings, and rapes. In some outlying towns, opportunists used the chaos as an opportunity to extort money from Jewish communities.

Abdallah Simon, the young Jewish Iraqi Army second lieutenant who had survived the RAF's wall of fire on the road to Fallujah, was in his family home in Baghdad when the riot and murder broke out. His father was barricaded in his office, unable to move through the anarchic streets; his younger brother Maurice was home with Abdallah. When the feared moment came and ten looters burst through their home's back door, Simon was ready in his army uniform, holding a revolver. "How dare you enter the home of an Arab officer!" he shouted at them in his most commanding voice. The invaders faltered, then fled in fear.

The reasons for the killing and looting were many. There was opportunistic profit seeking, an attempt by the police and army to recoup paychecks that had evaporated in recent weeks, all while prices skyrocketed. False rumors were spread by those who hated or wanted to profit from the deaths of Jews: that they had signaled to RAF planes during the war, that they were cheering the failed revolution for independence. There was the targeting of minorities in times of chaos, a commonplace often repeated in history, but this time with the sinister tinge of race purity, the ultra–race nationalism that went hand in hand with the fascism embraced by the Golden Square and its ilk. (Curiously, Fritz Grobba appeared not to favor using anti-Semitism as a tool for his work in Iraq. He was even criticized by more strident Nazis for having cultivated Iraqi Jews as allies.)

This was a horrific turn away from the pluralism that had existed in Iraqi lands for centuries, arguably the place that Jews had substantially made their home for the longest-ever period. That pluralism, while far from perfect equality, was based on the Koranic injunction that Muslims must protect the other children of Abraham in their midst. And during the midst of the terror, there were reports of imams stopping and shaming, using these religious grounds, those who attempted pillage and murder.

The tales of Muslim Iraqis defending Jews were many too. When the murder spree in Baghdad started, a Kurdish tribal leader gathered his fighting men and took up the defense of Sandur, an entirely Jewish village in his lands, declaring, as related by the village rabbi, "No one will ever hurt the Jews of Sandur, even if there were an edict from the authorities against the Jews, I will personally guarantee the Jews will not be harmed."

In Baghdad a high-ranking officer in the Iraqi Army warned his Jewish neighbors on the eve of the disaster that there could be horrible trouble and to barricade their home. As they sheltered on their roof, the family watched in horror as a mob descended on their house. But then they saw the officer's wife—the man himself was away—step from her neighboring door and angrily address the crowd, armed with a pistol. With fierceness she said she'd stop anyone who approached a Jewish home, and even—then brandishing it for all to see—would detonate a grenade.

During this bloodletting, Freya Stark listened miserably to the gun-fire popping around the city overnight. The next day a cohesive Iraqi battalion arrived from the north and, combined with those among the police who never joined in, began moving through the city, openly firing on the rioters and killing scores. It was over. In the coming days, the child king himself returned and a functioning Iraqi government coalesced.

This war for Iraq was over, yet this murder spree, which claimed around two hundred Jewish Iraqis or more, represented this episode's worst wound for what it seemed to say about the dark nature of race nationalism.[16]

10

"Go Abroad in the Land"

*How They Came to Syria-Lebanon: Jack Hasey
and Roald Dahl*

THE BATTLE OVER Iraq was also about Syria-Lebanon. For some among the Iraqi revolutionaries, the ultimate, eventual goal of the revolt was the union of Iraq and Syria-Lebanon in a united Arab kingdom friendly with the Axis. And in their treaty with the Golden Square government, the Axis promised to support the creation of this new kingdom in Iraq and the Levant in the postwar new world order. (And how they might explain this to their Vichy French vassals, whose colonies these were in 1941, and would cease to be in this agreement, the Axis left unsaid.)

But beyond the visions of certain pan-Arab nationalists and promises of the Axis, Syria-Lebanon was deeply connected to the Iraq war because of the aid its Vichy French leaders provided to the Germans, Iraqis, and Italians during the April and May 1941 conflict. The French provided air bases for the Luftwaffe and Italian air forces, sent weapons and vehicles to Iraq, and promised the Axis the use of a small, somewhat hidden Lebanese port. And Vichy colonial authorities hosted a Reich's ambassador for coordinating the delivery of French, and potentially German, weapons and ammunition by rail from Syria to Iraq. In the last week of May 1941, the Germans and French even agreed that Vichy Syria would host Iraqi officers for training, would share intelligence with the German high command, and would in a sense coordinate with them in Syria-Lebanon's air and naval defense against the Allies. This collaboration marked a new level of Vichy-Axis military cooperation, a terribly ominous development because of what greater wide-scale cooperation could mean for the world war.

And the British knew a good deal about this new collaboration, including the airfield and fuel accommodations that Vichy made for the Luftwaffe thanks to Enigma decryptions. This was a disturbing turn in the eyes of leaders in Cairo and London. For as long as Vichy was arguably neutral in the war, Turkey had far less to fear from Syria, and thus from Axis encirclement. But if Germany and Vichy were openly fighting side by side in the Levant, Turkey might well not be able to hold out. And then that prime west-to-east rail corridor through Anatolia leading to Russia and Iran might fall to the Axis. And then there was the prospect of several tens of thousands of Axis-friendly troops just to the north of Iraq, whose stability was far from certain even after the defeat of the Golden Square, and British Palestine with its weak garrison protecting the Suez Canal. In retrospect, too, the potential picture of hundreds of thousands of Jews in Palestine being held hostage by a combined German-Vichy force is deeply harrowing given the eventual fate of so many French Jews under the Vichy government.

So again there was a debate in Whitehall and in Cairo about what to do with the evidence of Vichy cooperation with the Axis over Iraq. The news from the Mediterranean was terrible—Crete and Greece had been lost in the past weeks, with new fears for Cyprus and Malta; the news from Egypt and Libya was alarming, as German general Erwin Rommel gained more and more ground and Allied counterattacks failed in the month of May 1941.

In late May, in Cairo, General Archibald Wavell received pressure from the War Cabinet, Free French leader Charles de Gaulle, and others to prepare a march on Syria-Lebanon. Wavell had already acceded to a risky assault on Baghdad by an almost ludicrously small force, and he warned Whitehall that he did not have enough men for a certain victory in Syria-Lebanon. If he undertook it, he would have to remove force from the fight with Rommel. Prime Minister Winston Churchill went so far as to tell Wavell he was prepared to accept the general's resignation if he didn't want to take responsibility for the job. Wavell acquiesced, saying he would find the men somewhere.[1]

This is where a young American, Jack Hasey, enters the story. Fate would soon take him to a hill outside Damascus, where his war would end in terrible suffering. But now he was landing at Port Sudan in early spring 1940, only a couple of months after Freya Stark had. But as she went north to Cairo, he went south to face the Italians. Yet how did a young man precede his fellow Americans into the global war by so long?

Jack Hasey started down this path much earlier when, in spring 1937, he sailed off for Europe. A son of Bridgewater, Massachusetts— handsome, with an all-American smile—he had spent the previous year as a freshman at Columbia University. Probably because of his Gregory Peck looks, he had been adopted by some wealthy and connected New York boys determined to show this kid from buttoned-up New England just how much fun life could be in New York after dark. The year had been a swirl of clubs, girls, Benny Goodman, and Guy Lombardo. He learned to be a swell and was good at it.

But at the end of the spring term of his freshman year Hasey wanted a change. In part, he wanted to escape the country before his parents received his grades, but he also wanted to distance himself from his upper-middle-class safety net. So he boarded a ship for France. He told his parents that he intended to improve his French, and that he might enroll at the Sorbonne (but he had no intention of doing that). He looked for work; it was the Great Depression, and finding something was a challenge. But his looks and nationality won him a job as an apprentice at Cartier Jewelers. The Cartier brothers wanted to cultivate him to become a salesman to American and British customers at the casinos and clubs of Cannes, Monte Carlo, and Paris. The job was to look like he belonged there, to be a bon vivant, until he could suavely issue an exclusive invitation to the Cartier showroom. The job was to wear tails well, and his year at Columbia had prepared him perfectly. He quickly climbed.

And he fell in love with France. Though popularity came so easy to Hasey, he especially admired what he saw as the French tolerance of the odd. And though he had thrived in bustling New York, he enjoyed even more France's unhurried culture, learning to savor the long moment rather than the quick thrill. He liked the cooking. And he liked the young women. He would make France home.

But very soon trouble came to this adopted home. Just before Jack Hasey arrived in France, Germany had annexed Austria; now Germany was massing troops on the Czech border promising to "reunite" German-speaking areas of that country with the "fatherland." And before long, Herr Hitler began murmuring about "reuniting" ethnic Germans in Poland. There was talk on the streets of another showdown with Germany on the Maginot Line, the economy fluctuating with every rumor. And with cash unreliable, the smart chorus girls came into the showroom with a series of beaus to have them buy the young women jewelry—sometimes simply unset stones.

By now, Jack Hasey took threats to France personally. It had been one thing to read about Hitler's and Mussolini's saber rattling in distant New York, but now he saw reservists putting on uniforms and boarding trains for the border. After saying goodbye to many new friends, Hasey tried to enlist and follow them, only to find that international treaty forbade it. He then tried to become a French citizen, only for a judge to reject his case.

So Jack Hasey and a group of international friends in Paris decided to form an ambulance unit. If they could not fight, they would at least help the soldiers of France if they fell. They bought their own truck, trained in the forest at navigation, dug "bomb craters" and trained at getting their truck out of them, practiced bearing each other on a stretcher around all kinds of obstacles. Cartier contributed silver badges that promised to make the ambulance unit the most glamorous on the battlefield.

Soon a sense that this was all glamor and no guts began to wear on Hasey and his comrades. The German threat was real and ever present, but did not yet manifest as war. Meanwhile, they chafed at sitting comfortably in Paris while their French friends garrisoned the lines.

Finally, in late fall 1939, there came a chance to help a beset country and to train for the coming war with Germany. The Soviet Union invaded Finland with an undisguised goal of expansion. Hasey and a small team of drivers and stretcher bearers hurried there to help, thrilled. To his mind he was finally going to fight for democracy against the bullies.

When the ambulance team arrived in Finland along with the winter, the grateful Finns gave them white coats and a white ambulance for camouflage. Only hours after that, the Soviets started bombing in the neighborhood. From that moment on, Jack and his friends were in danger, either speeding to the scene of fighting to carry out the wounded, suffering under bombardment, or defending themselves against the assault of life-threatening polar cold. Hasey had left America to free himself of his middle-class cocoon, and he had certainly succeeded. Safety was nowhere to be found when Soviet bombers operated freely without opposition. And as often as he was racing to rescue the wounded, he was helping in an operating room, covered in gore, or bearing away the dead.

Hasey not only passed that test, he actually thrived surrounded by blood, frostbite, and death. He thrived on purpose and comradeship and found that, while he was often scared, he managed his fear well. Then, one night, he and a friend were using blowtorches to get their ambulance's engine started and attracted a Soviet bomber. Too late they heard it diving, and they were nearly killed, a burst block of icy earth slamming into Hasey's arm, leaving it twisted in unnatural angles. The Winter War was over for him.

Now Hasey was the patient, and his friends evacuated him to Helsinki, and from there to the United States, where on his arrival he was overwhelmed by print and radio reporters. The "folks back home," it turned out, had followed his unit's adventures as something like the first Americans to fight in the terrible world war nearly everyone expected. For some he represented the best of the American conscience; for others he embodied a warning about getting dragged into Europe's troubles.

Those pushing for America to prepare itself to intervene adopted him, and a large, New York–based operation, the American Volunteer Ambulance Corps (AVAC), offered him a contract as an official spokesman. His new job was to talk about the pressing need in Europe, the threat of war, the opportunity to help by funding ambulances.

Soon after, he was shaken by news that Finland had surrendered to the Soviets, who swallowed a massive portion of the country. But he enjoyed a happy reunion with his family in Boston. Then there was a rally at a local school where they celebrated him like the guy who won the state football championship instead of getting beaten by the Soviets. Then Jack hit the road for a speaking tour, his arm in a sling. That road even led to the White House to have tea with Eleanor Roosevelt one day.

By then Hitler had acted on his promise to annex part of Poland, thus triggering war with Britain and France. France was still free, the Germans had not invaded, but everyone expected invasion soon, while the United States watched from the sidelines. Hasey was desperate to get back to his beloved France, but decided that for now he could do more by rallying American attention and encouraging material support in the form of ambulances.

After meeting the First Lady he met senators, governors, and ambassadors. He spoke to countless reporters. His favorites were the famous actors and actresses, who he found were actually the least likely to offer empty-headed bromides about how, gosh, they hoped it would all turn out okay in the end. They tended to hate the fascists.

As the weeks passed Jack Hasey grew increasingly impatient, as he saw little sign of his fellow Americans rising to the threat of fascism. He saved a special ire for Senator Burton K. Wheeler and Charles Lindbergh. Wheeler could be heard on the radio warning Americans that "satanically clever" propagandists—and "international bankers" (a code word for Jews)—were trying to drive Americans "like sheep to the slaughtering pens." And while Hasey was speaking to audiences, famous aviator Lindbergh was speaking to audiences for "America First!" and warning Americans that they must not be tricked into war with Germany, that war between the two nations would only sap the strength of the "white race," which must be preserved against any challenge by so-called lesser races. And, besides, Lindbergh argued that Germany could be negotiated with after its eventual victory. "The only reason that we are in danger of becoming involved in this war is because there are powerful elements in America who desire us to take part," he said, referring like Wheeler to an imagined Jewish conspiracy. "They represent a small minority of the American people, but they control much of the machinery of influence and propaganda."

Jack Hasey's lowest moment on the road came when he returned to his alma mater, Columbia, in New York. Speaking to the Student Union, he despaired over trying to make the students see the threat facing Europe. He felt they had a terribly misguided hope that even after Czechoslovakia and Poland, a peace could still be talked out or a revolution in Germany would remove the Nazi regime and restore sanity. He found the students naive and dreamy, as if they lived in a different world. Some even hectored, suggesting that Hasey was a fascist warmonger himself. He could not perceive a single potential ambulance driver among them. (Of course, only two years earlier, Jack had been the naive Columbia boy, and maybe a smart aleck, too, and quite possibly no one would have seen the eventual blood-soaked ambulance driver in him, either.)

Soon Jack started to feel like one of the chorus girls back in Paris: sent out every night to do the same song and dance. But that changed when word suddenly came over the radio of the German invasion of Denmark and Norway. France must be next. He quit his job with the AVAC, hung up his dancing shoes, and got on the fastest ship for Europe.

Landing in Portugal, he hurried overland to the French border and crossed it just in time to meet a rush of refugees fleeing Belgium and France in the other direction. Germany had invaded, the Maginot Line was overrun by German armor, and Paris was next. Still, Jack hurried on. He only succeeded in getting himself trapped.

Hasey made it to Biarritz, on the Atlantic coast just over the border from Spain. There he joined old friends and coworkers and tried to figure out what to do next. But very soon black Wehrmacht staff cars started rolling into town. They pulled up before the hotels, commandeering them for officers, and a sign went over the door of a fine restaurant that Hasey knew from his days selling jewelry: "For Officers Only." Then trucks came bearing troops; Jack figured there were about six thousand Germans garrisoning the town within hours. In the coming days the casino became the club for soldiers, and a German band was installed. The Germans tried to be social in their way—they made it clear that the local women should join them in their club. At first, all of the French women laughed off the idea of dancing with the invader. But within only days some began to go in. It was a matter of getting good food, which was already becoming scarce. The Germans combed the town for weapons, declared a 9:00 p.m. curfew, and hung swastikas. Lying low, Hasey bristled at the sight of those flags and those gray-green uniforms in his adopted France.

On the radio came the voice of Marshal Philippe Pétain, the new chief of state of occupied—what would become known as Vichy—

France. Pétain had been a hero in World War I, the "Lion of Verdun," who had bitterly defended that town from a German attack. But now, at age eighty-four, he was docile. When the Germans were bearing down on Paris, Pétain feared it would be left a broken ruin; when Churchill encouraged the French to carry on a guerilla war, Pétain argued it was hopeless. Ultimately, despite arguing that he had no choice but to oversee an armistice with Germany, Pétain seemed to welcome a regime that would restore old-fashioned ways, respect for the proper order, and quash the permissiveness of modernity. Soon Pétain's regime replaced France's old slogan of "Liberté, égalité, fraternité" to the more Teutonic "Travail, famille, patrie" (Work, family, fatherland). When the radio broadcast Pétain's voice, Jack Hasey switched it off.

In Biarritz's bars Hasey heard another name in the coming days: de Gaulle. It seemed one French colonel had done remarkably in the otherwise disastrous Battle of France. That May, Charles de Gaulle had won a lopsided victory in a battle of tanks and infantry at a critical crossroads in northeastern France. He could not hold it, though, for a lack of air support. When the Germans broke French defenses, de Gaulle called on his fellow officers to retreat from France so they could rally and keep up the fight. Some few thousand did. Having made it to Britain, de Gaulle called for resistance now over the BBC. Jack had not heard the broadcast, but others had, and when he talked to them Hasey could see the despair in their eyes replaced by light. De Gaulle, he decided, was his man. Now he only had to find a way to escape occupied France and join him in England.[2]

Hasey managed to get on a crowded refugee ship with other civilians—Poles fleeing yet another country, a group of nuns, a rabbi who blessed him—and escaped to England in August 1940. Having nowhere else to go, he phoned London's Cartier representative, who happily welcomed him to stay at his home in the green suburb of Putney. At first Jack tried to get involved in the war by forming a new American field ambulance unit. But he was rebuffed at Joe Kennedy's American embassy—the ambassador wanted less, not more American involvement in what he considered a purely European matter. Soon after, Hasey's host surprised him by having none other than Charles de Gaulle over for dinner. It turned out they were longtime friends. Two days later, Jack Hasey was enlisted with the Free French and reported to its headquarters west of London.

At first Jack thought he would serve in a field ambulance unit, but the Free French had not organized one yet. Until an ambulance unit could be formed, it was his strange fortune to fall in with a group of Foreign Legion officers practicing at a nearby rifle range. He learned that they had fought the Germans in Norway before being forced to retreat that spring. Henceforth they were called les Norvégiens. He returned to train with them the next day, and the next, until finally they invited him to join their unit. After some months of proving himself, the unit's officers voted to put Jack in charge of a section of forty legionnaires. And, a few months after that, in fall 1940, Jack Hasey himself was setting out on a British-Indian liner around Africa, hoping to drive the Italians from the Red Sea colonies.

Of course, Hasey had seen the French Foreign Legion depicted in the movies—Gary Cooper had practically made a career out of playing a legionnaire. But he thought the depictions of flinty antiheroes escaping a shadowy past were an exaggeration, everyone enlisting under false names, everyone a fugitive. Only it was more than half true, Hasey learned. Nobody asked Hasey's background; no one volunteered theirs. The only background was the one they shared: the battles they fought together, the son-of-a-bitch officer they endured. Their nation was, and loyalty was to, the Foreign Legion.

Still, Jack Hasey learned a thing or two about his men. There was Perez, who had fought for the German-supported nationalists in Spain until Francisco Franco's forces had bombed innocents and Perez switched sides to the Republicans. There was the graying, Teutonic ox Weisskopf. There was Blashiek, the mighty Pole. There were black West African veterans. One senior officer had been a Catholic priest. There were "unclassifiable" men of any or all races and nationalities named Jean and Roberto. There were also Miguel and Manuel: a great many were veterans of the Spanish Civil War who battled and lost to antidemocratic forces there and had fled to France. This gave the Thirteenth Demi-Brigade a particularly antifascist essence.* Jack had received his blood baptism many times over in Finland, but the Bridgewater boy was still keenly aware of the differences between him and these hard-bitten soldiers.

Things moved fast after Jack and the Free French landed in Port Sudan; they were the last arrivals of an international assembly set to attack the Italians and Vichy French in Eritrea to the south. Awaiting the Free French were Indians, Scots, and South Africans, who now all went by rail as deep into the desert as possible, then transferred to trucks as far they could advance among the scorched stones.

Then it was a battle from stony hilltop to hilltop as the Italians and their allies defended their strongholds high up. The Free French had brought their artillery, which was a godsend, and the British contributed some bombing, which the Italians could not answer until later in the campaign; but it was still a horrible labor, day after day with limited water, under an attacking sun and rock-shattering Italian artillery. Sometimes Hasey and his platoon crawled all day under fire; sometimes they fought many hours-long battles trying to relieve comrades pinned by elite Italian Alpine Savoie Chasseurs. Sometimes they listened to cries of wounded soldiers of many nations weakly echoing around hillsides under a burning sun, without water, without hope of being retrieved.

Once, when his section came upon some young Italian prisoners being led to the rear, Jack Hasey took the opportunity to talk to them.

"Whenever you see an Italian over forty years old, shoot him dead, don't take him prisoner," one said.

"Why?"

"Because they are responsible for all this. It's their war, not ours. They put Mussolini in power. We didn't."

Day after day, Hasey's legionnaires and the various prongs of British, Indian, and South African forces struggled eastward toward the critical

---

*As many as ten thousand antifascist refugees of the Spanish Civil War, from Spain and around the world, fled to France around 1939. Interred, they were offered the chance to enlist in the Foreign Legion, which some thousands gladly accepted, eager to deliver on their grudge against the Nazis. Some of these veterans were among the first to enter Paris in 1944, repeating the motto, "First Paris, then Madrid," hoping that the Allies would repay their sacrifices by liberating Spain.

Red Sea and port town of Massawa. Standing between them and Massawa were alpine strongholds defended by dug-in, cornered men. A Sikh company of the Indian Army's First Punjab Regiment, Third Battalion—who'd already seen fighting in Libya—were scaling a peak when a rain of grenades came down on them. Lance Naik (Lance Corporal) Babu Singh, a shard-slashed eye streaming blood, slung a boy from a neighboring village back in eastern Punjab over his shoulder and carried him down the hill. The safety of Charlie Company of the Scottish Cameron Highlanders would sometimes depend on a Hindu company of the Rajputana Rifles to defend their ridge; sometimes vice versa.

The most important bastion on the road to Massawa was the six-thousand-foot Mount Sanchil and its surrounding ridges, and the Allied fighters of many lands struggled to drive the Italians and their Eritrean troops from these heights for weeks. The Allies rushed it repeatedly, covered by their own artillery, but they would often arrive at a summit in such reduced numbers or cut-up shape that they could not defend their won ground afterward. One night, Richpal Ram, a twenty-year veteran of the Indian Army from southern Punjab, led his platoon up against Italian positions under brutal mortar and machine gun fire. He reached the objective, but he had only thirty men behind him who could stand. For the next four hours, from midnight to 4:00 a.m., he repulsed six Italian counterattacks before running out of bullets and leading the survivors back to Allied lines behind his bayonet. Somehow he was able to repeat the entire experience a few days later, leading a company melded from the survivors of two. In the fight up the rocks he had his foot blown off, yet he continued to try to wave his men up the hill until he was hit again, bleeding to death as he assured those around him, "We'll capture the objective." They did not. It took many more days of fighting to drive the Italians from the spot.

Finally, Jack Hasey and his legionnaires were under the incessant guns of the Italian fort at Massawa. As they moved slowly forward and up, Italian bombers appeared, unopposed by Allied air cover, and Jack and his men hurried for cover until the bombers exhausted themselves. Then moving in a daze, the legionnaires continued the crawl uphill to attack machine gun nests surrounding the place. This slowly advancing siege took days. One by one, the men in his section disappeared under the bombs and artillery, machine guns and rifles. Only later when he tried to find his men would he discover that only one in four could still stand. Hasey wondered at his survival and later thought of the nuns with whom he had fled France—and the rabbi's blessing.

He did not think, then, about the cause for which he was fighting—neither the good he was trying to do, nor the evil of war that led him to kill several men at once with a grenade. His fatigue- and artillery-numbed mind only mechanically moved his fingers: pull pin, throw grenade up hill, drop, wait for crash, peek up carefully, observe a motionless foot hanging out from the nest—a good sign. Advance, reach for another grenade.

Then the fort ran up the white flag and it was done. The key Axis air and submarine base in the Red Sea was won by the Allies.

The town of Massawa itself, which wanted nothing of the Italian fascists' fight, opened its doors to the Allied soldiers, who finally got a decent drink of water and much else. It was a moment to breathe before these legionnaires (though they did not know it) were to be shipped north to a brutal fight in Syria facing Vichy French soldiers. After a few days of recovery, with the Allied troops resting in former Italian barracks, a signal captain came into the officers' mess hall where Jack and some others were eating.

"One moment please," he said to the quieting room. "I have the honor to inform you gentlemen that in radio broadcasts in both Rome and Vichy, the following men have been condemned to death." He read a long list, on which was Jack Hasey.

Now a wanted man like the Spanish Republicans and others among the men, Jack truly was a legionnaire.

"A toast to the condemned," someone said, rising, and the men lifted their Italian wine to the wanted men.[3]

The next individual to enter this story cut a striking figure: he was six foot five or taller, with sandy hair and pale eyes. His parents were Norwegian, and Norwegian was his first language. He was named after the famous Norwegian Antarctic explorer, Amundsen, too. But Roald Dahl had grown up in Cardiff, Wales.

Dahl's route to Syria in June 1941 started two years earlier in British Tanganyika (now Tanzania) in southeast Africa. He was then twenty-three, working for Shell Oil, supplying fuel for mines and farm operations—bored, but learning Swahili and enjoying the country's landscape and wildlife. In summer 1939 he named the two lizards who invaded his Shell-supplied bungalow Hitler and Mussolini, one slight and one fat.

When Britain declared war on Germany in September 1939, Dahl enlisted in the local imperial force, the King's African Rifles, and the lanky twenty-three-year-old with no military experience whatsoever was immediately made a lieutenant. It was like this throughout the empire: wherever British men found themselves working for oil companies, or mines, or growing coffee and cotton in Africa or Asia they duly enlisted. And the British Empire being what it was, these men—mostly neophytes—were immediately commissioned as officers and put in charge of indigenous soldiers who very often had vastly more experience in soldiering than the white men. By the end of the war, truly experienced native soldiers were far more likely to ascend to higher ranks, but the British had to learn lessons the hard way in the intervening years.

Dahl's first job was to police the road out of British Tanganyika toward neutral Portuguese Mozambique and to seize any Germans fleeing the country that way as enemy aliens. This formerly having been a German colony before being lost in World War I, there were far more Germans in the country than British, and they were to be interned in camps near Dar-es-Salaam. Roald Dahl, at least, had the good sense to realize he was an utter amateur at this, and on this first mission took his platoon's sergeant aside and said in Swahili, "Look, Sergeant, I am sure you realize that I am not a soldier." The man had the good sense and good tact to suppress a smile and simply replied that he understood. "So, if you see me doing something silly, please tell me." The soldier politely agreed to do so.

After a couple of months of this, Dahl felt he wasn't truly doing his bit in the war, and enlisted in the Royal Air Force (RAF). After some training at a small base to the north in Kenya, he was sent for his real course at a vast base and flight school in the middle of a desert in Iraq: RAF Habbaniya. Dahl could hardly believe his eyes at the size of the place. How could this square mile of a city exist in what he considered the middle of nowhere? Great rows of barracks and bungalows and hangars and gardens and recreation halls; ludicrous street names like Bond and Regent.

He trained for six hours a day throughout spring and summer 1940 in the biplane Hawker Harts and Audaxes that Tony Dudgeon and his friends would use one year later, modified by them to carry racks of bombs for their desperate countersiege against the Iraqis. Dahl frankly hated the place. It was far too hot and desolate and, he wrote home, he would be thrilled simply "to see ordinary men and actual women doing ordinary things in ordinary places once more." Then his course was complete, and Dahl was rated an above average single-engine fighter pilot.

He was then ordered to Libya, where it would be his mission to fly Gladiators against the Italians above the battle lines. Dahl knew that the Gladiators were well out of date, and that the pilots defending London were in vastly more powerful Hurricanes and Spitfires, but for him a Gladiator was the most powerful and maneuverable plane he'd ever flown. Little did he know when he left Habbaniya that his first experience flying a Gladiator would be just about his last.

Arriving from Iraq in Egypt, he picked up his new Gladiator at a base on the Suez Canal and, having no training on the craft, was ordered west toward the frontline battle with the Italians. He took off, made some stops to fuel along the route and, at the last stop, received directions to his little makeshift airstrip in the desert, where he would find his new comrades of the RAF's Eightieth Squadron. This would be little more than a cleared patch of scrub, some fuel barrels, and tents—the kind of place where Tony Dudgeon was then being ground down daily, watching a succession of pilots fly off, never to return.

Roald Dahl, too, flew off in that direction, and never to return—at least by air. He had received bad directions or had misunderstood them, because the little airfield was nowhere to be seen once he reached the stated coordinates. He turned and turned, searched and searched, and found nothing but a vast plain of boulders. As the sun descended, Dahl grew desperate to find a place to land before full darkness; he'd simply have to walk for days back to Mersa Matruh or hope to be found by a passing plane. He picked a spot where he thought he'd have enough space to land before crashing into rocks, and he'd have to hope for the best.

The best was not in store for Roald Dahl. He touched down as the sun set and, still rolling at great speed, the Gladiator's wheels struck a large rock, the nose slammed deep into the gravel, and Dahl's head crashed into his gun site. He faded in and out of consciousness as he dragged himself away from his plane, which had started to burn. Machine gun ammunition started popping around him, as it would for the Italian pilot picked up by the Arab Palestinian they called Reading near Baghdad. Unbeknownst to Dahl, he had crashed in a no-man's-land between Allied and Italian forces and, lucky for him, some British soldiers saw the flames light up the dusk and dared to investigate.

It took six long months for the young Dahl to recover from his head injuries, burns, and ravaged face in a hospital in Alexandria. When the bandages came off he was just happy to find he wasn't blind, but to the surprise of all, he made a full recovery. After being recertified to fly, he was eager to finally join the Eightieth Squadron, which, he learned then in mid-April 1941, was in Greece. The relentless German drive through Greece had recently begun, and though the Greek resistance was determined, and the Allies had landed to back them up, the Axis numbers were overpowering. So Dahl reported to Ismailia on the Suez Canal to arrange to join his squadron across the Mediterranean, only to be told he would fly there himself in a new Hurricane.

The good news was that this was an utterly different craft from his usual 1930s-era biplanes; it was a modern, single-wing fighter that could go toe-to-toe with the Luftwaffe. The bad news was that Dahl had no training on it whatsoever. But he and the plane were badly needed in Greece, where there was almost no air support for the British expeditionary force on the ground, nor for the Royal Navy that would soon have to rescue them in their retreat. Dahl's superiors allowed him a few training flights in the Hurricane before he left for his destination, a small airfield outside Athens. He was horrified to learn that the RAF was spread so thin, that a single fighter and a single pilot could be so desperately needed that they would send him and this expensive, rare craft into a running battle with essentially no training. What hope, he thought, could there be for him, for the war?

A couple of days later he lifted off from the Suez desert, crossed hours of sea, and drained two external fuel tanks before locating his bleak makeshift airstrip in Greece. After rolling to a stop, he had to be lifted out of the small cockpit by two ground-crew, his six-foot-five frame was so badly cramped. They helped him down and let him untangle slowly in the sun, a gentler sun than Egypt's.

"I don't see the point of it," one of the men standing over him said. "You bring a brand-new kite, an absolutely spanking brand-new kite straight from the factory and you bring it all the way from ruddy Egypt to this godforsaken place and what's goin' to 'appen to it?"

"What?"

"Crash bang wallop! Shot down in flames! Explodin' in the air! Ground-strafed by the One-O-Nines [Messerschmitt 109s] right 'ere where we're standin' this very moment! Why, this kite won't last a week in this place!" To Dahl it didn't seem the man was trying to scare him, or even being unkind; he was truly exasperated by the waste.

Dahl tried to tell him that it couldn't possibly be that certain. The man replied that the German army and Luftwaffe were pouring south-ward in their direction with astronomically superior numbers, hundreds of fighters and bombers.

"What have we got?" Dahl asked.

"What we've got is exactly what you see on this ruddy field! Four-teen 'urricanes! No, it isn't. It's gone up to fifteen now you've brought this one out!"

If the ground crew officer's welcome was jarringly direct, Dahl's squadron leader was merely indifferent. Dahl reported to him in the shack that served as the ops room, with the man hardly reacting to Dahl's arrival. One more man, it seemed, and one more Hurricane wouldn't matter much; besides, the officer had probably sent many, many young men like this tall newcomer to death in the sky. It was better for the squadron leader, perhaps, not to learn every pilot's face.

Having only trained for seven flight hours in a Hurricane, not in-cluding his cramped flight across the Mediterranean, Roald Dahl was thrown into battle above Greece the morning after his arrival. He flew out by himself to patrol grounds over the coast and some friendly cargo ships and was met on the spot, as if it were a rendezvous, by six German Junker Ju 88 medium bombers, whose front and rear gunners poured bullets toward Dahl's Hurricane in a burning spray of tracers. He relished the power of his modern plane, which allowed him to throttle up to the twin-engine Germans and, almost to Dahl's wonder, shoot up one plane's engine. He'd maimed it, and it sunk toward a mountainside, and though he was thrilled with his first hit, Dahl was also happy to see three parachutes emerge from the Junkers.

Over the next days, though he was six months late to his job, and though it seemed like a hopeless task, Dahl discovered that he was actually quite good at casting his machine gun fire in front of Messerschmitts and Junkers. What's more, he had an extraordinary run of luck. In those mid-April hours over Greece, the British and Allies falling back and back toward the sea beneath him, Dahl was typically outnumbered ten to one in the air. His plane was roundly peppered with bullet holes. Yet somehow he lived on, even though he often flew three or four sorties a day. Within a week, though, three of his squadronmates were dead.

By the third week of April, General Wavell in Cairo ordered the man in charge of Allied forces in Greece, Lieutenant-General Henry Wilson—who would direct the battle for Syria-Lebanon in June—to complete a fighting retreat to the sea and evacuation. By that time, to cover this evacuation from the air, at least on the Eightieth Squadron's long stretch of Greek coast, there was only Roald Dahl and six other pilots. Dahl thought it a kind of deadly farce.

As the harried days of fighting wore on and the overwhelming numbers of German and Italian air and ground forces poured down the country, each sortie took on more of the character of a suicide mission. Some of the pilots quite naturally asked their commanding officer whether or not it made more sense to fly their Hurricanes to Egypt so they could contribute, at least, to the fight in the Western Desert. Keeping the precious Hurricanes in Greece meant only certain destruction.

"Our job is to keep these seven planes going so that we can give air cover to . . . the navy," responded the adjutant.

"With seven machines?" one of the pilots asked. "It's ridiculous!"
"I'm only passing on orders."

Later, when the adjutant wasn't around, one of the pilots said, "You know what I think? I think someone wants to say that the brave RAF in Greece fought gallantly to the last pilot and last plane." And Roald Dahl feared he was right. (Did a similar conversation take place among the Iraqi Army being pounded by RAF Habbaniya when they themselves had little air cover before they broke from their position on the plateau?)

Before long the conquering Luftwaffe arrived to bomb the Eightieth Squadron's airstrip, and its remaining seven planes and pilots retreated to a landing place farther down the coast, slightly more distant from the advancing Axis. The Luftwaffe, of course, found this quickly and bombed it, leaving only five Hurricanes now in one piece on this half of Greece, but no equipment, no ground crew, and only enough fuel to reach Crete. So, finally, their superiors gave up on any more resistance and Roald Dahl and his few remaining squadronmates were packed into a little old transport, which somehow dodged the Luftwaffe infesting the skies, and made it across the Mediterranean to safety—for now. That was about the day that RAF Habbaniya was besieged by the Iraqis.

Dahl had a much-needed rest in Alexandria before he received orders, near the end of May, to proceed from Egypt to Haifa in the north of British Palestine. He didn't know it yet, but there was about to be a lot of work for him in the skies over Syria.[4]

11

"He Who Practices Deceit"

Henri Dentz and Rudolf Rahn on the Eve of the War for Syria-Lebanon

IN CHARGE OF Vichy Syria-Lebanon was General Henri Dentz, and he was nothing if not a loyal soldier. He had been posted in Syria as a younger man, in the 1920s, as a midcareer army officer, in years when trouble simmered between colonial authorities and the Druze people of the south. Dentz followed orders from his superiors, then, to invite Druze leaders to Damascus to parley under the white flag. He also followed orders to throw those leaders in prison—white flag be damned—when they arrived.

Dentz, it seemed, would do as he was told, no matter the cost to reputation or conscience. This had been tested the previous spring, June 1940, when he was directed personally to surrender Paris to the Germans. And again he did his duty, however distasteful. From then on Dentz loyally followed Marshal Philippe Pétain and Vichy. Many thousands of soldiers fled France to keep up the fight, many tens of thousands in France's African colonies, especially, rallied to Charles de Gaulle and the Free French forces; but not Dentz. For him, a government that cooperated with Hitler's Germany was still his rightful government; those who refused to follow Pétain's orders were mutineers.

In early 1941 Pétain's government sent Dentz back to Syria-Lebanon to administer these colonies, the League of Nations "Mandates" that France had held since the defeat of the Ottoman Empire in World War I. For Dentz this was just another duty. He was not enthusiastic about the Germans or Italians in particular, though like many he had doubts about democracy's ability to survive. He distrusted the British and suspected some global conspiracy of the Jews, as did so many anti-Semites the world over. But his real motive in serving Vichy in the Levant was the same as it had always been: duty.

Tall and straight, with a thick, dark, Gallic mustache, General Henri Dentz was now, in May 1941, in the grand Résidence des Pins, the palatial headquarters of the Vichy French government of Syria-Lebanon. The place sat among the cedars at the edge of Beirut, and its arcades and arches turned pink when the sun sank into the Mediterranean below the city. It was impossible to call the building elegant—it was originally built to be a casino, after all—but it was at least grandiose. Today's business was anything but genial. Representatives of state and military intelligence offices arrived at the palace to report to Dentz that Beirut and Damascus were infested with agents.

By the terms of the armistice with the Axis, the French colonies would remain under the control of vassal France, their administrations left to Vichy, their colonial armies officially neutral in the world war. But after the capitulation, the Axis declared that there would be a special delegation posted to Beirut to facilitate commercial and political "harmony" between the new France and the Germans and Italians in the Mediterranean. Dentz, who had worked in military intelligence in the past, had to have known that the delegation was also a nest of Axis agents. The Italians were bad enough. French agents followed Italian agents from their headquarters in the St. George Hotel to meetings with various power brokers, newspaper editors, and Syrian informers. Their aim was to buy support for eventual Italian supremacy in the Levant, whatever the promises that conquered France could retain its colonial holdings.

But, as described by Dentz's military and colonial intelligence officers, the German conspirators made the Italians look like amateurs. These German men and women doubled as archaeologists or posed as journalists or even as Jewish refugees. Tailing the German agents from their headquarters in another fine Beirut hotel, the Vichy French discovered a stream of silver flowing to local Arab notables and journalists. The Germans rekindled old relationships with former Ottoman officers who had served beside them in World War I, and they built a spy network among the locals. Working in opposition to the Italians, they were laying the groundwork for the day when the Vichy were replaced by native puppet rulers—Christian in Beirut, Muslim in Damascus—whose strings were held by the Reich. If outwardly the Axis promised to preserve the integrity of the defeated French Empire, in fact they were already preparing to become the Levant's true masters.

Now there were reports of the most audacious subversion yet. One of the Reich's Foreign Office's men, one Werner von Hentig, hardly made a secret of his wooing of native leaders to Germany's side. Hentig had recently invited them to Beirut's Hotel Metropole for screenings of a film about the fall of France before the relentless tanks of the Wehrmacht. And he was spreading the idea that Germany was considering the creation of an Arab confederation in Iraq and the Levant, to be centered on Damascus.

The intelligence briefing over, Henri Dentz wrote an appeal to Vichy France for an intercession with the Germans and Italians to stop undermining his administration. Other than watch their activities, that was all he could do.

The Axis were not trustworthy partners, yet it was Dentz's duty to partner with them. Indeed, some weeks later, orders arrived from France telling Dentz to partner with their German conquerors more closely than ever. They were orders that might test any man less dutiful than Henri Dentz.[1]

On May 1, 1941, Rudolf Rahn, a diplomat in the Reich's Foreign Office, was enjoying a spring holiday with his family in the Bavarian Alps when a telegram arrived for him from his director. He was to rush up to Munich, the orders read, where he would find a plane waiting to take him to occupied Paris.

Rahn was forty-one, already a veteran of many diplomatic postings, tall with dark hair but softening in middle age. He was a Nazi, having joined the party early, and was on his way to becoming a favorite of the upper Nazi clique. But though an ardent German nationalist, he considered himself a staunch Francophile, and his dearest professional hope was that he himself might be central in bringing France and Germany together in this new German-led age for Europe and the world. And, though he didn't know it yet, it was this goal of harmony between the Reich and a reconstructed France toward which he would soon be working in the Levant.

Arriving at the embassy in Paris a few hours later, Rahn was guided by his chief toward the compound's garden, where they could talk unheard.

"You know the situation in Iraq," the man said. The fighting had just started at Habbaniya. "Should the Arabs resist the English invasion, it will only be with our help; otherwise, it is inconceivable. . . . As yet, the führer is unwilling to believe that the French are truly ready to be loyal. Only by showing him an example can we convince him. [Vichy head of state Admiral François] Darlan shares my opinion, and is prepared to instruct the High Commissioner in Syria, General Dentz, to grant passage to German troops and aircraft en route to Iraq and to provide weapons, upon request, for the Iraqi Army."

Rahn eagerly accepted his mission, handed to him instead of Werner von Hentig so as not to provoke General Dentz, who had recently complained about Hentig's meddling. Rahn was handed a case full of money and a radio transmitter, and was directed to an awaiting Heinkel where he met his traveling companion, a Vichy French official whose task was to assure General Dentz that this was the genuine will of Pétain's government. They took off.

That night they landed at a solitary airstrip on Italian Rhodes, where there were already two more Heinkels awaiting him. Also there was Fritz Grobba, on his way to Baghdad to head the German mission in Iraq. Rhodes was the easternmost point of Axis control in the Mediterranean, and from here Grobba couldn't avoid flying over Syria and refueling in Aleppo to reach Baghdad to begin helping the Golden Square. Grobba asked Rahn whether the three Heinkels could safely enter French airspace. Would the French attack them? Why else did he have a French official with him? asked Rahn. Rahn asked the Italian air officer in charge to have all the Heinkels' swastikas overpainted with French Air Force roundels—a veneer, indeed.

The next day, while the planes were being painted, Grobba and Rahn, two strange tourists, had an enjoyable time exploring the island's Crusader castle with its unique red stone. Then the two departed in their disguised planes, landing at Aleppo, Syria, hours later. As Grobba's planes refueled, the Luftwaffe personnel with them wanted to have a look around the city. These Luftwaffe officers became surly when Rudolf Rahn firmly insisted that they take off their uniforms before leaving the French air base. Why did they need to hide themselves, weren't they the conquerors? After that Grobba's mission flew on and Rahn was frankly happy to be rid of the haughty airmen. There was much for him to do, and diplomacy was called for.

Rahn found the reception of the French officer in command of this Syrian base quite cool, and a sign of the general reception that the Germany military might receive here, but the presence of the Vichy official and written orders from Paris helped. The next day Rahn flew on to Beirut in a French plane to better disguise his movements, and he was taken to the Résidence des Pins, where Dentz, also cool, was waiting. First the Vichy representative spoke to the general alone. Then, Dentz having Admiral Darlan's signature on the papers brought from France authenticated, Rahn was led through.

"My father departed the Alsace in 1871 so that his son would not be required to learn German," he began before Rahn could get a word out, "so you can imagine, Mister Ambassador, with what pleasure I welcome you."

The French, and the Dentz family in particular, had already experienced German incursion, when the Franco-Prussian War of 1870–71 saw the transfer of their ancestral Alsace from France to Germany. Dentz then complained about the undermining activities of Werner von Hentig, who had hinted to the Syrian Arabs that they would soon be independent of France in a new united Arab kingdom. But this speech, this show of resistance, was most likely for the purpose of Dentz's self-image or self-respect. In truth, Dentz's speech could only be just that, a show; for if Dentz kicked Rahn out of the country, there would be consequences for him personally and most likely for occupied—hostage—France. In fact, a few days before Rahn arrived, Dentz had already received a wireless message from the office of the Vichy War Ministry: "It is not impossible that you may shortly be faced with a German attempt to give assistance to Iraq. . . . It is not possible to treat the armed forces of Germany as hostile, but you would naturally oppose with force any intervention by the British forces." Dentz's compliance was already certain.

Rahn had the professional sense to let Dentz's anger pass, even thanking Dentz for his frankness. Rahn then made his diplomatic sally. Unlike Hentig, he said, he was there to join with Dentz and France. Syria's defense was untenable against British aggression and meddling without French-German cooperation. What was more, their cooperation here could help assure peace in Europe. Help him, Rahn asked, to supply the Iraqis with weapons, so that the English would be tied up for months fighting them. In the meantime, Rommel would have greater rein in the Western Desert. Then Dentz could resupply and dig in, preparing for any Allied attempt at retribution. Rahn spoke for an hour, persuading rather than ordering, and seeking to show why there could be little hope for British and French harmony—only French and German reconciliation and shared progress.

"That has a certain sense," Dentz said finally, acting like someone who had a choice. He had received instructions from Vichy to cooperate, because at that moment negotiations were taking place in Paris between the collaborationist government and the Germans; they were nearing their apparently successful end, in fact. The day that Rahn met Dentz, Vichy leader François Darlan and Adolf Hitler were speaking at the führer's mountain retreat at Berchtesgaden, working out the terms of German-Vichy military cooperation. Known as the Paris Protocols, and eventually signed later in May, they called for Germany to free almost seven thousand French prisoners seized during the conquest of their country, ease travel restrictions between the northern occupied zone of France and southern Vichy-administered zone, publicly disclaim any German interest in seizing French colonies in the Levant and West Africa, and reduce the charges Germany extracted from Vichy as the price of occupation. The Germans and Italians would also redistribute weapons they'd confiscated in Syria-Lebanon after the fall of France to the French forces in the Levant.

Besides the fact that the Vichy French were seeking better terms for their conquered country, and despite the fact that Pétain and Darlan expressed no public disdain for Nazism, many in the upper echelons of the Vichy military had a deep personal resentment for the British. If it hadn't started with the British Expeditionary Force fleeing before the German blitz, it started with the British destruction of the French fleet at the port of Mers-el-Kébir in Algeria in summer 1940. In that attack thirteen hundred French sailors died when the Royal Navy sunk six French warships to keep them out of the hands of the Germans. But it didn't end there: since the fall of France, the Royal Navy had continued to closely police French imports for possible war material, seizing 167 ships by spring 1941. Vichy accused the British of trying to starve and ruin them, a neutral nation.

When the Paris Protocols between Germany and Vichy France were signed later in May, the French offered the Afrika Korps rights to use a French Tunisian port farther away from the Royal Navy's Malta base, a French submarine base in West Africa, and a small, discreet port in Lebanon. They also codified French and German cooperation in the defense of Syria-Lebanon.

By the end of Dentz and Rahn's long meeting, they agreed to a plan. Rahn promised that German Luftwaffe personnel would stay out of Damascus and Beirut (Rahn himself would use the alias Renouard), and stick to their airfields, so as not to convince Arab nationalists that the Germans were there to liberate them from French rule. In turn, besides allowing the Germans the use of Syrian airfields, Dentz would facilitate the delivery of French weapons through Syria to Iraq—twenty thousand rifles, six hundred light and heavy machine guns, many tens of thousands of grenades, a battery of seventy-five-millimeter field guns, hundreds of thousands of rounds of ammunition, and some trucks. And Dentz promised to arrange for the Iraqis to be trained by French instructors on any unfamiliar weapons. They would both work together, in the meantime, to shore up the defense of the colony against anticipated British reprisals.

Only a week before this, Dentz had personally assured the US ambassador to Syria-Lebanon that he would strenuously resist any incursion of the Luftwaffe seeking to use Syrian airfields for an attack on Crete. The French had already resolved to lie if Luftwaffe planes were spotted in Syria. They would "deny all allegations," stated a German report, and if a British reconnaissance plane caught the Germans on the ground, they would claim they were "emergency landings made in error by aircraft of unknown origin purchased by the Iraq government." Vichy passed these instructions to Dentz. "Have received and understood your messages," General Dentz sent back.[2]

To disguise the fact that the smart young people at Bletchley Park were reading diplomatic book codes and decrypting German Enigma machine messages using a loudly clacking computer, the British gave themselves alibis, of sorts. When they sent Ultra-derived intelligence to the Middle East, they suggested in the messages that an agent in the field had made the discoveries, or perhaps a surveillance plane. For example, when one of Bletchley Park's computers decoded a German message to Luftwaffe forces in Greece, the subsequent report to Cairo read as if someone had actually seen something suspicious on the ground at a captured air base near Athens. In fact, they were reading Luftwaffe orders to its personnel in Greece to prepare the way for Grobba and Rahn to land there on the way to Rhodes and on to Syria.

> O.L. 261
> REPORT FOLLOWS FROM DIRECTOR OF INTELLIGENCE: EQUIPMENT IS BEING COLLECTED AT ATHENS-TATOI FOR NEW OPERATION STOP . . . LONG RANGE BOMBERS . . . PROBABLY WITH EXTRA TANKS . . . PERSONNEL EN-GAGED ARE TO REMOVE ALL BADGES FROM UNIFORMS AND CARRY THEM IN POCKET STOP OBJECTIVE MAY BE IRAK WITH OR WITHOUT LANDING IN SYRIA . . . 9/5/41

> O.L. 267
> FUEL SUPPLIES ON RHODES ARE TO BE MAINTAINED AT A LEVEL SUFFICIENT TO ALLOW FOR FUELLING AT ANY TIME OF JUNKERS NINE NOUGHT . . . OVER AND ABOVE THE FUEL REQUIRED BY [FORCES TARGETING CRETE] STOP THESE TRANSPORT AIRCRAFT ARE PART OF A NEW UNDERTAKING, WHICH MAY POSSIBLY BE THE ONE REFERRED TO IN 261, THIS SERIES. 11/5/41[3]

In his Beirut office on May 11, Dentz had told Rahn that it would take about three weeks to get the large shipment of French weapons moving out of Syria to the Iraqis. Rahn said that if that were the case, he might as well turn around to Germany: they must start the weapons moving in a day for them to be of any use in the war in Iraq. Dentz was taken aback, but reached for a pen and drew up the necessary orders.

The next day Rahn flew to the north of the country in a small French plane with a Vichy French army captain to make arrangements for the weapons to cross into Iraq, where an Iraqi train would be waiting to take them to Mosul. Part of the rail line would pass through Turkish territory, and the Turks had insisted on five days' notice any time weapons or troops passed through their lands. At Rahn's suggestion the French had told the Turks that the weapons were meant for French garrisons in northeast Syria because of trouble with the Kurds. The Turks believed it.

Once in Syria's far north, Rahn had a very difficult time reaching Grobba and the growing Luftwaffe base of operations at Mosul. The phone lines across the frontier were poor and depended on human operators at police stations who were not always at their posts. But eventually he coordinated with Grobba, who said a train was on its way; it would be carrying grain supplies that the French needed on account of a rash of war speculation and hoarding in Syria-Lebanon, grain required to keep Syria stable and to strengthen the resolve of Vichy garrisons if the British threatened.

After the weapons arrived via Turkey at the Iraq border, Rahn needed an engine to take them south into Iraq and a rendezvous with an Iraqi train. Rahn purchased the services of a Turkish engine and engineer, went aboard himself, and the long train full of French weapons rolled into Iraq. There'd been a rumor at the border station that the British had tipped off the local Bedouin to the approach of the train full of valuable cargo and, whether true or not, the horseback Bedouin did materialize out of the wilderness with a war cry about an hour and a half into Iraq. The Turkish engineer was petrified; he slowed and seemed about to reverse until Rahn drew his handgun, unlocked it, and strongly encouraged the engineer to speed past them.

Soon Rahn spotted the Iraqi train in the distance, along with a military escort and Grobba's car. The train came to a halt and, with the cars disconnected, the exchange was made. As the weapons proceeded toward Mosul, escorted by the Iraqis, a sole RAF bomber appeared, but its one heavy bomb landed far wide of its mark. Grobba and Rahn had their first success.

Now, two weeks into May, about the time Messerschmitts started attacking the Allied column from Palestine and Habbaniya itself, Rudolf Rahn was well integrated into General Dentz's operations. Dentz had provided Rahn with an apartment in Beirut with office furniture and equipment, connected his radio transmitter to a good antenna mast, and had given him and his staff use of three French official cars. Rahn and the Vichy representative who worked with him helped draft radio speeches for Dentz aimed at savaging de Gaulle and his "mutineers." Thirty German military staff had now followed Rahn's arrival, but they kept out of Beirut and even kept to their barracks in isolated Palmyra and at other airfields. Rahn got Dentz to step up his counterintelligence against Allied nationals, with the result that a Polish informer was caught in Rahn's new quarters and a shipment of mines was discovered in the trunk of a car linked to two Englishmen. Rahn also cautioned that the American embassy in Beirut must be watched as another pit of spies.

Rahn was even able to influence Dentz on military matters, with the help of Berlin. Dentz intended to maintain strong garrisons in Syria's far north in case Turkey joined the Allied aggression or tried to take advantage of the chaotic situation to seize northern areas of the former Ottoman Empire they'd long sought to reclaim. Rahn got the Reich's Foreign Ministry and the German embassy in Ankara to radio messages telling Dentz they doubted any such Turkish action. So Dentz instead poured those troops into southern Syria with eventual consequences that were terrible for the Allies.

The British, equipped with Ultra intelligence and with constant air observations, had approached Dentz about forty-eight hours after the arrival of Rahn's Heinkel demanding an explanation. Dentz responded that he was unaware of any German planes or personnel in Syria; if there were any, they might be lost; and if they truly were German, the planes would be interred. In sum, he stuck to the script provided by his superiors.

Rahn, after the British complaint, feared it was only a matter of time before they invaded; he had already seen a British surveillance craft in the Syrian sky. He only hoped that the Iraqi Army could tie the British down long enough for Rommel to do his work and for more German planes and weapons to arrive in Syria.[4]

With the passage of Luftwaffe planes through Syria confirmed by cracked Enigma intelligence, the RAF began eagerly hunting them at Vichy French air bases in Syria. On May 14 an RAF reconnaissance flight taking off from Transjordan spotted at least one German transport and several fighter craft at the isolated air base at Palmyra in central Syria. Back on the ground in Transjordan, the pilot asked his commander whether he could take a Blenheim fighter-bomber and catch them on the ground. His commander, in turn, put the question to the general leading Habforce, John Clark.

"Do you want to declare war on Syria?" he asked.

"That would be a bloody good idea," returned the airman.

General Clark approved the attack on the Germans, but what it really meant was that the former allies, France and Britain, were about to fire at each other in anger above Syria. A pair of modern metal-skinned Tomahawk fighters were found in central Palestine and rushed to eastern Transjordan, where they joined two Blenheim bombers and a Blenheim fighter-bomber. They lifted off, flew into French airspace, and attacked the airstrip. That's how the fight over Syria began, even before the fight for Iraq was over: with a few planes hunting the Luftwaffe on the ground. The pilot who initially spied the Germans at Palmyra was disappointed to see that the warplanes, probably Heinkels, had already left for Iraq; but he took some satisfaction in shooting up two German transports on the ground.

A few days after this, while Roald Dahl was in Egypt recovering from his narrow escape from southern Greece ahead of the blitzing Germans, his Hurricane, and at least five of the surviving Hurricanes from his Eightieth Squadron, went on a mission without him. Five RAF pilots from other Squadrons borrowed the Eightieth Squadron's Hurricanes, which had been air ferried to Lydda in British Palestine. They stopped in Amman, then took off for the airfield just outside Damascus, a place called Mezze. On the flight north to find their target, they failed to see it; but as they turned, disappointed, they found the airfield, as well as their dearest wish: Luftwaffe planes on the ground. They dipped to strafe them. Soon a three-engine Junkers transport was burning up and a Messerschmitt Bf 110 was shattered. Three French planes on the ground were also wrecked, along with many base vehicles. The Vichy troops, meanwhile, fired away at the Hurricanes.

The next day the five Hurricanes, holes patched, flew a tour of Palestinian towns, showing the flag. The message: Yes, the RAF had been able to offer little response to multiple bombings of Haifa and, yes, there might be new tension between Palestine and Syria, but the RAF was there, now, with some of its best fighters.[5]

On May 18, 1941, General Henri Dentz spoke over Levant Beirut:

> French, Lebanese, and Syrians, you have heard the appeal of Marshal Pétain; you have heard his moving words replete with firmness and wisdom, words inspired with ardent desire for peace and order.
>
> At the same moment in which he was speaking [over the radio], English airplanes attacked our aerodromes without warning. Once more after [the Port of Mers-el-Kébir] . . . England has spilled French blood and has attacked French soil.
>
> The British Government, in order to justify this aggression against France, has accused it of failing to forcibly expel German airplanes flying over Syria, some of which were forced to make landings. Nothing can justify this accusation. Marshal Pétain has confirmed that France has no aggressive intentions against England. The privileged move by our former enemy was strictly within the terms of the armistice.
>
> This is the truth. All the accusations of Britain against France are only calumnies and criminal pretext. But we will act accordingly with calm and dignity.[6]

The British, the Free French, and other allies had long feared an Axis-occupied Syria for the dire threat it would pose to Palestine and Transjordan, for the way it might encourage pro-Axis actors in Iraq, and for the way it would encircle Turkey. All this would lead to the further peril of the Suez Canal and the oil fields of Iraq and the refinery at Abadan, Iran. But the Enigma decryptions in early May, then the arrival of the Luftwaffe about a week later, meant that long-held worries turned into an immediate crisis. Yet General Archibald Wavell struggled to scratch up a bare minimum number of troops for the relief of Habbaniya, let alone answer the threat in Syria with force.

In Westminster in early May 1941, the deputy prime minister, Clement Atlee, floated a potential solution: in return for Syrian Arab support in driving out the Vichy and Axis, the British would openly support a future Arab Federation in the Middle East. In other words, Atlee suggested that the British make a similar pledge as had the Germans to the Iraqis. It was similar, too, to the promise the British had made to Lawrence of Arabia's Arab allies in World War I in return for fighting against the Ottomans, a promise that T. E. Lawrence felt was deeply betrayed later. Others in the War Cabinet poured cold water on the idea, saying the Syrians were too divided among themselves to unite, let alone unite with a kingdom like Iraq or that of Ibn Saud. Churchill was also too eager for forceful action to agree to such an uncertain scheme. Instead the War Cabinet wondered about the capability of the Free French to lead the attack.

Charles de Gaulle and his commander in chief of the Free French forces, General Georges Catroux, had aimed to reclaim Syria and win over its large, modern army of forty thousand since early spring 1941. They saw Syria as a strong base, naturally defensible, from which to recover their strength before continuing the fight for the liberation of continental France. It was also their goal to recover the French Empire from the collaborationists and the Axis, and Syria was the jewel in that imperial crown. General Henri Dentz, of course, thought the same thing of Syria; and neither side envisioned true independence and democracy for the people of Syria or Lebanon anytime soon.

Free French leaders began pushing General Wavell in Cairo for an invasion of Syria-Lebanon in spring 1941, well before the Iraq war. But

Wavell hardly had any forces to commit to Iraq, let alone Syria. De Gaulle and his staff assured Wavell that if six thousand Free French troops marched north out of Palestine, the Frenchmen and French colonial troops on the other side would take courage and join the resistance. Wavell was unwilling to gamble on that rosy reception, so de Gaulle and General Catroux's requests were pushed off. Some in the British War Cabinet, meanwhile, still hoped in early May that Dentz would not be able to stomach the Germans in Syria and would reject collaboration. Those with better access to secret intelligence knew better.

But that only lasted a few weeks, because by then Dentz had proven that he was quite willing to follow orders to host the Germans and Italians; thus, the RAF was bombing Syrian air bases. From the second week of May 1941 it was only a matter of a short time before a war must be fought for the Levant.

It started with some sharply pointed propaganda beamed, dropped, and handed out in Syria-Lebanon commencing a few days after the discovery of the Luftwaffe landings. That is, the Allies increased radio broadcasts from the Palestine Broadcasting Service and secret transmitters in Syria, dropped leaflets, and had their network of Arab and Jewish spies on the ground disseminating propaganda. The French-language propaganda called out the Vichy military collaboration with the Germans; the Arab propaganda played to hatred of the colonial master. Some deserters from the Vichy ranks took to the radio to call upon their brethren in Syria-Lebanon to join them in Palestine; while, on the other hand, Vichy propaganda airing on Radio Levant had long charged the British with fleeing during the fall of France and stated that British calls for defections were because they wanted to fight the war with the blood of other nations.

US president Franklin Delano Roosevelt contributed to the pressure campaign on Vichy Syria-Lebanon in these days after Churchill sent him a private message in early May outlining his fear of an Axis Syria: "If the German air force and troop carrier planes get installed in Syria they will soon penetrate and poison Iraq and Persia [Iran] and threaten Palestine . . . Hitler may quite easily now gain vast advantages very cheaply." A few days after the discovery of German planes in Syria, Roosevelt had a warning message drafted, then aimed at Vichy. The United States, it read, based its relationship with conquered France on the fact that it would not collaborate militarily with the Axis, but any "collaboration . . . will in reality imply their alliance with a military power whose central and fundamental policy calls for the utter destruction of liberty." That, Roosevelt concluded, would void any expectation France had for the respect of its territory and mean that France was now a menace to the free world. The United States was neutral, but at least the president wanted to bring pressure to bear on the Vichy leaders and let them know that America implicitly condoned the fight coming its way in Syria. (In early May the Vichy chief of state had promised the American ambassador in France that the nation would not collaborate militarily with Germany.)

There were desertions from the Vichy Army of the Levant, but they were not enough to make a large difference in the end. The most famous was the case of Colonel Philibert Collet, leader of a cavalry regiment made up of Circassians, men descended from exiles from the Black Sea. Collet was a sort of French Lawrence of Arabia—even known as Collet of the Circassians—and was a popular figure among the French in the Levant and at home. He had an English wife, and was rumored for a long time to be considering desertion. Finally, three weeks into May, he rode for the Transjordan border before an arrest he knew was coming. There was hope among the Free French leadership that such a figure might start a flow of deserters, but it did not. In fact, the vast majority of the several thousand Circassians he commanded stayed at their barracks and stables; only a few hundred followed him. The rumor was that most feared for their families and feared for their pensions if they deserted.

Crossed over, Collet warned his new Free French superiors that he foresaw no further defections. This should have been a warning sign for those many who hoped that the Vichy soldiers would put up a token defense before they inevitably changed sides to fight the Axis. In another dark omen, a Free French airman defected to the Vichy in Syria from Palestine in a stolen plane—a precious, modern twin-engine Glenn Martin fighter-bomber—about the same time.[7]

As May 1941 turned to June, Freya Stark left Baghdad, the city recently scarred by murder and mayhem. Her plane passed over Fallujah, and she was relieved to look down and see the main mosque's minaret, rumored to have been destroyed by the Allies, still standing. And she distinctly saw the iron bridge over the Euphrates for which many men had recently given their lives. Stopping at RAF Habbaniya, she was surprised to find that it didn't look like a place that had been besieged for an agonizing week. After a change of officers coming and going from the base, her plane continued on to RAF Lydda in British Palestine.

By nightfall that day she was installed in a room at the King David Hotel, the vast stone edifice that doubled as a headquarters for the civilian Mandate government and the British Army in Palestine. And at 10:30 p.m. she was in dinner attire, having a lavish meal framed by champagne, while elegant men and women moved across the dance floor nearby. She usually relished such a scene, but after weeks of rationing food, of fear and sorrow in Baghdad, it struck her as ugly.

For the next few early June days, Freya would stay at the King David before returning to Cairo to check on her Brotherhood of Freedom circles there. The hotel was a hive of activity, with officers pouring in and out, ascending and descending the stairs to the top-floor Army headquarters. She saw the Free French General Catroux under his round kepi cap emblazoned with oak leaves; he was sixty-four, but to Freya he seemed youthful. There were Syrian Arab allies, old friends of Stark's, and intelligence officers, and soldiers who had evacuated before the German conquest of Crete only days earlier.

This crowd, this energy, existed because this was the headquarters of the battle for Syria-Lebanon, which was just about to launch. Amid it all, the man responsible for the whole invasion found time to have lunch with Freya Stark. General Henry Maitland Wilson, nicknamed Jumbo for his portliness, had been in Greece during the resistance to the Axis invasion there and the eventual Allied evacuation that Roald Dahl had struggled to cover from the air. Rations had been short, and the general was for the moment less than jumbo. In those days, a saying circulated in Jerusalem that he had succeeded in extracting "eighty-five percent of our army and seventy-five percent of himself." Still, Wilson was happy to talk with Stark for a while, surprising her with his calmness at such a moment.

They spoke about how flat-footed Baghdad's British embassy had been in failing to anticipate the Golden Square coup or at least failing to detect the pulse of feeling in Iraq. And, speaking of feeling on the street, Wilson told her that recently he had been asked by Palestine Mandate officials whether he could send around the country some tanks on a kind of tour, a showing-the-flag sort of thing like the Hurricanes of the Eightieth Squadron had done, a show of strength and security "to improve the morale of the villages." The officials told him that just three tanks should do the trick.

"The sight of three tanks," he replied to them, "would improve my own morale."

Jumbo Wilson had very few tanks for the invasion of Syria-Lebanon, and those were light, thin-skinned machines the size of sedans—more like covered Bren carriers than tanks—but he enjoyed more firepower than had those invading Iraq less than a month before. This good news was due to bad news: Wilson could employ some of the troops who'd evacuated from Crete and Greece. These included Australians of the sorts David Smiley had physically corralled in the dive bars of Alexandria. There were six Australian infantry regiments; two Free French regiments, including Jack Hasey and his battalion of the Foreign Legion, numbering about six thousand altogether; and a regiment of the Indian Army arriving from hard duty in the war for northeastern Africa.

In reserve were the veterans of the fight for Iraq, including the Arab Legion, Reading and the Household Cavalry, Jack Bartlett and his friends pulling their twenty-five-pounders, John Masters and Dr. Dutt of the Gurkhas, Bill Slim and the Lancers, and Harry Chalk and the First Essex. The Transjordanian Frontier Force, some of whose soldiers had refused orders to march on Iraq, would participate too, eager to prove themselves. And this time the Royal Navy, always the greatest strength of the British military, and in the area in which it never ceased to have the advantage over the Germans and Italians generally, would be able to cover Allied troops in coastal areas. In sum, the Allies could commit around thirty thousand troops to the battle if they reached into reserves, and around fifty aircraft—some the most modern, like Roald Dahl's Hurricane.

Still, the invasion, called Operation Exporter, was forced on Freya

Stark's friend General Wavell by Churchill and the War Cabinet. Wavell wanted to focus his power on the contest with Rommel, and felt he didn't have enough troops to achieve overwhelming force against the highly professional troops of Dentz's nearly forty-thousand-man Armée du Levant. Nor did he have the planes to spare to provide the kind of cover that the Allied troops would really need against the large, well-served Vichy French Air Force of over 250 aircraft. And General Dentz had around ninety tanks at his disposal, some heavy, while the Australians and Free French in Wilson's force had at most thirty, all light. In Westminster, those around Churchill were hardly delighted at splitting attention between Rommel in the west and the French in the north, either. They were "too late for surprise" and too early to go in overwhelming force; but delay, the foreign secretary felt, would mean the "French will have time to consolidate, get their breath and German help. Vichy has sold out . . . [we must] go ahead with what must be a gamble."

The relaxed lunch over, Freya Stark and the general parted ways. Then she joined a car of friends pointed south toward Cairo, and they passed Australian guns being pulled north for their destiny in Lebanon. The fighting would begin the next day.[8]

12

"There Is No Blame on the Blind Man"

The Invasion of a Global Army Begins

> My belief is we will, in fact, be greeted as liberators. . . . I think it will go relatively quickly.
> —US vice president Dick Cheney, speaking of Iraq on CBS's *Meet the Press*, September 14, 2003

GENERAL WAVELL OFFERED nearly the last word on the eve of the Syria campaign in a June 5, 1941, cable to the War Cabinet—really to Churchill: "Force is not anything like as large as desirable and operation is obviously in nature of a gamble, dependent on attitude of Vichy French." Success, in other words, might depend on the choices of those who must either side with Marshal Philippe Pétain and fight their former allies and Charles de Gaulle, or lay down their arms.

The battle for Syria-Lebanon, launched three days later on June 8, was preceded by a promise of independence for the people of Syria-Lebanon—Arabs, Circassians, Druze, and many others. The day before Allied troops invaded, Free French General Georges Catroux led the way on the airwaves: "I come to put an end to the Mandatory regime and to proclaim you free and independent. You will . . . from henceforth be sovereign and independent peoples, and you will be able to form yourselves into separate states or unite into a single state." A British broadcast followed, giving its blessing to this promise, one that was supposed to depict the Free French as liberators in the eyes of the people in Syria-Lebanon, maybe even in the eyes of Vichy colonial troops. But events would suggest that the people of Syria didn't understand how one set of Frenchmen making far-off promises was better than another set of Frenchmen making far-off promises.

More germane to the fight was the work of spies and saboteurs—
Arab, British, and Jewish—on the eve of the attack. These agents had
been held on a leash by Wavell and the Special Operations Executive
(SOE) for months in the hope that General Henri Dentz might come
around to the Free French someday, or at least to keep from antagonizing
him and have Dentz round up suspected Free French sympathizers. But
now the gloves were off. Arab and Jewish agents in Syria-Lebanon copied
and distributed leaflets, while Jews who had immigrated from Syria to
Palestine, those who could speak the Syrian Arab dialect and pass as
Arabs, served as observers and were equipped with transmitters. Scouts
gathered on the Syrian border, ready to guide the leading elements into
the country, while in the days running up to the invasion the Royal
Engineers infiltrated the country with explosives.

Even before the shooting began, British and Jewish saboteurs began
their work. They cut phone lines, took up observation posts, set fire to
fuel stores—at least in one instance with a time bomb lowered into place
from a warehouse skylight. When the battle began, teams of Royal Engineers and Sabotage and Subversion Section (SO2) agents, totaling about
fifty, disabled trucks, burned police posts, and ignited gas stations. They
even managed to wreck two tanks and bombed a house in Beirut containing members of the Axis Armistice Commission. Sometimes anti-
Vichy Frenchmen and Arabs in Syria helped.

An earlier attempt at sabotage failed when, about a week after the
initial Luftwaffe landings in Syria, the British and their Jewish Palestinian
allies attempted to destroy the oil refinery at Tripoli. The facility was
then receiving oil pumped from Kirkuk, Iraq, as part of the Golden
Square's deal with the Axis. And it was this oil supply that could have
saturated the Axis war machine, had it been secured. The Allies could
not simply bomb the French refinery in northern Syria—at the moment
the Royal Air Force (RAF) confined itself to striking airfields receiving
German craft. So it fell to an SOE agent and twenty-three commandos
of the Jewish Palmach. SOE agent Anthony Palmer was twenty-six, tall,
a long-jump champion, and a baronet—another of those who, like David
Smiley, did something useful with his privilege. Palmer's colleagues of the
Palmach commando were veterans of the Haganah, the Jewish paramil-

itary, some of whom served in the field with British troops and police during the mid-1930s Arab Revolt in Palestine, some who had earlier worked against the British as double agents.

Very early on the chilly morning May 18, the saboteurs heavily loaded their police patrol boat with explosives, tools, landing dinghies, and rations for the trip from Haifa to Tripoli, over a hundred miles up the coast. The boat lay low, and the sea outside the Haifa breakwater was very high. The plan was to hit and run, but if things went badly, the men were given cash and the locations of safe houses in the region, including that of an Arab agent in Beirut. If the worst happened, they could abandon the mission and turn their boat for safety at Cyprus.

The good boat *Sea Lion* moved out of Haifa Harbor, and Palmer and his men waved goodbye to their crew and handlers on the breakwater; that was the last anyone saw of them. After a radio check-in at 11:00 a.m. reporting that all was well, nothing more was heard. The observer waiting for them in Tripoli never saw the boat. The worst did happen, and there was no turning for Cyprus. At some point, not far from the coast of Lebanon, their ship disappeared: the deep-riding boat foundered, or one of the heavy explosives among the gear exploded, or it was intercepted. A sole shirt that seemed to have belonged to one of the commandos washed up in Lebanon, but that was the extent of any clues.[1]

In the final hours before the Allied invasion, Rudolf Rahn was rushing to prepare. He succeeded, he believed, in cultivating a good relationship between the Vichy naval commander in the eastern Mediterranean and the head of the Luftwaffe mission in Syria, and they all discussed potential coordination in the coming battle. Rahn, meanwhile, asked that the British consul in Beirut be expelled, which Dentz saw to; and Rahn asked that the consul of the United States, still neutral, also be expelled, but Dentz did not agree. Rahn also asked to headquarter some German military staff in Beirut with Dentz, but the high commissioner replied that his officers and men would not gladly stomach Wehrmacht uniforms among them; it would be wiser, he said, to keep the German staff at the country's air bases. Rahn complied. And while he was unhappy about the defection of Colonel Philibert Collet of the Circassian Cavalry, at least

Rahn saw that Dentz changed certain defensive measures of which Collet had been aware before becoming a turncoat.

Rahn's next project was to find Arab nationalists to take up arms against the invaders, offering that such fighters would have a say in the kingdom of Iraq and the Levant in the new world order; but he was disappointed, even disgusted by the lack of Arab response. So instead Rahn issued implicit threats far and wide that any social upheaval during the fighting would be answered with a severity that would make the German name feared.

On the eve of the battle, Dentz asked Rahn and Vichy leaders to withdraw German planes from Syria. "The presence of German units in Syria can only serve as a pretext for an attack," he said. The war for Iraq was now lost, the Luftwaffe was no longer needed there, and Dentz was unwilling—for now—to have the German Air Force appear to be providing direct air cover for French troops. It was important that the Armée du Levant appear to be fighting to defend the sovereignty of the French Empire to avenge the dead sailors at the Port of Mers-el-Kébir and not for the sake of the Germans. Events would soon prove that Dentz could compromise on this.[2]

In mid-May 1941 Jack Hasey and his battalion of Free French Foreign Legion departed Massawa, Eritrea, on a day of 115-degree heat, heading north to enter the Suez Canal. As they steamed up the canal, they were cheered by Free French garrisons at their guard posts until the legionnaires docked at a rail station and continued up to Gaza on the coast. From there they moved to a more northerly camp in trucks, passing rows of ripening oranges, a place where they could easily visit Tel Aviv for beer and nightlife. Hasey met some recent German Jewish refugees there who told him they were eager to return home after the Nazis were driven out. After all, they told him, that was their native land, and in spite of everything, they loved it. Hasey also revisited some of the tourist sites he had seen years earlier as an eighteen-year-old, upper-middle-class American tourist. Now he wondered when, if ever, people would once again travel about the world in something other than military uniforms.

One day a lieutenant from the Vichy French Foreign Legion appeared in the camp straddling the borders of Palestine, Syria, and Transjordan, there to join the Free French. As an officer, he was guided to the officers' quarters.

"I am not an officer in the Foreign Legion, sir. I am a private," he said. "I escaped from Syria in this officer's uniform."

"Where's the officer?" a captain asked.

"He is still there, sir." And in the tradition of the Foreign Legion, no more was asked about the fate of the man who'd owned the uniform, nor how the private had gotten to Palestine. He was simply issued a new Free French private's uniform.

Camped near Hasey were Australian troops, the Twenty-First Australian Brigade, the largest core of the invading force. Having been brought up from the Egypt-Libya border, they numbered several thousand of Australia's total contribution of almost eighteen thousand. There was also a battalion of the First Punjab Regiment and one of the Rajputana Rifles, a total of about two thousand, who contributed an outsize share of the fighting, and with them several hundred native British troops attached to the Indian Army. Among the forty-five hundred or so Free French nearby were several dozen Free French Spahis, North African Arab cavalrymen renowned for their riding skill. They had been stationed in Syria when France fell to Germany a year earlier, and about one man in four in the regiment then crossed the border into Transjordan to keep up the fight. Since then they had served in Eritrea, where their horses and camels had served the Allies well in very rough terrain. The Spahis faced the prospect of battling their friends in their own regiment when the order to move was read several days later.

The Australians moved out before the rest, moving west; they'd turn north at the coast toward Lebanon. Then Jack Hasey and the Free French and the Indian Army troops headed north together. Their transport was improvised, like that of the force that had invaded Iraq a month earlier, with about two hundred vehicles, including buses and trucks of a vintage and type the American could hardly identify: jalopies, Hasey called them. Some of their tires were worn down to fabric, and parts were held on with tape. In the weeks before this, Hasey and his comrades heard rumors that modern American weapons would reach them any day. They hadn't; instead, American school buses had reached them.[3]

The Indians camped beside Jack Hasey and now rolling north toward the border with Syria with him were the men of the First Punjab Regiment and the Sixth Rajputana Rifles. They were from northwest India, today's Indian and Pakistani region of Punjab and India's Rajasthan. They were Hindus, Muslims, and Sikhs from many ethnic communities. Some of the troops going north in this column were Free French West African troops—Muslims as well.

Those men had not left their belief and religious practice behind when they enlisted. They worried whether they were observing Koranic injunctions against wars of aggression, for example; they worried whether surrendering to a vicious enemy or fighting past their last bullet would violate their religion's prohibition of suicide.

Generally speaking, the British and Free French were at least adequate in providing their Hindu, Muslim, and Sikh troops accommodation to observe religious practice. For this their motives ranged from genuine respect to grudging awareness that disrespecting believers invited mutiny. Of course, there were European bigots—usually newly arrived nonprofessional officers. In case of offense or prejudice, soldiers tended to alert more senior officers, who got such offenders chastened or transferred. For example, in one extreme case, an Anglo-Indian Indian Army officer obscenely denounced the Koran with the result that several soldiers swore themselves to vengeance. The commanding officer sent for the offending man, dressed him down, and ordered a written apology to the battalion's Muslims and a personal apology to the unit's senior Muslim officer. Peace prevailed.

Probably the most visible aspect of belief in those dusty camps was daily prayer. With few exceptions, Muslim troops were able to follow their prayer schedule when in camp, sometimes marking out with stones a little square of ground as a makeshift mosque. Marching or fighting precluded praying multiple times daily, and Muslim soldiers tended to take this in stride as practical. As with other practices, the British and Indian armies tried to respect non-Christian burial rites and Hindu cremation.

In those camps on the Transjordan frontier, diet also set Indian men apart, with multiple mess kitchens and cooks dotted among the tents. Pork, of course, was forbidden among the Muslims and ritually slaughtered meat was required. Hindus avoided beef and they, along with Sikhs, preferred food from only their community's hands. Again, observing these things was far easier in the barracks than in the lines, though even on a fighting campaign Muslim soldiers sometimes enjoyed the services of a halal butcher who worked with their quartermaster. In the field the devout often had to make a practical choice of consuming the ubiquitous tin of bully beef or mutton—halal or no—or sticking to chapatis, if available, or at least biscuits. (Later in the war, some Muslim troops slogging through the cold rain of Italy facing off against the Germans thought a beneficent God would forgive them for chasing away the chronic chills with a little rum.) Only when they were not on campaign could Muslim soldiers observe Ramadan and its ritual of fasting; otherwise, the enervating effects of hunger, often combined with heat, made it too dangerous.

Dietary requirements tended to enforce a certain minimum level of separation among units of different religions. One mess hall would be filled with cigarette smoke, another smoke-free. One might serve alcohol, another would not. On the other hand, Arab legionnaires were noted for eating next to their British counterparts on the Iraq and Syria campaigns. Units in the British Army and Indian Army battalions were usually segregated at the level of the company—roughly one hundred to two hundred men. Yet veterans recall relatively good relations among these groups—British, Hindu, Muslim, Sikh, and even between the Jews and Palestinian Arabs who served together in British units in Palestine.

The Indian Army military brass, along with politicians, were concerned that the rivalries between Indian communities would stir strife among the forces. And they were concerned that Muslim Indian nationalism might sow discord or hurt recruitment in the core recruiting grounds of northwest India. They linked this nationalism with Islam, leading them to do things like spy on their troops at prayer on occasion, in case prayer turned into rally for an independent Pakistan. Scotland Yard, meanwhile, circulated agents among Muslim gatherings in London during the war years. The British Muslim community loudly professed its loyalty in word and deed at the same time.

Given the natural desires of so many Indians to have their own nation free of British overlordship, why would they fight for the British in the global war? Why choose one European interloper over another—especially before the world came to know the true extent of German and Japanese genocides? After all, no Indian sepoy fighting on the Allied side was ever conscripted.

The reasons for enlisting were as varied as the enlistees; but for many it was simply a well-paying, reliable, respectable job. The core of the Indian Army at the outbreak of the war were Muslim men of Punjab—comprising 25 percent of the total force—whose fathers and uncles had fought in Europe and the Middle East in the Great War. In the Punjab, especially, soldiering was a family tradition.

Take the case of one young man whose unit, the First Punjabi Regiment, was preparing to march on Syria. In 1935 Punjabi Sikh Babu Singh became a sepoy in the regiment's third battalion, a battalion that would become famous in its day for hard and far-flung experience in multiple World War II theaters and campaigns. Singh's uncle was a World War I veteran, and so was an older cousin; yet another cousin, Bakhtawar Singh, was in the battalion with him. Another cousin was in the Indian Army's Frontier Force Regiment. Three of Bakhtawar's brothers-in-law fought in World War II as well.

Among enlistees in the Indian Army, some fought for what was called izzat, a sense of personal worth as reflected in the eyes of their local communities. They would do their village proud as a soldier. Besides, Indian Army soldiers swore an oath over salt. Other Indian troops made the simple calculation that their war pay and perhaps heroics might lead to a better marriage on their return home.

Still others were tempted, as young men the world over had been for ages, by the promise of romance and glory. Jumma Khan, a Pashtun sepoy, told his officer that the glint and polish of an Indian Army parade had set him on the course to fighting the Wehrmacht in the Greek Isles. In India a team of Muslim soldiers' wives toured with a recruiting group exhorting young men to enlist.

For some enlistees there was a feeling that they had joined a struggle to make the world safe for what one Indian journalist embedded among Indian Army troops could only nebulously call "ordinary, decent living." And if Indian soldiers had not joined to protect a democracy that they did not possess, some had a sense that the only way to achieve it, and achieve dignity for themselves and all common men, was to fight the Axis.

The stories of these Muslim recruits are in some ways similar to those of young men (and, in the fields in which they were able to contribute to the war effort, young women) from Allied countries around the globe: a sense that if their "country"—however they defined that— was at war, they were obligated to participate; an opportunity for steady pay; personal pride and the expectation of one's townspeople; the promise of excitement embodied in a display of monstrous tanks and exploding mortars; the menace of an enemy who might appear some day on the horizon; or the indeterminate decision-making of the eighteen-year-old mind.[4]

In late April 1941, with the battle for Iraq about to begin, the unflagging Reich's Foreign Office staff in charge of bringing India and the Middle East to the side of the Axis had an interesting meeting. They hosted a visitor, an Italian figure recently arrived in Berlin, unknown to them. It was one Orlando Mazzotta—or so the man's false passport read; he was neither Italian nor named Mazzotta. He was Subhas Chandra Bose, a former president of the Indian National Congress, now in violent opposition to Britain's war effort, and a fugitive from house arrest by the British in Calcutta. (It was this escape that Santi Dutt's sisters took to the streets to celebrate.) The Reich's Foreign Office worked a subtle diplomatic spell to help move Bose from a hideout in Afghanistan to Russia to Berlin, with German consuls in twenty-four cities reporting the man's progress across the face of Asia and Europe. And now, after two and a half months of traveling, Bose was in Hitler's capital.

Bearing proposals for how the Germans and the Indians might coordinate efforts to defeat the British, Bose was another who had decided the enemy of his enemy was his friend. Like Amin al-Husseini, Bose was a charismatic figure who had abandoned national liberation through politics for liberation through violence. He had discovered fascism in prison after the British arrested him for sedition in the 1930s, and in it he saw a path toward Indian unity, strength, and efficiency—the chimeric promises of authoritarianism that seduced the Golden Square and so many around the globe. Back then, released from prison, young Bose traveled to Germany and Italy to cultivate relationships with political leaders there, meeting personally with Mussolini, whom he particularly admired. Then, Hitler declined to meet with Bose, but Bose published his admiration for both. Despite this admiration, by the later 1930s, it proved impossible for Bose to ignore the racial framework that supported German-style fascism. It disappointed him, and Bose hoped eventually to convince Nazi leaders to alter their public statements on the inferiority of nonwhite peoples. (Another monumental Indian nationalist, Jawaharlal Nehru, was consistent in his public anti-Nazi and antifascist views.)

Now, in the spring of 1941, and convinced of ultimate Axis victory, Bose was willing to put aside his distaste for Nazi race ideology for the sake of defeating the British. He left no record of how he imagined India would navigate its freedom in the Axis new world order, but he must have convinced himself that Nazi leaders no longer conceived of the Germans as the highest master race and the Indians a subject race, possessing corrupted blood. And, later, Bose must have imagined he could somehow preserve Indian freedom from those other blood supremacists, the Japanese Empire.

While neither Hitler nor the foreign minister had welcomed Bose back in the 1930s, on this April morning the German Foreign Office welcomed him. Small, with a soft face and round spectacles, Bose did not look the part of an anti-democratic revolutionary. But in the global contest, the Reich's diplomats hoped that he might provide an edge for the Axis, and they now discussed how to make India a front in the war.

To Bose's mind, Britain in 1941 was a dying man seizing India in a death grip that only tightened as he died. And if Britain did not die, if it were only wounded in the global war, the empire would rebuild its strength by sapping India's lifeblood and then start a new fight against the victorious Axis. Thus Britain, Bose believed, must be utterly destroyed. As Bose and the Germans spoke, they arranged that the Indian should set up a provisional "free Indian" government in Berlin on the model of the Polish government in exile in London, with Bose receiving a residence, stipend, and staff. They discussed how they might coordinate radio propaganda to India from Afghanistan, where Bose also had in mind a military and logistical headquarters. From there, with the aid of German military advisers, a revolutionary regime would direct sabotage throughout the subcontinent. Bose calculated that around fifty thousand German or Italian troops would need to muster there for an eventual march on India. But the real force in this Indian-Axis alliance, Bose believed, would be the Indian Army itself. Most of the Indian Army was ready to defect at any time, he told the Germans.

At the end of May 1941 Bose listened as Berlin radio announced the defeat of the Iraqi revolt, in part at the hands of Indian troops landed in Basra. It struck Bose as only the latest case of the British spreading imperialism through the exploitation of Indian soldiers. The Germans, he told his Foreign Office contacts, should make a joint declaration about their intention to free the Arab countries of the Middle East and India together. That way, he told his Foreign Office liaisons, Germany would enjoy a bloc of allies "from North Africa on the one side and right up to Japan in the Far East."

Time would prove that Japan posed the gravest threat to India late in the war. And had the Japanese Army, which was on the door of eastern India in 1944, visited even a fraction of the atrocities and mass killings on India as it did at the rate of tens of millions in China, Korea, the Philippines, and elsewhere, the blood price of a "free India" would have been incalculable. Germany wasn't the only country whose racial supremacy resulted in racial bloodbaths.

Among those soldiers at the eastern gate of India in 1944 were Indian soldiers of the so-called Indian National Army, allies of the Japanese, many recruited by Bose himself. The core of this army, which numbered about forty thousand, consisted of former Indian prisoners whom the Japanese captured at the fall of Malaya and Singapore. Such prisoners were given the choice of remaining prisoners—laboring under frequently brutal conditions, and poorly fed—or taking up arms for the "liberation" of their homeland. Pressure to enlist was intense, and those who spoke against collaborating were sometimes tortured.

In April 1941 a troopship bound for Malaya was turned to Basra instead. The fates sent some Indian Army troops from the harbors of Bombay and Karachi west—to a bitter fight in Iraq, Lebanon, and Syria—and some the fates sent into the hands of the Japanese in Malaya and Singapore, to be recruited by Subhas Bose himself.[5]

Finally, with the RAF strewing conciliatory leaflets ahead of them, Syria-Lebanon's invaders crossed the border after midnight on June 8. Middle East Command in Cairo and General Henry "Jumbo" Wilson organized a three-pronged attack that marched north out of Palestine and Transjordan. One prong marched up the coast, under the guns of twenty ships of the Royal and Allied Navy, aiming for Beirut; the second marched up the middle road between the great Lebanon and Anti-Lebanon mountain ranges to seize a series of towns in that valley and cut Beirut off from Damascus; and the third prong was in the east, rolling over the high plain toward Damascus. The coastal or western prong comprised Australian infantry, artillery, and a precious dozen or so light tanks (most armed with machine guns, not cannons); the middle prong was made up of more Australian infantry and guns, along with some British infantry and horse-backed cavalry brought up from Egypt or northeastern Africa, like the Royal Fusiliers, along with its small handful of light tanks and guns; and the eastern prong was manned by battalions of the First Punjab and Fourth Rajputana, a few British infantry units attached to the Indian Army, a dozen armored cars, their share of Australian guns, and Free French units including Jack Hasey's Foreign Legion, Senegalese infantrymen, and a dozen more Free French light tanks.

When those Free French drove northward in the dark over the Syrian border, they left a small group of officers behind. Among them were a Foreign Legion colonel and captain who refused to fight their fellow citizens in Syria who, they said, were simply following orders and fighting under the flag of France. In addresses to those Free French troops waiting to cross the border, General de Gaulle had pronounced that "you could in all conscience refuse to take part"; but in private he was furious with the officers who refused since, de Gaulle shouted, *he* was the highest representative of French military honor. The vast majority of Free French pilots refused to take part in the campaign as well, with dire consequences for the men on the ground stalked by Vichy planes.

This harks back to an incident in Transjordan in early May when one squadron among the ranks of the Transjordan Frontier Force (TJFF), Jordanian Arab and Palestinian cavalrymen, had effectively mutinied, refusing to ride into Iraq. According to the terms of their enlistment, they'd said, they were not an army intended for foreign engagements. And they'd also refused orders because some, at least, had been convinced by Axis radio propaganda that they should not make war on other Arabs fighting for their "independence" in Iraq. That squadron had been dismissed or given early retirement. The remainder, including their Arab junior officers, were prepared to fight, and some would soon die in Syria. Along with the Free French in the eastern prong of the invasion were several squadrons of the TJFF, on horseback and in Fords, armed with rifles and even a few valuable Bren machine guns.

The first twenty-four hours of the invasion was a strange mix of optimism, accidents, blood, and bad omens. The Syrian town of Kuneitra, north of the Sea of Galilee and near the Golan Heights, overlooked the northward road and was the first target of the Royal Fusiliers, men and boys mostly from London. With them was a Free French captain, a recent defector from the Armée du Levant who'd garrisoned the town only weeks before. He told the British just the route to approach, and the place was taken without a shot.

On another northern road, east of Kuneitra and just over the Transjordan border, was a critical rail bridge over the rocky gorge at Tel Shehab. There was an ancient village there, a stop on the ages-old caravan route, sprayed by a waterfall. It was held by a watchful Vichy garrison, ready to trigger explosives poised to drop the bridge over the churning water of the Yarmuk River into the gorge. In the dark, first hours of the invasion, a platoon of Rajputana Rifles crouched one hundred yards above the valley. Captain Adam Murray, a twenty-four-year-old Belfast boy, told his Indian havildar (sergeant) Goru Ram to stay put with the platoon while he and a Free French guide snuck across the bridge to cut the main wire leading to the explosives on the bridge or at least eliminate the sentries. Because Murray couldn't count on spotting the lead wire in the dark, the riflemen stood ready to rush the bridge and frantically search for TNT fuse wires to pull before the French could trigger them. If things went wrong, it would be a kind of horrible scavenger hunt, a race to find the fuses before a Vichy soldier flipped the switch and sent all the searchers plunging to eternity.

Murray, armed with a Thompson submachine gun, and the Frenchman crawled away from the Rajputs, cut through some barbed wire, and crawled toward the Vichy sentry post composed of sandbag-surrounded tents. For a while, the waterfall covered the sound of the two men, but eventually a French guard heard them.

At the racking of a rifle bolt and sounds of alarm, Goru Ram could no longer stand back. He rushed to the scene with his own tommy gun just as the firefight broke out. With flashing and rattling, the Rajputana Rifles charged the bridge and two other guard posts. And the French sentries were killed before they could detonate the bridge.

Cases like Kuneitra, Tel Shehab, and some other instances of tactical Vichy retreats in the first few hours of fighting—the Arab townspeople of Tyre cheered the unopposed arrival of the Australians up the coastal road on day one—led some among the Allies to draw the wrong conclusions. A TJFF trooper in the eastern, most successful prong of the attack wrote in his diary at the end of the first day that "the invasion seems to have gone off well and we ought soon to be in Damascus," which was only around sixty miles away.

Back in Britain, the voice on the BBC had some optimistic things to say at the end of the first day of the invasion: "Penetration into Syria by Allied forces continues. Points between twenty and thirty miles inside the frontier have been occupied. . . . It is understood that some opposition has been encountered from the local French troops, but this is not believed to have been on considerable scale. It has been stated in Cairo, according to news agency reports, that French officials in the country already occupied are co-operating with the Allies."

The story from the Syrian town of Deraa was different. Ahead of several companies of the First Punjabis, a staff car flying a white flag drove toward the French-held town in the first daylight hours of the war, key because it, too, straddled both the north–south highway and railway. In the car was a British officer of the Punjab Regiment, a Free French officer, and a British civilian official of the Transjordan government. As it drove up the highway, a sharpshooting French gunner put an antitank shell neatly into the car's engine. The orders for the day from General Wavell in Cairo stated that "the enemy is not hostile until he proves himself otherwise." Yet the attack on their car didn't apparently convince these three of the Frenchmen's hostility, because they got out, dusted themselves off, and continued walking toward the town, holding their white flag high. Lucky for them, they were not murdered, as well, as they walked and shouted a prewritten litany, inviting the French to "fight alongside the Allies against the Germans." They were rebuffed by the Vichy officer in command and thus turned away, surviving a nerve-wracking walk back to the sepoys behind them. Battle commenced— fierce, but successful for the experienced Punjabis.

So if there was initial success, the experience of the first day or two at least disabused those who thought the Vichy soldiers might cross from line to line at the sight of the invaders or that, in a joke some of the Australians told themselves, it was going to be "just a bus ride to Beirut." The orders for most Allied troops who crossed first were to not shoot first, to carry a white flag, and seek parley. Many of the leading Australian infantry had been ordered to wear their characteristic slouch hats instead of their helmets in the hope that the Vichy soldiers might be willing to surrender to Australians rather than the Free French "mutineers" or to the British who'd bombed their navy and abandoned them in spring 1940. But this proved a sad joke. Some Australians in their slouch hats, and bearing the white flag, were machine-gunned.[6]

The invasion did mark a success, if bloody, for the Jewish-Palestinian Palmach commando, which had recently suffered the loss at sea of its total strike force bound for the Tripoli, Lebanon, refinery. In the final days before the invasion, Palmach officer Moshe Dayan had scouted the Palestine-Lebanon frontier in advance of the Australian incursion. Not knowing the area well, he relied on local guides to show him good tracks and bridges passable by vehicles. (The owner of a Beirut travel agency who'd explored back roads in the guise of picnicking with his family also provided the Allies a map of unknown paths.) It was a frontier ranged by smugglers and those who moved in shadows; when seeing others in their night reconnaissance, Dayan and his guide, Yitzak the Druze, would mutter a curt greeting in Arabic and both parties would move on, eyes down, no questions asked. In those explorations Dayan identified two key bridges just over the border that would have to be secured or at least cleared of potential explosives if the Australians were to advance successfully on the first day of battle.

Thus, on the night before, two teams crossed the frontier to disable any potential TNT like the Rajputs did at Tel Shehab around those same hours. There were sixteen men total: five Palmach men, ten Australians, and one Arab, Rashid Taher. Taher led Dayan's team of eight through the dark at 2:00 a.m. and crawled up to the vital bridge. Finding that the French had not wired it, the team breathed a sigh of relief, and now they only had to hold it and await the Australians' trucks, due at 4:00 a.m. The men slid down a ravine and closed their eyes for the moment.

They were awakened by the sound of approaching fire. It was dawn, the Australians had not yet arrived, and the team was badly exposed by the rising sun. Taher knew of a stone police post nearby, and the commandos hurried to it for some cover. Finding it already occupied by a small group of Vichy troops, the raiders had to fight for it. A machine gun was mounted on a terrace on the building's upper story, and it tried to keep the commandos pinned down while another French team tried to flank the Allies through some trees. But Taher was deadly accurate with a rifle and successfully covered the dash of Dayan and a friend who managed to get to the base of the stone outpost. From there a couple of lobbed grenades silenced the machine gun up above. After that the whole team rushed the building and the French inside surrendered.

The men then climbed to the roof and put the mounted machine gun back in working order. From there they could command a wide area with the weapon and with an invaluable mortar found nearby; they could even provide good observations for the invasion force, if only it would come down the road. But it did not. It turned out that a stretch of the coastal road had been dynamited by the French; that explained why they hadn't bothered with this bridge. Another commando team of Australians had assaulted a Vichy Algerian cavalry post in the night, and the Algerians had managed to trigger explosives that dropped a broad cliff face onto the motorway. Subsequently, the Australians had spent hours clearing the debris. Those were hard hours for the eight men in the French police outpost, but they were well stocked with captured weapons put to constant use as Vichy troops kept arriving to surround them.

During the battle, as he looked for the source of some incoming fire from his rooftop position, Moshe Dayan raised his field glasses to his eyes, when suddenly a rifle bullet drove into the very lens of the binoculars and exploded it. Dayan's hand was cut by the flying metal and glass and, worse, shards were driven into his eye. He fell unconscious.

Hours later the Australians arrived at the police post and drove off the Vichy French siege party. Dayan and two injured Australians were placed in the back of a captured truck and they made their agonizing way to the ambulance station in the rear of the column before being sent onward all the way to Haifa, with Rashid Taher at Dayan's side. Twelve hours after his eye was destroyed, Dayan was taken into surgery to remove the scatter of metal from his head.[7]

In the coming days, the news media back in Vichy France reported indignantly on the Allied invasion of its colonies. "The hereditary enemy throws off its mask," proclaimed one magazine; the ancient enemy of France, in other words, was no longer pretending not to covet France's possessions. Another magazine wrote of the betrayal of the Free French, whom it preferred to call "Gaullists"—not freedom fighters, but men duped by de Gaulle into mutinying against lawful authority. "Here is revealed the horror of Gaullist disloyalty. It is inconceivable that the English would consent to accept the backing of the Gaullists under these circumstances."

Learning of the Allied invasion back in Vichy on the morning of June 8, Marshal Philippe Pétain was said to have responded to the news, "if we do not defend ourselves, the Germans will seize [French] North Africa." Within a few hours, he was speaking to the defenders of Syria-Lebanon over stratospheric radio waves beamed from France:

Frenchmen of the Levant! The countries where you live and for
whose prosperity you have worked for many years are today the
subject of an unspeakable attack. This attack was led . . . by
Frenchmen under a rebel flag. Supported by British Empire
forces, they do not hesitate to spill the blood of their brothers
defending the unity of the Empire and French sovereignty. . . .
Trickery preceded violence. For several days, the propaganda
which formed the basis for the aggression claimed that German
troops were landing in our ports. . . . You who are on the spot,
you know that to be false. You know that several aircraft, which
had stopped over in our territories, have today left Syria.[8]

The Luftwaffe truly had evacuated Syria. There was no need for it to base
there, with the war for Iraq over; and Dentz had personally requested
the German air withdrawal because it threatened some French troops'
morale. And Dentz and his masters in Vichy were not ready, at least at
first, to fight alongside the German military in the field or air.

Rudolf Rahn was at Dentz's elbow the morning after the invasion.
Dentz waved his orders from Vichy to resist at all costs in Rahn's face,
saying, "And now the Orient is truly on fire, and you lit the flame." The
diplomat replied that he hardly thought he'd lit the spark; but if there
were a fire, let it be used to weld together Germany and France in a sensible partnership for Europe.

Still, though Rahn suggested it, Dentz resisted direct military coordination with Germany because he feared that his soldiers and airmen
might outright refuse. And he and some in Vichy feared that the Allies
might then consider all the French Empire fair game, too. But that didn't
mean there was no coordination at all, of a kind. The Vichy minister of
defense radioed Dentz hours later, stating that the Luftwaffe, flying from
the Aegean, would help by attacking the Allied fleet and Palestinian and
Transjordanian air bases. "For reasons of morale," he said, "the intervention of the German air force will have to take place without overflight
of Levant territories. . . . [The Royal Navy and] other targets which are
equally important for current operations are the airfields at Amman,
Haifa, and Lydda, as well as the Haifa port installations."

In the dark of night, therefore, a day after the Allies crossed the Syrian border, the Luftwaffe sent twenty light bombers from Italian Rhodes to attack Haifa. Their targets were the Royal Navy and the harbor area, but most of their bombs fell wide in the darkness and some Arab townspeople were hurt when the bombs fell in their neighborhoods. A Vichy bomber joined in targeting Haifa two days later. Then the Germans returned the next night, striking Haifa and Tel Aviv. Over the course of the next month and a half, the Axis and Vichy air forces dropped no fewer than three hundred bombs on Palestine, hurting dozens, mining the Haifa Harbor, and killing around a score, including Axis prisoners in their barracks.[9]

13

"These Curses Shall Come Upon You and Overtake You"

The Allies at the Edge of Defeat

We gave our superiors our word as soldiers of France that we would fight. They told us we must fight to preserve French honour.

—Unnamed Vichy officer, captured in June 1941, to Henry Gorrell of the United Press, in Henry Gorrell and Kenneth Gorrell, *Soldier of the Press: Covering the Front in Europe and North Africa, 1936–1943*

[The British] press was causing great fuss that it had new and founded grievances against us. Or not founded? We can debate it. . . . [But] for the soldier, "the enemy" is the one who fires on him or one on whom he opens fire; the term expresses a state of affairs with certain categorical imperatives.

—Pierre Guiot, Vichy French captain of the destroyer *Valmy*, based in Beirut, in *Combats Sans Espoir (Guerre Navale en Syrie 1941)*

We're professional soldiers obeying orders and you came here on a deliberate aggression. You think it would have been easy for us to quietly submit . . . ? The Boche keep threatening us. They say they will take reprisals [in occupied France] and they mean it.

—Unnamed Vichy officer prisoner of war to journalist Alan Moorehead, June 1941, in *African Trilogy*

While some wallowed in self-pity day after day, indulging in the belief that we're a decadent people, they, the fighters of Syria, have shown the world that a defeated France retained enough pride to defend its honour. A people like ours do not give in after one day's trial when they reconnect to the purest traditions of their history.

—Aviation writer Gilbert Poincelet, writing in unoccupied southern, or Vichy, France, late summer 1941, in *Dans le ciel de Syrie*

I would like to go to Syria. With a lot of my comrades, I made a request
to be sent there. [An official] asked for a list of volunteers in the prison
camp. . . . You know how happy I'd be to go over there. That would
make you forget that bad June of 1940.
> —Captain Edouard de Lamaze, writing to his family from a prisoner
> of war camp in Bavaria, June 1941, in Jean de Lamaze, *Oflags*
> *(1940–1945)*

But how beautiful you were in our eyes, you men who honourably carried
out this war of despair! We will remember them with growing pride as
we learn about the magnificent resistance of the French fighters of Syria.
> —Novelist Jean Damase, writing in occupied France, 1942, in *Ici, Paris*

IT WAS 2:30 A.M. on June 15, 1941, when a British force was shocked and
scattered. They were feinting northward to try to convince the Vichy
French that the attack on Damascus was imminent from the southwest
rather than the southeast. There were two armored cars, three tracked
Bren carriers, and not quite one hundred Royal Fusiliers on the Damascus
road when they, instead, were surprised in the dark by Vichy tanks and
armored cars. It was all the British could do to escape south down the
road to their headquarters in Kuneitra, a largely Circassian village that
had been taken with ease almost a week before. Most escaped the am-
bush, but fifty Londoners of the Fusiliers were caught by the French.

Back in Kuneitra, those who made it told their lieutenant colonel
that a large but uncounted armored force had emerged from the night
and could only be closing the sixteen miles that now separated them. The
Fusiliers had started the war as hardy, professional troops stationed in
India, attached to the Indian Army; but they had left well over one hundred men in graves cut out of the Eritrean Desert after horrible fighting
with crack Italian grenadiers that April. These had been replaced one
month earlier in Palestine by a majority of green newcomers from Britain.
There were 475 Allied men in the village to defend against around 1,750
attackers coming down the road behind eleven medium tanks.

The Vichy French also had almost a dozen armored cars that they
first put to use cutting off four crossroads leading out of Kuneitra at
dawn. Circassian Cavalry, meanwhile, patrolled the tightening snare. The

terrain was very rough under the shadow of the Golan Plateau and largely impassable by wheeled vehicles off road; that meant the French could besiege it with ease just by controlling the crossroads. After they realized that the British had no tanks of their own and only two remaining armored cars, the French knew they had time. The Vichy besiegers would attack the next morning.

This was the moment for the Allies to have attacked by air, punching through the Vichy roadblocks with armor or armored cars, rushing twenty-five-pounders or at least antitank guns to the scene. But in this campaign, "in the nature of a gamble," there were chiefly only planes enough to cover the Royal Navy, and only a handful of tanks spread across three invasion routes, some which had already broken down in the harsh landscape. Artillery, including antitank guns, were the Allies' fiercest weapon, which made its distribution a question of the highest importance; and the force defending Kuneitra, in short, was not important enough. A desperate message delivered in person to the brigadier leading this half of the invasion pleading for antitank weapons was declined. Such guns, if sent to Kuneitra, would leave another force defenseless against French tanks.

Hell for the defenders of Kuneitra, therefore, came over the horizon before 5:00 a.m. The besieged men had piled stone barricades over the routes into town, but the eleven-ton Renault tanks pushed through and rolled over them. At places the Fusiliers imagined were strongpoints, they situated men with about fifteen long Boys antitank rifles and started firing away. But the half-inch hardened-steel bullets skimmed off the tanks' one-and-a-half-inch steel plate, at any range, leaving hundreds of spent shells littering the various defense posts on the village perimeter. Instead the French tanks turned their cannon and machine guns on these posts and cleared them out. The inexperienced Fusiliers did not fall back in any kind of order; they scrambled out of crumbling stone and mud houses and into the next one they saw, until the defenders lost contact with one another.

And the British men began falling. A Fusilier manning a long Bren gun behind a stone wall was shot through by a tank's machine gun. A corporal who'd worked a World War I–era machine gun to death flung it aside and grabbed one of the five-foot Boys rifles to take on a tank, only to be exploded. A man with another of the precious Bren guns died in a duel with a French sniper. Some battalion truck drivers joined in and, requesting a supply of grenades, formed a tank-hunting squad trying to stalk close enough to lob one in an open turret or wreck a tank tread.

All the while, the commanding British officer reported to his headquarters over the wireless set of his collapsing defenses and helplessness before the French tanks. He also told three Free French liaisons with the Fusiliers to try to escape the village on foot; he had every reason to fear that they would be summarily shot as renegades if the Vichy caught them. They scampered and dodged, and successfully crossed twenty-five miles to the rear and safety.

The French tanks having wrecked the defenses of Kuneitra, and the British defenders having collapsed around one remaining strongpoint, Vichy Senegalese troops followed the tanks into action. The British answered their charge with accurate mortar fire. Then came a Vichy Circassian cavalry charge, led by a Frenchman on horseback with his saber drawn, as if from another era. He was shot from his horse. The Circassians, invading a predominantly Circassian village, rode on. Vichy French infantry, meanwhile, rousted out isolated British defenders from their barricades and hiding spots with grenades. The fight began before dawn, and now it was 1:00 p.m.

Throughout the afternoon, the French worked slowly to isolate the last British defenders. They were methodical, but like the defenders, the French were also exhausted. The British were holding out for relief that would never come until, finally, in the early evening a Polish lieutenant of the Vichy Foreign Legion approached the defenders in their last stone holdout with a Fusilier prisoner at his side. Waving a white handkerchief, he pleaded for parley, and then practically begged the young Allied lieutenant colonel to surrender so that he no longer had to fire on the British. The defenders were nearly out of ammunition, and surrendered to avoid a massacre by the eleven French tanks visibly poised not far away.

The Vichy Foreign legionnaire accepted the Fusilier officer's surrender gratefully and took him to the Vichy commander to make arrangements to bury the twenty British dead and help the many wounded, some soon to die. Roughly three hundred Fusiliers were now prisoners, while a score had managed to escape during the fighting, and more hid and later slipped away in the dark, scampering toward the Palestine border.[1]

The Vichy counterattack in the third week of June also targeted the village of Ezra on the road to Damascus from the south, which had been won with relative ease by the Allies in the first few days of the campaign. Vichy Tunisian infantry and other units succeeded in taking it back during the encircling counteroffensive, and it was now garrisoned by about two hundred French and colonial troops. If this important north–south corridor were cut, the Allies pushing on Damascus would be in trouble. In his diary, a Free French soldier called it a mortal threat to their line of communication, and it fell on the Allies to improvise a response.

The main unit at hand was the Transjordan Frontier Force (TJFF), the Palestinian and Jordanian cavalrymen who ranged the hills and deserts policing bandits and smugglers. A different troop of the TJFF had also refused orders to participate in the Iraq invasion a month earlier, arguing that the terms of their enlistment barred it, and some also objecting to being used against other Arabs. This squadron, though, wanted to fight. They formed the nucleus of a makeshift army of one hundred men and many languages. There were European Free French marines, Free French infantrymen of Chad, a Sikh platoon with two Bren carriers, a dozen Royal Fusiliers from London, and one antitank gun. This hodgepodge attacked Ezra in the midafternoon heat of June 17.

The Vichy's two hundred men in hardened positions and a small fortlike barracks had many machine guns firing from loopholes in response, and the Arabs of the TJFF and the others had to bullseye those loopholes to try to quiet those devastating guns sweeping back and forth. The Allies' sole antitank gun they used like artillery, though those stone walls tended to shrug off the shots. The French, in turn, answered with their own seventy-five-millimeter gun and mortars. The Free French marines, meanwhile, launched rifle grenades back at the Vichy strongpoints. The officers of the army of many languages fell wounded or dead at a terrible rate. Yet finally, the Allies poured enough fire through those slits and windows to quiet the French machine guns and the Vichy surrendered.

Fourteen men of the international force of one hundred were dead, as were around thirty Vichy soldiers, with around 170 of the latter now prisoners. This was a monstrous rate of death, even for this vicious war. Afterward, the captured French captain in charge of Ezra's defense wrote in his diary, "we are sick of this fight against Frenchmen [with] . . . ours killed by Frenchmen. . . . We are convinced we're doing our duty. But what a painful duty!"[2]

The day that the Vichy tanks stalked Kuneitra in preparation for their successful attack, the Allies lost yet another strategic position. Marjayoun was a town to the northwest, in southern Lebanon, built on a hill that commanded a north–south road between the Lebanon and Anti-Lebanon mountain ranges. It was a kind of defensive gate to the valley; indeed, a Crusader castle stood nearby precisely for that reason. On the first day of the Syria-Lebanon war, the Australians could not take it, even though they had with them the Allies' main handful of tanks.* Rebuffed, their Australian commander patiently awaited the arrival of fresh guns from Palestine, perhaps the same ones that Freya Stark had seen coming up the highway from Egypt. Having arrived, the Australians punishingly drove the Vichy French and Algerian defenders of Marjayoun northward.

These Vichy forces took up a new, strong defensive position in the direction of Beirut, and thus this central prong of the invasion force was successfully blocked and almost a stationary week passed. The Australian commander of the forces occupying Marjayoun grew impatient and didn't want to mount a static defense; that is, he didn't want to wait for the enemy to come to him, a tactic that seemed exploded in this new age of mobile warfare. So he received permission to flank the French through the hills and attack a more northerly town straddling an east–west pass through the Lebanon range.

*The fight had been proceeded by the customary approach under a white flag by several representatives: an Australian captain, a Jewish Palestinian guide, and a Free French liaison. When the Free French officer climbed a stone wall to plea for parley, he surprised a group of North African infantrymen. They held their fire, but their European officer shouted, "Shoot! Shoot this fool with a flag." A bullet went through the collar of the Free French officer, but he managed to get back to his lines.

It was then, of course, that the Vichy tanks sprung their attack from the north back against Marjayoun, supported by the American-made Glen Martins of the Vichy Armée de l'air. Behind them came Circassian cavalry on horseback and legionnaires and Senegalese in trucks, the battle beginning at the height of the hot summer afternoon. In the town was only one company of Australian infantry and two hundred troopers of the Scots Greys cavalry whose horses had long before been taken away— horses who would have served them quite well in this rough environment. This time the defenders had antitank artillery, which did slow the Vichy advance. The Allies also had some serious field guns and steadfast gunners who made the advance horrible for Vichy legionnaires, among whom they dropped shells with incredible skill. Still, the French thrust their way into the town, led by the tanks.

The outnumbered Australian and British defenders were not having it. Most ran, though their guns were having good effect. Trucks started racing down the road to Palestine, not fifteen miles behind them, though no order to retreat was ever heard. It was chaos. And the Vichy planes enjoyed playing on the chaotic stream of vehicles until the single Australian antiaircraft gun at work pierced one of them, sending it crashing into the rocks.

Some of the Scots Greys tried to dig in and resist the French, but weren't trained for such things and, besides, in the mad environment there was no coordination nor provision for supplying them with ammunition. After a few terribly thirsty summer hours, those who dug in raised their hands until the Vichy troops lined them up along the road out of town. They were about to be loaded into trucks for the winding drive to Damascus when a Scots Grey lance corporal shuffling into one of the trucks was approached by a Vichy legionnaire. "Where you from, Jock?" the stranger asked him in Scotch-inflected English. This Vichy legionnaire, who had overheard the lance corporal's Scottish accent, told him that he himself was from Glasgow. Not to worry: he had been shooting over the heads of the Australians and British, he assured his countryman.[3]

As Rudolf Rahn noted in Beirut with pleasure, there were over five hundred British prisoners taken in Kuneitra and Marjayoun, and the French had captured valuable weapons and ammunition in doing so. In addition, they could send prisoners back to Europe for safekeeping, possibly to be swapped later. The counterattack had been a certain success.

Working with sympathetic members of General Henri Dentz's senior staff, Rahn had encouraged this counterattack in part to bolster the morale of the French officers, in part to discourage a static defense that could only sap hard-to-replace supplies, and in part to exploit the blockheadedness of the British. Rahn could hardly understand why they had only sent troops northward up the obvious routes, routes well worn down by Babylonians, Romans, and medieval Crusaders. They were narrow paths, and lines of communication could only run back the same obvious paths, which the superior numbers of the Armée de l'air could easily find. The strongpoints along these paths were few and equally obvious. Thus, flanking the Allied advance and cutting through its lines of communications had been quickly done.

Had the British invaded from the direction of Iraq, which is what Rahn and his Vichy liaison had feared before the fight began, the French in Syria could answer with only small numbers spread over great distances. He frankly found it incomprehensible, and reported to Berlin, therefore, that "the English command was obviously inferior to the French."

Rahn, meanwhile, was trying to raise some kind of force in the direction of Iraq in case the British came to their senses and reoriented their attack. The answer seemed to be Fawzi al-Qawuqji, a veteran of the Ottoman Army originally from Tripoli, Lebanon, who had fought shoulder to shoulder with the Germans in Palestine in the Great War, winning an Iron Cross. He had bitterly watched the British and French carve up Arab territories after the war and became their mortal enemies. Most recently, in the name of casting out the British from Iraq, Qawuqji had commanded a mobile group of around several hundred raiders—many little better than bandits—against Allied flanks in Iraq in May. Now Rahn wanted to put them to better work in the Syrian southeast. This raised an eyebrow among Dentz's staff, who hated Qawuqji as an anti-French revolutionary; they even had a price on his head. But knowing that war made strange bedfellows, the French consented and reprieved Qawuqji.

Rahn contacted him through Fritz Grobba's connections, redubbed him a "freedom fighter," and encouraged him to sabotage the oil pipeline to Haifa while stalking the borderlands.

Generally, though, the Nazi Rahn was disgusted by Arabs and Syrians, whom he called an "unlovely mixture of races and religions." They were corrupt, greedy, vacillating intriguers, he thought. The French had been too lenient with them, spoiled them. A few days after the Allied invasion, an embassy from the prime minister of the native Lebanese council came to visit Rahn. The army was coming up the coast, the Royal Navy was destroying whole villages. Please, they asked, would the minister use his influence with General Dentz to have him surrender Beirut, declare it an open city, before the Allies leveled it?

As if he was there to protect the interests of Levantine property-owners, Rahn thought, disgusted. "I admire the indulgence of the High Commissioner [Dentz]," he said. "In his place, I would have had Prime Minister . . . strung up on the highest cedar of Lebanon."

Rahn was also still trying, with his new French ally, Vice-Admiral Pierre Gouton, to encourage closer air force and navy cooperation between Dentz and the Luftwaffe. The Royal Navy was moving too freely off the coast of Lebanon, and its guns had claimed thousands of Vichy defenders' lives on the coast, where entire strongpoints had been pulverized. Striking at the Royal Navy's air support, striking the ships themselves with Luftwaffe dive-bombers, could change the equation south of Beirut. Besides, Rahn could see it all in his mind's eye, what he considered a "logical chain": the French would agree to German help against the ships off Lebanon, then against the British mechanized forces, then finally accept a commitment of German ground forces. The harmony he envisioned would become reality.

And, indeed, General Dentz told Rahn in the second week of June that he was won over to once again welcoming the Luftwaffe in Syria, especially for the purpose of bombing the Royal Navy. The "immediate intervention of *Stukas* based in Syria . . . would be decisive," Dentz radioed Vichy. "Rahn confirms that the visitors will depart immediately after the business is settled." Back in Bletchley Park, deciphers of Enigma-coded Luftwaffe communications revealed this alarming development.

In response to Dentz's decision, the Vichy air minister flew to Syria to inspect the situation, assessing whether airfield facilities and fuel and ammunition supplies were sufficient to support the Luftwaffe in any numbers. Assessments quickly revealed this was doubtful. Plus, the Vichy regime still recognized that there would be a price to pay in military and national morale for openly fighting beside the Germans; if France were to do so, it must be worth it militarily. Furthermore, at the scale required to turn the tide against the Allies—and many thought it might turn the tide, given recent French successes—the plan practically meant a massive occupation of Syria by Germany. The Vichy regime was fighting res- olutely against Britain to preserve its colony; this could hardly be fur- thered by handing the Levant over to the Germans, regardless of such promises from "visitors."

Dentz kept asking, but Vichy kept demurring, in part because fur- ther negotiations for lightening the weight of German occupation terms in France were bogging down. Had the Germans convinced the Vichy French that they would loosen their shackles and respect their sovereignty in places like Syria-Lebanon, the French might very well have accepted fighting partners with perhaps decisive consequences.

Still, the looser sort of coordination between the Luftwaffe and French continued. And Vichy France, meanwhile, was pouring planes into Syria-Lebanon from North Africa. The last Vichy stopover before flying across the Mediterranean was an airfield at Eleusis, Greece, which had been Roald Dahl's first posting as a fighter pilot, and the place where he tried to slow the German advance while his new friends died around him.[4]

Roald Dahl had a one-month break in Alexandria after his narrow escape from the Germans in Greece, with time to send a letter to his mother in England with the sort of hair-raising details of his experiences that moth- ers do not want to read about their children. He probably thought he was being reassuring when he concluded, "Anyway, I don't think any- thing as bad as that will happen again."

Dahl then received his orders to report to Haifa at the end of May, and he bought a used 1932 Morris Oxford—horrid brown, with a max- imum speed of thirty-five miles per hour—and set off into the desert, like

John Masters flogging Ol' Man Mose across American open spaces. Dahl crossed the Suez Canal on a cable-towed raft, then headed up through the Sinai Desert, relishing the perfect isolation and a landscape he imagined Mars must be like. Of course, the old workhorse gave up in the inhuman heat; but after Dahl slept the night in the back seat, the car was ready to go again in the morning. A watermelon sustained him until he reached the green coast of British Palestine. As he drove north, he wondered at the citrus fruit dropping from laden branches, littering the sides of the road with sweet luxury, a fragrance that in rationed England was the stuff of distant memory. And soon he descended to coastal Haifa, with its port and air base near the sea. Here gathered the Eightieth Squadron, its few survivors from Greece, and some fresh pilots. With an Australian unit, this squadron was the core of the air force for the Syria-Lebanon campaign: Roald Dahl and eight other young men. He parked his exhausted Morris next to a corrugated iron shed, sure he'd lose the car either because he'd soon advance to the next local theater to fight or because this base would be evacuated, like those he'd abandoned in Greece.

On June 8, with the rest of the Allied force, Dahl and the Eightieth Squadron flew into battle. Some of his squadronmates turned toward the air base at Rayak, Lebanon, east of Beirut, to try to shred Vichy fighter planes on the ground. But unfortunately for the Royal Air Force and the Australians, these were scrambled in time and they, with other French planes, were bloodily effective on the first day of the invasion. The French strafed the long lines of Allied vehicles on their obvious, narrow paths northward; and they killed four Australian pilots, while sending two others bailing into the sea. A French pilot who'd shot down four German and seven Italian planes over France in 1940 killed an Allied Hurricane pilot over Damascus that day.

On that first day, the Royal Navy started dealing out heavy blows against Vichy coastal defenses, but the French Air Force offered an outsized threat in return, because a single plane with a heavy bomb could send a ship quickly to the sea floor while offering, in turn, a very small and fast target. Dahl's job at the commence of battle and for many days to come was to protect the fleet that rode out, like he did, from Haifa.

At the start of the war for the Levant, with the help of a ground crewman, the lanky Dahl squeezed into the narrow green aluminum cockpit, sitting on his parachute. Over his canvas parachute straps, the two fitted a second pair that pinned him hard to his hard seat. Then the crewman rolled the Plexiglas hood narrowly over Dahl's head. Left hand on the throttle, right hand on the ring atop the stick, and feet on the rudder bar, Dahl steered into position and pushed the slight throttle lever forward. In no time he was over the Allied fleet.

It was early afternoon when Dahl saw a twin-engine fighter-bomber coming for the ships. It was either a French Potez 63 or a Junkers 88; it really didn't matter which to Dahl. His job was to destroy them before they could bomb the fleet; the job of the front and rear German and Vichy gunners, meanwhile, was to send Dahl into the sea.

A trick of glass and optics, called a reflector sight, made an orange circle appear to be floating near the windscreen of his Hurricane. He had eight guns in his wings, and these were targeted to converge on a focal point 150 yards ahead of him; there was no way to aim them except to aim the whole plane as if it were a gun itself.

This he did, over that French or German fighter-bomber, sending out bursts of his eight guns at one of its engines until he saw smoke pour out. It sunk, then, and limped toward the sea. That day Dahl flew five missions: one over land, seeking French planes to strafe, three over the Mediterranean, protecting the fleet, and one searching out—and finding—the two downed Australian pilots in the water.

One day it was his role, with some wingmates, to attack a Vichy Lebanese air base where some fighters had started arriving from Vichy North African colonies. Coming in low, they caught five planes on the ground. Fingers over the brass firing buttons, they were preparing to cut them up when Dahl glimpsed people on the ground—people in brightly colored clothing: women. He could make out bottles on one of the French plane's wings; the French pilots, it appeared, were enjoying some wine with some of their guests, showing off their planes.

Dahl and his friends held their fire and watched the young women toss their glasses and hurry away in their impractical shoes. Meanwhile, the French air defenses opened up and the Hurricanes started getting pocked. On their second pass, the gloves came off, and Dahl's raiders destroyed the planes before they could get in the air.

But most of Dahl's time had to be spent over the Allied fleet, where every day he dueled with the Germans and French. Friendly antiaircraft guns from the Royal Navy exploded among the Junkers, and when Dahl got close, the exploding shells made his Hurricane hop too. On June 15, the same day the French made successful counterattacks against the Allied ground forces, the Luftwaffe nearly sunk the destroyer HMS *Isis*. The *Isis* had two Vichy destroyers on the run when Ju 88s appeared and dive-bombed, damaging the *Isis*'s engines. The destroyer HMS *Hero* rushed to the *Isis*'s aid, handing it a tow cable, and began pulling the destroyer back toward Haifa. Along the way, though, the cable snapped. Still, *Isis* eventually managed to start its engines and crawl toward its home at Haifa. All the while, flying in relays all day, Dahl and his comrades had to fend off Junkers and other planes still trying to finish the limping *Isis* off.

Back in Britain, the BBC reported that "continuous support has been given to our troops in Syria by aircraft of the Royal Air Force and the Royal Australian Air Force." But in reality, instances like the pummeling of the *Isis* are why the Allied men on the ground, like those overrun at places like Kuneitra and Marjayoun, usually had no help from the air.[5]

Bomb splinters tore through the air above Jack Hasey, the young man very far away indeed from his home in Bridgewater, Massachusetts. His face, the usually dark beard now bleached blond by the Syrian sun, was pressed against shale that burned like coals. Only minutes earlier, he and his platoon had waved to the planes passing overhead, hoping they were there to deliver food and water; but they had delivered exploding steel instead. He and many hundreds of the Free French Foreign Legion were trying to press toward Damascus, but it had been slow going, in infernal heat, for days.

There was a string of peaks and ridges here south of the capital. Beyond them was a green plain that invited the traveler to Damascus, the City of Jasmine, just visible on the horizon from the ridgetops. These heights also commanded an important road and railway to the capital, and must be seized before the Free French and Indians could attack Damascus itself.

For five days, from June 15 until this day, June 20, the Free French and their partners, the Punjabis and Rajputs, had been fighting for these rocks against a large force of Vichy units, highly professional soldiers from France, Morocco, and Senegal whose aim, the Free French admitted, was extraordinary. To expose one's head for even two seconds, a legionnaire remembered, was to die. Both sides had some artillery and mortars, while the Vichy French had bombers that killed or wounded no less than half of Jack Hasey's platoon.

Both sides fought with the discipline of professionals but were also motivated by rage against the other. There was charge and countercharge from one rocky crevice to another. The men howled. "Mort aux meurtriers!" (Death to the murderers!) cried the Free French; "Mort aux gaullistes!" (Death to the Gaullists!) cried the Vichy soldiers. The Free French soldiers of Chad wielded machetes, and Vichy soldiers of Morocco responded with bayonets. This continued for days, with men brutalized by sun and thirst, by the smell of corpses that could not be recovered. Companies lost as many as one-third of their men. A Vichy tank charge on a trajectory to crush Jack Hasey's platoon was turned away by Free French seventy-five-millimeter field guns that appeared just in time to drive them off. Near another hill, a squadron of Vichy Spahis performed a cavalry charge from the direction of Damascus. The Indians defending against it hesitated to fire, whether mesmerized, or disbelieving, or sorry to fire on the animals, until at last, they had to. Afterward, out of the dust, trotted a pitiful squadron of riderless horses back in the direction of Damascus.

Jack Hasey's fight came to an end amid this brutality. It was during another of the countless duels for the high ground among the stony hills, and Hasey was leading the remnants of his platoon when he was surprised by a curious sensation that he described as being numbly pushed backward while walking forward. Then his neck and chest stung. He next became conscious that he'd been shot, and was mildly disappointed that he didn't think glorious thoughts of fate or sacrifice or service to his beloved France. He simply thought, Oh, hell.

He had stumbled upon a Vichy machine gun nest. A bullet had torn through his neck and jaw, wrecking its hinge so that his mouth hung open. When he put his hand up to close his mouth, he realized that it, too, had been shot through. Another bullet passed clear through his chest, under his clavicle.

In the tradition of the Foreign Legion the fallen legionnaire remained where he dropped, knowing he'd be there until the battle was won. But Jack Hasey was lucky that this didn't apply to officers, and his Polish attendant managed to drag him back, tie up his wound at a dressing station, and get him evacuated in a truck to the rear. There he tried to talk to an officer, only to find that he couldn't work his hanging jaw. That night he was operated on in a farmhouse in a small Syrian village, a surgeon inserting a tracheostomy tube to assure Hasey could keep breathing. He received last rites. Given water, it would pour out of the hole in his neck. So the next day, without the aid of any anesthetic, another surgeon in another village had to insert a tube directly into his stomach so the American wouldn't die of dehydration and hunger.

And the young man with the ravaged face lived on, moved from station to station, all the way down to Jerusalem, tended to by Australian and Scottish doctors. Along the way he was sowed, patched, and partially reassembled. He was on a long, slow road back to Bridgewater.[6]

In the days following, in the battles for the ridges south of Damascus, it was said that two enemies startled each other, one holding a grenade and the other a bayonet. Each hesitated just long enough to recognize his enemy: his brother. Neither had seen nor heard from the other for over a year. It was just one of countless strange encounters between the internecine fighters. For example, Jack Hasey and his friends were awoken from a leaden sleep one night to find newcomers dropping exhausted into their camp: they were unaware Vichy soldiers, and were soon sent to Palestine as prisoners of war. Some Australian soldiers on the Lebanese front, meanwhile, captured an Australian legionnaire.

A few days before this, on June 16, Colonel Philibert Collet, who'd crossed lines to the Allies with several hundred Circassian Cavalry only weeks before, was maneuvering against a group of Vichy Druze cavalry who had successfully interrupted an Allied supply line. As the time approached for Collet to strike, he gathered his officers to plan. When they learned they were to attack the Druze, they told Collet forthrightly that they did not want to attack "their countrymen." Collet could hardly believe his ears: the insubordination was enough, but to hear his officers call the Druze "their countrymen" was too much: the two communities had generations of bad blood between them. Yet now they seemed to envision themselves as conationals. Luckily for Collet, he did not have to figure out what to do with his men on the verge of mutiny; in the distance, the Vichy Druze Cavalry began riding off. They were deserting for the same reason: they were unwilling to fight their compatriots. In another instance, two Circassian companies—one Vichy, one Free French—fell on one another with embraces rather than rifles. And in another, opposing Foreign Legion companies refused to fire on each other.[7]

But there was no such conciliation for the Indian Army men and boys sent to capture Mezze. As the fight for the hills south of Damascus viciously ground on, the Allied brigadier commanding this sector decided to send the Punjabis and Rajputs on a bold operation. To the west of the string of hills here was the road leading southwest out of the capital. The main village commanding that road and a nearby airfield was Mezze. For the several Indian companies the brigadier intended to send, it meant striking blind into a countryside with uncounted Vichy forces, facing potentially superior numbers in Mezze, the possibility of encountering Vichy tanks, and the potential of house-to-house fighting with all of its uncertainty and savagery.

The brigadier summoned the British lieutenant colonel who would lead the Indians, showing him the proposed flanking strike on a heavily creased map. Hugh Greatwood, the forty-one-year-old colonel of the Rajputs, looked at the plans, compared his own map, checked some figures, and then looked at the brigadier in the eye: "I think you are condemning my men to death, Sir."

"If you won't do it, I'll have to find somebody who will."

After a long, quiet breath Greatwood answered, "In that case, of course I'll do it."

That night, Greatwood duly led his Indian companies into the dark unknown toward Mezze so that others would not have to. He and well over one hundred Indian soldiers he'd known for years would be dead or dying within forty-eight hours.

The first danger was a long, twelve-mile march of half the night through enemy territory with untried defenses. And Greatwood's fears were confirmed when the Indians, marching through a grove, were shocked by dug-in machine gun emplacements with carefully laid lines of fire, the ground strewn with barbed wire. Men quickly started falling.

While some struggled to quiet those machine guns, others skirted the stream of tracers and headed toward the defense of Mezze, now awakened by the machine gun rattles. The sepoys cut barbed wire and charged Vichy guard posts with their cry of, "Allahu 'akbar!" Naik (Corporal) Abdul Rahman led his platoon on a pillbox, knocking down its defenders with Thompson submachine gun fire; then he led them to the next, and onward toward the center of town. Subedar (Warrant Officer) Mohammed Akbar, separated from his company during the machine gun trap in the grove outside Mezze, led a handful of men he gathered against the town's defenses, surprising and taking down two gun companies who were watching for allied trucks and tanks.

There were no Allied tanks coming, but there were Vichy tanks in the town and these, in turn, surprised Akbar and his men. As two tanks approached their position at the edge of town, Akbar dove out of sight behind a low mud wall until one of them was even with him. He then sprung up to lob a grenade, attracting rifle fire from Mezze's defenders, and the grenade damaged a component of the tank and the three-man French tank crew scrambled out, only to be shot down by the Indians. A second Vichy tank approached, and Akbar repeated his charmed grenade lob; this crew was taken prisoner. At the site of another defensive post on the edge of Mezze, Colonel Greatwood was not so lucky; he was shot in the chest and now lay at death's door.

Dawn was behind them, and so continued all day the localized, intense fighting throughout the crowded little town of Mezze. By night it was in the hands of the Punjabis and Rajputs, having driven off or wrecked the tanks defending the place and claiming forty prisoners, French and Moroccan Spahis. Most of the French garrison fled to fight another day. Hugh Greatwood's men, meanwhile, laid him in a large stone house surrounded by gardens, the new company headquarters.

The attack on Mezze achieved the desired effect of distracting the French. A Vichy officer phoned in to Damascus a dark report: "Éléments ennemis ont pris pied dans le village de Mezze. L'attaque a été menée par des fantassins attaquant au coude a coude avec de tres nombreuses mitraillettes. . . . La fusillade était intense." (Strong enemy elements gained a foothold in the village of Mezze. The assault was led by infantry attacking shoulder to shoulder with submachine guns. . . . The fire was intense.) The headquarters in Damascus was startled at this news from the west of the days-old battlefront, and it convinced the Vichy French to start an orderly withdrawal from the capital. Ultimately, it led to the drawdown of resistance along the front south of Damascus, where Jack Hasey and his comrades were fighting and dying. But before that, much of the French force was redirected and thrown at Mezze itself the next day.

The supporting units that were supposed to cover the Indians' flanks hadn't succeeded. The three red flares that the Punjabis and Rajputs launched into the dim morning signaling success went unanswered by Allied units that were supposed to be around the countryside. They were alone.

The horror for the isolated Indians started with a barrage of deadly accurate professional gunnery upon the town by the Vichy French that rarely enjoyed such an exposed target in this war. After the French guns came a squadron of those thick-hulled French tanks that had already bulldozed so many Allied defenses in these weeks. Behind these were Senegalese riflemen and legionnaires. At first the Indian men guarding the perimeter had been able to hold off the approaching infantry. But the thirty-five-ton machines smashed their makeshift defenses across the roads and around the village. Most of the defenders' antitank ammunition was lost with the captured supply trucks, and the scrambling men quickly ran out of grenades. When they took cover, and fired from behind walls, the tanks simply smashed those walls. When the men dodged from house to house, the tanks shot through windows and doors. The Punjabis and Rajputs did what they could to answer or at least delay the advancing tanks and the troops covering behind them. But there was little they could do.

And they fell back and back until the big stone house and its wall became their last holdout. They picked fruit from the trees and dug up some vegetables in the garden since they had no rations. They tore up bedsheets to use as bandages. They crawled among the bodies of the fallen, looking for ammunition. Night fell and they fought on, trying to make every shot count. The gardens had a lot of low brush, which helped cover the defenders, but they had very few antitank rounds remaining, and they had to be rationed to keep the tanks guessing about how many the Indians possessed. So they improvised to keep the tanks at bay: the house, it appeared, belonged to a well-to-do European employee of the Iraq Petroleum Company, and was nicely supplied with wine. The besieged Punjabis and Rajputs poured the vintage out and replaced it with gasoline, with which a small garage was also nicely stocked, though the car was long gone. These Molotov cocktails made the tanks keep their distance for now. Still, the attackers knocked down the garden walls, piecemeal.

The next morning the sleepless siege continued with no relief in sight for the Indians, most of whose officers were now dead. Heroes holding out in a barricaded house against an outnumbering force of savages: it's such a commonplace trope. The Alamo comes to mind, or Charles George Gordon at Khartoum, or the Siege of Lucknow. They're clichéd allegories, meant to contrast the stolid courage of the white man with the frenzy of the barbarians at the gate. But the scene in Damascus in 1941 neatly turns this around. The resolved defenders—Havildar (Sergeant) Abdul Aziz was said to have even been downright cheerful as he encouraged his men—were from what is today India and Pakistan. The men in the tanks and at the artillery were French.

In the light, the attackers rolled artillery up the village streets and started pounding away at the stone house turning the inside into a mess of dust and collapsing masonry. The enemy fired a rifle grenade through a window, the shrapnel cutting one of the Punjabis' senior officers, who would later die from the wound. A tank turned its predatory muzzle on the roof and exploded a corner. Stone, tiles, and beams fell on the wounded who had been lying in the attic.

Until now, they had outwitted or outrun death, or gotten lucky, these Indian Army men. In many months of soldiering in Libya and northeastern Africa, on hills and rocks and deserts, they'd survived mortar, bomb, and bullet many times over. But today, behind collapsing brick and splintered mortar, they were dying. The Hindus and Sikhs among them were subject to Karma and the cycle of lives, the Christians and Muslims to God's predestination or providence. But now very few of them would escape their fate, very few would walk out of the stone house alive. Only about thirteen Indians could still fight at the moment of their surrender (or overrunning) on June 20. About two hundred more in and around the stone house were wounded or half dead from thirst. Earlier, over one hundred were killed and many score had been injured or scattered by the machine gun fire south of Mezze. Several hundred lay dead or dying at their defensive posts around the village. In total the casualties numbered 738. The Punjabi and Rajput battalions of this army were essentially out of the battle.[8]

The cost in blood was rising, and the Allied invasion could still turn into a total reversal, as had happened in Greece. These terrible battles south and west of Damascus, along with a pulverizing struggle up the coast for the Australians and Scots south of Beirut, cried out for a change in Allied plans. With time dragging, figures in Cairo, Freya Stark's friends and colleagues, began to fear that politicians might accept an armistice in Syria-Lebanon that would leave the collaborationist Dentz in power there. The other thing they feared was a possible Vichy retreat into neutral Turkey, claiming a kind of sanctuary of the "neutral." Charles de Gaulle, meanwhile, worried such outcomes would leave him without a chance to recruit from among the tens of thousands in the Vichy Armée du Levant.

Back down in Jerusalem, at midnight on June 29, fed-up Australian general Thomas Blamey knocked on the door of Freya Stark's friend, the man in charge of the invasion, General Henry "Jumbo" Wilson. Told the general was asleep by a guard, Blamey brushed in and demanded he be awakened. A sentry went off. The large man, awake only minutes, soon came downstairs and walked into a barrage. The force was too weak, insisted Blamey. Men were dying by the minute, and something had to

British twenty-five pounder field gun in action during the advance into
Syria, June 1941. *(Credit: Courtesy of Imperial War Museum Collections)*

Australian troops pose near captured French Morane fighters. Photo taken
July 24, 1941, Syria. *(Credit: © G. Silk, courtesy of Australian War Memorial)*

A Bren gun carrier of the Sixth Australian Division Cavalry Regiment passing through a wood during the advance into Syria. Photo taken June 1941.
(*Credit: Courtesy of Australian War Memorial*)

Australian soldiers cool their feet in an ancient Roman aqueduct in Syria, June 1941.
(*Credit: © Frank Hurley, courtesy of Australian War Memorial*)

Indian Army troops of the Fifth Indian Infantry Brigade (foreground) watch a Bren gun carrier drive on conquered Damascus. A ruined French tank sits in the background.

(Credit: © Military History Colletion/Alamy)

Allied troops search the ruins of Palmyra, July 1941.　　*(Credit: British Crown)*

An Allied cavalryman inspects the ruins of a German Heinkel destroyed on the ground at Palmyra's airstrip. Its Swastika had been hastily painted over, but someone has chalked-in its outline. *(Credit: Courtesy of Australian War Memorial)*

An RAF officer investigates the bombed ruins of an Iraqi gun on the plateau above
the RAF base at Habbaniyah, Iraq, in May 1941.

(*Credit: RAF Photographer, courtesy Imperial War Museum Collections*)

Roald Dahl (second from right) and friends posing before the Euphrates at Habbaniya during their fight training in 1940.

(*Credit: © Roald Dahl Story Company/Roald Dahl Museum and Story Centre Archive*)

Nazi Rudolf Rahn (seated, smiling) in Tunisia, where he was the Reich's chief liaison to the ruling Vichy French authorities, circa late 1941.

Vichy soldiers waiting to cast their votes on the subject of joining de Gaulle's forces or returning to France. Photo taken August 24, 1941. Beirut, Syria.

(Credit: Courtesy of Australian War Memorial)

French soldiers boarding the ship *Sinaia* to be convoyed across the Mediterranean to Vichy France. Beirut, Syria, August 29, 1941.   *(Credit: Courtesy of Australian War Memorial)*

change; they needed reinforcements, and they needed a shift in the direction of the attack.

Strangely, help for the ground-down Allied invaders was available because of failures on another front. General Archibald Wavell's recent counterpunch against Rommel on the Egypt-Libya frontier, Operation Battleaxe, had failed. Thus, some units were freed of responsibility there, meaning more men, particularly Australians, could be brought up through Palestine to the Syria-Lebanon fronts. Jumbo Wilson asked and received them.

As for shifting the direction of the attack, Wilson agreed to that too. He asked for reinforcements from Iraq to drive on Syria from the east. This meant that Jack Bartlett, Harry Chalk, John Glubb and his Arab legionnaires, the Arab Palestinian called Reading, and David Smiley were in for more fighting in this war for Iraq and the Levant.[9]

14

"They Too Suffer as You Suffer"

Reinforcements: The Indian Army and the Cavalry Drive on Syria

> Palmyra, 11 Dec. 2016, 14:00. We are completely surrounded by Daesh. The terrorists also fully control the al-Bayarat highway [west of Palmyra]. There is no place to retreat. Thank God that the General is with us, he finally got in touch with the authorities and sent six Mi-28 helicopters to accompany our retreat through gardens. They successfully covered us with fire from the right and left flanks. We managed to break out of the encirclement.
>
> —Report of Syrian soldier Omar Dirmam, who escaped the Islamic State of Iraq and the Levant's siege of Palmyra, 2016

ON JUNE 21, 1941, Reading awoke before dawn on the western Iraqi sand, wrapped in an army greatcoat. Though the days were scorching, nights in west-northwestern Iraq were chilly, even in June. His boss, the fastidious member of Parliament turned intelligence officer for whom Reading translated, had a portable cot, laid out every night and packed up every day by his servant and driver; no sleeping on the sand for him.

The past month had not been easy going. Practically shanghaied from Haifa to serve as an interpreter, he had rushed across an Iraqi desert overflown by Messerschmitts and past the wreckage of Fallujah toward war outside Baghdad, where he would've died had an incoming artillery shell not been a dud. But for all that, Reading had come to see this as the life for him. He'd decided that he wanted to transfer to intelligence, and he told his boss that. While he would see the campaign through with him, afterward Reading would appreciate his help getting a commission to train as an intelligence officer.

But that was for the future. For now, Reading got up off the cold ground and prepared for the next leg in his journey across these deserts: today he would pass over the frontier into Syria. After a predawn breakfast, he climbed back into the stalwart artillery-shell-dented American car he'd inhabited for a month in Iraq. And, after dawn lightened, a vast body of trucks began rolling northwest, away from the Haifa–Kirkuk oil pipeline and toward Palmyra, about 150 miles away in Syria. Palmyra, while small, was a key location, with an oasis, grand Roman-era ruins, an airfield, a stone fort, a pumping station for the Iraqi oil pipeline to Lebanon, and a desert crossroads. It also had a Crusader castle topping a steep stony hill overlooking everything. Eight centuries earlier, the strong fortress kept watch on the crossroads; so did it now.

Most of Habforce, the relief force for the Royal Air Force (RAF) base at Habbaniya, was on the move into Syria that day in order to draw the Vichy French away from the bitterly stubborn defense of Beirut and Damascus. Ultimately the goal was to overrun Palmyra and push on to Homs, farther west in Iraq, effectively cutting Syria in half and forcing a French capitulation, in a bleak shadow of the German slice across northern France a year earlier. At the same time that Reading was crossing here, the Indian Army was about to invade, driving on the town of Deir ez-Zor, an eastern Syrian provincial capital on the Euphrates north of Palmyra. Another Indian Army group was headed for far northern Syria to block any thought of a French retreat to Turkey and to command the railroad that Rahn had used to ship weapons to the Iraqis. There were, in sum, three invasion forces entering Syria about this time, the first day of Syrian summer.

Around Reading, spread out so as not to present a good target for enemy planes, rolled over a hundred trucks bearing multiple cavalry troops. There were also Jack Bartlett and the big quads of the Lincolnshire gunners; again, their twenty-five-pounders were the most powerful ground weapon in this war and could destroy the French tanks that had so devastated the Allies in the past few weeks—if only they could draw a bead on them. Operating freely ahead of and around this dispersed mass were the homemade armored cars and Chevy pickups of

John Glubb and the Arab Legion. They would sometimes barrel in, confer with officers, and then disappear, leaving clouds of dust.

Once an Arab Legion car full of men arrived to speak to Reading's boss and compare maps and bearings. A pale Englishman was among them, an RAF airman learning the lay of the land from the legionnaires. He introduced himself as Pilot Officer Mosley, a name that brought Reading's boss up short. Yes, this man confessed, answering the obvious question, he was related to the British archfascist Oswald Mosley. That was his cousin, who had preached cooperation with Germany before the war and was now imprisoned in London as a public enemy.

Coming up behind Reading, the cavalry, the gunners, and Arab Legion was Harry Chalk and the First Essex Regiment, their stolen Iraqi Bren carrier borne with them on a flatbed truck. Chalk hadn't been much impressed by Baghdad, which he'd wanted to look more like something out of the Arabian Nights tales, but he wouldn't have minded seeing more of Iraq. Still, he took it rather personally that the French had hosted the Luftwaffe, which had gunned the Essex on their way to Habbaniya. He understood that he would face the French Foreign Legion somewhere up this road, and that thought was a bit daunting, though Chalk didn't rate the French very highly generally.

Within a few bright hours, Reading's car approached two piles of stones on either side of the poor, rutted dirt track they'd been flanking. Some more stones were strewn out in short lines on either side: what passed for a border demarcation. They were almost halfway to Palmyra.[1]

In Amman, the Arab Legion happily received its orders to invade Syria too. It had returned to a provincial headquarters in Mafraq, Transjordan, after chasing the Golden Square from Baghdad, regrouping in Habbaniya, and policing some tribal raiders—maybe encouraged by Fawzi al-Qawuqji—who'd crossed into the country from Syria, taking advantage of the war's chaos. On the eve of the legion's joining the fight in Syria, Emir Abdullah I came north to address them, as around 350 legionnaires formed a square around the pacing prince.

"The moment for freeing Syria has come," Abdullah said. "I rely on you to seize this golden hour in the history of the Arabs." For many among the gathered troopers, this was a war of liberation, a chance to throw out those French who'd occupied Damascus for a generation. After three cheers, the legionnaires mounted their armored cars and trucks and drove north and upward, through lava fields of sprinkled dark boulders, before emerging into a gravelly highland and onward to the oil pipeline. There they were greeted by French planes that strafed them. The widely dispersed vehicles weathered this well before rolling onward and finding the Household Cavalry, the gunners towing their twenty-five-pounders, some RAF armored cars, and others. Then it was time to push into Syria, the legion dispersing in small groups to accompany various British units as guides and scouts.

One truck, out scouting ahead of its British charges, came upon a French outpost on the dusty plain, just a collection of tents, men with binoculars, and a wireless set for warning Palmyra of any approach. As fast as the Arab legionnaires raced, they could not reach the lookouts before they radioed back to Palmyra that the invaders were here. The legionnaires rushed to smash the wireless set, only too late; soon the sky would be filled with Vichy bombers searching them out. Still, the Arab Legion captured a French officer there and, questioned about the garrison at Palmyra ahead, the small man with broken spectacles was forthcoming. Why not? he mused. You must already know everything, since Colonel Philibert Collet came over to you with all the detailed knowledge he possesses of French defenses. The outpost also contained some helpful papers; less helpful was the French translation of Adolf Hitler's *Mein Kampf* found among them.[2]

Inevitably, not long after this, the Vichy Armée de l'air found Reading's dispersed column. Three Potez 63 bombers came straight down the line of trucks, cars, and gun limbers, and dropped their seventy-five-pound bombs at their leisure. There was little the men on the ground could do to resist the bombers, and no air cover for them, so men dove flat on the gravel. One of the Australians rushed up from Egypt to participate in the invasion, a gunner with a priceless antitank unit, had his arm blown off as craters blew open on the plain.

After the planes had exhausted their bombs, Reading's column moved off again to catch the Kirkuk–Tripoli pipeline and make their final turn toward Palmyra. They hoped to rest and resupply at an oil pumping station there, one of the stations that had recently kept Iraqi oil flowing to Vichy Lebanon; it doubled as a fortified outpost, with stockpiles and a water well. Arriving at the walled and barbed-wired station, they found it occupied by a Vichy French garrison. So some of Jack Bartlett's friends in the 237th Field Battery tried a twenty-five-pounder against the buildings in the fort, only to find the shells bounced off its big granite blocks. There'd be no respite here, so the column pushed around the fort, west toward Palmyra, leaving a small force to harass and hold down the French inside so they would think twice about sallying forth and attacking the column's rear.[3]

That small Allied force had a terrible destiny. About forty-eight hours later, the small section watching the place, troopers of the Warwickshire Yeomanry, were dug into position, all eyes on the quiet French-held station, while behind them Allied vehicles occasionally kicked up dust as they traveled westward, deeper into Syria. It was brutally hot, but some helpful officers circulated to keep the besiegers supplied with precious water. Then, to their surprise, a group of five three-ton Chevys approached the besiegers at first light, flying a white flag. It seemed that those in the stone outpost had had enough, and the Warwickshire men came out of their positions to parley with those in the leading vehicle. That's when Vichy Senegalese troops led by French officers leaped from the backs of the Chevys and opened up a spray of fire with Thompsons. Then French armored cars sped from behind the screen of trucks. It turns out they had not emerged from the fort; they were a relief force from somewhere. The British troopers who'd emerged to hail the white flag were slaughtered in cold blood. Now a French light gun opened up from the fort. Some British troopers escaped. Eight were murdered. Five were badly hurt. And five were captured.

French officers were rounding up their prisoners and preparing to abandon the oil pipeline station—they left one injured British officer with the wounded, dying, and dead—when an Arab Legion truck happened to come on the scene. A British soldier with the legionnaires didn't understand what he'd come upon—the French officers he mistook for British—and by the time the man realized his mistake, he and the Arab troopers were surrounded.

So some Arab legionnaires joined the captured Warwickshire men as prisoners, soon packed up and sent westward into still secure Vichy areas. They were eventually transported by air to German-occupied Greece, and later all the way to conquered France itself.[4] (Their remarkable story appears in the pages to come.)

Reading and those in his column would hear of this tragedy only later, and meanwhile pushed on toward Palmyra, not twenty miles to the west. For Reading and the cavalry around him, the recent bombing of the column south of the Kirkuk–Tripoli pipeline changed things; this was going to be a different affair from the drive on Baghdad. In that campaign, it was the RAF that dominated the sky. True, there had been the harrowing threats of Axis fighters, which strafed Allied units with deadly results: Reading had seen their handiwork up close in the wrecked bodies of Arab legionnaires. But these French planes had devastated the surface of the Syrian plain. The threat from them was not that you might be singled out for strafing, but of general, widespread destruction. Reading knew as well as any that death hovered close in this war: he was alive because of a dud artillery shell. But now he took up a pen to write his last words to his family in Haifa, making two copies; one he put in his breast pocket, the other he gave to his officer to send in case nothing in his breast pocket remained.

Both copies were almost annihilated. The vehicles of the Household Cavalry were west of the pipeline fort and still a few miles east of Palmyra on a plain about two by three miles in area. Somewhere in the direction of Palmyra, entrenched machine gun positions were blocking the approach of the head of the column. Therefore, Reading's American car was stationary, spaced widely from its neighbors to make a poorer target for air attack, yet the air attack came in the afternoon, when the western horizon filled with Potez bombers. Reading and the driver rushed away from their vehicle; the intelligence officer, meanwhile, tumbled out, grabbing a rifle in a vain attempt at resistance, while the French prisoner with broken spectacles remained motionless in the car, fatalistic. Black bursts framed with yellow sand erupted from the plain all around Reading. Then French fighters followed the bombers rattling away at the men and vehicles. The attack lasted hours and was the beginning of an all-out air offensive on the would-be besiegers of Palmyra. It was in many ways a mirror of the Battle of Habbaniya: a small, outmanned garrison holding out in a vital position, with mainly air forces capable of keeping the besiegers—lacking air cover—at bay.

The ground all around the dispersed column alternatively heaved with heavy bombs or erupted in little explosions from cannon and machine gun fire. Reading's intelligence officer had stopped firing at the planes with a rifle and instead bizarrely took up a camera to photograph them as if he were documenting a crime. Then the man was shot in the leg and he collapsed into the car. The French prisoner, who'd never left the car in the attack, managed to start it, even though it'd been shot through in several places, got it into gear, and weaved off, bearing Reading's boss toward an ambulance.

Now Reading was alone on the hellish plain, hunted from above. At some point, minutes or hours later under this terror, his reason left him, his higher-order mind disconnected. Instinct set in, and it only knew that it wanted to get away from the explosions. His body started ambling as if of its own accord eastward, back in the direction from which they'd come, the desert still blooming with dust and fire behind him. Toward the east, only death awaited him, whether from thirst and heat, strafing planes, or guerilla raiders; so Reading was lucky that someone picked him up and drove him eastward toward the field dressing station about twenty miles to the east and south, an emergency room under canvas, at a deep valley called Juffa. He was lucky, too, that Fawzi al-Qawuqji's raiders didn't come upon his rescuers' vehicle, as they had others, and that his ambulance or truck wasn't strafed by the French, as happened to others. Eventually the vehicle carrying him approached Juffa, and the care of doctors; it passed under an antiaircraft gun mounted on hills ringing the station like a sentinel against the French planes. (The French, though, would soon find the place.)

Reading was not wounded, but saw nothing of the world around him. The doctors did what they could for him, but they didn't even know who he was other than the fact that he was in a British Cavalry uniform. They wanted to know who his next of kin were, but didn't find the letter to his family in Haifa in his breast pocket. When Reading's wounded intelligence officer arrived at the station—his ambulance had been strafed by the French—they finally pieced together who the young Arab was. The officer asked to see Reading, sure that the young Palestinian man would recognize him and snap back to himself.

No, the doctor told him, shaking his head; he wouldn't.[5]

Not far from Reading's column, David Smiley and another group of the Household Cavalry drove on Palmyra from a different direction, more northward, along the oil pipeline to Lebanon. The nationalist guerilla fighter Fawzi al-Qawuqji, who'd entered into an uneasy partnership with Rudolf Rahn and General Henri Dentz, had been raiding near the pipeline, along with Allied supply lines, and Smiley's group came upon a station looted by them. Only a few months earlier, Smiley himself had done such "irregular" warfare in northeastern Africa against the Italians. He's heard some repulsive rumors about what some Arab guerillas did to those they captured, which allowed him to make a hard distinction between their guerilla raiding and his own in the Sudan borderlands.

Smiley pushed past the looted pumping station toward Palmyra, only to come upon the ongoing devastation on the plain southeast of the town. They were Glenn Martins, Smiley noted, made in America; and the two-hundred-pound bombs they dropped had originated in Britain. Smiley's driver did his best to cross the plain as quickly as possible, but there were burned-out vehicles all around, as well as boulders and other hazards. Smiley disliked the bombers, of course, but he particularly hated the way the fighters appeared without warning, often out of the desert sun, and their ability to better target the moving vehicles.

The approach to Palmyra was clogged by over three hundred vehicles, and much of the landscape was covered by French machine guns and artillery. Smiley's column was forced to stop on the plain, and the men hurried away from their dispersed vehicles and immediately cut shallow trenches into the sand and gravel. Inevitably the unopposed planes came out to sow their bombs. Smiley was in a trench with a friend when they both saw a bomb sailing silently toward them—straight toward them.

This is it, he said to himself. Smiley had wanted to get his polished cavalry boots dirty and did so in many countries and fights; he had wanted to serve in the heart of the action, and this was truly it. He closed his eyes to await his end.

The bomb made impact twenty yards away, and its shards sliced through the air above the two men lying in their shallow slit in the desert. The steel splinters cut through a nearby truck in several places.

The constant French attacks continued. Later that day, yet another fighter strafed the plain, coming in very low above the trenches containing Smiley and several others. The men fired from where they sat, two of them shouldering their rifles, Smiley firing his personal Mauser machine pistol. One cavalry trooper, perhaps relishing the opportunity to fire back at his tormenters, climbed out of his trench and squatted behind a fifty-pound World War I–era machine gun on a tripod, badly exposed in this duel.

But to the delight of the four men, they knocked out the fighter as it screamed overhead. It twisted slowly and dived to its death five hundred yards behind them. Rushing to the smoking ruins, Smiley found that the plummeting plane had struck and killed one of their own men. They also found a few remains of the French pilot, which they buried in the desert under a jury-rigged cross.

That day Smiley's column alone suffered four deaths and more wounded, with seven trucks shot through or burning on the plain. Night finally brought respite from the unceasing pounding, and under the cover of darkness Smiley and his comrades were able to advance closer to Palmyra's columns and escape the plain of horrors for some cover.[6]

Jack Bartlett and his friends from Lincolnshire were spread out in several batteries around the edges of Palmyra. The lucky team was on the north side of the town, where there were some hills that offered decent cover. But Jack was on the south side, firing on a modern fort, pillboxes, and an airstrip. His and the other twenty-five-pounders were the only real answer the Allies had for the TNT pinning the force down and ending lives all around Palmyra. In daylight, the First Essex Regiment and cavalry couldn't cross the flat ground before the town to assault it—or be cut down by French machine guns that commanded the landscape.

The French planes, meanwhile, were making Jack and his fellows earn every shot. They'd dug in as best they could, and stayed low in their trenches; they piled stones around their guns to provide some kind of shelter. But for Bartlett, it was a nightmare of unremitting heat, noise, and destruction. It was 125 degrees in the shade, and water was scarce. Flies constantly nagged, and snakes found their way into sleeping places. Periodically, vehicles nearby exploded. A gun on his team was wrecked by a bomb, and another nearby battery had a gun destroyed. Men ran from trench to trench. A colonel running between guns brought a strange rumor that, in some distant world, Germany had just invaded Russia. That could mean very little to those living in this hell, on this day on which 112 French sorties were flown against the besiegers of Palmyra.

The days wore on, and the siege continued, with no air support to keep the tormenting fighters and bombers at bay. At least some long-nosed Australian Bofors antiaircraft guns eventually arrived from the rear to protect the batteries. The gunner was seated next to the gun's breach, and with just a subtle turn of a wheel he could swing the whole gun up, down, and around to target an enemy. This didn't end the air onslaught, but it helped keep the fighters from strafing low and at their leisure, at least.

Once a Bofors gun hit a French fighter above Bartlett. The pilot ejected and began to drift to earth, but something was wrong: the chute appeared, but was not opening. To his horror, Bartlett realized that the chute had failed, and the pilot soon struck the ground not far from him. Jack inspected the chute, cutting it free and eventually mailing the precious silk to his mother in rationed England. Perhaps she never learned of its bleak origins.

One day some friends in another battery were killed when they'd sheltered under their quad. A French fighter lit it up, burning the sheltering men and killing one. On another day, a French pilot came down not far from Bartlett; the man, he learned, had escaped conquered France at Dunkirk, and had then served in the RAF; was shot down over northern

France and captured; was given the option of serving in the Vichy Armée de l'air; and had been rushed to Syria at the outbreak of this war to fight his former Allied comrades. Jack wondered whether the pilot might now reenlist in the RAF.[7]

Harry Chalk and the First Essex Regiment had the unenviable task of besieging Palmyra. They'd suffered, too, running the gauntlet of the approach to the town, when a pair of comrades driving their water truck were killed by a strafing French fighter. Then followed days of ducking and maneuvering among the tumbled ruins of an ancient Roman quarter. Once, when they tried to approach the modern part of the town and its Vichy Foreign Legion strongpoints, sniper fire pinned them down. The tracked Bren gun carriers were called up, as they were less vulnerable to the sniping, but soon armor-piercing rounds started coming through their steel walls. The Essex only had a few carriers, and when one went into a ditch on its side, with its five men exposed, it was time for the carrier *Southend-on-Sea*—stolen from Iraq—to shine. It, along with a second, hurried to cover the men tossed out of the beached vehicle. Now rifle fire pelted all three carriers from cover one hundred yards distant, more men were hit, and the Brens rattled back at the attackers. Thus covered, men hopped out of the *Southend* and dragged their comrades to cover before lifting them into the surviving carriers and retreating. They all lived, in part thanks to the robbery of a Bren carrier in Iraq. But the experience was a cautionary tale for the Essex commanders: Palmyra could not be stormed by infantry without paying a high price.[8]

Around this time, David Smiley was operating near Harry Chalk, learning the same thing as he probed the defenses of Palmyra after dark. One night, setting off on a scouting mission, he heard in the darkness a Cockney voice saying, "In peacetime, blokes pay cash to come and see these bloody ruins, and here we are doing it buckshee [free of charge]." With a squad of ten, Smiley crouched and crawled among the ruins of the Palmyrene and Roman Empires, observing enemy defenses and examining possible routes of attack. He noted the lay of the land, for later reporting to his superiors, but good paths of attack seemed closed.

Along the way he sent a pair of men to check the status of the Crusader castle on the hill overlooking the town; the place was alternatively held by Allied and French forces throughout the siege. After some hours, with dawn approaching, the two men had still not returned, and Smiley was burdened with the loss of two more lives in this miserable campaign. He waited for their return too long, in fact, and his patrol was spotted by the Foreign Legion when dawn illuminated them. Machine guns and rifles opened on them from the direction of the modern town and for Smiley and his patrol it meant a fraught hour of scampering, diving, and crawling among the ancient rubble to escape.

About forty-eight hours later, the lost men reappeared in the cavalry lines, without their boots and rifles. They told of crawling up to the Crusader castle to investigate, only to be attacked and surrounded by the town's inhabitants, who removed their rifles and boots at gunpoint. Smiley knew the men pretty well and thought it far more likely that they thought better of approaching the dark and dangerous fort, and instead found a place to sleep, having their rifles stolen, meanwhile, by an opportunistic local resident.

A couple days later, with the siege still grinding on in the dust and the French Air Force still punishing the Allies, a rare victory lifted Smiley and the entrenched men's spirits. Six French Glenn Martin bombers appeared on the horizon to make their usual uncontested strafing run. It seemed only a question of who would share the fate of the Essex water tanker crew, the ambulance that had been shot up, and the burned men who had sheltered under their quad. But this time six Tomahawks suddenly emerged from the sky to take on the French. It seemed that six Royal Australian Air Force P-40s, on escort duty for some Blenheims bombing elsewhere, had caught sight of the French bombers and seen an opportunity.*

*A terrific, but false, story later circulated among the Allied soldiers suffering around Palmyra that the six P-40 Tomahawk pilots had been at their base in Palestine when they intercepted pleas for air cover at the approach of the French bombers. They then leaped in their fighters without orders and scrambled to the rescue. Thinking they'd be court-martialed upon their return to base, one was immediately awarded a Distinguished Service Medal. This fantasy accords with the mens' belief that the air force brass were stingy in protecting them from the air, and with the reputation of the Australians as being of flexible discipline.

On the ground, cheers went up all around at this almost unheard-of appearance of air cover. The French pilots seemed shocked, and started taking a rain of machine gun fire. Smiley watched as, one after another, the six French planes broke, burned, and collapsed. Somewhere a man was calling the action like a boxing announcer: "A right, and a left. And another—and another!" A series of white parachutes soon stood out against the blue Syrian sky. It was supremely satisfying for the men on the ground who'd been hunted for over a week, and they shouted with bloody joy.

David Smiley, though, was about to be taken out of the war for a month. He was quickly descending into fever and listlessness. He had malaria. (Dr. Ernest Altounyan, an old friend of T. E. Lawrence, and a doctor who was volunteering with the Arab Legion, improbably had a telescope with him on the campaign and later diagnosed malaria via blood sample.) So, after the cheers, Smiley collapsed on a cot in a cave.

There in a makeshift sick ward, Smiley had a neighbor. One of the French parachutes had been outlined by fire during its descent that day. And the pilot dangling from it, though he survived the fall, was later carried into the cave, horribly burned. Soon the doctors worked away on him, removing large patches of burned skin from the Frenchman. That night, Smiley and the pilot were placed in the same truck to be removed to the rear, and Smiley listened to the delirious man's moaning for many hours. His previous delight in watching the French planes catch fire was long gone now. By midnight, a Catholic chaplain arrived to whisper over the Frenchman, who did not last until dawn.[9]

Over coastal Lebanon and southern Syria, Roald Dahl's squadronmates were dying at a steady rate; of the nine who had started in the air war, only five were left by the end of June. (By another calculation, based on what Dahl gathered, 30 percent of his friends from flight training at the Habbaniya air base were now killed or missing in the war at large.) He'd been flying as much as his tall frame could bear, sweating profusely all the while, his plexiglass canopy functioning as a perfect greenhouse. He spent as many as seven hours a day in the air, strafing, circling the fleet, scrambling to catch French or Germans, of whom he'd shot down one and four, respectively. Dahl was now livid with the French, whom he considered Nazi collaborators, for the loss of life he considered unnecessary; he would never forgive them.

One day Dahl's squadron leader approached him and asked him to go look at a new landing spot about thirty miles away from Haifa. Because the port had now come under increased attack from the Vichy Air Force and the Luftwaffe operating from the Aegean Islands, the squadron leader was afraid their Haifa base was too exposed. If their small force was shot up on the ground, a vast part of their total force in the region would disappear.

"Fly over there and have a look at it," the officer said. "It's meant to serve as a small secret hideaway where those Ju 88s could never find us." Dahl took off and was over the designated spot in a flash. Below him, he could just make out a strip cut from a field of corn. It was hidden enough.

Dahl took the chance of trying out the landing, and the ground was firm and fast. He switched his engine off to have a look at this green place when, suddenly, several dozen children rushed out of the corn to point and shout. The Hurricane was clearly a wonder to them. Then a tall bearded man approached whom Dahl was sure was a twin of the Prophet Isaiah, his eyes shining with energy.

"Welcome to our little settlement," the man said, offering his hand. Dahl took it, though the man's German accent was an instinctual red flag to someone who'd started the war tasked with rounding up Germans in Tanganyika.

"I didn't think anyone knew about this," Dahl said.

"We cut the corn ourselves and helped roll out the strip."

"But who are you and who are all these children?"

"We are Jewish refugees. The children are all orphans. This is our home." The man led Dahl into a small wooden house beside fig trees. A silent woman inside, whom the bearded man did not introduce, lit a small kerosene burner and made them coffee.

Dahl had been out of touch from the dark developments for Jews in Europe in the foregoing years, in part because of his isolation in East Africa.

"So where do you go from here, you and your orphans?"

"We don't go anywhere," the man said, offering bread; "we stay here."

"Then you will become Palestinians, or perhaps you are that already."

"No, I do not think we will become Palestinians."

Dahl was confused. He had not learned of Zionism, the movement for a Jewish nation in Palestine, what Zionists called Eretz Israel, the land of Israel. And yet nationalism—be it French, Iraqi, Jewish, or Syrian—was always close to the heart of this war. Dahl took to the air in his Hurricane several times a day to undergo a kill-or-be-killed trial because the Vichy French sought to protect their national integrity and redeem their national pride. The people of Syria, meanwhile, tended to revile French overlordship and hoped the Allies were freeing them to form their own nation; the Arab Legion hoped that they were freeing their Arab cousins, too. The Iraqi war was born in the authoritarian nationalism of the Golden Square. Palestinian Arabs, whether militant like the Mufti Husseini, or broad-minded like Reading, or liberal like Freya Stark's friend Lulie Abul-Huda, a pan-Arabist, hoped for their own sovereign nation someday as well.

The bearded man did his best to explain what he was doing in Palestine; Dahl felt rather naive. They drank their coffee. "We need a country of our own," the man said. "Even the Zulus have Zululand. But we have nothing."

Dahl was still unsure about what the man meant, and wouldn't understand this conversation for years to come.

"You have a country to live in . . . therefore you have no problems," the man told Dahl.

"No problems! England is fighting for her life! I've got problems myself in just trying to stay alive."

"That is a very small problem. Ours is much bigger."

"Don't you care whether we beat Hitler or not?"

"Of course, I care. It is essential that Hitler be defeated. But that is only a matter of months and years. Historically, it will be a very short battle. Also, it happens to be England's battle. It is not mine. My battle is one that has been going on since the time of Christ."

The dark-haired woman washed the dishes, and the man led Dahl back outside. "You have a lot to learn. But you are a good boy." He slapped Dahl's back. "You are fighting for freedom. So am I."

The children were still looking at the Hurricane in wonder. Some older boys watched over them to make sure they didn't touch the plane. Dahl prepared to climb in.

"Do not think we are not grateful. You are doing a fine job. I wish you luck," the man said.

"You, too." Dahl still didn't understand the conversation he'd just had. He started the engine, wheeled around, and roared off.

As the end of June approached, Dahl started suffering overwhelming headaches when he flew. A doctor examined him, and said it had to do with his crash in Egypt and the consequences for his head. The prognosis was poor. Finally, not long after, the doctor grounded him; Roald Dahl was out of the war. And he soon boarded a transport for the long journey around the Cape of Good Hope for England.[9]

The Arab Legion had a victory in those long, hot days around Palmyra as July approached. But they, too, had to suffer the unopposed attentions of the French Air Force, first. They were based at Juffa, the rearward base situated in a crater-like depression southeast of Palmyra. Reading, now on his way to a more rearward hospital, had passed through Juffa in a state of shock; David Smiley then passed through, stricken with malaria. Reading and Smiley were lucky to be gone when the Vichy French found the place and started paying it a lot of unwelcome attention, flying multiple sorties a day, bombing it with incendiaries, dueling with the Bofors gun crews who bravely swiveled and pounded back at them.

One day, two civilian trucks arrived in the camp. Out leaped Za'al ibn Mutlaq, a sheik of the Hawaytat Bedouin of Transjordan, his gray hair braided under his kaffiyeh. The Hawaytat were famous for having contributed the core of the raiders against the Ottoman Turks in World War I's Arab Revolt, for having fought with Abdullah I of Jordan, Faisal I of Iraq, and T. E. Lawrence. Many tribesmen leaped out behind the sheik, singing a war song and firing their guns into the air, which didn't quite accord with British Army rules in force in the camp. But the singing Bedouin relished the opportunity to fight: when they had heard that the French were to be driven from Syria, that glory and spoils were in the offing, they hurried to Juffa. Glubb, the Arab Legion commander, knew these men well; he had recruited from among them and other Bedouin communities.

The day after their arrival, the French air raiders made their inevitable return, the air-raid whistles blowing around the valley. The Hawayti, including Za'al, were scattered around the camp. When others leaped for their slit trenches, Za'al picked up his rifle, took off his cloak, and quickly loped up the slope ringing the place, ignoring the pleas for him to take cover in a trench. At the top of the ridge, easily distinguishable to those below by his white shirt against the blue horizon, he shouldered his long rifle and took aim at the approaching bombers. They fired away too as they roared past him and eastward. He repeated his duel against the lower, louder fighters, who seemed to pass only feet above his head and his shouted challenges and dares.

After the raid was over and the French planes returned westward to refuel and reload, Za'al came down from the heights, picked up his cloak, rested his rifle, and found a kettle of coffee. "There is no joy in war nowadays," he said.

Joy for the Arab Legion and some of the Hawayti adventurers was to come. The next job for the legion armored cars and trucks was to open contact between units besieging Palmyra and the Indian Army to the north, which was driving west up the Euphrates and aiming for Deir ez-Zor. That meant capturing the village of Sukhna, midway between the two towns, a couple days after Za'als duel with the Armée de l'air. When the legion and some Hawayti Bedouin approached the town out of the hills, its Arab inhabitants came out to greet them in a better reception than nearly any other experienced by the Allies in the campaign. The French-Syrian police had already deserted their station there, but the townspeople warned the legionnaires that there was a French mechanized column operating to the north in the direction of the Euphrates, news consistent with Allied reports of French raiders operating in the area.

So the legion's armored cars and some infantry trucks drove north looking for that Vichy column, probably a company of the Light Desert Force. A day's search through the hot hinterlands between Sukhna and the Euphrates turned up nothing, and the legion's scouting force, three armored cars, thirty troopers, a pickup, and some heavier trucks camped on a hill north of the village. The next morning, while some men gathered brush for the coffee fires and breakfast and others watched a crossroads north of their position, an alarm went up. Unidentified vehicles were approaching from the east, moving in a close row at a leisurely pace, with no armored car leader: a supply convoy of the Indian Army operating north of here—lost, perhaps?

Still, Sergeant Fahad ash Shuraiti didn't like the looks of them. "There are no troops east of us here," he said. For the sake of caution, the three legion armored cars in the group got in ready position, while Shuraiti and a comrade hopped in a pickup to examine this unexpected convoy, the men in camp looking on. When the legion pickup got within about a mile of the approaching vehicles, the rattle of machine gun fire—probably from an armored car—floated back up to the camp. Shuraiti could be seen whipping his truck around and firing a red signal flare, though it was now unnecessary, since all eyes were on him. The Allied scouting force on the hill was badly outnumbered at around five to one, but they seemed to relish this opportunity to square off against the French. The armored cars hurried to a position across the road down which the enemy was driving, while the troopers also strung out in a line and lay or crouched in gravel. They were at a slight elevation above the oncoming French. Someone hurried back down the road toward Sukhna to alert the Household Cavalry and Arab Legion troopers there.

When the Vichy force got within about five hundred yards they halted, their troopers pouring out of the tarp-covered trucks and forming their own firing lines, some with light machine guns. A legionnaire who rose up was hit, and he fell on his face. But, the firefight erupting, the Vichy force was soon taking casualties too. Eventually some of the Arab Legion simply could not abide this firing at a great distance, this faceless exchange. Troopers Shali Auda, Huwaimil Bunaiya, Sa'ad Kuleiban—old warriors, and one an Arab Revolt veteran—rose up and charged, calling to the men strung out beside them, "Where are the gallants? Where are they?"

The Vichy—they were indeed the Second Light Desert Company, comprising French and Syrian troops—were surprised at the audacious charge across open ground; many were overrun, shot, or captured. Even the French trucks and several armored cars spun their wheels in the gravel and sped away. Now the legion's armored cars, along with legion pickups and Household Cavalry trucks that were just appearing from Sukhna, started chasing them. The Vichy vehicles raced eastward in the direction of Deir ez-Zor, about seventy-five miles away. The Arab Legion vehicles could not meet up with the road without wasting precious time, so they bounced over the gravel parallel to the road. The French sent machine gun fire spraying in the direction of the Allies, but would not slow down enough to take careful aim. The Arab legionnaires, all the while, fired with their rifles, to similar effect, and shouted their challenges to the wind. The race soon reached speeds of over sixty miles an hour, with Arab Legion commander John Glubb joining in the chase driving his staff car, legionnaires having jumped in with him. A man clung to the side of the car, riding the running board, and when he stuck his wind-blown head in to encourage more gas, Glubb realized it was one of the Hawaytis. Glubb had no idea how he'd gotten there.

As the chase wore on, the Arab Legion and Household Cavalry vehicles were able to edge closer and closer to the road and the French without losing distance. It seemed that the enemy feared eventually being cut off, and they turned left off the road, apparently heading for a hilly area to the north. They rolled up and down the gravel until they came to a break, a dry riverbed, that cut them off. They then turned in search of a crossing, but that brief delay was all it took for their pursuers to catch them. One Vichy truck plunged down and across, managing to escape, but the rest were cornered. The legionnaires rushed the enemy before they could organize a defense, and the French and Syrians were soon on the ground, disarmed in a matter of minutes. Between the firefight and the chase, the Second Light Desert Company lost eleven men, six armored cars, and four trucks. Eighty were now prisoners bound for Sukhna, along with three French and one Syrian officer who was placed in Glubb's staff car. One of the French officers had been behind the white flag ruse and slaughter of cavalrymen at the Tripoli pipeline fort.[10]

Soon after Reading and Smiley crossed into Syria, Indian Army troops commenced another thrust in the invasion of Syria from the east, following the Euphrates. Some of these men were those who'd occupied Basra, and some of the professional soldiers among them resented that they'd "missed out" on the fights at Fallujah, Habbaniya, and the outskirts of Baghdad. And it didn't help that they would start their westward drive a few days behind the other prongs—aiming first at the eastern provincial capital of Deir ez-Zor, then meaning to drive on Raqqa, then Aleppo. Deir ez-Zor was garrisoned by Foreign Legion and Light Desert Company troops; it had some artillery and an airstrip. The town also defended two critical Euphrates bridges, the only crossings in the region. Essentially these bridges were the gateway to eastern Syria from Aleppo and Damascus; if the Allies could seize them, they would make it extremely difficult for the French to supply their forces in a huge swath of the country.

Just before setting across the Syrian frontier, Major General Bill Slim talked to some of the armored car crews of the Thirteenth Lancers at their base camp on the Euphrates. "How do you like Iraq?" he asked a risaldar-major, the seniormost cavalry captain in the regiment. The man was tall and wiry, with a neat beard and a hawk nose under a black cavalry beret. He had most recently patrolled the turbulent frontier between India and Afghanistan.

"A bad country, sahib," replied a Pashtun.

Slim agreed. He'd been in Iraq (then Mesopotamia) as a far younger man, in World War I. Back then his fellow soldiers called it "miles and miles of Sweet Fanny Adams, with a river runnin' through it." That is, miles and miles of nothing, on either side of the Euphrates.*

"Bad country," continued the Indian cavalry officer, "bad people, and a bad war—no fighting."

"Well risaldar-major, sahib, we haven't had much fighting up to now, but I promise you a proper fight one day."

"If it is the will of God."

And so it was. But first, these Lancers, the Frontier Force Rifles, the Gurkhas, and some Royal Artillery with eighteen-pounders had to endure a scorching desert crossing, while the Sikh Regiment held the frontier base, periodically visited by the strafing Vichy Air Force with bloody effect.

*The term "Fanny Adams" is a euphemism for "fuck all," meaning "nothing." It came about because of the terms' shared initials, F. A.

Captain John Masters was in a truck with Gurkha riflemen and signalers, skirting the Euphrates bound into Syria. They baked in the cab,
the desert sun unremitting. The road was a whiter glare in a world of
glare, and the trucks ahead and behind disappeared in wavering light.
The Indian Army was famous for its water discipline: they never drank
unless they were near a source of water for refilling their canteens. Before
long, every cell in Masters's body pled with him to drink, but he'd be
damned before he'd break water discipline in front of the Gurkhas. A
man named Naru, beside him, seemed to perceive his suffering and suggested that Masters have a drink from his canteen, but Masters wouldn't.
One of his men had collapsed from heatstroke in Basra, and Masters was
sure he would lose consciousness soon.

After enduring this for unknown hours, palms seemed to appear
before them, but by now Masters wasn't sure he could trust his sight.
But in fact they were at an oasis, and Colonel William Weallens bought
up a cartload of watermelons and quickly distributed them to the men.
The fading Masters dove into his slice as the rind poked both his ears.
Then he felt his brain recomposing itself, his whole body, as this heavenly
thing drew life back into his cells.

Besides the desert, the Frontier Force, Gurkhas, and Lancers had
to endure more attention from the Vichy French Armée de l'air. Luckily
for the Indian Army men, they were well into digging their slit trenches,
as was mandated every time they stopped, when the first Glenn Martin
bombers found them. They hugged the earth close as the heavy bombs
crashed all around them. When the planes flew back west and the dust
began to settle, two Gurkhas were found hurt and were hurried to physi-
cian Santi Pada Dutt. Jamedar (Warrant Officer) Sarbdhan Bura, with a
mustache that drooped over the sides of his mouth, had a reputation for
quiet shyness and bravery. Now he lay quiet as Dutt examined him and
found just a small puncture on his side, high up under his armpit. But
this hole alone was enough: Dutt would have to operate to remove the
shrapnel. As an operating tent was set up, Dutt went to Masters and the
company subedar major to tell them that it was critical, that he'd soon
anesthetize Bura to operate.

The Gurkha took Masters's hand when the two went in to see him, already on the operating table. Bura had helped Masters when he had first joined the Gurkhas in 1938 as a trainer of boys, playing the role of "grandfather" to the recruits so far from home in Nepal, and for the first time. Masters held it tight. "You'll feel better tomorrow," he assured Bura, until it was time for Dutt to lead him away and administer sleep. Bura did not live until morning.

The next day the Indian Army column continued the drive westward and were repeatedly attacked from the air, leaving burning vehicles and columns of smoke in the desert after every visitation. Air support for this region came from Habbaniya, and amounted to four Hurricanes and four Gladiator biplanes. Only a few days earlier, Masters had been in Habbaniya; he could now picture pilots with iced drinks, chatting up nurses in the club back at the base. He imagined them doing so now, as his men were killed or hurt and trucks wrecked. On the approach of the fourth attack that day, this one of nine Vichy planes, Masters scanned the horizon in the direction of Iraq and, sure enough, saw dark specks approaching. He pointed and shouted to the Gurkhas around him, "Hurricanes! Now watch!"

But as the Hurricanes closed with the French raiders, perhaps too eagerly and too early opening fire, the sound of machine gun and cannon fire faintly reaching the ground, and smoke billowed from first one, and then the other, RAF plane. One did a crazy turn toward the ground. The other, also hit, grazed a French bomber with its wing, and then it, too, fell. The Gurkhas to whom Masters had shouted triumphantly did not meet his eye.

The final push on Deir ez-Zor was accompanied by a titanic dust storm, which engulfed the region, pelting the men besieging Palmyra to the south, too. Units lost contact with their rearward base, the wireless sets rendered useless except to issue crazy keens of ricocheting electrons. The vehicles in the convoy lost sight of each other too. When Dutt couldn't see any truck ahead of him, he was afraid he'd lagged too far behind, so he stepped hard on the accelerator. In fact, he was too far ahead of the others, so that he arrived at the rendezvous point in front of Deir ez-Zor well before the rest of his column. Thus, the Indian Medical Service spearheaded the drive that day. Fortunately for Dutt, the dust storm also kept the French bombers at bay.

Now that Dutt and the Indian Army had arrived at Deir ez-Zor and the dust storm had subsided, the Allies started taking fire from French seventy-five-millimeter guns and machine guns, as well as bombers. Bill Slim knew that a simple frontal assault on the town would be very bloody, with the Vichy French well aware of their presence, guns dug in, and pillboxes vigilant. That meant the Indians needed to flank the town, both to divide French fire and keep the French from simply driving west out of the town to another stand in Raqqa or another strongpoint in the direction of Aleppo. A persistent fear among the Allies was that the French would draw out the fight, take to the hills, or slip away into Turkey. So the Lancers and Frontier Force Rifles would loop south of Deir ez-Zor, just under the horizon, pass around, and come back at the town from the west. (In fact, they would drive through the territory that had been haunted by the Second Light Desert Company until that unit was routed by the Arab Legion.) Once the flanking units were in place, the Gurkhas would storm the town's defenses from the east under cover of the eighteen-pounders.

This attack was yet another Allied gamble common in the Iraq-Syria war because it was performed on the force's last drops of fuel. The Indian Army units had made a successful fast run out of Iraq, but that made resupplying fuel, which arrived in clutches of four-gallon tin cans that had a tendency to rupture, very difficult; and more could not arrive in time. Every drop, therefore, was siphoned from any vehicle not essential in the flanking attack. And if the attack were delayed or shoved back, or if the flanking route simply consumed more fuel than was calculated, the entire Allied force would be stranded or even sit prey to Vichy armored cars that could literally drive circles around them. French bombers, meanwhile, would return day after day to annihilate them.

As it happened, the flanking vehicles did not run out of gas and the attack from both west and east went off on the morning of July 3. The few Indian Army guns pounded away, answered by eleven French ones, over the heads of the Frontier Force and Gurkha riflemen who loped and crawled forward, attacking cement blockhouses, answered by machine gun fire. The Pashtun Lancers sped on the town, meanwhile, to draw fire away from the riflemen and try to keep French heads down. Vichy fighters and bombers appeared to attack the Indians, hitting the ambulance section and medical evacuation area. There was a duel at one of the Euphrates bridges when Vichy forces moved to blow it up, two Indian mortar teams holding off the French soldiers rushing it until the eighteen-pound guns could get in place.

The fierce battle lasted from morning to midafternoon before the last French vehicles, mainly occupied by officers, ran for their lives and French-Syrian snipers were hunted down throughout the town. After that, uncounted scores of French-Syrian troops simply threw away their uniforms, unwilling to do die for their French occupiers, and went home. The Indians took over a hundred prisoners and captured priceless fuel, vehicles, and parts. They'd removed an airstrip and several planes from Vichy hands, and they started to cinch a noose around Dentz's armies.

Now John Masters and the Fourth Gurkha Rifles, along with some Lancer armored cars, refueled from the newly acquired French supply of gasoline and rushed eighty miles west up the road and the Euphrates toward Raqqa. There they learned that Fawzi al-Qawuqji's irregulars had come through, frightening the townspeople. The fleeing French had already passed through, too, heading north and edging toward the Turkish frontier. Masters and the Gurkhas then pursued and were hunted, in turn, by French Morane fighters.

Then, arriving after dark, Masters, his riflemen, and some Lancers reached the fort of Tel Abyad, where they hoped to catch the retreating French almost at the border. They were instead greeted by the townspeople's' rifle fire. An Arab guide riding with a Lancer armored car shouted their identity into the dark streets of Tel Abyad, and the firing soon stopped. (The town was heavily Armenian; many were refugees from Turkey's own bloody frenzy of race nationalism in the 1910s.)

The Gurkhas learned that they'd just missed the fleeing French once again. At dawn, John Masters and his friends looked around the village, its fort surrounded closely by homes, orchards, and the abandoned trenches and barricades the Vichy forces had meant to defend. John found on one wall a message left by the French, perhaps just the day before: "Wait, dirty English Bastards, until the Germans come. We're running away now, so will you, soon." The message didn't anger him, but saddened him at its perversity—a perversity he thought the whole war in Syria embodied.

The next morning the French Moranes appeared and opened a blazing stream of fire. Masters hit the dirt in an orchard as the plane's guns fired so fast that they didn't rattle, but made a constant single roar. Peeking up, he saw two young Nepalis, Deba and Ghanbahadur, in a clearing nearby, methodically setting up a tripod and mounting a Bren gun. One crouched, shouldering the long gun, while the other loaded and held the ammunition belt. Two fighters above singled them out and roared out their blast; the ground around the Gurkhas was ripped up. The exposed nineteen-year-old boys fired back into the sky. Minute after minute of the duel passed, and they fired on. Tears came to Masters's eyes as he thought, this was what we are fighting for: survival and self-respect, a refusal to be terrified by sheer force. Finally, on the last planes' last attack, a streak of black smoke emerged from one of the Moranes.[11]

The day that Deir ez-Zor fell, Palmyra fell. It seemed that when the men of one of the units defending the town, a Vichy Light Desert Company, learned of the capture of their brother company by the Arab Legion a couple of days earlier, they left their positions and crawled out through the Allied siege. This reduced the number of defenders by almost half, and none could be spared. Besides, it had been a grueling defense against superior Allied numbers who, even if they were mauled by planes, had the artillery edge thanks to the Lincolnshire gunners' twenty-five-pounders. In another strange mirror to the Allied defense of Habbaniya, the French had been resupplied only with difficulty by planes that had to land under the fire of the besiegers. With the loss of Deir ez-Zor and Sukhna, Palmyra couldn't hope for a relief column, either. So that day a Vichy officer emerged from the Palmyra fort with a white flag and three British cavalry troopers as hostages in tow—probably a wise move, given the dubious French respect for the white flag in this campaign. Harry Chalk had been poised to storm Palmyra's fort with his friends just prior to its surrender; when he learned of the white flag, he breathed a sigh of relief, happy not to square off against the Foreign Legion.

When the Essex and Household Cavalry marched into Palmyra to take its defenders as prisoners, they were shocked to find there were only 165. Eighty-seven were members of the Foreign Legion, the majority of whom were German and Russian, whose countries, now that Hitler's Operation Barbarossa had just launched, were in a life-or-death struggle. Only twenty-four remained of the Light Desert Company. Some were not infantry at all, but French Air Force personnel pressed into defending the town. The Allies also found many of the defenders perfectly drunk. With the fatalism of true legionnaires, they had helped themselves to the officers' wine supply the hour that they accepted their hopelessness.

The fall of Deir ez-Zor and Palmyra began a litany of bad news for the Vichy French. French planes, as horrible as they remained for those they strafed and bombed, were dwindling at a fast rate. In the last week of June, the French lost planes at a rate of seven to one to Allied planes, whether in the air or on the ground, or lost them to mechanical failure. Vichy tried to pour in planes from Europe and North Africa as quickly as possible, but it was a slow and treacherous business, and some broke down en route. Meanwhile, when airstrips like that at Mezze were captured by the Indian Army, or Palmyra captured by the Essex and Household Cavalry, the RAF and the Royal Australian Air Force were quick to move in and exploit them, thus putting them closer to their French targets.

In late June, Dentz believed that he had reinforcements on the way; he just needed to hold on. The Vichy French and Germans were negotiating the release of men and material from France for shipment to Syria-Lebanon: over three thousand Algerian, French, and Foreign Legion soldiers; antiaircraft and antitank guns; and nine tanks. Meanwhile, calls for volunteers went out in France and even among French prisoners of war in German camps. But there wasn't much time for such reinforcements to be organized and moved. The Germans authorized the troop releases, and the first infantry battalion from France moved by rail to the Greek port of Salonika, but there remained the question of how it would reach Syria.

Though the Axis and Vichy navies and air forces were a constant, capable threat, the Royal Navy remained supreme in the Mediterranean, and moving the Vichy troops by sea was a dangerous prospect. Far better would be transportation by rail through Turkey. Approached by Vichy France, the Turks balked, even though they allowed the Germans to move oil through the country to Syria. Supplies of ammunition, desperately needed parts, and a few hundred troops had been shuttled throughout June on French planes flying at night, but something bigger was needed. General Dentz inquired about German air transport help. But the possibilities of a mass German airlift of the type that had won them Crete dried up with the Operation Barbarossa invasion of Russia.

So by sea it was. At the end of June, two French transports of troops and supplies prepared to load up in occupied Salonika, Greece, while two Vichy destroyers sallied out of Beirut Harbor in the dark on July 1 to escort them. From Rayak, days away from being seized by the Indian Army, three French Glenn Martin bombers attacked Haifa to cover the destroyers' run out of Beirut. Reaching Greece, they guided the transports out and turned for Syria. Then the Royal Navy pounced. One transport ship was hit, with forty-six men killed; but it was struck in a Turkish port, so 266 made it to shore and were held in neutral Turkey. The Royal Navy chased the other transport to the relative safety of an Italian-occupied port. The two Vichy destroyers, meanwhile, were hunted and corralled by nine ships and a submarine and were forced to run for Salonika. Only one ship with supplies, a fast destroyer sailing direct from Toulon, France, reached Beirut during the month of June, and it was badly damaged from the air the day after it dropped anchor.

Again the young women and men of Bletchley Park played a large role in these Allied victories, necessary but sometimes horrible. The Vichy Navy communicated its ships' positions to the German Navy to avoid friendly fire; the Germans thus broadcast the news to their Mediterranean forces over the air. Those Enigma-scrambled Morse code chirps were picked up by listening stations, relayed home, and entered into the cryptographic computer in green Milton Keynes, England. Thus, when the French submarine *Soufleur* arrived off Beirut at the end of June to fend off British incursions, the Royal Navy was expecting them, and the days of *Soufleur*'s young men were shortly numbered. The captain of the British submarine *Parthian*, never knowing where the information came from, was already stalking the intercepted coordinates for the French. One dark early morning, the *Soufleur* was at rest on the surface about six miles off of Lebanon, recharging its batteries, while a few young men swam and a few remained on deck at lookout. From a distance, the *Parthian* fired a spread of four torpedoes, and one struck right beneath the French conning tower, breaking the submarine in half and quickly sinking it 125 feet to the sea floor. The men and boys inside had no chance. Of the six on the surface, five survived the blast, and they tried to swim to the Beirut shore on the far horizon. Four survived the swim. One was said to later defect to Charles de Gaulle's Free French forces.

Reinforcements and resupply for Dentz were not coming by sea. The Vichy French were putting up bloodily effective resistance, especially in the hills south of the capital, Beirut; but resistance required food, ammunition, and fuel. The Allies, meanwhile, activated their logistic systems, which stretched to Palestine and beyond to the Suez Canal; Basra was quickly turning into the effective depot that Churchill and Roosevelt had envisioned at the same time. Royal Indian Army Service Corps trucks and Indian drivers were arriving at a steady pace from across the Persian Gulf. And these drivers would soon contribute to a system of logistics that helped supply the Soviet defense from the south. If the war depended on a million single contributions, those of "mere" Indian truck drivers were as indispensable as any.

At the beginning of July, the Allied troops in Syria started coming upon abandoned tanks, useless because they were out of fuel. Some British troops found nine outside Damascus; some Free French troops found two more north of Damascus. Fuel started running very low for the Armée de l'Air, in part because of earlier sabotage and in part because RAF and Australian raiders targeted enemy fuel tanks.

Thanks to the mortal sacrifices of the Punjabis and Rajputs at Mezze, along with Jack Hasey's men and hundreds of others battling around the city, Damascus surrendered on June 21. Then Palmyra and Deir ez-Zor fell on July 3, and the Indian Army hurried west across Syria in its own drive on the sea. Town after town in central and northern Syria fell in the week following. To add personal insult to injury, the RAF located Henri Dentz's headquarters at the Casino turned villa, the Résidence des Pins, and on a Sunday afternoon at the end of June dropped two bombs in the middle of it. The general was not at home.

Meanwhile, Rudolf Rahn, always at Dentz's elbow, pressed the general to fight on after the fall of Damascus, counting on German and Vichy aid to arrive by air and sea in late June. He proposed a French surprise attack on Haifa: "Take away their oil supply if they'll take your Mediterranean fleet's!" (In the days to come, he and the Italian legation in Beirut would plead with Dentz to destroy Tripoli's refinery.) Rahn proposed an expansion of Fawzi al-Qawuqji's irregular forces. But then Qawuqji himself was shot five times in a battle with an Allied supply column in eastern Syria, barely managing to escape capture and run for Aleppo. Rahn met him there and saw him off by air to occupied Europe for medical treatment. After that, Qawuqji's irregulars became little better than marauders out for their own benefit, resulting in looting—of which Masters and the Gurkhas saw evidence in north central Syria. Rahn managed to pay for the services of a few hundred Bedouin, but they never moved, let alone fought, and must have had a good laugh at the expense of the haughty Nazi.

Even as the Indian Army cut the country in half with its successful drive to Aleppo, General Dentz placed his last hope in a Vichy rally at Homs and the holdout of Beirut until help could arrive. Earlier he'd ordered Allied prisoners sent to France in case a prisoner swap was possible.

There was one final battle to be fought, this one at the coastal town of Damour, the last defense of Beirut, mainly between Australians and Vichy Foreign Legion and colonial troops. It lasted three horrible days, beginning the night of July 5: a fight on peaks and ridges, yet another battle for a bridge, and a duel of artillery. Australian doctors were constantly at work trying to save young men's lives, if not their limbs; chaplains were deputized to administer anesthetics, and the convalescing wounded were asked to donate blood. There was a colossal rain of naval guns that left more bombarded men with broken psyches, while Rudolf Rahn watched the naval guns flash in the darkness from the balcony of his hotel in Beirut. In the end, the remnants of the Vichy units retreated north past Beirut, and the Australians' few light tanks could drive on the city.

In the first few days of July, the politicians in Vichy imagined they could still make the fight so costly to the Allies that they might leave the defeated Vichy French in political control of Syria-Lebanon. But after the fall of the last defense of Beirut, they authorized Dentz to ask for peace without such conditions. As the Australians were setting up their gun batteries just south of the town and Arab politicians and notables pleaded with him to surrender the city before it was destroyed, General Dentz crossed Beirut to the US residence and handed the American consul a note to pass, in turn, to the British, asking for an armistice.[12]

15

"The Beginning and the End"

> The accumulation of stressors may contribute to making the soldier an ineffective combatant on the battlefield. An overly-stressed combat soldier is likely to be one who is physically able, but is otherwise psychologically unable or unwilling to continue the fight as he/she experiences phenomena often referred to as combat fatigue, combat stress reaction or even in contemporary trends, may be categorized as Posttraumatic Stress Reactions.
>
> —*Handbook of Military Psychology: Clinical and Organizational Practice*

OVER TWO THOUSAND soldiers, sailors, and airmen died in the battle for Syria-Lebanon, men and boys from all over the world, from Senegal to Syria, Punjab to Nepal, Britain to Australia. Australian mothers and fathers suffered the worst, losing 416 children. The Vichy side, and Axis air forces, lost slightly more than the Allied. Unrecorded numbers of Syrian bystanders died in the crossfire of those house-to-house battles of Ezra, Kuneitra, and Marjayoun. No one counted them.

There were far more wounded. Some Vichy troops had been told that the Free French were shooting prisoners—some French airmen didn't bother wearing parachutes for that reason—and were surprised to find themselves in the good hands of Australian doctors or American volunteer nurses. On the other hand, when those nurses reached wounded Free French POWs in Vichy French hands, they were livid to find many treated, to their minds, worse than dogs. They received the treatment—or rather, neglect—of mutineers, as they were in the eyes of their Vichy captors.

When peace was signed, David Smiley was in Palestine after an arduous evacuation from Syria, a slow, dangerous route that Reading also followed. Smiley recuperated from his attack of malaria at Sarafand, the

British base south of Tel Aviv, and when his health recovered he took some time to visit the many wounded cavalry in nearby Jerusalem. Among them was Brigadier Joe Kingstone, the leader of the relief column for Habbaniya known as Habforce, and the Syrian invasion prong pointed at Palmyra named after him: Kingcol. Practically, the flinty brigadier was responsible for the successful drive on Baghdad, and was the type to chew up and spit out officers for not observing blackout discipline and the like. But just like one of the Golden Square colonels under the bombs of the Habbaniya countersiege, Kingstone lost the ability to function under the French bombs outside Palmyra. Now he sat in the hospital, silent, eyes open but unfocused.

Doctor Ernest Altounyan, that old companion of T .E. Lawrence and Faisal I, had been outside Palmyra with Smiley and was now there at the hospital in Jerusalem, and he reflected on cases like Kingstone's. The doctor had been badly wounded under a barrage at Passchendaele in World War I, but would sooner return to Passchendaele than the horror outside Palmyra, he said. "[At Passchendaele] you had a tremendous deal of moral support," he explained. "You had a great deal of noise on your own side; a great artillery barrage firing over your head. You had the feeling of being in it with others. In this type of desert warfare you are left all alone . . . and out of the clear sky you are set upon by one of these fighters. It is a purely personal form of persecution. . . . There is a limit to the amount of horror that the human mind can take in, and it soon reaches saturation point."

Like Kingstone's, Reading's mind had reached its limit, and he was somewhere in Palestine, perhaps at Jerusalem or Sarafand, unseeing—like Joe Kingstone—for now. For the moment, brigadier and translator, Englishman and Palestinian, inhabited the same silent realm.

Harry Chalk and the First Essex Regiment had reached their limit on the rocks of Gallabat on the Sudan-Ethiopia frontier one year earlier, "persecuted" from the air by the Italians. They suffered the same thing at the hands of the French around Palmyra, but they somehow endured. After Palmyra fell, Chalk enjoyed the Roman ruins, which he found interesting. His company then headed north to Deir ez-Zor to hold the town while the Indian Army kept pushing west and north. A week later, just after the peace, the Essex was ordered to parade smartly—as smartly as it could, given recent experiences—before a dignitary. It turned out to be—to Chalk and his friends' minds—just some "frog." Later he learned that it was in fact Charles de Gaulle, there to see the liberators of Palmyra. Chalk didn't care a whit about him and, after his experiences in Syria, reviled the French. In the next few weeks, Harry and his friends were given liberty in Beirut in small groups, which they found nearly un-touched by the war and where they started feeling human again. Mail caught up to them, too, and Chalk soon learned that a cousin in the Royal Navy had died in his submarine, in the dark like the young men of the *Soufleur*, and sharing the same grave.

Beirut was a scene of celebration when the Australians rolled in, crowds lining the road from the south to welcome them with constant applause. A truck stopped and an old Lebanese man approached and slapped the backs of young, sun-darkened Australians. A Lebanese boy hitched a ride in one Australian truck, conspicuously proud of himself. Coffee vendors moved among the people, the squares were sites of celebrations, the people happy to watch the French go and ready for independence.

There was some tension in the coming months, both between the new Free French commissioner of the Levant, General Georges Catroux, and the Syrians and Lebanese, as well as between the British and Free French. The Lebanese and Syrian people did not want to see Henri Dentz's rule simply replaced by Catroux's, and they protested signs of French reentrenchment. When the Free French acted harshly or appeared repressive, the other Allies stepped in—usually politically, but sometimes physically, and almost to the point of combat. The Free French accused the British of meaning to shove them out of the Levant, perhaps to spread British influence there. The British, in turn, reminded the Free French that on the eve of invasion they'd both promised Lebanon and Syria their independence, and that this was a war of liberation, not conquest. Of course, such lofty aims the British did not have in mind in their own colonies or informal spheres—whether in India, or for the Arabs of Pales-tine, or in their informal sphere in Iraq.

Freya Stark's role as a propagandist and spy was to convince the

Arab Middle East that backing the Allies was in its best interests politically and spiritually. In other words, she wanted to convince the Arab world that its national future would benefit from cooperation with the British, and that fascism was a spiritual corruption spread by evil men. She always insisted her job was simply to show people what they already knew was true, never to coerce or deceive. But her all-too-close observation in the Baghdad embassy showed her that the British were not very convincing as "helpful partners" in Iraq, in part because they complacently continued to back Iraq's old power brokers without developing new relationships with younger nationalists who felt cut out. Some of that generation, in turn, had felt little bothered when a section of the anti-British military ascended to power in the form of the Golden Square. Stark was frustrated.

In response, as she worked in Egypt and elsewhere in the Middle East in later 1941 and 1942, then took off for America to try to garner American support for a benign British imperialism in the Middle East on the tea circuit, she wrote a book, *East Is West*, laying out by example the kind of future Arab Middle East she envisioned. It was a gentle admonishment to the British to be helpful and not just controlling, and a genial call for liberal Arab countries to modernize, including in their treatment of women. She was disappointed by events and all parties, including the Americans, who were obvious in their intent to claim a greater role in the Middle East after the war.

General de Gaulle came to pin a medal on Free French soldier Jack Hasey in bed while Hasey endured months of healing and plastic surgery outside Jerusalem—or at least the patients around Jack thought it was de Gaulle. It was actually Hasey's Foreign Legion colonel and captain, there to give him the Croix de Guerre. Jack still couldn't speak to tell his fellow patients of their error.

A series of surgeries between June and fall 1941 restored Hasey's voice and, to the credit of his surgeons, even his good looks, despite the scars running down his chin and neck. Hasey's irrepressible charm, the stuff that had first made him a star jewelry salesmen, returned; and as winter 1941 approached, he frequently had a date for the movies or was hosted for drinks by the Americans now appearing in greater numbers at the King David Hotel. A few weeks before his appointed day to begin a series of flights back to Massachusetts, the Japanese launched a surprise attack on the American naval base at Pearl Harbor, Hawaii, which was followed by a German declaration of war. So, at last, Hasey's fellow Americans joined him in his war.

If the Free French set down a tense road in Syria-Lebanon until the end of the war, the Lebanese and Syrians were at least happy to see Dentz and the Vichy French forces go. The Allies clearly stipulated in their peace terms that they would facilitate the safe return to France of any Vichy French soldier and official who wished to depart. The arrangements were made, and troopships in France given safe passage to the Levant to pick them up, while the Free French and Allies tried to persuade as many men as possible to stay and fight with them. British and Free French soldiers visited Vichy officers in POW camps in Palestine, sometimes berating them as Nazi stooges, sometimes gently seeking to persuade. But many of the officers had families in France, and they feared retribution should they join the rebels. And, of course, some simply hated the turncoat Free French too much to ever side with them. Others, like the Polish lieutenant who pled with the last British holdouts in Kuneitra, about to be pulverized by tanks, to surrender, were relieved to join de Gaulle. About a thousand European French soldiers joined the Free French, along with about twenty-five hundred North Africans and West Africans, and seven hundred legionnaires. But thirty-two thousand French troops returned to Vichy France instead. The British tried until the last moment, making each soldier about to board a troopship for France pass through an enclosed tent, where a British officer asked each man alone, one last time, whether he wished to remain and fight the Axis. Very few did. Some men, in fact, had painted "Vive Pétain" and "Vive Dentz" on the sides of one of the eight steamers that took them back to German captivity.

As the Australians had approached Beirut, Rudolf Rahn removed himself and his staff to Tripoli, up the coast, frustrated that he had failed to convince Dentz to blow up the refinery there. A note reached him the next day explaining that the British demanded all German agents' evacuation from the country as condition of any armistice and that Rahn needed to cross the Turkish border by midnight. So he and his staff, with their radio equipment, fled, frustrated. If only fifty Luftwaffe transports could have been spared, Rahn thought, the five French battalions they could have delivered from Europe could have turned the tide, allowing Beirut to be a beachhead for a second front in Rommel's campaign. Always considering himself a sincere friend of France, Rahn headed to French Tunisia several months later to pursue further French-German cooperation there.

Rahn's Foreign Office colleague Fritz Grobba, on the other hand, continued to focus on the unification of Iraq and the Levant under a regime friendly to the Axis. He continued to plan for the day Germany returned to Iraq and the Levant, drafted proposals for cooperation between the Reich and its "partner" in Iraq or a kingdom of Iraq and Syria, and organized propaganda. But his project was badly hampered by increasingly sour disputes between the various Arab exile factions in Berlin, including Rashid Ali al-Gailani's, Amin al-Husseini's, and Fawzi al-Qawuqji's groups each of which naturally hoped to be on top when Germany eventually drove the British and French from the Middle East. In the meantime, each had to appear the most powerful, the most diehard, the most popular, the best investment to their German hosts. They in turn drew various personnel in the German Foreign Office into their jostling and feuding. Al-Husseini went so far as to go around the Germans and approach the Italians to receive greater recognition from them. He also pushed to recruit a fighting force among Arab POWs and Balkan Muslims, but he never attracted many, and they were notoriously unreliable for the Germans, while local Muslim leaders preached against al-Husseini.

In the last hours before the peace had been negotiated, General Dentz ordered all navy ships to sail for France and the air force to take its remaining several dozen planes or so to Vichy North Africa via occupied Greece. Meanwhile, he ordered over fifty Allied officers and NCOs onto those ships and planes to be sent to France by rail upon landing in Salonika. These included the officers of the Fusiliers, taken after their desperate defense of Kuneitra; the Warwickshire Yeomanry, deceived by a white flag; Arab and Indian NCOs; and others. These Allied officers boarded ships or transport planes at Aleppo and Homs and sailed or flew west in the dark.* Then they had a strange tour of occupied Europe. Greek civilians, grateful for the Allies' doomed attempts to defend their country, snuck them food; they encountered French guards who reviled them, and others who clearly sympathized with them; and they were interviewed by unremittingly courteous Gestapo officers. When the French separated three Arab officers from the British, saying that "natives" must be segregated, the British officers went on strike—refusing to appear for roll call—until their comrades were returned, and the French grudgingly gave in. So through Greece and Yugoslavia, Austria and Germany, all the way to southern France, the prisoners rolled by train. In Yugoslavia some guards pointed out where resistance guerillas had bombed a track and shot up a German train, the sort of act that could end in civilian executions. On a German troop train in southern Germany, the Allied officers heard a harmonica playing "It's a Long Way to Tipperary." This all came to an end after imprisonment in Marseilles, when the Allied men were eventually sailed back to Beirut in small groups after the Vichy troops arrived from the Levant.

Eventually indeed. Henri Dentz was still in Lebanon in late August 1941. To British eyes, Vichy France was dragging its feet in returning the final Allied officers. Eventually General Henry "Jumbo" Wilson in Jerusalem had enough of the dragging and ordered General Dentz arrested, along with a number of Vichy officers equal to those Allied officers still imprisoned in Marseilles. Delivered to Jerusalem and placed under house arrest, Dentz vehemently objected to his incarceration. General Wilson personally visited Dentz and told him in no uncertain terms that Dentz had effectively torn up the peace protocols that guaranteed the repatriation of POWs and that he was shocked at the stories of mistreatment of his officers in captivity. The implications for Dentz's future accommodations were made clear to him, and Dentz pled that none of this was his fault, and all that of Vichy.

*In one, somewhere over Cyprus, a British officer ducked up toward the cockpit and spoke with the French pilot. He could simply turn the plane for Cairo, the Englishman said. The pilot, who'd desperately fought off the German invasion of France, struggled with his conscience, but refused: his extended family in occupied France depended on his serving Vichy. But in later years, the pilot would pass air force–related information to the French Resistance. Targeted by the Gestapo, he eventually fled to Britain and flew missions between England and resistance contacts in occupied France.

Wilson's hostage-taking caused action, and when the Allied officers duly appeared, the final French officers were released. All but one French officer: Dentz himself, that is. That's because a sole Indian jamadar (warrant officer) was still missing. The French said that the Indian had fallen ill before departing France. General Wilson by this time didn't trust the Vichy French to return him in a timely manner so he kept his one last hostage; Dentz was said to be bitter at being equated to an Indian non-commissioned officer. The jamadar eventually appeared, and Dentz finally returned to France, where he took on an administrative office for the rest of the war.[1]

The Francophile Nazi Rudolf Rahn returned disappointed to Berlin, having failed to realize his vision of Axis-Vichy military success, but having, it seemed, won the approval of Adolf Hitler himself. Briefly given an audience, Hitler said, "I let you down, down there in Syria." Rahn was soon sent back to Paris and then to French Tunisia in late 1942 where, once again, he would stoke French resistance to the Allies in the name of a new French-German partnership. The American invasion of northwest Africa, along with more Allied and Free French victories around El-Alamein, sent Rahn packing from North Africa in early 1943. After the Allied landings in southern Italy, Rudolf Rahn was then sent as one of the rulers of an Italian puppet state in northern Italy in late 1943. While there, his office oversaw the arrest and transportation of eight thousand Roman Jews to a concentration camp and death in Austria.[2]

Roald Dahl, having left the Middle East in August 1941, surprised his mother in the early fall at her home in England after his convoy on the Atlantic dodged U-boats and German bombers operating out of France. He brought a bag of lemons and limes picked up in Sierra Leone, precious in tightly rationed Britain, though such treasure had lain rotting in heaps at roadsides in Palestine. Dahl tried to get back into the air as a flight instructor in England, but it didn't work; his throbbing head wouldn't allow it. In a chance meeting with an Air Ministry official, Dahl's good looks and conversation impressed, resulting in a posting to the British embassy in Washington, DC. There his role was to be charming and make inroads among the Americans on the cocktail circuit and tell the stories of his harrowing experiences in the eastern Mediterranean. Though by that time the United States was in the war, there was much isolationist instinct still to be overcome among the Americans, and some calls for the United States to only fight for narrow ends, especially against the Japanese. Dahl also reported on his conversations in an official capacity, becoming a sort of spy along the lines—though not the importance—of Freya Stark. When the famous novelist C. S. Forester (also working in a propaganda role in the United States) asked Dahl for notes about one of his harrowing flying experiences, Dahl wrote up his crash on the Libyan frontier. Forester changed very little, accept to attribute the crash to the enemy, not bad directions, and asked the tall RAF man, "Did you know you were a writer?"

Jack Hasey's charisma, too, combined with the sacrifice he made during the siege of Damascus, meant that his next war duty was also on the charm offensive. After rejoining his family in Massachusetts, he returned to service in the Free French Foreign Legion in London, acting as a liaison between the Americans and the Free French and resistance headquarters. De Gaulle always refused to be a pet of Churchill, or of Roosevelt or Dwight D. Eisenhower, and Hasey had a lot of smoothing over to do in the coming months and years. After the war Hasey helped de Gaulle write his wartime memoir and shared his observations on the president of France with American officials. These skills and his winning personality eventually resulted in a job with a new US department called the Central Intelligence Agency.

It was a sad joke that Tony Dudgeon got caught in the siege of Habbaniya, because he'd been sent there to rest after the stress of running a bomber squadron in the Egyptian desert. After the utterly frenzied air countersiege, Dudgeon, naturally, was worse off. He couldn't sleep; he would break down in tears or break out in anger. No one offered him treatment, nor did he seek it out, except in the form of whiskey and companionship in Cairo's dark corners. He was assigned a desk job in that city and thought he would remain there.

But Dudgeon's work at Habbaniya seemed to have won the right attention in London; a promotion came through, and with it new responsibilities that seemed to save him. His new job was to collect American and British reinforcement planes at Ghana and ferry them by air straight across Africa to the Middle East, a long trek that invited a lot of challenges and enterprise. Later, in the year leading up to the Normandy invasion, Dudgeon helped plan its air logistics, even learning to pilot a glider for firsthand knowledge of what he would ask his pilots to do. He remained in the Royal Air Force, specializing in tough jobs in planning and organization, retiring as an air vice marshal.

Jack Bartlett of the Saturday Soldier gunners of the 237th Field Battery had more hard fighting to do. From Syria he went to Egypt and in the fall of 1941 had a series of horrible duels with German Panzers in the Western Desert, from which he barely escaped and many friends did not. Then he was reunited with Harry Chalk's First Essex Regiment in India, where they trained in jungle warfare before heading to the Burma-India frontier to defend India from the Japanese and their Indian National Army allies. Bartlett and Chalk's role would be to open up a supply corridor through occupied Burma, in many ways operating as guerillas. They lost their big quads and twenty-five-pounders, which were replaced by mules and mortars. The 237th and the Essex already had a bond, but in the jungles of Burma they shared a bond of misery: hungry, often ill, living in mud, frequently living in close quarters to the skeletons of the Japanese who also died hungry and sick, the jungle claiming everything but their bones very quickly. Bartlett somehow survived to return to England in 1945, where he met a young woman of the Auxiliary Territorial Service and, after five years of fighting French, Germans, Iraqis, Italians, and Japanese, and still only twenty-five years old, tried to reclaim a normal life working for a corn company and as a farmer.

Like Jack Bartlett, Harry Chalk lost a lot of friends to German tanks in Libya outside Tobruk, the Essex leaving the better part of a company in graves there. In later 1942 he boarded a transport in Port Said and sailed for Bombay, where, like Bartlett, he hanged up his khakis for jungle green before heading for Burma. Bill Slim, who'd led the Indian Army into Syria, was now put in charge of driving the Japanese away from India. The jungle was horrible, smelling of death, and Chalk always seemed to have sores. After over two years in Burma and India, Chalk's number came up to go home. He was among the only surviving original members of his battalion.

Back in Southend, Chalk found work as a tiler, then felt lucky to get a job as a supervisor with a home building contractor. But even as supervisor, he didn't make enough money to buy one of the homes he was building, managing only to rent a single room in a house with a number of workmates. Someone organized a march down the middle of Southend, some signs asking "Where are the homes fit for heroes?" Harry's oldest brother joined in, and they nearly ended up in jail for that one. But this, like everything, the still boyish Harry Chalk took in stride. He took it in stride, too, when a few years later, now twenty-nine and a reservist, he got a letter to report for duty: he was bound for Korea.

John Masters and the Fourth Gurkha Rifles Battalion drove back to Baghdad and then into Iran in August 1941 when the British and Indian armies invaded neutral Iran from the west and the Soviet Army invaded from the north. The Allies justified their invasion by citing Iran's refusal to dismiss around one thousand German diplomats, merchants, and others in the country. But while the experience of Iraq and Syria did show the influence that a small contingent of German representatives could have, their main reason was actually the Allies' desperate need to run a supply lifeline for the Soviet resistance to the Wehrmacht up through Iran's rail corridor.* The British, meanwhile, could then directly take up the defense of the precious oil supplies of Abadan. A safe bet in summer 1941 was that it was only a matter of time before German tanks, having overrun the Soviets, would directly threaten Iran from the north, and afterward the Levant.

---

*Thinking him gun shy and worn out by the stresses of leading Middle Eastern and North African forces, Churchill moved General Archibald Wavell out and replaced him with General Claude Auchinleck from India, and Wavell took Auchinleck's place in Delhi. From there, in July 1941, Wavell looked at Iran with great unease writing to the Chiefs of Staff in Westminster, "It is essential to the defence of India that the Germans should be cleared out of Iran now, repeat now. Failure to do so will lead to a repetition of events which in Iraq were only just countered in time."

Masters was then nominated for officer school, which meant a return to India for training at Quetta and a sad departure from Santi Pada Dutt and the Nepali officers and young riflemen. Masters was then a brigade major, in charge of around twenty-four hundred men of an Indian Army brigade of Gurkhas, British regiments, and a Nigerian regiment. Like Bartlett and Chalk, he was sent to the Indian eastern frontier and Burma, sometimes walking deep behind Japanese lines as what were called Chindits, or deep penetration columns. On one of these expeditions, in an isolated spot in northern Burma, his brigade was discovered and besieged for over two weeks by the Japanese. Already hungry, with many ill and wounded, Masters had to give the order to retreat—a retreat on which the mortally ill and wounded of his men could not follow. Horribly, he felt it was his responsibility to euthanize the dying men painlessly rather than let them fall into Japanese hands before leading the break out of the Japanese siege.

Masters, too, survived the jungle. After the war, the breakup of the Indian Army with the partition of India into the new nations of India and Pakistan left him personally dejected, both for the Indian Army and for India, and without a happy professional home. He moved to the United States, having been enamored of the country—and especially the Southwest, which reminded him of parts of India—since exploring it in Ol' Man Mose just before the war. He was exceptional for hating racial prejudice, not liking what he saw of Jim Crow operating there. It was fitting, too, that Masters was antiracist, because he learned some years after coming to America that a distant grandparent was a Muslim woman of Delhi. Masters cast around for work in the United States until he, like Roald Dahl, stumbled into a lifelong career of writing after trying an initial piece about his wartime experiences.

Santi Pada Dutt had his own horrors ahead of him. With the Gurkhas he was bound for North Africa and its monstrous seesaw battles of artillery and tanks. A year after their war in Iraq and Syria, Dutt and his Gurkha battalion were southwest of Tobruk during the Battle of Gazala, Rommel's greatest success, when they got cut off and had to improvise a stand against guns and tanks, their only cover some hastily scratched-out trenches. Under a rain of shells Dutt tried to do what he could for the men being torn apart, but it was only a matter of time before the Germans overran them. The doctor never left the side of his wounded men, even after defeat, and pressed the Germans to provide him supplies and the ability to care for them. He then followed them to a series of prison camps in Italy.

Not everything was blood and captivity, however. In Basra, seeking out a place for a makeshift hospital, Dutt met an Armenian school teacher who leant her space. Knowing that the Indian Army circulated throughout the Middle East, she gave the doctor the name of her sister in Cairo, whom he sought out. Married in the middle of the war, they were together fifty-eight years before dying within the same year in San Francisco.

David Smiley kept doing his best to put himself in harm's way. After recovering from malaria and following the Household Cavalry to Iran for a brief period, he also participated in the trial by fire in the Western Desert. Because of his earlier commando work in northeastern Africa, and his performance in Iraq and Syria, he was then recruited by the Special Operations Executive and parachuted into occupied Albania in 1943 and 1944 to conduct guerilla warfare against collaborators, Germans, and Italians, blowing up bridges or ambushing the enemy, as Fawzi al-Qawuqji had done to the Household Cavalry and other units. Then Smiley was off to Thailand to terrorize the Japanese and their puppet regime, nearly dying by one of his own booby traps intended for a Japanese officer. After the war, he spent over twenty years as a commando and spy, an agent of a collapsing British Empire that advanced its interests through cloak-and-dagger rather than departed colonial governors and viceroys.

The survivors of the First Punjabis and the Sixth Rajputs—Hindu, Muslim, and Sikh—who scaled the heights of Eritrea and suffered so badly outside Damascus were released from French captivity in July and August 1941, some having taken the grand tour of occupied Europe to Vichy France. Starting in the fall of 1941, they were in northern Libya, in battles between tanks and artillery, where human bodies didn't belong. Platoons disappeared and companies were reassembled out of those who could still walk and those not in German and Italian POW camps. Both battalions then went to Italy in 1943, where they fought alongside the

Americans and Poles along the Winter Line, trying to take Rome. It was like Eritrea all over again, scaling peaks and ridges under fire, but instead of the sun burning their necks, sleet sloshed down on them. In the dark in January 1944, the veteran sepoys sprung from rock to rock near Monte Cassino, illuminated as if by strobe lights by short-lived German flares, tossing grenades up and ahead since they couldn't easily bring their rifles to bear on those above them. But they slipped in mud, got caught in barbed wire, and were shot down by cornered Germans.

While it's true that the Punjabis and Rajputs were usually segregated by ethnicity and religion at the level of the company, they still served and lived shoulder to shoulder in battalions for years of shared hardship. There are relatively very few anecdotes of racial or community tensions within the Indian Army during the war, especially among those serving overseas in battle zones. In India itself, tension and violence between communities flared especially after the war years, and the flavor of irreconcilable hatred between nations on display in World War II, and between the two would-be nations of France in Syria-Lebanon in 1941, erupted between Indian communities even prior to the cataclysmic partition in 1947. During that terrible event, the Indian Army veterans of World War II performed impartially, broadly speaking, trying to contain the violence of the partition itself, in which at least one million died from massacre and hardship. But that was like trying to contain an inferno. And battalions that had formerly been only segregated at the company level became completely ripped apart, with Muslim soldiers going to Pakistan and Hindus and Sikhs going to India. On top of this, the veterans of Bose's Indian National Army, which collaborated with the Japanese, tended to be celebrated in postindependence India as freedom fighters; the veterans of the Allied Indian army felt scorned, linked to the hated imperialists.

Intercommunal violence bore on the Arab Palestinian known as Reading too. The year after the partition of India came the partition of British Palestine, resulting in war, massacre, and hardship. Whatever exactly happened to Reading himself is lost to history, but the fate of his home of Haifa, targeted by Germans, Italians, and Vichy French during World War II, is emblematic. Before the bloody events of 1947–48,

Haifa's population of around 135,000 was split almost evenly between Jews and Arabs (Christian Arabs and Muslim Arabs). After the partition and violence, barely a few thousand Arabs remained. Moshe Dayan, who lost an eye in one of the first missions of the Syria-Lebanon war, fighting beside an Arab comrade, had the job of administering part of conquered Haifa and taking supplies from emptied Arab homes for the new Israeli Army's needs. The chances are that Reading no longer had a home after 1948.[3]

Notes

Chapter titles come from the holy books of the Abrahamic religions, many parts shared among them. Chapter 1: Revelation 6:4; chapter 2: Job 22:10; chapter 3: Quran 29:65; chapter 4: Exodus 14:3; chapter 5: 1 Kings 18:19; chapter 6: Quran 2:142; chapter 7: Jeremiah 51:12; chapter 8: Ezekiel 4:3; chapter 9: Exodus 11:9; chapter 10: Quran 62:10; chapter 11: Psalm 101:7; chapter 12: Quran 24:61; chapter 13: Deuteronomy 28:15; chapter 14: Quran 4:104; chapter 15: Revelation 22:13.

Chapter 1

1. On the likelihood of Hitler preserving the British Empire in some form to police some of the world, see John Lukacs, *The Legacy of the Second World War* (New Haven, CT: Yale University Press, 2010), 60. For Hitler's likelihood of keeping the empire as a sort of police state and his apparent fondness for the film *Lives of a Bengal Lancer*, see Lawrence James, *Churchill and Empire: A Portrait of an Imperialist* (New York: Pegasus, 2014), 205. For the probability that Iraq and the Levant would always be a "vassal" no matter what promises the Axis made, see Francis R. Nicosia, *The Third Reich and the Palestine Question* (Austin: University of Texas Press, 1985), 201 and elsewhere. For Muhammad Khan of Skinner's Horse, see his commendation in the National Archives, WO/373/29, 395. William Joyce, Lord Haw-Haw, is quoted in Andrew Stewart, *The First Victory: The Second World War and the East Africa Campaign* (New Haven, CT: Yale University Press, 2016), 50.

2. For this bleak period in the state of North Atlantic convoys, see Kevin Smith, *Conflict over Convoys: Anglo-American Logistics Diplomacy in the Second World War* (Cambridge: Cambridge University Press, 2002), 30 and elsewhere. For Churchill's "breaking all our hearts" see Winston

Churchill, *The Churchill War Papers*, vol. 3, *The Ever-Widening War,
1941*, ed. Martin Gilbert (New York: Norton, 200), 409. For an assessment of Istanbul's inability to defend against an armored assault from the
west, see Bernard Fergusson, *The Trumpet in the Hall, 1930–1958* (London: Collins, 1970), 80–83. For the American ambassador to Turkey
and the British Foreign and War Offices watching Turkey's neutrality
anxiously and linking the fate of Yugoslavia and Turkey in their minds,
and linking Turkey's neutrality and defensibility to the outcome of Iraq
and Syria emergencies, see Christopher Catherwood, *The Balkans in
World War Two* (Basingstoke, England: Palgrave Macmillan, 2003), 38,
157, 161–62. For the murder of thirty-six random Belgrade inhabitants
by the German Army in April 1941, see Gerhard Gronefeld, "Ich kann es
nicht vergessen—und ich will es auch nicht," Freelens, https://www.free-
lens.com/magazin-archiv/ich-kann-es-nicht-vergessen-und -ich-will-es-
auch-nicht/. For Rommel's leap from Tripoli and the Ultra intelligence
that led to British complacency, see Srinath Raghavan, *India's War:
World War II and the Making of Modern South Asia* (New York: Basic
Books, 2016), 151–52. For a quick summary of the consequences of the
Suez Canal falling, see Bevin Alexander, *How Hitler Could Have Won
World War II: The Fatal Errors That Led to Nazi Defeat* (New York:
Random House, 2002), xi. For more on the significance of the Suez
Canal, see Ashley Jackson, *The British Empire and the Second World
War* (London: Hambledon Continuum, 2006), 99–100, and on the
Madagascar plan for the Japanese Imperial Navy, 340–41. For how the
Suez Canal hovered around all of Roosevelt and Churchill's big plans for
US logistical and eventual troop intervention in the war, see for just one
example, Warren F. Kimball, ed. *Churchill and Roosevelt: The Complete
Correspondence*, vol. 1, *Alliance Emerging: October 1933–November
1942* (Princeton, NJ: Princeton University Press, 1984), 163–65.

3. Of course, public opinion polls are a difficult source on which to base
an argument, but in this case they provide one piece of data among many
indicating widespread opposition among US respondents to intervention
in the war; for this and other details about Roosevelt's maneuvering in
these days, see Steven Casey, *Cautious Crusade: Franklin D. Roosevelt,*

American Public Opinion and the War against Nazi Germany, 1941–45 (Oxford: Oxford University Press, 2001), 28 and elsewhere. For Mussolini's conversation with his German military liaison, see Enno von Rintelen to OKH [German Army Supreme High Command], April 13, 1941, Imperial War Museum, AL 1007.

Chapter 2

EPIGRAPH: Tony Blair, *BBC Newsnight*, February 6, 2003, quoted in Ali Haider, "Why You Can't Explain the Iraq War without Mentioning Oil," The Conversation, http://theconversation.com/why-you-cant-explain-the-iraq-war-without-mentioning-oil-59352.

1. For Eden's time in Egypt, Transjordan, and Palestine, including the meeting between Eden and Emir Abdullah I, see Anthony Eden, *The Reckoning: The Memoirs of Anthony Eden* (Boston: Houghton Mifflin, 1965), 154–56; "Mr. Eden to Egypt and Palestine," *Spectator*, 24 October 1940, 1; and John Bagot Glubb, *A Soldier with the Arabs* (New York: Harper, 1957), 41–42. We know that Abdullah was aware of Amin al-Husseini's presence in Baghdad in 1940, but it is hard to assess whether Abdullah could gauge the degree to which he might contribute to the threat of collaboration with Germany; on this, see Yoav Gelber, *Jewish-Transjordanian Relations, 1921–48* (London: Cass, 1997), chap. 8, and for Abdullah's announcement that he would fight on with the "Free British" if it came to it, 152. For Abdullah's support of Britain in these days, see the history by Arab legionnaire Ma'an Abu Nowar, *The History of the Hashemite Kingdom of Jordan*, vol. 3 ([Oxford]: Ithaca Press, 2001), 18–19, which includes how war speculation made things hard on the ordinary soldier; he also sensed that Abdullah knew partnership with Britain was better than being under the heel of the Axis (18). See also Syed Ali el-Edroos, *The Hashemite Arab Army, 1908–1979: An Appreciation and Analysis of Military Operations* (Amman: Publishing Committee, 1980), 222. Glubb reports on the meeting and on the rumors and nervousness in Jordan, including the false rumor that Ibn Saud had a secret pact with Germany; see John Bagot Glubb, *The Story of the Arab Legion* (London: Hodder and Stoughton, 1948), 251; Glubb also thought Abdullah acted out of a sense of pride in steadfastness in the old alliance, 254; for opinion on the street that the Germans would soon be in Syria, 252–55; and on Abdullah's offer to fight in the Western Desert, 251. For Eden and Wavell's review of the troops, his being "moved" and "exhilarated" at the sight of the Arab troops, and their review of the Syrian border, see Eden, *The Reckoning*, 155–56. For their warning to Glubb that the Arab Legion might have to stand alone, though they would try to arm them somewhat better, see Glubb, *Arab Legion*, 252–53.

2. The details of this conversation in a Palestinian café come from a police officer who was present at the scene; see Roger Courtney, *Palestine Policeman: An Account of Eighteen Dramatic Months in the Palestine Police Force during the Great Jew-Arab Troubles* (London: Jenkins, 1939), 88–90; Courtney was far from romantic about the Palestinian Arabs, so his evidence is especially credible. For Radio Bari, including invented uprisings and mosque destruction, see Massimiliano Fiore, *Anglo-Italian Relations in the Middle East, 1922–1940* (Farnham, England: Ashgate, 2010), 45–46. For Axis radio eventually targeting Emir Abdullah as a stooge of "the Jews," calling him Rabbi Abdullah, see Dafnah Sharfman, *Palestine in the Second World War: Strategic Plans and Political Dilemmas, the Emergence of a New Middle East* (Brighton, England: Sussex, 2014), 13.

3. The most complete account of the bombing suffered in Mandatory Palestine during the war, and the source of many details here, is Nir Arielli, "'Haifa Is Still Burning': Italian, German, and French Air Raids on Palestine during the Second World War," *Middle Eastern Studies* 46, no. 3 (2010): 331–47, which includes Italian assessments of the importance of the Haifa oil terminal. For these raids, as well as plans for German-occupied Palestine, see Sharfman, *Palestine in the Second World War*. For the SM.79's reputation, see Jon Lake, *The Great Book of Bombers* (Minneapolis: MBI, 2002), 151. For some details of the July 24, 1940 raid, including observations of tall columns of water generated by falling bombs and other scenes, see *New York Times*, July 25, 1940; *Times* (London), July 25, 1940; and *Palestine Post*, July 25, 1940. For the raid in which Tel Aviv was hit, see *Palestine Post*, September 10, 1940. For the Acre bombing, the quoted villager, and children collecting fragments, see *Palestine Post*, June 26, 1941. Iraqi and British Palestinian military figures come from Adrian Fort, *Wavell: The Life and Times of an Imperial Servant* (London: Cape, 2009), 218. For concerns in Britain in July 1940 that the Germans might make a move on Syria and Palestine, see F. H. Hinsley, E. E. Thomas, C. F. G. Ransom, and R. C. Knight, *British Intelligence in the Second World War*, vol. 1, *Its Influence on Strategy and Operations*, 1st ed. History of the Second World War (London: Stationery Office Books, 1979), 251, and for concerns in later 1940 including conclusions that Germany would make a run for Iraq's oil, 254–56. For an interesting speculative assessment of what might have occurred had the Axis focused much more on crossing the Greek islands into Syria, see John Keegan, "How Hitler Could Have Won the War," in *What If?: The World's Foremost Military Historians Imagine What Might Have Been*, ed. Robert Crowley (New York: Putnam's, 1999), 295–310. Details about British planning for an invasion of Palestine come from Ronald Zweig, "British Plans for the Evacuation of Palestine in 1941–1942," *Studies in Zionism: Politics, Society, Culture* 4, no. 2 (1983): 291–303. Further details about the creation of the Palmach and British-Jewish agency cooperation in planning for intelligence, sabotage, and the like in the event of German occupation comes from Ian Black and Benny Morris, *Israel's Secret Wars: A History of Israel's Intelligence Services* (New York: Grove, 1992), 32–33. Further evidence that the Palmach was trained by the British comes from an interview with Jewish member of the East Kent Regiment Franz Ferdinand Levi, Imperial War Museum, catalog no. 17600. Fascinating evidence of Jewish spies, referred to as "our friends," in Syria-Lebanon is in National Archives, HS 3/211. For the fate of Libyan Jews during the war, see Renzo De Felice, *Jews in an Arab Land: Libya, 1835–1970* (Austin: University of Texas Press, 1985), chap. 6. For Jewish intelligence leaders' meetings with Arab leaders bitterly opposed to al-Husseini and fearful of German invasion, see Hillel Cohen, *Army of Shadows: Palestinian Collaboration with Zionism, 1917–1948* (Berkeley: University of California Press, 2008), 180, 187; and Ezra Danin, *Zionist be'chol tnai* [in Hebrew] (Jerusalem: Kidum,

1987), 157–58. For Lehi and its attempts to coordinate with the Germans and Italians, see Sasson Sofer, *Zionism and the Foundations of Israeli Diplomacy* (Cambridge: Cambridge University Press, 2007), 253–54; Joseph Heller, *Stern Gang: Ideology, Politics and Terror, 1940–1949* (Oxford: Routledge, 1995), 70, 84–87, 116; and Arie Perliger and Leonard Weinberg, "Jewish Self-Defence and Terrorist Groups Prior to the Establishment of the State of Israel: Roots and Traditions," *Totalitarian Movements and Political Religions* 4, no. 3 (2003), 107–8.

4. For 1930s Iraqi politics, see Majid Khadduri, *Independent Iraq: A Study in Iraqi Politics since 1932* (Oxford: Oxford University Press, 1951), 1–205, esp. 156–205. Khadduri's study is fascinating in that the author was able to interview some of the actors in the politics of the 1930s and 1940s; as such, and given its proximity to the events in question, it is handled as a primary document. For Grobba working with Ernst Woermann on broadening influence in Iraq and driving a wedge between Iraq and Great Britain, see Nicosia, *The Third Reich*, 184–89; and Francis R. Nicosia, *Nazi Germany and the Arab World* (Cambridge: Cambridge University Press, 2014), 42 and elsewhere. Details on Grobba also come from Francis R. Nicosia, "Fritz Grobba and the Middle East Policy of the Third Reich," in *National and International Politics in the Middle East: Essays in Honour of Elie Kedourie*, ed. Edward Ingram (London: Cass, 1986), 206–28. Biographical and other details also come from Edgar Flacker, "Fritz Grobba and Nazi Germany's Middle Eastern Policy, 1933–1942," DPhil. diss., London School of Economics, 1998. The physical description of Grobba is from Sir Archibald Clark Kerr, British ambassador to Iraq, quoted in Flacker, "Fritz Grobba," 18, and the "Arabomaniac" comment is on 186. Other details on the quickening of the "German option" come from Lukasz Hirszowicz, *The Third Reich and the Arab East*, Studies in Political History (Toronto: Toronto University Press, 1966), 105–11. For a careful scholarly study of the inroads of fascism into Iraq in this period—as opposed to numerous poor-quality polemical texts on the subject of fascism and the false monolith "the Arabs"—see Peter Wien, *Iraqi Arab Nationalism: Authoritarian, Totalitarian and Pro-Fascist Inclinations, 1932–1941* (Abingdon, England:

Routledge, 2008). For the intelligence that yielded warnings of serious trouble for the British in Iraq in these months, see Hinsley et al., *British Intelligence in the Second World War*, 1:366–67. For the crown prince and regent's escape, see Jackson, *The British Empire and the Second World War*, 147. For the Nazis' problem of trying to get Arab help while denigrating the Semitic race, see Stefan Wild, "National Socialism in the Arab Near East between 1933 and 1939," *Die Welt des Islams* 25, nos. 1–4 (1985): 140–43, which includes Hitler's "half-ape" comment of 1939, as well as the idea that the Nazi regime would keep the British Empire at least partly intact in the postwar period in the role of caretakers of "lesser" races in the Middle East and India (142). For the Golden Square, see Mohammad A. Tarbush, *The Role of the Military in Politics: A Case Study of Iraq to 1941* (London: Campaign, 1982), 285. For Arab anti-Nazi writing pointing out how Nazi racism made cooperation with them worse than foolhardy for Arabs, see John Broich, "Did the Muslim World Really Fall for Hitler?" March 2017, *Slate*, http://www.slate.com/articles/ news _and_politic/fascism/2017/03/islamofascism_and_anti_fascism_in_the _arab_world_during_world_war_ii.html.

5. Rashid Ali al-Gailani and the four powerful army and air force officers known as the Golden Square did not spring their coup on German instructions. It caught the Axis by surprise. That is a good thing, because given time to prepare for it, Germany might have ordered an airborne garrisoning of Iraq instead of Crete and almost certainly would have succeeded in the absence of any British ability to resist. For the connections between the Golden Square's pro-German stance, the German-trained officer's statement about the Blackshirts, and the new Royal Iraq Army's role in unifying Iraq and its close relationship to Germany, see Ibrahim al-Marashi and Sammy Salama, *Iraq's Armed Forces: An Analytical History* (London: Routledge, 2009), introduction, chaps. 2–3, and especially 28. For the spread of paramilitary uniform in Iraqi schools, see F. al-Samir, "The Role of the Army in the National, Social, and Political Development of Iraq," in *The Military as an Agent of Social Change: XXX International Congress of Human Sciences in Asia and North Africa*, ed. Claude Heller (México City: Colegio de México, 1981), 115. For the statement that pro-Axis members of the military were convinced that the timing of the coup was perfect and that Axis forces would help them drive the British from the eastern Mediterranean, see Italian ambassador Luigi Gabrielli's report of April 10, 1941, in *German Foreign Ministry Records*, cited in Geoffrey Warner, *Iraq and Syria* (Cranbury, NJ: Associated University Presses, 1974), 94. For al-Gailani and the multifaceted politics of Iraq in this period see Wien, *Iraqi Arab Nationalism*. For fierce Palestinian Arb anti-Nazism, see Najati Sidqi, *Al-Taq lid al-isl miyya wa-l-mab di al-n ziyya: hal tattafiq n?* [The Islamic Traditions and the Nazi Principles: Can They Agree?], in Israel Gershoni, "Why the Muslims Must Fight against Nazi Germany: Muḥammad Najāti Ṣidqtī's Plea," *Die Welt des Islams* 52 (2012): 471–98. A stirring passage from Sidqi reads, "The Easterners and the Muslims support the democratic cause in principle and in deed. This is not because they are ingratiating towards the Allies or fear them, as Hitler's propagandists and spies suggest; they support it because democracy is essential to their life, because the freedom of the peoples… is their supreme, ultimate ideal… the Muslims who adhere to the humane message of Islam cannot feel uncertain, not even for a moment, about their obligation to fulfill their historical duty to defeat the enslavement and idolatry that threatens to destroy the globe" (497). Most of the details about Sidqi's *al-Taq lid al-isl miyya* come from Gershoni. Other details about Sidqi come from Salim Tamari, "Najati Sidqi (1905–79): The Enigmatic Jerusalem Bolshevik," *Journal of Palestine Studies* 32, no. 126 (2003): 79–94. For Iraqi anti-German campaigning, see Orit Bashkin, "The Barbarism from Within—Discourses about Fascism amongst Iraqi and Iraqi-Jewish Communists, 1942–1955," *Die Welt des Islams* 52 (2012), 405 and elsewhere. For the Egyptian antifascists, see Israel Gershoni, "Liberal Democracy versus Fascist Totalitarianism in Egyptian Intellectual Discourse: The Case of Salama Musa and al-Majalla al-Jadida," in *Nationalism and Liberal Thought in the Arab East: Ideology and Practice*, ed. Christoph Schumann (New York: Routledge, 2010), 166–69 and elsewhere. For British Muslim leaders' arguing that world Islam from England to the Soviet Union to North Africa should support democracy, see Yusuf Ali, "Islam as an Influence in the War," paper presented at a meeting at the Chatham House, January 23,

1941, Chatham House Library, catalog no. 8/691, 5 and elsewhere. For this generally, as well as the Iraqi left in these years, see Bashkin, "The Barbarism from Within," 403. For the Jewish teachers who promoted Arab nationalism and another who took a stand against anti-Semitism, see Orit Bashkin, *New Babylonians: A History of Jews in Modern Iraq* (Stanford, CA: Stanford University Press, 2012), 78–79. See also Daniel Silverfarb, *Britain's Informal Empire in the Middle East: A Case Study of Iraq, 1929–1941* (Oxford: Oxford University Press, 1986), chaps. 12 and 13. For al-Gailani's calculations over these days generally, see Silverfarb, *Britain's Informal Empire*; and Warner, *Iraq and Syria*, 90–91. The British ambassador to Iraq reported to London that there was little sign of support for the al-Gailani regime among outlying tribes and top Shiite representatives in an April 28 message to Eden; Middle East intelligence reported something similar earlier in April; see Kinahan Cornwallis to Anthony Eden, April 28, 1941, and MICE to various department heads, April 7, 1941, in Alan de Lacy Rush, ed., *Records of Iraq 1914–1966*, vol. 9 (Slough, England: Archive Editions, 2001), 436, 460. For al-Gailani's maneuvering, see Walid M. S. Hamdi, *Rashid Ali al-Gailani and the Nationalist Movement in Iraq, 1939–1941* (London: Darf, 1987), 48–52. For al-Gailani's speech before Parliament, see Kinahan Corwallis to Anthony Eden, 28 April 1941, in Alan de Lacy Rush and Jane Priestland, eds., *Records of Iraq, 1914–1966,* vol. 8 (Slough, England: Archive Editions, 2001), 456.

6. For the War Cabinet meeting of April 7, 1941, see National Archives, CAB 65/18/15. Details about inquiries to Wavell in Cairo and his response come from Compton MacKenzie, *Eastern Epic* (London: Chatto & Windus), 1951, 89–91. For this episode generally, see Warner, *Iraq and Syria*, 88–90.

7. Biographical details about Auchinleck, including the suggestion that years patrolling in the tribal areas taught him a habit of vigilant watching for threats come from Philip Warner, *Auchinleck: The Lonely Soldier* (London: Buchan and Enright, 1981), chaps. 1 and 2. For Auchinleck's antiracism, see Daniel Marston, *The Indian Army and the End of the Raj*

(Cambridge: Cambridge University Press, 2014), 86. For Ambassador Cornwallis's April 11, 1941, telegrams to the Foreign Office suggesting that troops should not land at Basra until some test case be tried, see National Archives, FO 371/27064; in this same file are the viceroy's objections, as influenced by Auchinleck. For Auchinleck's messages to New Delhi, see Warner, *Iraq and Syria*, 91; and MacKenzie, *Eastern Epic*, 91–92.

8. Churchill's reaction to the Iraqi demands comes from Winston Churchill, *The Second World War*, vol. 3 (London: Cassell, 1965), 226. The Foreign Office response is in Archives of the Commonwealth of Australia, series A1608, quoted in Warner, *Iraq and Syria*, 93; see also British Embassy from Foreign Office, secret telegram, April 22, 1941, in Rush and Priestland, eds., *Records of Iraq*, 8:453–54. For the meeting of al-Gailani, al-Husseini, and others with the Italians on April 24, 1941, see telegram from Italian Ambassador to Iraq to German Foreign Office, April 25, 1941, in *Documents on German Foreign Policy*, Series D: 1937-1945 (hereafter, *DGFP*), vol. 12 (Washington, DC: Department of State, 1962), 634–35. The terms of the secret treaty signed the next day, April 25, 1941, are transcribed in the National Archives, FO 371/27099. Hamdi suggests this treaty is a fake, that the original was lost and the first iteration of it was a French translation. He believes it was British wartime "dirty trick" meant to paint the coup plotters as Axis stooges to discredit them as loyal nationalists. See Walid M. S. Hamdi, *Rashid Ali al-Gailani and the Nationalist Movement in Iraq, 1939-1941*, DPhil. diss., University of Birmingham, 1987. With respect, I find that this is a solution in search of a problem. There is no positive evidence that it is a fake, and the terms would not seem necessarily to paint al-Gailani and his supporters as bad nationalists. Trading oil for aid in their revolution was only practical. Hamdi also suggests that the Hitler regime would have been unlikely to make such terms with the "lesser" Arab race. This seems rather belied by the fact that he made alliances with the likes of the "Slavic" Soviets (whom, of course, he betrayed), the Japanese, and others. See Hamdi, *Rashid Ali al-Gailani*, 55. Further, internal German Foreign Office documents show that al-Gailani's government already informally offered Iraqi oil for aid in a top secret telegram from the Italian embassy in Baghdad shared with the German Foreign Office, April 19, 1941, in *DGFP*, vol. 11, no. 372, 587. For 1940s plans between Germany and Italy to share in the exploitation of the Middle East after dislodging the British, including sharing its oil, see Ernst Woermann's memorandum to the German diplomatic establishment abroad, August 20, 1940, in *DGFP*, vol. 10, 516–17. More directly, see Heinz Tillmann, *Deutschlands Araberpolitik im Zweiten Weltkrieg* (Berlin: Deutsche Verlag der Wissenschaften, 1965), 241, which references a memorandum of Emil Wiehl, head of the Department of Trade Policy, "Handakten Wiehl," in the Politisches Archiv des Auswartigen Amtes, Irak, Serie 4740H, E 233200. On the Haifa oil pipeline shut down, see Hamdi, *Rashid Ali al-Gailani*, 54; and Nicholas Rankin, *A Genius for Deception: How Cunning Helped the British Win Two World Wars* (Oxford: Oxford University Press, 2009), 331. For the Italian Foreign Ministry memorandum of September 5, 1940, see Ministero Degli Affari Esteri, *I Documenti Diplomatici Italiani, 9ª Serie: 1939–1943*, vol. 5 (Rome: Libreria dello Stato, 1965), 543–44. For German offers to buy up Iraqi commodities in return for credits prior to the spring 1941 war, see "Irak, vol. 1," German Foreign Ministry Files, National Archives, GFM 33/2108. On the Iraqi Army being placed on standby and reinforcements arriving in Baghdad, see the coded radio message from intelligence source in Basra to Air Officer Commanding, Iraq, April 4, 1941, National Archives, AIR 23/5933.

Chapter 3

EPIGRAPH: Dean Bailey, *Crawling Out of Hell: The True Story of a British Sniper's Greatest Battle* (Stroud, England: Fonthill, 2017), https://books .google .com/books?id=4oMlDwAAQBAJandpg=PA61anddq=we +landed +in+basraandhl=enandsa=Xandved=0ahUKEwj27Yuf4uvYAhWIx4MKH Ty0CTMQ6AEINDAC.

1. Details for Masters and his eastward voyage toward Britain come from John Masters, *Bugles and a Tiger; A Volume of Autobiography* (New York: Viking, 1956), 83, 89, 241, 250, 259, 269–89; and John Clay, *John*

Masters: A Regimented Life (London: Joseph, 1992), 77, 78–79, 192, and elsewhere. This valuable biography draws on letters from Masters to his family in England and other unique papers.

2. Details from this section come from my conversations with Leila Sen, daughter of Dutt, who generously gave her time and shared unique documents with me, along with her biography of her father and mother, *Aegis of Kali, 1939–1945: A Time of Love and War* (self-published, 2017), which includes transcriptions of her father's diary and many letters; and John Masters, *The Road past Mandalay: A Personal Narrative* (New York: Harper, 1961), chap. 2.

3. The unit that sailed to Malaya in April 1941 while these units sailed west and joined the Indian National Army at a rate of around 90 percent was the 5/11 Sikh Regiment. The Jind Infantry Battalion (a princely state unit) was also in the convoy. For this and the SS *Varella*, see Gurbakhsh Singh, *Indelible Reminiscences: Memoirs of Major General Gurbakhsh Singh* (New Delhi: Lancer 2013), 23–25; for Singh's brother's account from the point of view of the 5/11 Sikhs, see Harbakhsh Singh, *In the Line of Duty: A Soldier Remembers* (New Delhi: Lancer, 2009). Information about the Third Field Regiment, Royal Artillery attached to the Indian Army comes from its war diary, March–April 1941, National Archives, WO 169/1444. For the young man from southern India "overjoyed" to learn he was heading to Singapore, see John Baptist Crasta, *Eaten by the Japanese: the Memoir of an Unknown Indian Prisoner of War* (Bangalore, India: Invisible Man, 1999), 5. For the kinds of training that units of the Tenth Indian Division like the 2/4 Gurkhas and 4/13 Frontier Force Rifles (aka Wilde's Rifles) performed, and for details in particular about the experiences of the 4/13, see William Edmund Hunt Condon, *The Frontier Force Rifles* (Aldershot, England: Gale and Polden, 1953), 211–30; Condon was a veteran of the 6/13 Frontier Force Rifles. Information about the 4/13 Frontier Force Rifles also comes from its war diary from this period, National Archives, WO 169/3449. This document also includes comments on how shipboard life was totally new to most in the 4/13 Frontier Force Rifles. For the Indian men who became officers in command of British subordinate officers, see Marston, *The Indian Army*, 86. Information about the Thirteenth Duke of Connaught's Own Lancers comes from its war diary from this period, National Archives, WO 169/3406; John Gaylor, *Sons of John Company: The Indian and Pakistan Armies 1903–1991* (Stroud, England: Spellmount, 1992); Kaushik Roy, *The Army in British India: From Colonial Warfare to Total War 1857–1947* (London: Bloomsbury, 2013), 120 and elsewhere; and Francis Ingall, *The Last of the Bengal Lancers* (Novato, CA: Presidio, 1988), 1–5. Among the World War I veterans in the harbors of Bombay and Karachi in those weeks were S. K. Furney (4/13 Frontier Force Rifles), H. V. P. Sealy, and F. D. Clarke (2/8 Gurkhas). Details about the 2/4 Gurkhas come from John Masters, *The Road past Mandalay*, 3–72. For how this unit had been intended for Malaya, see MacKenzie, *Eastern Epic*, 90, and Masters, *The Road past Mandalay*, 15, and for the young woman who died in the Café de Paris, page 16. Details about the activities of the various units on board the *Devonshire*, *Lancashire*, and *Varella* come from their war diaries; see, for example, for the happy sighting of porpoises and flying fish, 2/4 Gurkha Rifles 1941 war diary, April 29, 1941, National Archives, WO 169/3460. For Masters and Dutt's conversations about why Indians should fight in the war, see Masters, *The Road past Mandalay*, 17–19. Some details about Dutt come from his obituary; see Susan Sward, "Santi Pada Dutt," SFGate, http://www.sfgate.com/news /article/SantiPada-Dutt-2960799.php. Other details come from my conversations with Dutt's daughter, Leila Sen, and from her biography of her father and mother, *Aegis of Kali*. Details about embarking on the ships, the novelty of ocean travel, the trip from Bombay to Basra, the number of troops in the *Devonshire*, and political discussions with British officers about Britain's rule over India also come from Satyen Basu, *A Doctor in the Army* (Calcutta: Sri Brojendra Nath Bose, 1960), 19–24. Anup K. Dutt seemed more inclined to think Britain's war was his; see Anup K. Dutt, *Fight No More: The Reminiscences of an Indian Medical Service Officer, 1940–1947* (London: Hazelwood, 1994), 9, 19–20.

4. For the loading of the *Lancashire*, see the 2/8 Gurkha Rifles war diary, April 18, 1941, National Archives, WO 169/3463.The tale of the *Lan-*

cashire captain's racist remarks on Indian hygiene come from Ken Ross, "With the 2/8th Gurkhas in Iraq, 1941–1942," *Red Flash: Journal of the 8th Gurkha Rifles Regiment Association* 22 (2004): 54, and for preparations on the *Lancashire* for an opposed landing using lifeboats, 54–55. For the *Devonshire* and John Master's thoughts, see Masters, *The Road past Mandalay*, 18–19.

5. For some landing details, see the 2/8 Gurkha Rifles war diary. April 18, 1941, National Archives, WO 169/3463. For the extraordinary porters of Basra and other observations about the scene, see Basu, *A Doctor in the Army*, 25. For the "black-veiled women," see Masters, *The Road past Mandalay*, 23. For more details on the first landing in Basra, see MacKenzie, *Eastern Epic*, 92. For details about the King's Own Royal Regiment landing, in particular, see E. N. Everett-Heath and R.A. Westworth, *The Flying Fourth* (Lancaster, England: King's Own Royal Regiment Museum, 2005), 1–6. For Rashid Ali al-Gailani in these days, see Hamdi, *Rashid Ali al-Gailani*, 50–52, 190–91; an

6. For al-Gailani's anger, see Ambassador Cornwallis's report to the Foreign Office, April 28, 1941, in Rush and Priestland, eds., *Records of Iraq*, 8:459. For civilian evacuations to the embassies and Habbaniya, see Jackson, *The British Empire and the Second World War*, 149; and Seton Lloyd, *The Interval: A Life in Near-Eastern archaeology* (Oxford: Alden, 1986), 80. Further details come from a recorded interview of John Terrance Cooper, officer with the Iraq Levies, Imperial War Museum, catalog no. 4515.

Chapter 4

EPIGRAPH: Phil Klay, quoted in "In 'Redeployment,' Former Marine Explores the Challenges of Coming Home," *Fresh Air*, March 20, 2015, National Public Radio, https://www.npr.org/2015/03/20/394280459/in-redeployment-former-marine-explores-the-challenges-of-coming-home.

1. Weather and other details about Habbaniya come from National Archives, AIR 29/893; see also Jackson, *The British Empire and the Sec-*

ond World War, 149–50. Other details come from Naida Smart, *Forgotten Victory* (Houghton Regis, England: Bound Biographies, 2012), 31, 37, 90. The tale of Dudgeon's guilt at outfoxing the Italian who drowned, as well as other details about his time in Egypt and Iraq, come from A. G. Dudgeon, *The Luck of the Devil: An Autobiography 1934–41* (Shrewsbury, England: Airlife, 1985), 154 and elsewhere. More details about RAF Habbaniya come from an interview of former RAF Levies officer John Dutton Frost, Imperial War Museum, catalog no. 4430. The exchange of letters about Habbaniya's apparent indefensibility, as well as other details, comes from A. G. Dudgeon, *Hidden Victory: The Battle of Habbaniya, May 1941* (Stroud, England: Tempus, 200), 15, 34, 47–66, and elsewhere. For the activity of the armored cars, artillery focusing on the hangar area as opposed to the civilian areas, and other details, see Christopher Morris, "The RAF Armoured Car Companies in Iraq (Mostly), 1921–1947," *Royal Air Force Historical Society Journal* 48 (2010), 33 and elsewhere; Christopher Buckley, *Five Ventures: Iraq, Syria, Persia, Madagascar, Dodecanese* (London: HMSO, 1977), 17; and Stephen H. Longrigg, *Oil in the Middle East: Its Discovery and Development* (Oxford: Oxford University Press, 1955), 291. Generally, see also Ashley Jackson, *Persian Gulf Command: A History of the Second World War in Iran and Iraq* (New Haven, CT: Yale University Press, 2018). For other details, including the Gladiators' inability to catch the Iraqi Douglas-Northrops, and casualty numbers, see Bisheshwar Prasad, ed., *Official History of the Indian Armed Forces in the Second World War, 1939–45: Campaign in Western Asia* (New Delhi: Government of India, 1958), 79 and elsewhere. Details from the ground at the Habbaniya air base also come from a letter of RAF armored car radio operator Egerton Spybey to Harry Spybey, January 4, 1944, transcribed and generously shared by Alan Spybey via the RAF Habbaniya Association; see "Text of a Letter Written by a Young and Uneducated Serviceman to his Eldest Brother during the Later Stages of World War II," http://habbaniya .org:80/pdf/; see also intrepid Assyrian Levy chronicler Gaby Kiwarkis's interview of Levy veteran Baijan Peku: Gaby Kiwarkis, "RAB Emma Baijan Peku MC," n.d., Assyrian RAF Levies, http://assyrianlevies.info/rab-emma-baijan-peku-mc.html. For the BBC misinforming listeners that the

Iraqis had struck first and implying that the Indian Army was passing through the country, see BBC radio broadcast transcripts for May 3, 1941, 8:00 a.m., British Library, Newspaper Library, BBC Radio Home News Bulletins, MFM.MLD218, film 56/57.

2. Hans Kroll to German Foreign Ministry, May 2, 1941, in *DGFP*, vol. 12, 686. For the context, see Francis Nicosia, *Nazi Germany and the Arab World*, 169.

3. The battle over a northern Ethiopian mountain fortress was Amba Alagi, which began on May 4, 1941. For Wavell's tough position before and during the breakout of war in Iraq, see Warner, *Iraq and Syria*, 88–90, 106–7; and Jackson, *The British Empire and the Second World War*, 148. For Wavell's responses to the War Office, including his outburst, see Harold E. Raugh Jr., *Wavell in the Middle East, 1939–1941* (Norman: University of Oklahoma Press, 2013), 211. For the assurance that the Golden Square had gone off at "half-cock" and accepting responsibility for draining men from Palestine and perhaps Egypt, see the War Office telegram to Commander in Chief, Middle East, May 6, 1941, National Archives, CAB 105/4, 18. For Churchill thinking Wavell seemed "tired out," see Churchill, *Second World War*, 3:228–29.

4. For Habbaniya as an intelligence center, see Nicholas Van der Bijl, *Sharing the Secret: A History of the Intelligence Corps 1940–2010* (Barnsley, England: Pen and Sword, 2013), 65 and elsewhere; Priya Satia, "The Secret Center: Arabia Intelligence in British Culture and Politics, 1900–1932," PhD diss., University of California–Berkeley, 2004, 558; Satia makes the point here that the intelligence officers operated illegally—that is, without any authority in the Anglo-Iraqi Treaty; see also the book that grew out of that dissertation: Priya Satia, *Spies in Arabia: the Great War and the Cultural Foundations of Britain's Covert Empire in the Middle East* (Oxford: Oxford University Press, 2010), 275–83. See also Hinsley et al., *British Intelligence*, 1:411. For the Middle East Intelligence center organization, see Hinsley et al., *British Intelligence*, 1:190–98, 570–71; and E. E. Mockler-Ferryman, *Military Intelligence*

Organization (1952), National Archives, WO 33/2723, 154–64. The Air Liaison Officer's reports for late April 1941 are in "Coup d'Etat April 194: Intelligence Reports," National Archives, AIR 23/5933; see, in particular, the reports of the air liaison officer for April 28–29, 1941, as well as the summary from MICE, Cairo, on April 29. For the sort of bribes paid, the resentment engendered among the Iraqis, and their close observation of the air liaison officers' comings and goings, see Air Ministry memo, "Activities of Royal Ari Force Liaison Officers," January 4, 1938 including the cover letter of Air Vice Marshal Christopher Lloyd Courtney, National Archives, FO 371/21849.

5. The story of the second day and night of the Habbaniya countersiege comes from Dudgeon, *Hidden Victory*, 64–95. For the women racing to contribute their efforts before being forced to evacuate, see Smart, *Forgotten Victory*, 126. Tony Dudgeon's account of Air Officer Commaning (AOC) Smart having a nervous breakdown is confirmed in Arthur Tedder, *With Prejudice: The War Memoirs of Marshal of the Royal Air Force Lord Tedder* (London: Cassell, 1966), 87, 92. Many elements from Dudgeon are reinforced by an official war diary made by two student members of one of the squadron's subdivisions, "C Squadron." James Dunford Wood, the son of one of these pilots, C.D.C Dunford Wood, generously digitized this valuable source; see "'C' Squadron Historical Record, No. 4 SFTS, Habbaniya, Iraq May 1941," https://storyofwar .com/background/c-squadron-historical-record-no-4-fts-habbaniya -iraq -may-1941/. Other information for this section comes from C.D.C Dunford Wood's personal diary for these days in early May 1941. For the RAF armored car officer who shot himself in the foot, see Egerton Spybey to Harry Spybey, "Text of a Letter Written by a Young and Uneducated Serviceman." Details about the airlifts come from Hamdi, *Rashid Ali al-Gailani*, 117.

Chapter 5

1. Details about the 237th Battery, Sixtieth Field Regiment Royal Artillery come from Jack Bartlett and John Benson, *All the King's Enemies* (Boston, England: Kay, 2000), 3–16, 32–36, and elsewhere.

2. David Smiley's details come from his Imperial War Museum interview, catalog no. 10340 (1988); David Smiley, *Irregular Regular* (Wilby, England: Russell, 1994), chaps. 1–3; and *Times* (London), January 14, 2009. For "Lords," "Honourables," and "Dukes," see officer roll, war diary of the Household Cavalry, National Archives, WO 169/1380.

3. For details about Harry Chalk's background and experiences, see his interview at the Imperial War Museum, catalog no. 31420; see also the memoir he created with James H. Hills, 2005, in the Private Papers of Harry Chalk, Imperial War Museum, Document 16935. See also Antony Brett-James, *Ball of Fire: The Fifth Indian Division in the Second World War* (Aldershot, England: Gale and Polden, 1951), chap. 2; and Ronald Lewin, *Slim, the Standardbearer: A Biography of Field-Marshal the Viscount Slim* (London: Cooper, 1977), 66–67. For the story of the day, and Jayanto Nath Chaudhuri being ordered to intercept the retreating Essex, see J. N. Chaudhuri with B.K. Narayan, *An Autobiography* (New Delhi: Vikas, 1978), 124–25.

4. For the British envisioning the role of the mechanized Arab Legion, see the memorandum from Army HQ, Jerusalem, to Middle East Command, Cairo, December 16, 1940, National Archives, WO 201/2667. For other details about the formation of the Arab Legion, securing its trucks, and so on, see Glubb, *A Soldier with the Arabs*, 39–41 and elsewhere. See also Glubb's March 1979 interview at the Imperial War Museum, catalog no. 4410, especially reel 4; and John B. Glubb, *The Changing Scenes of Life: An Autobiography* (London: Quartet, 1983), 121–22. For anxiety in Amman and Emir Abdullah I needing to be talked out of riding on Baghdad, see High Commissioner for Palestine Harold MacMichael to Colonial Office, May 8, 1941, National Archives, FO 371/27069, 1. Glubb relates this anxiety, too, in *The Story of the Arab Legion*, 255–56, and his story of being summoned by Jumbo Wilson is on 257–58. More on the Arab Legion, including insights into why young men enlisted, comes from Katharina Lange, "Proud Fighters, Blind Men: World War Experiences of Combatants from the Arab East," in *Translocality: The Study of Globalising Processes from the Southern Perspective,* ed. Ulirke Freitag and Achim von Oppen (Leiden: Brill, 2010), 91–92 and elsewhere.

Chapter 6

EPIGRAPH: Frank Miller, quoted in Special Inspector General for Iraq Reconstruction, *Hard Lessons: The Iraq Reconstruction Experience* (Washington, DC: GPO, 2008), 125.

1. Details about the Fifth Indian Army Division come from a veteran of the division, Antony Brett-James, in his *Ball of Fire: The Fifth Indian Division in the Second World War* (Aldershot, England: Gale and Polden, 1951), prologue and chap. 1. For Freya Stark's life, including her early foray into Druze lands, Iran, and Yemen, choices include Jane Geniesse, *Passionate Nomad: The Life of Freya Stark* (New York: Random House, 1999); and Molly Izzard, *Freya Stark: A Biography* (London: Hodder and Stoughton, 1993). The episode on the Red Sea comes from Freya Stark, *East Is West* (London: Century, 1945), 43–49, and especially 47, where Stark describes the Sikh officers' happy reaction to the news of the forthcoming raid. See also Freya Stark to Sidney Cockerell, September 7, 1940, in Freya Stark, *Letters*, vol. 4, *Bridge of the Levant, 1940–1943*, ed. Lucy Moorehead (London: Russell, 1977), 89–90. The advice of the cook to get the harem to wish what Freya wished is in Freya Stark to Stewart Perowne, February 9, 1940, in Stark, *Letters*, 4:10–11. The scene from the harem in which the older wife made special claims for her breasts is in Freya Stark to Flora Stark, March 5, 1940, in Stark *Letters*, 4:34–35. Stark's considerations on the relative power and freedom versus imprisonment of the wives comes from Stark, *East Is West*, 30–31, 35.

2. Details for this section on Freya Stark in spring 1941 in Cairo and Amman, and her arrival in Baghdad come from Stark, *Letters*, 4:117, 123–27, and elsewhere. Details about Lulie Abdul-Huda come from Stark, *East Is West*, 69–75; for more on her life, see Alan Rush, "Princess Lulie Abul-Huda Fevzi Osmanoglu (1919–2012)" (obituary), *Al-Ahram Weekly*, http://weekly.ahram.org.eg/News/ 682.aspx. For more on Stark, including her exchanges with General Wavell, see Geniesse, *Passionate*

Nomad, chap. 16. For Abdullah I's concern over how the Transjordanians could possibly answer a Vichy threat, and for tribal leaders' stating they would remain with Britain but could not realistically resist, see Alec Kirkbride, *A Crackle of Thorns: Experiences in the Middle East* (London: J. Murray, 1956), 130-1. For George Antonius's beliefs, see his *Arab Awakening* (New York: Putnam's, 1946), 170, 268–69, 392. For Stark's meeting with Antonius and al-Husseini, see Stark, *East Is West*, 142–43 and Stark, *Letters*, 4:127.

3. Sources for this section on Freya Stark's trip to Iran and rush back to Baghdad to find herself besieged come from Freya Stark, *Dust in the Lion's Paw: Autobiography 1939-1946* (London: J. Murray, 1962) 83–87, 130; and Stark, *East Is West*, 143–60. She sadly wrote in later years that the British eventually lost their influence in the Middle East because of "a lack of clearness and faith in our own values." See Peter B. Flint, "Dame Freya Stark, Travel Writer, is Dead at 100," *New York Times*, May 11, 1993. Other details about the embassy scene, Adrian Bishop, the airplane components being dumped down the well, and Seton Lloyd come from his memoir: Lloyd, *The Interval*, 79–83. We know that oil secrets were burned in the embassy grounds bonfire because in place of where they should be in the embassy records there's a note indicating as much: Baghdad Embassy files, National Archives, FO 624/22, no. 127. More on Adrian Bishop comes from Petà Dunstan, *The Labour of Obedience: The Benedictines of Pershore, Nashdom and Elmore* (Norwich, England: Canterbury, 2009), 131–32. For the fate of the air liaison officers, their Iraqi associates, and others whom Iraqi police associated with the British and robbed, see National Archives, FO 624/26, no. 572. The many British Iraqi officials who embodied a range of attitudes included C.C. Aston, Ernest Dowson, Cecil Edmonds, and Alec Kinch. As an RAF intelligence officer in Palestine, Patrick Domville directed the Peace Bands in Palestine during the 1936–39 Arab Revolt, which engaged in brutal communal punishment.

4. This scene of Freya watching the incoming bombers is drawn from Stark, *East Is West*, 90–91. The fact this bombing run was that described by Dudgeon is based on Dudgeon, *Hidden Victory*, 89; it is further corroborated by the diary of C.D.C Dunford Wood, "'C' Squadron Historical Record."

Chapter 7

EPIGRAPH: Thomas Hamill, Paul T. Brown, and Jay Langston, *Escape in Iraq: The Thomas Hamill Story* (Accokeek, MD: Stoeger, 2004), 18.

1. For the Household Cavalry's lack of experienced drivers, see Everard H. Wyndham, *The Household Cavalry at War: First Household Cavalry Regiment* (Aldershot: Gale & Polden, 1952), 52. For the presence of the Royal Engineers and their dynamite intended for Kirkuk's oil fields, see the interview with a veteran of the Third Field Squadron, Royal Engineers, William Lionel Vickers, Imperial War Museum, catalog no. 17378, reel 2. For a number of details, including the "black ribbon" quote, see Thomas A. Martin, *The Essex Regiment, 1929–1950* (Brentwood, England: Essex Regiment Association, 1952), 46 and elsewhere.

2. Somerset de Chair writes that the Sixth Cavalry Brigade, of which the Household Cavalry was a part, was headquartered at Hadera, a village outside Haifa, and had signal personnel based there. De Chair writes that Reading came from force headquarters. The Sixth Cavalry Brigade war diary and Household Cavalry war diary make no mention of nonarmy supernumerary, nor of an individual seconded from another unit. In case De Chair was wrong, and Reading was in fact a police interpreter, I appealed to the veterans of the Palestine Police Association, but that yielded no memories of an interpreter named Reading. Later in the campaign, Reading asked De Chair whether he would support Reading's application to Army Intelligence. We do not know whether he was Arab or Christian. We might speculate that he was educated at the American University of Beirut, but there's no evidential basis for that, only that he somewhere learned the confidence to speak and deal with someone like De Chair on a solid footing and had a degree of cosmopolitanism sufficient to enlist in the British Army. Since De Chair never provides Reading's name, we are at a great disadvantage. My historian's choice was to push back against the historical record's disregard (and De Chair's orientalist disregard and racism) and lift him from obscurity even though our evidence for him is slight. For how interpreters who worked with the British took on aliases, see Fergusson, *The Trumpet in the Hall*, 30. Reading first appears in Somerset de Chair, *The Golden Carpet* (New York: Harcourt, Brace, 1945), 16. For the brutality of the British suppression of the Arab Revolt, including violence toward noncombatants, see Matthew Hughes, "From Law and Order to Pacification: Britain's Suppression of the Arab Revolt in Palestine, 1936–39," *Journal of Palestine Studies* 39 (2010): 6–22.

3. For the remarkable assembly and journey of Grobba's mission, see Dudgeon, *Hidden Victory*, 109–13; for Dudgeon's flight to warn Habforce, see the Sixth Cavalry Brigade HQ war diary, May 14, 1941, National Archives, WO 196/1259.

4. For details about wrestling with the vehicles in the heat, and the legionnaire doing the gunner's target practice for him, see Bartlett and Benson, *All the King's Enemies*, 86, 89. For details about the Arab Legion's first days and weeks in Iraq, see Glubb, *Story of the Arab Legion*, chap. 14 and elsewhere. Many details, including the experiences of Reading, come from De Chair, *The Golden Carpet*, 16–44 and elsewhere. Details about one troop's Transjordan Frontier Force mutiny come from the Foreign Office file on the subject, National Archives, FO 371/27143. For the Haifa taxi as staff car, see Wyndham, *Household Cavalry*, 28. For Harry Chalk's views of Glubb versus the men of the Arab Legion, see his 2008 Imperial War Museum interview at the Imperial War Museum, catalog no. 31420, reels 3–4.

5. For the arrival of Grobba and his party in Baghdad, his paying al-Gailiani and al-Husseini, and his appeal for planes, see Gehrcke to Foreign Ministry, May 11, 1941 (two wires on that date), in *DGFP*, vol. 12 775–76. For the strong impression that Grobba identified as the "German Lawrence," see Flacker, "Fritz Grobba," 120–211 and 318n66; for Germans civilian aids in Iraq who could relay data and propaganda, 139;

and for the Schutzstaffel office in Tehran devoted to Iraq, 222. For the departure of Werner Junck, the ghost column of tanks from the direction of Mosul, and Grobba's persistent belief in the presence in Iraq of British tanks, see Fritz Grobba, *Macht und Männer im Orient* (Göttingen: Musterschmidt, 1967), 245.

6. Details about this scene of the duel between the Arab legionnaires and the Messerschmitts come from Glubb, *The Story of the Arab Legion*, 273–74; and De Chair, *The Golden Carpet*, 41–42, 240–41. See also Smiley, *Irregular Regular*, 43.

7. Details about the last day of the Habbaniya siege come from Dudgeon, *Hidden Victory*, 97–99. Others come from Everett-Heath and Westworth, *Flying Fourth*, 12–13. See also Smart, *Forgotten Victory*, 130.

8. This story comes from the unique firsthand account of a Jewish officer in the Royal Iraqi Army that's a small part of Abdallah H. Simon and Edwin E. Simon, *Vintage Years: A Memoir* (N.p.: Simon, 2009), 44–45 and elsewhere. For the urban Jewish middle class of Iraq, see Orit Bashkin, "Arabic Thought in the Radical Age: Emile Habibi, the Israeli Communist Party, and the Production of Arab Jewish Radicalism, 1946," in *Arabic Thought against the Authoritarian Age: Towards an Intellectual History of the Present*, ed. Jens Hannsen and Max Weiss (Cambridge: Cambridge University Press, 2017), 65–66; and Esther Meir-Glitzenstein, *Zionism in an Arab Country: Jews in Iraq in the 1940s* (London: Routledge, 2004), 4–6.

9. Details in this section come from Dudgeon, *Hidden Victory*, 97–99 and elsewhere. For the scene of devastation along the road to Fallujah, see the interview of Mornington Samuel Wentworth, armored car driver for the RAF at Habbaniya, Imperial War Museum, catalog no. 4768, reel 5.

10. For the fractures and morale breakdown in the Iraqi military, see Silverfarb, *Britain's Informal Empire*, 133–36, 139. For the matter of Iraqi morale at Habbaniya, other clues to why the besiegers routed, and the devastation to the retreating and reinforcing columns, see Hamdi, *Rashid Ali al-Gailani*, 122–23. For the idea that the Iraqis believed the British were flying in artillery, see "The Siege of Habbaniya," National Archives, AIR 41/30, II. For the breakdown of Colonel Fahmi Said at Habbaniya, see al-Marashi and Salama, *Iraq's Armed Forces*, 63; and Military Intelligence, Cairo to RAF Habbaniya and Shaibah, May 15, 1941, National Archives, AIR 23/5933.

11. Winston Churchill, *The Second World War,* Volume 3: Grand Alliance (New York: Bantam, 1962), 236.

12. For the scene at the Baghdad embassy on May 7, 1941, Stark thinking British policy in Palestine was near the root of troubles in Iraq, and her feelings on Grobba, see Stark, *Dust in the Lion's Paw*, 96–97, 107, 130.

13. On the activities around Basra on May 7–8, 1941, see Frontier Force Rifles war diary, National Archives, WO 169/3449 4/13; Masters, *The Road past Mandalay*, 19–29; H. J. Huxford, *History of the 8th Gurkha Rifles* (Aldershot, England: Gale and Polden, 1952), 163; B. R. Mullaly, *Bugle and Kukri: The Story of the Tenth Princess Mary's Own Gurkha Rifles* (London: Blackwood, 1957), 257; and the war diary of the 3/11 Sikhs, April–May 1941, National Archives, WO 169/3444. For Queen Victoria's Own Madras Sappers and Miners' participation in the battle for the Big House and their casualties, see R. A. Lindsell, *A Short History of Queen Victoria's Own Madras Sappers and Miners during World War II* (Bangalore: QVO Madras Sappers and Miners, 1949), 8. Details for William Russell Willoughby Weallens come from Masters, *Road Past Mandalay*, 12; *London Gazette*, 1 Jan. 1918, 13 June 1919, 2 May 1941; and his medal card at the National Archives, WO 372/21/50919.

Chapter 8

EPIGRAPH: Ross Caputi, "I Am Sorry for the Role I Played in Fallujah," *Guardian*, December 22, 2011, https://www.theguardian.com/commentisfree/2011/dec/22 /fallujah-us-marine-iraq.

1. Harry Chalk's comment about the Brylcreem Boys comes from James H. Hills's terrific video interview of his grandfather, kindly shared with me. Jimmy Roosevelt's arrival is described in De Chair, *The Golden Carpet*, 51; they are confirmed in the war diary of the Household Cavalry HQ, May 20, 1941, National Archives, WO 169/1259.

2. For "Captain Ben-Moshe," see David Raziel and J. Bowyer-Bell, *Terror out of Zion* (New York: St. Martin's, 1977), 55–56; Saul Kelly, "A Succession of Crises: SOE in the Middle East, 1940–45," *Intelligence and National Security* 20 (2005): 125–26; Andre Gerolymatos, *Castles Made of Sand: A Century of Anglo-American Espionage and Intervention in the Middle East* (New York: Macmillan, 2010), 90; Shlomo Lev-Ami, *By Struggle and By Revolt: Haganah, Irgun and Lehi, 1918–1948* [in Hebrew] (Tel Aviv: Mis rad ha-bit ah on, 1977), 154–55 (with thanks to Mordy Pelleg for the translation of this source). There are many sources for Irgun terror in the 1930s, including Raziel and Bowyer-Bell, *Terror Out of Zion*; Tom Segev and Haim Watzman, *The Seventh Million: The Israelis and the Holocaust* (New York: Holt, 2005), 39; and, for just one of any number of reports from the period, "Haifa-Bombs Fell Scores; Arabs Are Killed and Wounded in Palestine Blasts," *New York Times*, June 19, 1939.

3. For the Arab Legion's activities during this period, see Glubb, *Story of the Arab Legion*, 280–87, 289. This includes the later discovery that the engineers' dismantling of the rails was observed and immediately reported: a very disturbing bit of information for the Golden Square and their sympathizers who had hoped to continue their resistance from Mosul until Axis soldiers appeared.

4. MacKenzie tells the story of Queen Victoria's Own Madras Sappers and Miners and their ferry in *Eastern Epic*, 102–3. Details for the first and second battles for Fallujah come from Martin, *The Essex Regiment*, 49–52; Bartlett and Benson, *All the King's Enemies*, 91; De Chair, *The Golden Carpet*, 49–53, 56–57, and, on the comparison to ruined Flanders towns, 69; Dudgeon, *Hidden Victory*, 124–25; Prasad, *Official History*, 96. For more details, see Everett-Heath and Westworth, *Flying Fourth*, 18–21. For the smell emanating from the ruins of Fallujah, see the Household Cavalry Headquarters war diary, May 22, 1941, WO 169/1259. On the comments about the Assyrians and the Iraqi tanks, see De Chair, *The Golden Carpet*, 57; Martin, *The Essex Regiment*, 50; and Kiwarkis, Peku interview.

5. Details for this section come from Sami Zubaida, "Contested Nations: Iraq and the Assyrians," *Nations and Nationalism* 6 (2000): 363–82; and Reeva Spector Simon, *Iraq between the Two World Wars*, 2nd ed. (New York: Columbia University Press, 2004), 111–13. See also Silverfarb, *Britain's Informal Empire*, 36–37. For firsthand accounts of the terror sowed in Assyrian lands, see Sargon Donabed, *Reforging a Forgotten History: Iraq and the Assyrians in the Twentieth Century* (Oxford: Oxford University Press, 2016), chap. 3. The quote from Levies veteran Odisho Moshe is from Gaby Kiwarkis's interview: Gaby Kiwarkis, "X-343—RAB Khamshi (50) Odisho Moshe 1919–2005," n.d., Assyrian RAF Levies, http://assyrianlevies.info/rab-50-odisho-moshe.html. Kiwarkis's interview of Iskhak Dinkha provides the tale of the Assyrian artillery officer in the Iraqi Army who was nearly shot by the Levies; Gaby Kiwarkis, "1061- RAB 50 Iskhak Dinkha," n.d., Assyrian RAF Levies, http://assyrianlevies.info/rab-50-iskhak-dinkha.html.

6. Details come from Gaby Kiwarkis's interviews located at https://assyrianlevies .info. See also the award recommendation of Robert Brian James of the First Essex, National Archives, WO 373/27. Harry Chalk describes the fight to maintain Fallujah in an interview, Imperial War Museum, catalog no. 31420, reel 3. The story of the surprise defeat of an Iraqi tank comes from Kiwarkis, interview with Moshe, and is confirmed by Kiwarkis, interview with Peku. For details about the killed men of the King's Own Royal Regiment, see King's Own Royal Regiment Museum, "Photo Gallery: Graves and Memorials, Habbaniya War Cemetery, Iraq, Second World War," http://www.kingsownmuseum.com /gallerycemeterieshabbaniya.htm. For the names of the fallen Assyrian Levies, see, Gaby Kiwarkis, "Roll of Honor," Assyrian RAF Levies, http://assyrianlevies .info/roll-of-honor.html. For the rumor of the British destroying the chief mosque in Fallujah, see Bashkin, *New Babylonians*, 114. The story of the Bren carrier *Southend-on-Sea* comes from Martin, *The Essex Regiment*, 59.

7. For Grobba's frustration and efforts to motivate Berlin, see Grobba, *Macht un Männer*, 243; see also Flacker, "Fritz Grobba," 239. With regard to the apparently sabotaged A-17s, sources suggest more than one problem, and a problem that might have extended beyond those planes, solely. For one thing, it appears vital components were stolen, as suggested by Kelly, "A Succession of Crises," 126. For another thing, the Royal Navy had indeed intercepted a shipment of machine guns, probably not for the A-17s, on the US merchant ship *Brooklyn Heights* just before April 1941; for that, see the relevant Foreign Office file in the National Archives, FO 371/27090.

8. Prasad, *Official History*, 106–7. John Connell, *Wavell: Scholar and Soldier* (London: Collins, 1964), 443–45.

Chapter 9

EPIGRAPH: Raad al-Hamdani, quoted in "Interview: Lt. Gen. Raad Al-Hamdani," *Frontline*, February 26, 2004, PBS, https://www.pbs.org /wgbh/pages/frontline /shows/invasion/interviews/raad.html.

1. Glubb, *Story of the Arab Legion*, 279–80, 285–86. Glubb recounts more of his talk with the Dulaimi in a June 10, 1941, memorandum to the British Baghdad embassy, National Archives, FO 624/26, no. 589.

2. For the Indian Army's activities around Basra, see MacKenzie, *Eastern Epic*, 103–5; and Prasad, *Official History*, 107–9. My characterization of Slim comes from Lewin, *Slim, The Standardbearer*, 67–69 and elsewhere; and Robert Lyman, *Bill Slim* (London: Bloomsbury, 2011). For the Sikh signalers of the Twentieth Indian Infantry Brigade Headquarters, including how they couldn't fit in their Fords, see the war diary for this period, National Archives, WO 169/336.

3. The story of the northern column's approach to Baghdad is told in Bartlett and Benson, *All the King's Enemies*, 91–97; Glubb, *Story of the Arab Legion*, 287–97; Wyndham, *Household Cavalry*, 27–30; Smiley, *Irregular Regular*, 43–48.

4. De Chair, *The Golden Carpet*, 69–110.

5. For the perspective of Freya Stark on May 29, 1941, see Stark, *Dust in the Lion's Paw*, 109–10.

6. Grobba, *Macht und Männer*, 243–45, and for Grobba's persistent belief that the Allies had tanks, even in 1967 when he wrote his account of the episode, 244. Flacker, "Fritz Grobba," 240–41.

7. Al-Gailani told this story himself in a letter to Iraqi historian Abd al-Razzaq al-Hasani, quoted in Hamdi, *Rashid Ali al-Gailani*, 158–59. For the train route to Khaniqin, see Grobba, *Macht und Männer*, 246.

8. Grobba message to German Foreign Ministry, 29 May 1941 in *DGFP*, vol. 12, 917.

9. De Chair, *The Golden Carpet*, 77–84.

10. Martin, *The Essex Regiment*, 55–56; Wyndham, *Household Cavalry*, 29–30; De Chair, *The Golden Carpet*, 92–93.

11. Stark, *Dust in the Lion's Paw*, 111–12.

12. For the 237th Field Battery's presence at the embassy, see its war diary, National Archives, WO 169/1482. For Chalk, his preference for a beer, his thoughts about Iraq, and his Jewish friends in the Essex, see the IWM's manuscript, *Biography of Harry William Chalk*, 21, 26. For the Arab Legion, see Stark, *East Is West*, 120. For the Iraqi representative's quote about fifty tanks, see De Chair, *The Golden Carpet*, 116. For rumors about the fate of the Golden Square, see Stark, *Dust in the Lion's Paw,* 114; and De Chair, *The Golden Carpet*, 118, 137.

13. Masters, *The Road past Mandalay*, 32–33.

14. For David Smiley's experience among the Kurds, see Smiley, *Irregular Regular*, 48–50; Smiley, 1988 interview, Imperial War Museum, catalog no. 10340; and Wyndham, *Household Cavalry*, 32–33. For Grobba's flight from Iraq, see Grobba, *Macht und Männer*, 246–47. On the Jews of Kirkuk living on edge with the Germans in their town, see Mordechai Zaken, *Jewish Subjects and Their Tribal Chieftains in Kurdistan* (Leiden: Brill, 2007), 305.

15. De Chair, *The Golden Carpet*, 127.

16. Stark, *Dust in the Lion's Paw*, 114–15; Simon and Simon, *Vintage Years*, 45. By far the most rigorous scholarly source on the Farhud is Bashkin, *New Babylonians*, 117–25. For the tale of the Kurdish agha who personally guarded the village of Sandur, for tales of extortion, and for those who shamed potential criminals on religious grounds, see Zaken, *Jewish Subjects and Their Tribal Chieftains*, 211–12, 305–9.

Chapter 10

1. On the terms of the Paris Protocols of May 23, 1941, see Nicosia, *Nazi Germany and the Arab World*, 170. For the use of the small port of Chekka, Lebanon, see Henri de Wailly, *Syrie 1941: La guerre occultée, vichystes contre gaullistes* (Paris: Perrin, 2006), 161.

2. For convoys creeping past Massawa in the darkness, see Dutt, *Fight No More*, 11–12. Most material from this section comes from John F. Hasey and Joseph F. Dineen, *Yankee Fighter: The Story of an American in the Free French Foreign Legion* (Boston: Little, Brown, 1942). Wheeler's radio remarks come from *Vital Speeches of the Day*, vol. VII (New York: City News, 1941), 203–5. For Lindbergh's radio address, see Charles A. Lindbergh, "Our National Safety: Let Us Turn Our Eyes to Our Own Nation," May 19, 1940, Ibiblio, http://www.ibiblio.org/pha /policy/1940/1940-05-19a.html. This speech was a consistent variation on the same message Lindbergh had been conveying for over a year.

3. Most of this section on John Hasey comes from Hasey and Dineen, *Yankee Fighter*, 194–96, 219, 230, 247, 250, 256. On the antifascist flavor of the Thirteenth Demi-Brigade of the Free French Foreign Legion, see Wailly, *Syrie 1941*, 102. For more details about the Spaniards and other prorepublic fighters who fought with the Free French, including their liberation of Paris, see Evelyn Mesquida, *La Nueve 24 August 1944: The Spanish Republicans Who Liberated Paris*, trans. Paul Sharkey (Hastings, UK: Christie, 2015). The veterans themselves appear in a documentary; see Alberto Marquardt, *La Nueve, the Forgotten Men of the 9th Company* (Paris: Point du Jour, 2009), video. For the 3/1 Punjabis and Babu Singh, see Ravi Inder Singh, *As Told by Them: Personal Narratives of Indian Soldiers Who Fought during World War II* (New Delhi: Quills Ink, 2014), 37. On the Cameron Highlanders and Rajputana Rifles relying on one another, see Peter Cochrane, *Charlie Company* (London: Chatto and Windus, 1977), 61 and elsewhere. Subedar Richpal Ram's last stand comes from his Victoria Cross award recommendation, National Archives, WO 373/28, 602; K.C. Praval, *The Red Eagles: A History of Fourth Division of India* (New Delhi: Vision, 1982), 36; and Yasmin Khan, *India at War: The Subcontinent and the Second World War* (Oxford: Oxford University Press, 2015), 64-67

4. For Roald Dahl's air route to Syria, Donald Sturrock, *Storyteller: The Authorized Biography of Roald Dahl* (New York: Simon and Schuster, 2010), 116, 120, 165–66, and elsewhere; Roald Dahl, *Going Solo* (London: Cape, 1986), 26–27, 59, and throughout; and *Roald Dahl Museum Archives, folder RD 14/4/42-59.*

Chapter 11

1. For the appearance of the Résidence des Pins, which was recently restored, see Pierre Fournié and Denise Ammoun, *La Résidence des Pins: Beyrouth* (Paris: Courbevoie, 1999). For Dentz's history, see Dorothy Shipley White, *Seeds of Discord: De Gaulle, Free France, and the Allies* (Syracuse, NY: Syracuse University Press, 1964), 240 and elsewhere. The Druze, even those who later emigrated to the United States, retained a hatred for Dentz for this dishonorable act; see E. D. Beynon, "The Near

East in Flint, Michigan: Assyrians and Druses and Their Antecedents,"
Geographical Review 34 (1944): 269, 274. For more on Dentz's moti-
vations, see the relatively sympathetic Adrienne Doris Hytier, *Two Years
of French Foreign Policy: Vichy, 1940–1942* (Geneva: Droz, 1958), 279
and elsewhere. For Dentz's enmity toward the British and Jews, see A. B.
Gaunson, *The Anglo-French Clash in Lebanon and Syria, 1940–45* (New
York: St. Martin's, 1987), 20. For the Italian "armistice commission" in
Beirut, as well as details from the Vichy counterespionage files in Beirut,
see Götz Nordbruch, *Nazism in Syria and Lebanon: The Ambivalence
of the German Option, 1933–1945* (Abingdon, England: Routledge,
2009), 89–93. For the activities of the Germans in particular, including
the audacious Werner von Hentig, see Warner, *Iraq and Syria*, 72–74;
and George Eden Kirk, *The Middle East in the War* (Oxford: Oxford
University Press, 1952), 87–88. Besides dealing with the Arabs behind
Dentz's back, agents like Hentig offered Dentz all kinds of "suggestions."
When Dentz demurred in the interest of maintaining some kind of independence for France, the same requests would later arrive from the Vichy
regime. It's impossible to know whether the anecdote is genuine, but a
Nation reporter told the story of a conversation between Dentz and another journalist, with Dentz saying, "As long as these Boches, Hentig and
Rosen, are here I am really not High Commissioner at all. They appear
humble and helpful and courteous, but every suggestion of theirs that I
turn down comes through a few days later as orders from [Vichy head of
state, Admiral François] Darlan. . . . I can save time by obeying my [Ger-
man] bosses here." Peter Stevens, "Can Vichy Hold Syria?" *Nation*, June
14, 1941, 689.

2. Hermann Weiß, *Biographisches Lexikon zum dritten reich* (Frankfurt:
Fischer, 2011), 363; Nicosia, *Nazi Germany and the Arab World*, 173
and elsewhere; Rudolf Rahn, *Ruheloses Leben: Aufzeichnungen und
Erinnerungen* (Stuttgart: Europäischer Buchklub, 1951), 224–30 and
elsewhere; Rudolf Rahn, "Report on the German Mission in Syria From
May 9 to July 11, 1941," July 30, 1941, in *DGFP*, vol. 13, 237–65;
White, *Seeds of Discord*, 240. For Dentz's own picture of the meeting
with Rahn and the days surrounding it, see Henri Dentz, *Affaires de Syrie*

(memorandum), 1945, Hoover Institution Archives, item no. ZZ035, 9–13. For the wireless telegram from Vichy war minister General Charles Huntziger, see George Kirk, *The Middle East in the War* (Oxford: Oxford University Press, 1965), 92–93. The obscure Lebanese port with a single crane was Chekka, and Dentz offered it as an out-of-the-way place that would not draw attention; see Wailly, *Syrie 1941*, 161. See also Jafna Cox, "The Background to the Syrian Campaign, May–June 1941: A Study in Franco-German Wartime Relations," *History* 72 (1987), 441. For Dentz's reply, see Isaac Lipschits, *La Politique De La France au Levant: 1939–1941* (Paris: Pedone, 1963), 94. For Darlan and the Vichy regime's bitter feelings toward the British in spring 1941, see Colin Smith, *England's Last War against France: Fighting Vichy 1940–1942* (London: Phoenix, 2010), 167–68. For other details, including Darlan's contemporaneous visit to Berchtesgaden, and a May 21, 1941 memorandum by Dentz on the terms of his cooperation with Germany, see Georges A. J. Catroux, *Dans la Bataille de Méditerranée. Égypte-Levant-Afrique du Nord, 1940–1944* (Paris: Julliard, 1949), 106–11. For Vichy's prepared lies about the Luftwaffe planes, if spotted, see German Embassy, Paris, memorandum to Reich's Foreign Ministry, Berlin, May 5, 1941, in *DGFP*, vol. 12, 719.

3. Hinsley et al., *British Intelligence*, 1:413. For the Enigma decryptions, see National Archives, HW 20/1, O.L. 261 and O.L. 267; see also O.L. 237.

4. Rahn "Report on the German Mission," 242–46 and elsewhere. For Dentz's lies, see White, *Seeds of Discord*, 241. For the lie about the Kurds causing trouble, see Cox, "The Background to the Syrian Campaign," 442.

5. Christopher F. Shores, *Dust Clouds in the Middle East: The Air War for East Africa, Iraq, Syria, Iran and Madagascar, 1940–42* (London: Grub Street, 1996), 182–205.

6. Text of radio speech translated and published in the *Chicago Tribune*, May 19, 1941.

7. For Free French thinking about Syria as their ideal base, see Charles de Gaulle, *Mémoires de guerre*, vol. 1, *L'appel (1940–1942)* (Paris: Plon, 1954), 149. For the idea of making a public statement in Syria in support of an Arab federation and the subsequent discussion, see Defence Committee, Operations, minutes for May 8, 1941, National Archives, CAB 69/2/7, 3–4. For de Gaulle's optimism about the Free French reception in Syria-Lebanon, see Smith, *England's Last War*, 172. For Allied propaganda, including Jewish Palestinian spies, as well as Radio Levant propaganda, see Meir Zamir, *The Secret Anglo-French War in the Middle East: Intelligence and Decolonization, 1940–1948* (London: Routledge, 2015), 66, 70; and Sharfman, *Palestine in the Second World War*, 75. For deserters from the Vichy Army of the Levant appealing over the radio, see N. E. Bou-Nacklie, "The 1941 Invasion of Syria and Lebanon: The Role of the Local Paramilitary," *Middle Eastern Studies* 30 (1994), 514n21. For Churchill's letter to Roosevelt about the threat of an Axis Syria, see William Langer and S. Everett Gleason, *The Undeclared War, 1940–1941* (New York: Harper's, 1953), 497. For the story of Collet and for one example among many of the idea that the Vichy French would not fight the Free French committedly, see Anne Collet, *The Road to Deliverance: Damascus–Jerusalem–Damascus* (Beirut: Les Lettres Françaises, 1942), 121. On the other hand, for Collet himself warning Catroux not to expect defections or a cakewalk, see Wailly, *Syrie 1941*, 165–69. For the defection of Free French pilot Lieutenant Labas, see Edward Spears, *Fulfillment of a Mission: The Spears Mission to Syria and Lebanon, 1941–1944* (London: Archon, 1977), 93. For Collet's imminent arrest, see Anthony Mockler, *Our Enemies, the French* (London: Cooper, 1976), 67. For Roosevelt's public statement about Vichy cooperation that implied its national and imperial integrity need no longer be respected, see Franklin D. Roosevelt, "Statement Condemning Vichy Collaboration with Germany," May 15, 1941, American Presidency Project, http://www.presidency.ucsb.edu/ws/?pid=16116; see also Michel-Christian Davet, *La Double Affaire De Syrie* (Paris: Fayard, 1967), 91–92. For Pétain's promise to US ambassador William D. Leahy not to collaborate with Germany beyond the strict terms of the armistice, see *Foreign Relations of the United States* 1941, vol. 3 (Washington, DC: GPO, 1970),

161–62. The foreign secretary described his anxiety in Eden, *The Reckoning*, 249.

8. Stark, *Dust in the Lion's Paw*, 116–18. Freya Stark to Sydney Cockerell, May 30, 1941, in Stark, *Letters*, 4:133. Stark, *East Is West*, 96–8.

Chapter 12
EPIGRAPH: Dick Cheney, interview, *Meet the Press*, CBS, March 16, 2003, quoted in "'We Will, in Fact, Be Greeted as Liberators'—Cheney," Information Clearing House, http://www.informationclearinghouse.info /article5145.htm.

1. On the Special Operations Executive SOE and especially SO2 (sabotage section) the Sabotage and Subversion Section (SO2) in Syria and Lebanon Syria-Lebanon generally, and their being held off in the hope that Dentz might come around, see Saul Kelly, "A Succession of Crises: SOE in the Middle East, 1940-45," *Intelligence and National Security* 20 (March 2005)," 126. The memoir of veteran agent David Hacohen tells of British-Palmach cooperation, the tale of the doomed strike on the Tripoli refinery, the boat captain who was a double agent, and also tells about Arab anti-Vichy spies and propagandists, and tells of the Syrian Jewish spies operating during the invasion; in David Hacohen, *Time to Tell: An Israeli Life, 1898–1984* (New York: Cornwall Books, 1985), 125, 137–39. Details about Royal Engineer, Jewish saboteur, and SO2 successes come from "SOE in Syria," including SO2 Jerusalem summaries for May 30, June 2, and June 20, 1941, UK National Archives, HS 3/211, also, "Report on SO2 Activities in Syria," directed to General Archibald Wavell, 12 June 12, 1941, UK National Archives, HS 3/154. For the disappearance of the *Sea Lion* and its commandos, see "SOE in Syria," SO2 Jerusalem memorandum for Cairo and London, May 28, 1941. UK National Archives, HS 3/211.

2. For Rahn's hurried preparations, his disgust at the Arab response to his call to arms, and the idea that Vichy in Syria were fighting to avenge the French Navy at Mers-el-Kébir, see Rahn, "Report on the German Mission," 247–48. For Dentz's request that the Luftwaffe and military mission evacuate, see Cox, "The Background to the Syrian Campaign," 447; and Warren, *Iraq and Syria*, 141–42.

3. John Hasey's experiences up to the invasion of Syria, including the sites of Palestine, his talk with German refugees, and the Vichy defector come from Hasey and Dineen, *Yankee Fighter*, 258–63. Confirming and adding details is the diary of Free French soldier Gabriel Brunet de Sairigné; see Gabriel Brunet de Sairigné and André-Paul Comor, *Les Carnets du Lieutenant-Colonel Brunet de Sairigné* (Paris: Les Nouvelles Editions Latines, 1990) 75–78.

4. For religious observance, see Mahmood Khan Durrani, *The Sixth Column: The Heroic Personal Story of Lt.-Col. Mahmood Khan Durrani* (London: Cassell, 1955), 2–3. For those who viewed their soldiering through a religious lens, including thinking about what the Koran told them regarding appropriate action, see H.M. Close, *A Pathan Company* (Islamadad: National Book Foundation, 1994), 129; and Dunkirk survivor Muhammad Akbar Khan's *The History of the Army Service Corps*, vol 2, Royal Indian Army Service Corps (Karachi: Islamic Military Science Association, no date data), 166. (Pathans was what their British contemporaries called the Pashtuns.) Francis Ingall of the Sixth Duke of Connaught's Own Lancers argued that the Indian Army strove hard to respect all religious observation; see Ingall, *Bengal Lancers*, 97. On this and other aspects of the British seeking—and sometimes failing—to accommodate Indian Army troops, see Tarak Barkawi, *Soldiers of Empire: Indian and British Armies in World War II* (Cambridge: Cambridge University Press, 2017), 55, 73, 75, and elsewhere. For more observations on the prayer and other practices of Madrassi versus Punjabi Muslims in the Indian Army, see Antony Brett-James, *Report My Signals* (London: Hennel Locke, 1948), 80; and Fazal Hussain, Indian Medical Service nurse, interview by Stephen Irwin, Blackburn Museum, 2007. For the varying degrees of ability to pray and observe other rites in the Arab Legion, including dining with the British, see John Bagot Glubb, *War in the Desert: An R.A.F. Frontier Campaign* (New York: Norton, 1961), 146;

Glubb, *A Soldier with the Arabs*, 51; and Glubb, *The Changing Scenes of Life*, 128–29. For Muslim soldiers' provisions, see Christopher Alan Bayly and Timothy Norman Harper, *Forgotten Armies: The Fall of British Asia, 1941–1945* (Cambridge, MA: Harvard University Press, 2005), 368–69. Mohammed Sadiq, a sailor in the Royal Indian Navy, recounts receiving halal provisions in a unique Youth Action documentary of 2012 (unpublished). For Muslims observing food prohibitions, though sometimes allowing themselves a little rum, see Royal Indian Army Service Corps veteran George Boyagis's 1984 interview by the Imperial War Museum, catalog no. 8706. For halal butchers in the field in Italy, the difficulty of performing prayer in dangerous conditions, see Khadim (Atta Mohammad) Hussain, 2007 interview by Stephen Irwin, Blackburn Museum. For Ramadan accommodations, see Brett-James, *Report My Signals*, 78; see also the Imperial War Museum interview of John Basil Ready, Camel Corps, Sudan Defence Force, catalog no. 3997, reel 2. On respecting rites like proper burial, see Martin Gilbert, *Routledge Atlas of World War II* (New York: Routledge, 2014), 234; and Ingall, *Bengal Lancers*, 97. Information on good relations between religions and sects comes from my conversations with Santi Pada Dutt's daughter, Leila Sen. See also the Imperial War Museum interview of Franz Ferdinand Levi. On the other hand, the most negative comment on relations between Hindu and Muslim troops (outside of the Indian National Army, where such relations were prominent between prisoners of war and enlistees), describing "coolness" between the groups, comes from the interview with Ian Hallam Lyall-Grant, catalog no. 22088, reel 19. The observations of US colonel William J. Donovan regarding mixed Arab and Jewish battalions in Palestine in the *Daily Mail*, March 27, 1941, 5, describe relations as harmonious. Maurice Louis Spector, in his Imperial War Museum interview notes that dietary differences were the main outward enforcer of difference; IWM catalog no. 22092, reel 2. The experiences of Muslim Indian Army troops Sardar Ali, Ali Akbar Khan, and Mohammed Sadiq come from a filmed interview by Stephen Irwin, Blackburn Museum. Experiences of Fateh Mohammed (Bengal Engineers) and the Singh family, who served in the 3/1 Punjab and elsewhere, come from the fascinating collection of transcribed talks with Indian Army veterans in Singh, *As Told By Them*. For the idea that boys joined in hope of adventure, see Ghul Hassan Khan, *Memoirs of Lt. General Ghual Hassan Khan* (Krachi: Oxford University Press, 1993), 4. War Cabinet minister Sir Stafford Cripps was sent to India in 1942 to negotiate with top leaders, seeking to get their official support for the war in exchange for a promise of some kind of home rule after the war, but the mission failed. Still, many there and in Britain believed a de facto deal was made, which did contribute to British decolonization. Francis Yeats Brown, *Martial India* (London: Eyre and Spottiswoode, 1945), 15–16, notes that Brown expected some kind of independence within ten years after the end of the war; and, for the Muslim women who recruited, see *Then Came Hazrat Ali: Autobiography, 1972* (Bombay: Popular Press, 1972) documents, among other things, Indians' lack of animosity toward the Germans and resentment of the British (199). For his understanding of the common Indian soldiers' motives in joining up, and what they were fighting for, see D. F. Karaka, *With the 14th Army* (London: Crisp, 1945), 29–30, and on finding that ordinary soldiers expected democratic change after the war, 29. For similar findings, see Florian Stadtler, "Britain's forgotten volunteers: South Asian contributions to the Two World Wars," in *South Asians and the Shaping of Britain, 1870–1950: A Sourcebook*, ed. Ruvani Ranasinha (Manchester, England: Manchester University Press, 2013), 27–28.

5. For Foreign Office official Ernst Woermann working with the Italians and Soviets to move Bose from Afghanistan to Berlin, see Sugati Bose, *His Majesty's Opponent* (Cambridge, MA: Harvard University Press, 2011), 195–96; and Mihir Bose, *Raj, Secrets, Revolution: A Life of Subhas Chandra Bose* (Norwich, England: Grice Chapman, 2004), 183–85. For Bose and his fascist sympathies, and attempts to convince Nazis of revising their statements about Indians and race, see Romain Hayes, *Subhas Chandra Bose in Nazi Germany: Politics, Intelligence, and Propaganda 1941–43* (New York: Columbia University Press, 2011), xxv, 46. In *Mein Kampf*, Hitler was spittingly contemptuous of the Indian independence movement; see Adolf Hitler, *Mein Kampf*, trans. Ralph Manheim (Boston: Houghton Mifflin, 1998), 655; and for Hitler's theory of blood-worthiness for empire and his and Alfred Rosenberg's ideas about the corrupt nature of "Indian" blood, 31, 149, 654–55. Hitler's unpublished manuscript is described in Adolf Hitler, *Hitler's Second Book: The Unpublished Sequel to Mein Kampf*, ed. Gerhard L. Weinberg, annotated ed. (New York: Enigma, 2006), 154; see also Alfred Rosenberg, *Der Mythus des 20. Jahrhunderts* (Munich: Hoheneichen, 1934), 31, 82, 455. For what India might be like in the new Axis world order, there are some hints in Hayes, *Subhas Chandra Bose in Nazi Germany*, 200n5: it would probably be dominated by Germany as it had been dominated by Britain; or, if Britain could only be brought to heel, the tamed British would continue to dominate it as clients of the Reich. For Nehru's antifascism as compared to Bose's profascism, see Rudrangshu Mukherjee, *Nehru and Bose: Parallel Lives* (London: Penguin, 2014). For this meeting, Bose's subsequent draft of the plan the men discussed, including assurances that the Indian Army would defect, see *Documents on German Foreign Policy, 1918–1945*, series D, vol. 12 (London: HMSO, 1962), 442–43, 499–502, 527–28. For Bose listening to the radio, hearing of the Golden Square's defeat, and writing to Woermann that the Germans should make a declaration about their intention to free Arabs and Indians and thus enjoy "a string of friendly countries," see Bose, *Raj, Secrets, Revolution*, 197. For the torture of those who appealed to comrades to refuse to enlist, see Mahmood K. Durrani, *The Sixth Column: The Heroic Personal Story of Lt. Col. Mahmood Khan Durrani* (London: Cassell, 1955), 52, 57; and John Baptist Crasta, *Eaten by the Japanese: The Memoir of an Unknown Indian Prisoner of War* (Bangalore: Invisible Man, 1999), 26.

6. Order of battle details come from J. C. McAllester and S. Trigellis-Smith, *Largely a Gamble: Australians in Syria, June–July 1941* (Sydney: Headquarters Training Command, Australian Army, 1995), 230–31. On the refusal to fight by some of the Free French, and for the three-man commando team at Tel Shehab, see Wailly, *Syrie 1941*, 203–4, 258–59. For the Transjordan Frontier Force's Arab officers and willingness to fight in Syria, see W. L. Milner-Barry Papers, Imperial War Museum, catalog item 16758, 119–22. For the white flags that were sometimes shot upon, see White, *Seeds of Discord*, 247. On the theory of the slouch hats, and the "bus ride to Beirut" joke, see H. D. Steward, *Recollections of a*

Regimental Medical Officer (Carlton, Victoria: Melbourne University Press, 1983), 43. For the murdered Australians bearing the white flag, see Henry T Gorrell and Kenneth Gorrell, *Soldier of the Press: Covering the Front in Europe and North Africa, 1936-1943* (Columbia, MO: University of Missouri Press, 2009) 119. The story of the capture of the Tel Shahab bridge comes from the medal card of Havildar Goru Ram, National Archives, WO/373/27; see also Smith, *England's Last War*, 220; W. G. Hingston, *The Tiger Strikes* (Calcutta: Directorate of public relations, 1943), 128, and MacKenzie, *Eastern Epic*, 109. For the Arabs of Tyre cheering the Australians, see Wailly, *Syrie 1941*, 231. The diary entry of Transjordan Frontier Force officer Walter Milner-Barry for June 8, 1941, comes from his private papers at the Imperial War Museum, catalog no. 16758. The transcript of the BBC broadcast from 9:00 p.m. on June 9, 1941, comes from the British Library, Newspaper Library, BBC Radio Home News Bulletins, MFM.MLD218, film 58/59. The story of the pinpointed staff car approaching Deraa comes from the war diary of the 3/1 Punjab for June 8, 1941, National Archives, WO 169/3423; this diary also included the orders stating that the enemy was not to be considered hostile. See also MacKenzie, *Eastern Epic*, 109.

7. The tale of Moshe Dayan comes from Moshe Dayan, *Story of My Life* (New York: Morrow, 1976), 65–71; other details come from Wailly, *Syrie 1941*, 230. It is confirmed by an internal memorandum of Cairo Special Operations Executive head George Pollock, June 16, 1941, National Archives, HS 3/154. The case of the Beirut travel agent and his picnics comes from Military Intelligence Organization, National Archives, WO 33/2723 163.

8. Philippe Pétain, *Paroles aux français* (Coulommiers, France: Deterna, 2010), 118–19.

9. On the Vichy press's reaction and Pétain's reported words on learning of the battle, see Cox, "The Background to the Syrian Campaign," 448–49. The story of Dentz waving the telegram in Rahn's face comes from Rahn, *Ruheloses Leben*, 248. For General Charles Huntziger's message about the Luftwaffe aiding the battle for the Levant by striking Palestine, see France: Comité d'histoire de la 2e guerre mondiale, *La Délégation française auprès de la Commission allemande d'armistice: Recueil de documents publié par le Gouvernement français*, vol. 4, *19 Janvier–21 Juillet 1941* (Paris: Costes, 1957), 542. For the bombing of Palestine during the Syria-Lebanon campaign, see Sharfman, *Palestine in the Second World War*, 20–21.

Chapter 13

EPIGRAPHS: Henry Gorrell and Kenneth Gorrell, *Soldier of the Press: Covering the Front in Europe and North Africa, 1936–1943* (Columbia: University of Missouri Press, 2009), 122; Pierre Guiot, *Combats Sans Espoir (Guerre Navale en Syrie 1941)* (Paris: Couronne littéraire, 1950), 9, 16–17; Alan Moorehead, *African Trilogy* (London: Landsborough, 1959), 165; Gilbert Poincelet, *Dans le ciel de Syrie* (Paris: Sequana, 1941), 97; Jean de Lamaze, *Oflags (1940–1945)* (Paris: La Marquise, 2003), 56; Jean Damase, *Ici, Paris* (Paris: Les Éditions de France, 1942), 25.

1. For the desperate story of the Kuneitra counterattack, see MacKenzie, *Eastern Epic*, 114–15; Smith, *England's Last War*, 224; Wailly, *Syrie 1941*, chap. 15; and C. Northcote Parkinson, *Always a Fusilier* (London: Sampson Low, 1949), 86–89.

2. For the battle of Ezra, see the interview with Shan Hackett, 1991, Imperial War Museum, catalog no. 12022, reel 1; the award recommendation for Elias Khalil Attallah, National Archives, WO 373/27/109; Wailly, *Syrie 1941*, 289–90, which includes the quote from Captain Le Roche; Sairigné and Comor, *Les Carnets*, 79–80; and Long, *Greece, Crete, and Syria*, 407.

3. Wailly, *Syrie 1941*, 251–58. François Garbit was the Free Frenchman whose collar was ruined; see François Garbit, *Dernieres Lettres d'Afrique et du Levant, 1940–1941* (Paris: Éditions Sepias, 1999), 75. See also Smith, *England's Last War*, 233.

4. Rahn reveals his thinking during the French counterattack, his race thinking about Syrians, and his threat to hang those who wanted peace in Rahn, "Report on the German Mission," 247, 250, 253–55. For al-Qawuqji, see Laila Parson, *The Commander: Fawzi Al-Qawuqji and the Fight for Arab Independence, 1914–1948* (New York: Hill and Wang, 2016). See also Rahn, *Ruheloses Leben,* 249–50. Dentz's request for Stukas based in Syria is in the Archiv Nationale and quoted in Wailly, *Syrie 1941,* 246. The British intercepts of these developments are embodied in a cable of June 16, 1941, National Archives, HW 20/2, O.L. 594. For Vichy France assessing the practical and political angles of hosting the Luftwaffe in mid-June, and for the way negotiations between France and Germany did not appear promising for France in these days, see Warner, *Iraq and Syria,* 144–46. On the Vichy use of German Eleusis, see Christopher Shores and Christian-Jacques Ehrengardt, *L'aviation de Vichy au combat,* vol. 2 (Paris: Lavauzelle, 1987), 30.

5. Dahl, *Going Solo,* 150, and chap. 14; Shores, *Dust Clouds,* 205–24; Smith, *England's Last War,* 213. Roald Dahl, *Pilot's Flying Log Book,* entries from May and June 1941, Roald Dahl Museum Archives, item no. RD1501. For Dahl assuming they'd either advance or evacuate, abandoning his car, and for the citrus littering the ditches, see Roald Dahl to Sofie Dahl, June 2, 1941, Roald Dahl Museum Archives, folder RD 14/4/42-59. For the BBC rosily reporting good air support for men on the ground, see the transcript of the BBC broadcast from 9:00 p.m. on June 9, 1941.

6. For the Free French push from the south on Damascus in the third week of June, see Hasey and Dineen, *Yankee Fighter,* 269–77; Roger Barberot, *A Bras Le Coeur* (Paris: Laffont, 1972); Sairigné and Comor, *Les Carnets,* 80–86; and Wailly, *Syrie 1941,* 298. For the ill-fated Spahi cavalry charge, see Fergusson, *The Trumpet in the Hall,* 110–11.

7. The tale of the two brothers, which Jean Damase claimed he heard from a former Free French veteran of the Syria fighting, comes from Damase, *Ici, Paris,* 39. For the Australian legionnaire, see Gorrell, *Solider* *of the Press*, 122. For the twin mutinies of the Circassians and Druze, see Bou-Nacklie, "The 1941 Invasion," 519. For the Circassians and legionnaires who wouldn't fight, see White, *Seeds of Discord*, 248; and Catroux, *Dans la Bataille*, 132–33.

8. For the story of Hugh Greatwood, see Fergusson, *The Trumpet in the Hall*, 111–12; and Mockler, *Our Enemies, the French*, 139. For Abdul Rahman and Mohammed Akbar, see their medal cards, National Archives, WO/373/27. For the unhappy Vichy report from Mezze, see Wailly, *Syrie 1941*, 301. For figures, see I. S. O. Playfair, *The Mediterranean and Middle East: The Germans Come to the Help of their Ally, 1941* (London: HMSO, 1956), 212.

9. For the midnight waking of Jumbo Wilson, see Norman D.Carlyon, *I Remember Blamey* (Melbourne: Sun Books, 1981), 59. For the thoughts of Freya Stark's friend Miles Lampson and also De Gaulle, see Lord Killearn, *The Killearn Diaries, 1934–46*, ed. Trefor E. Evans (London: Sidgwick and Jackson, 1972), 182. For the failure of Operation Battleaxe freeing up help, see Wailly, *Syrie 1941*, 292.

Chapter 14

EPIGRAPH: Omar Dirmam, "Chronicle of Fight in Palmyra from Serviceman of Syrian Army," n.d., South Front, https://southfront.org/chronicle-of-fight-in-palmyra-from-serviceman-of-syrian-army/.

1. Reading's thoughts of joining the British Army and experiences entering Syria and approaching Palmyra are in De Chair, *The Golden Carpet*, 198, 204–36.

2. Glubb, *Arab Legion*, 310–16; De Chair, *The Golden Carpet*, 208–9.

3. De Chair, *The Golden Carpet*, 210–12. Bartlett and Benson, *All the King's Enemies*, 103.

4. For the story of the slaughter of the Warwickshire Yeomanry detachment, see Private Papers of N. G. P. Boswood, Imperial War Museum, Document 16086, box 08/108/1; and Private Papers of L. Flanakin, Imperial War Museum, Document 15520. Other details come from Glubb, Arab Legion, 319–20; and Household Cavalry Headquarters war diary, National Archives, WO 169/1259. Some sources mistakenly blame al-Qawuqji for this massacre. Firsthand accounts make clear he was not involved, but that he was raiding lines of supply in the area.

5. Household Cavalry Headquarters war diary, National Archives, WO 169/1259; De Chair, *The Golden Carpet*, 210–36; Glubb, *Arab Legion*, 323.

6. For David Smiley's entry into Syria, see Smiley, *Irregular Regular*, 52–54; Wyndham, *Household Cavalry*, 37–39; and Shores, *Dust Clouds*, 237.

7. Bartlett and Benson, *All the King's Enemies*, 101, 104–7. Interview of Arthur Hooper, signaler attached to the Sixtieth Field Regiment during the Syrian campaign, 1994, Imperial War Museum, catalog no. 13852, reels 6–7. Hooper's second operator, Jack Spencer, was with Joe Kingstone when his Dodge utility van was hit by a French bomber and burned out. According to Hooper, that's when Kingstone suffered his nervous breakdown. See also Smith, *England's Last War*, 248.

8. Martin, *The Essex Regiment*, 62–65; Chalk, *Biography*, 21–22. Smiley, Irregular Regular, 54–56; De Chair, The Golden Carpet, 234; Shores, Dust Clouds, 243–45. The tale of the renegade Royal Australian Air Force pilots comes from Bartlett and Benson, All the King's Enemies, 106–7.

9. Roald Dahl to Sofie Dahl, June 20, 1941, and June 29, 1941, Roald Dahl Museum Archives, folder RD 14/4/42-59; drafts of Dahl's *Going Solo*, Roald Dahl Museum Archives, RD 2/25/2/40.

10. For the Hawaytis, their role in the Great War, and their relationship with Glubb, see Yoav Alon, *The Shaykh of Shaykhs: Mithqal al-Fayiz* *and Tribal Leadership in Modern Jordan* (Stanford, CA: Stanford University Press, 2016), 107–8; and Eliezer Tauber, *The Arab Movements in World War I* (London: Routledge, 2013), 128. For this scene generally, and the later battle north of Sukhna, see Glubb, *Arab Legion*, 324–36; and Long, *Greece, Crete, and Syria*, 466. For this and for the capture of the officer responsible for the white flag betrayal, see Wyndham, *Household Cavalry*, 43.

11. Masters, *The Road past Mandalay*, 37–52. For the two Hurricanes' failed attack above Masters and the Gurkhas, see Smith, *England's Last War*, 257. For the Indian Army units' experiences, see William Slim, *Unofficial History* (London: Corgi Books, 1970), 151–60. On the effects of the dust storm, and for the Deir ez-Zor battle, see Prasad, *Official History*, 238–49; and J. N. Mackay and C. G. Borrowman, *A History of the 4th Prince of Wales's Own Gurkha Rifles*, vol. 3, 1938–1948 (Edinburgh: Blackwood, 1952), 33. For the significance of the loss of the Euphrates crossing at Deir ez-Zor, see Wailly, *Syrie 1941*, 335.

12. For the fall of Palmyra, see Prasad, *Official History*, 225–26; Mockler, *Our Enemies, the French*, 174–75; and Long, *Greece, Crete, and Syria*, 477. For Palmyra's supply airlift, see Shores, *Dust Clouds*, 241. Harry Chalk tells of his nervousness about attacking the Vichy Foreign Legion in their fort at Palmyra in the video interview his grandson James H. Hills generously shared with me. For the losses of planes, see Shores's day-by-day, blow-by-blow accounts for these late June and July days in chapter seven; and Smith, *England's Last War*, 258. For solicitations for volunteers in France and in prisoner of war camps, see Wailly, *Syrie 1941*, 336–38. For troop movements from France, Turkish resistance, and Vichy naval and air activities, see Shores, *Dust Clouds*, 247. For naval activities, see Playfair, *The Mediterranean and Middle East*, 214. The signal communicating the location of the doomed *Soufleur* can be found in National Archives, HW 20/2, O.L. 622. Thanks to Enigma decryption, the Royal Navy was also aware of the French destroyer headed from Toulon to Syria with ammunition, but failed to catch it at sea; National Archives, HW 20/2, O.L. 625. Dentz's request for a German airlift can be found in National Archives, HW 20/2, O.L. 667. For the sinking of the *Soufleur*, see Julie H. Ferguson, *Through a Canadian Periscope: The Story of the Canadian Submarine Service* (Toronto: Dundurn, 2014), 120; and Warren Tute, *The Reluctant Enemies: The Story of the Last War between Britain and France, 1940–1942* (London: Collins, 1990), 180. For the tanks abandoned without fuel, the fuel shortage for the air force, and the battle of Damour, see Mockler, *Our Enemies, the French*, 179. For the bombing of the Résidence des Pins and the direct hit, see Carlyon, *I Remember Blamey*, 59–60; and Mary Borden, *Journey down a Blind Alley* (New York: Harper, 1946), 176. For Rahn's experiences and Dentz's hope for Homs, see Rahn, "Report on the German Mission," 260–62; that source has Rahn's proposal for a surprise attack on Haifa, as does Rahn, *Ruheloses Leben*, 263. For Vichy France hoping to administer a conquered Syria-Lebanon, see Wailly, *Syrie 1941*, 292. For the doctors constantly at work and other details, see Steward, *Recollections*, 51–52.

Chapter 15

EPIGRAPH: Stephen V. Bowles and Paul T. Bartone, eds. *Handbook of Military Psychology: Clinical and Organizational Practice* (Cham, Switzerland: Springer, 2017), 420.

1. Casualty figures come from Steward, *Recollections*, 54; see also Smith, *England's Last War*, 269 and elsewhere. For the rumor that the Free French did not take prisoners, see Ferguson, *The Trumpet in the Hall*, 107. For Vichy troops being cared for, see Steward, *Recollections*, 47; interview of nurse Josephine Pearce, 1976, Imperial War Museum, catalog no. 831, reel 10, which explains that the Free French wounded were kept in conditions that were abhorrent compared to those of the British and Vichy wounded. For Smiley, De Chair, Kingstone, Altounyan, and Reading, see De Chair, *The Golden Carpet*, 230–35; and Smiley, *Irregular Regular*, 56. For Chalk's experiences after the fall of Palmyra and the visit of "some frog," see Chalk, *Biography*, 22–23; Chalk's experiences are also in the video interview provided to me by his grandson, James H. Hills. For the scene in Beirut at the peace, see Kenneth Slessor and Clement Semmler, *The War Diaries of Kenneth Slessor, Official War Cor-*

respondent 1940-1944 (St. Lucia: University of Queensland Press, 1986) 294-95. For the stress between the British and the Free French after the victory as the Lebanese and Syrian people waited for genuine independence, and for the ways in which the United States, preeminent after World War II, got involved, see Christopher D. O'Sullivan, *FDR and the End of Empire: The Origins of American Power in the Middle East* (New York: Palgrave, 2016), 143–45. For the British and the Free French nearly coming to blows in the Levant Crisis, and other stresses, see Edward Hampshire, "Alfred Duff Cooper," in *The Paris Embassy: British Ambassadors and Anglo-French Relations*, ed. Rogelia Pastor-Castro and John W. Young (Basingstoke, England: Palgrave Macmillan, 2013), 24–26. For Hasey, see Hasey and Dineen, *Yankee Fighter*, 278–85. For Koshonofski joining the Free French, see Parkinson, *Always a Fusilier*, 94–95. For attempts to persuade Vichy officers and soldiers to join De Gaulle, see Mockler, *Our Enemies, the French*, 227–33. For "Vive Pétain" and "Vive Dentz," see Steward, *Recollections*, 63. For Grobba's headaches with jockeying would-be Arab leaders, see Flacker, "Fritz Grobba," 282–83. For the poor success of al-Husseini as a recruiter, see Raphael Israeli, *The Death Camps of Croatia* (New Brunswick, NJ: Transaction, 2013), 124 and elsewhere. For al-Husseini's efforts to win influence in Berlin, see Philip Mattar, *The Mufti of Jerusalem: Al-Hajj Amin Al-Husayni and the Palestinian National Movement* (New York: Columbia University Press, 1988), 99-107. On Dentz's orders for the navy and air force to head to France or North Africa via Greece and take the Allied officer prisoners to Europe, see Wailly, *Syrie 1941*, 359. For Bernard Cordier, the French pilot who regretted not turning his plane full of prisoners of war to Cairo, "Bernard Cordier (1912–1993)," memoir, http://henri.eisenbeis.free.fr/bernard_cordier_pilote_trappiste.htm. A terrific account of the Arab, Australian, and British prisoners' experiences in Syria and en route to France is in the Papers of N. G. P. Boswood, Imperial War Museum, Document 16086. See also the account of Household Cavalry officers in the Fourth Cavalry Brigade Headquarters war diary, National Archives, WO 169/1259. For some other officers' experiences, those taken by sea, including some short-lived escapes, see Parkinson, *Always a Fusilier*, 92–94; and "Repatriated Prisoners of War

Tell of Adventures inside Occupied Europe," *Egyptian Mail*, August 19, 1941. For the prisoners' refusal to parade until their Arab allies were returned, see Glubb, *Arab Legion*, 320. For the arrest of Dentz, see Henry Maitland Wilson, *Eight Years Overseas 1939-1947* (London: Hutchinson, 1951), 123.For Wilson's dressing down of Dentz, see Miles Lampson to Anthony Eden August 21, 1941, National Archives, FO 954/15A/85. Dentz's apparent outrage at being equated to a jamadar comes from Fergusson, *The Trumpet in the Hall*, 115.

2. Weiß, *Biographisches Lexikon*, 363; Rahn, *Ruheloses Leben*, 270–71; Nicosia, *Nazi Germany and the Arab World*, 230–31. Rahn was awarded the "Knight's cross" by Hitler in 1943. Rahn's underlings were mainly involved in the death sentence of those Italian Jews, but Rahn was fully aware of the action, because the term *liquidiert* (liquidate) was included in the orders from Berlin to Rome; see Robert Katz, "The Mollhausen Telegram, the Kapler Decodes, and the Roundup and Deportation of Roman Jewry: The New Documents, 2000–2001," in *Jews in Italy under Fascist and Nazi Rule, 1922–1945*, ed. Joshua D. Zimmerman (Cambridge: Cambridge University Press, 2009), 231–3.

3. Dahl's experiences come from Dahl, *Going Solo*, 204; and Roald Dahl, "Lucky Break: How I Became a Writer," in *The Wonderful Story of Henry Sugar and Six More* (New York: Knopf, 2001), 171-206. Hasey's experiences come from Alex Chadwick, "American John Hasey, French Legionnaire During WW II," May 12, 2005, National Public Radio, https://www .npr.org/templates/story/story.php?storyId=4649471 ; and Joe Holley, "John Hasey Dies at 88; French Foreign Legion, CIA Operations Officer," *Washington Post*, May 11, 2005, http://www.washingtonpost.com/wp-dyn /content/article/2005/05/10 /AR2005051001415.html. For Tony Dudgeon, see Dudgeon, *The Luck of the Devil*, 200; and "Air Vice-Marshal Tony Dudgeon" (obituary), *Telegraph*, January 9, 2004, http://www.telegraph .co.uk/news/obituaries/1451197/Air-Vice-Marshal-Tony-Dudgeon.html. For Bartlett's experiences, see Bartlett and Benson, *All the King's Enemies*, 254–55, 267, 271–72, 277. For Chalk's experiences, see Chalk, *Biography*, 26, 30–39. The July 1941 quote from Wavell comes from

Connell, *Wavell*, 26. For the invasion of Iran for the purpose of controlling the north–south Trans-Iranian Railway and securing its oil supply,
see Ervand Abrahamian, *A History of Modern Iran* (Cambridge: Cambridge University Press, 2008), 97 and elsewhere. Masters's experiences
come from Masters, *The Road past Mandalay*; John Masters, *Bugles and
a Tiger: A Volume of Autobiography* (New York: Viking, 1956), 269–
89; and Clay, *John Masters*, 12–13, 77, 78–79, 192, and elsewhere. Information on Dutt comes from my conversations with his daughter, Leila
Sen, and her biography of her father and mother, *Aegis of Kali*; and
Dutt's award recommendation, National Archives, WO 373/47/535. For
David Smiley, see his autobiographies: David Smiley, *Arabian Assignment*
(London: Cooper, 1975); David Smiley, *Albanian Assignment* (London:
Chatto and Windus, 1984); and Smiley, *Irregular Regular*; see also his
1988 interview, Imperial War Museum, catalog no. 10340. For the fates
of the 3/1 Punjabi and 4/6 Rajputana, see Hingston, *The Tiger Strikes*,
142–46; W. G. Hingston, *The Tiger Kills: The Story of the Indian Divisions in the North African Campaign* (London: HMSO, 1944), chap. 3;
and Cochrane, *Charlie Company*, 113. See also Raghavan, *India's War*,
360–61 and elsewhere; and Yasmin Khan, *The Raj at War: A People's
History of India's Second World War* (London: Vintage, 2016). For the
way many Indian Army veterans of World War II felt resented after the
war for their association with the British, see the interviews of veterans
in Andrew Williams, *BBC Timewatch: The Forgotten Volunteers: The
Indian Army at War* (London: BBC, 1999). For Dayan in Haifa, see Shab-
tai Teveth, *Moshe Dayan: The Soldier, the Man, the Legend* (London:
Quartet, 1974), 159.

Acknowledgments

I could not write books without the help of highly trained, expert, and hardworking archivists and librarians. I thank them, including the professionals at the United Kingdom's National Archives; the British Library, including the India Office Records section; the Imperial War Museum; and the National Army Museum. I also thank those at the Ames South Asia Library, Chatham House Library, and Kelvin Smith Library.

My research for this book was funded in part by the History Department at Case Western University and very generously by the Baker–Nord Center for the Humanities, which also provided me a fellowship, freeing writing time for this project. I thank the center's leadership, staff, and founders for marching tenaciously upcountry as if through Euphrates-flooded mud in hostile territory.

I thank many others with whom I've corresponded while writing this book, and those who have contributed in many ways, including in no particular order, Lior Lalieu-Smadja at the Mémorial de la Shoah, Joy Wheeler at the Royal Geographical Society, Ruth Williams at the Roald Dahl Museum, Stephen Walton of Imperial War Museum Duxford, Stephen Irwin at the Blackburn Museum, and Graham Kay. I thank Leila Sen, who spoke with me about her father, Santi Pada Dutt, as well as James H. Hills, who communicated with me about his grandfather, Harry Chalk. Thanks also go to Mandeep Singh Bajwa, William Claspy, Shoaib Daniyal, Valerie Deacon, Raghu Karnad, Gaby Kiwarkis, Meade Klingensmith Jr., Katherine Lange, and Dan Marston. I thank Orit Bashkin and Priya Satia for their trailblazing work on this period in Iraq's history. I also thank Robert Lyman for his *First Victory* on the Iraq campaign and his *Iraq 1941*, the maps and other details of which helped tremendously in sorting out the various movements and allocations of troops. And I thank Henri de Wailly for his *Syrie 1941: La guerre oc-cultée, vichystes contre gaullistes*, which is a model of humanity in its perspective.

Thank you to the steadfast crew at The Overlook Press and Abrams Press, including Chelsea Cutchens, Adam O'Brien, Lauren Roberts, and many others contributing to *Blood, Oil and the Axis*, including design-ers and my copy editor. It was a sad thing to lose the monumental Peter Mayer recently, but I feel so lucky that mine was one of the last projects he took on and that I learned a great deal from his lifetime of editorial experience. Thank you, Peter.

And thank you very much to my agent John Silbersack, from whom I continue to learn so much.

Like my last book, *Squadron*, the present volume is dedicated to my wife and son. I also dedicate it to my students, past and present, who inspire me and for whom I write.

Index